Walt Disney and Europe

Frontispiece: Illustration for Snow White and the Seven Dwarfs *(1937)*
by the Swedish artist Gustaf Tenggren. © *Disney Enterprises, Inc.*

WALT DISNEY AND EUROPE

European Influences on the
Animated Feature Films of Walt Disney

ROBIN ALLAN

INDIANA UNIVERSITY PRESS

Bloomington and Indianapolis

Library of Congress Cataloguing in Publication Data

A catalog record for this book is available from the Library of Congress.

ISBN: 0-253-33652-X (cloth)
ISBN: 0-253-21353-3 (paper)

1 2 3 4 5   03 02 01 00 99

First published in 1999 and distributed throughout the world, except in
North America, by
John Libbey & Company Ltd, 13 Smiths Yard, Summerley Street,
London SW18 4HR, England

and in North America by
Indiana University Press, 601 North Morton Street, Bloomington, Indiana 47404-3797

This book makes reference to various trademarks, marks and registered marks
owned by Disney Enterprises, Inc.

Manufactured in Malaysia by Kum-Vivar Printing Sdn Bhd, Rawang, Selangor.

TO JANET AND BILL

Contents

Acknowledgements

This study is an extension of my Doctoral Thesis for the University of Exeter and I am grateful to Dr Richard Maltby, then of the School of American Studies, for his help and encouragement. I owe a special debt of thanks to my then Principal of the College of Adult Education, Manchester, William Tyler, for his initial support. I should also like to thank Brian Sibley for reading the manuscript, for making many helpful suggestions, and for providing the Preface. Errors of fact or judgement, however, are entirely my own.

I should like to record my thanks to The Walt Disney Company, and especially Margaret Adamic for allowing me to reproduce Disney copyright illustrations, and to David R. Smith, Archivist Extraordinaire for granting me access on many occasions to the invaluable resources of the Walt Disney Archives.

I should also like to thank the many people and institutions on both sides of the Atlantic that have helped me; it would be invidious to single out idividuals, some of whom have now shuffled off their mortal coils. In alphabetical order then I thank: Charlotte Alexander, Jim and Persis Algar, the Staff of The American Academy of Motion Picture Arts and Sciences, Ken Anderson, Ray Aragon, Art Babbitt, Mike Barrier, Kathryn Beaumont, Giannalberto Bendazzi, Lee Blair, Ann Boulton, Ray Bradbury, the staffs of The British Film Institute and British Library, Victoria Bryan, Alan Bryman, John Canemaker, Adriana Caselotti, the staff of the Central Library Manchester, Tony Cierichetti, Claude Coats, Bill Cottrell, Matt Crandall, Jack and Camille Cutting, Roald Dahl, Michael Darby, Marc and Alice Davis, Andreas Deja, Richard Dixon, Olive Duncan, Sebastien Durand, Bruno Edera, Didier Ghez, Eyvind Earle, Jules Engel, Elfriede Fischinger, Gary Geller, Tony Glyn, the staffs of the Goethe Institutes of London and Manchester, Eric Goldberg, Joe and Jennie Grant, Howard Green, John Halas, Teddy Hall, Theo Halladay, John Hench, Jennifer Hendrikson, Muir Hewitt, Richard Holliss, Kath Hull, Dick and Marilyn Hulquist, Don Iwerks, Rush Johnson, Ollie Johnston, Bob Jones, Jo Jürgens, Milt Kahl, J.B. Kaufman, Jim Keeshen, Ward Kimball, Richard King, Jack and Jane Kinney, Daniel Kothenschulte, Irene Kotlarz, Martin Krauss (Bilfinger-Berger, Mannheim), Garda Krug (MAN Augsburg), Don Laffoon, Lionel Lambourne, Mark Langer, Carsten Laqua, Eric Larson, David Lebrun, Gordon Legg, Scott MacQueen, Kaye Malins, Manchester Education

Committee, Bill Matthews, Mark Mayerson, Elizabeth Meador, Karen and Russell Merritt, Diane Disney Miller and Ron Miller, William Moritz, Rose Motzko, Herwig Müther (Krupp Essen), Grim Natwick, Robert Neuman, Walt Partymiller, Jayne Pilling, the staff of the Portico Library Manchester, Graeme Pye, Herb Ryman, Mel Shaw, Frau Schoback, Paula Sigman, The Society for Animation Studies, Charles Solomon, Frank Thomas, Richard Todd, Adrienne Tytla, the staff of the Victoria and Albert Museum, the staff of the Walt Disney Studio Library, West Surrey College of Art, Colin White, David Williams, Richard Williams, Edith Wilson and Retta Scott Worcester.

Acknowledgement should also be made to the editors of *Animation Journal*, *Animatrix* and *A Reader in Animation Studies* where shorter versions of Chapters 2 and 7 first appeared. Finally I owe a warm debt of gratitude to my wife Janet, who has made many helpful suggestions, and to my family for their long-suffering patience and support.

Illustrations and annotations

Many people and institutions have kindly allowed me to reproduce pictures from many different sources; illustrations are individually acknowledged or are in the author's or other private collections. All copyrighted illustrations are acknowledged, and every effort has been made to clear all rights. The author and publishers will be pleased to hear from any copyright holders whom it has not been possible to locate.

In order to avoid excessive notation, all Disney story conference notes are dated in the text and come from the Walt Disney Archives, unless otherwise acknowledged. All uncited quotations come from interviews with the author; a list is at the end of the bibliography. Spelling has been Anglicised.

Preface

What's an Englishman doing writing about an American institution? That was the question – posed in an incredulous tone bordering on outrage – which I was asked some years ago, while researching an earlier book about Walt Disney. The questioner was American and worked at the Disney Studio, and he had a point. Disney *was*, after all, a national institution.

Can there have been a child who grew up in America after 1928 who didn't know Disney's name, or who couldn't have immediately identified that engaging entourage of cartoon characters led by a Mouse called Mickey? Surely everyone must have been able to recite the stories of Disney's animated feature films from *Snow White and the Seven Dwarfs* onwards, or to sing from memory, any one of a dozen hits with such positive, up-beat titles as 'Whistle While You Work', 'When You Wish Upon a Star' or 'Who's Afraid of the Big Bad Wolf?'

Later, the famous name became a famous face when his avuncular personality joined the likes of Lucille Ball, Jack Benny, Walter Cronkite, Johnny Carson and the rest of America's extended TV family, And, having been admitted into virtually every American home, Disney then invited the people of America over to his *place*, to that extraordinary kingdom of daydreams, immodestly called Disneyland, where children of all ages could literally enter a three-dimensional realisation of his fantasies.

All that certainly makes Walt Disney an American institution, an original or a legend, call him what you will. Indeed, over sixty years, he's been called *most* things: some of them wise and many of them foolish; described in terms that are occasionally true but more frequently false.

But Walt Disney is also an *international* institution. There is scarcely a corner of the globe untouched by the Disney culture, and that includes Britain and the rest of Europe, where people have had a very particular (sometimes loving, sometimes hating) relationship with Disney. This is scarcely surprising since a significant part of the Disney Studio's film output has drawn its inspiration from the fairy-stories, folk-tale and literary classics of Europe.

Not everyone, of course, admired Disney's appropriation of Lewis Carroll's *Alice in Wonderland* or the process by which J.M. Barrie's *Peter Pan* became transmogrified into Walt Disney's *Peter Pan*. British critics were quick to carp about both those films *and* Disney's versions of *Winnie-the-Pooh* and *The Jungle Book*: while, as long ago as 1940, the Italians were protesting at the treatment received by their children's classic, *Pinocchio*, and, more recently the French were up in arms over the Disneyfication of *The Hunchback of Notre Dame*.

For good or ill, Disney turned to European folklorists and storytellers – from Aesop, Grimm and Perrault to Hans Anderson, Kenneth Grahame and A.A. Milne – as sources for his animated films; while the works of other writers – including R.L. Stevenson, Jules Verne and P.L. Travers – provided storylines for many of his live-action movies. At the same time, Disney's ambitious dreams for Disneyland were, in part, a response to the pleasure gardens of Europe.

Walt Disney – who proudly traced his ancestry back to France via England – was a frequent traveller in Europe. Following every visit, he would return home with armfuls of illustrated story-books, either as potential film projects (he bought the rights to T.H. White's *The Sword in the Stone* and Dodie Smith's *The One Hundred and One Dalmatians* long before they became classics) or simply to inspire the imagination of his writers and artists.

Perhaps, after all, it is not so ridiculous for an Englishman to write about Disney. Particularly when the Englishman in question is a scholar and an enthusiast of the calibre of Robin Allan. Not only does Dr Allan know and love the Disney films, he also knows about – and cares passionately for – those authors and illustrators whose books have, over the years, received the Disney treatment. His observations on the way in which the European sensibility represented in these works has been adapted and absorbed into American popular culture are original and perceptive.

It is almost thirty years now since I first met Robin Allan and, in that time, he has repeatedly, and generously, shared his knowledge and trenchant opinions with myself and others writing about Disney. I have long entertained the hope that he would, one day, write his own book on the subject. That he has now done, and the resulting work is uniquely his own. The insights to be found in these pages offer a new and vital perspective to our understanding and appreciation of that American – and, it can now be said, *European* – institution known as Walt Disney.

Brian Sibley

Introduction

There are many Walt Disneys. There is the man who died in 1966; there is the company which Disney created and which goes from strength to commercial strength; there are the theme parks and associated merchandising, and finally, there are the films and media which generate and contribute towards this economic buoyancy. For me Walt Disney means film and the magic of the moving line, a line that can be made to move anywhere, do anything, with colour that can be changed and blended to any and every hue within the time-span of the film.

This book examines one aspect only of an enormous subject, the creative roots of the Disney empire. These were the early animated films, especially the features. The films were made by an American who drew upon a European inheritance of literature, graphic and illustrative art, music and design as well as upon European and indigenous cinema. I identify some of these sources which were utilised and transformed by Disney into a new art form.

I limit my study to those films undertaken in Walt Disney's lifetime, with a brief look at the early years and then a detailed examination of the feature films from *Snow White* to *The Jungle Book* thirty years later. Fourteen of the seventeen fully animated feature films made before Disney died in 1966 have European sources. I consider some of the individual artists who made major contributions to the films but who were subsumed into the studio machinery. Popular acceptance of Disney operates on a number of complex levels; everyone has their own Disney in their conscious and sub-conscious mind and the modern child, unlike my own generation which could only see the films occasionally in the cinema, cannot escape the all-pervasive iconographic power of Disney imagery. Aesthetic, cultural, socio-political and feminist attacks upon all aspects of Disney proliferate, but the films continue to be popular, their layered richness proclaiming their classical status as the twentieth century draws to a close. I seek to address some of the European influences upon these radiant works of art.

I also look at Disneyland, the first and only theme park completed under Walt Disney's personal supervision, and in a final chapter I touch upon The Walt Disney Company today and its continuing use of European sources both in new animated feature films and in its theme park near Paris.

I have based my study on a number of primary sources. Firstly I have the good fortune to have grown up with many of the feature films under discussion, and over the last sixty years have seen – and re-seen – most of them on their first release. I remember my first Disney cartoon, which was a *Silly Symphony, The Spider and the Fly* (1931). I saw this in 1937 at the age of three and saw *Hercules* on its release in 1998 sixty years later. Thus I have a double experience of the films, the child's memory and the adult's reassessment through cinematic re-release and video. Secondly, the Walt Disney Archives have a wealth of primary source material in the form of story sketches, preliminary drawings, props and designs as well as original conference notes taken by a stenographer at the story meetings held between Walt Disney and his colleagues. These have all been generously made available for study. Thirdly I have been able to interview a number of men and women who worked closely with Walt Disney himself and who, though now elderly (and in some cases alas deceased since my research began in 1985) spoke with lucidity and a remarkable consensus of opinion about their work in general and about European influences in particular. I interviewed members of Disney's family and artists, colleagues or relatives of artists, between 1985 and 1992 on a number of visits to California, New York and Massachusetts. Sometimes I was kindly granted more than one interview. Walt Disney's associates have original art work which I was able to examine, record, and in some cases borrow for an exhibition of Disney Art at the Portico Library in Manchester in 1990. Finally there is a small body of scholarly work currently being undertaken which is based on primary source material to which I have referred. This is largely centred upon the Society for Animation Studies whose research has been made available since its first Annual Conference in 1989.

Robin Allan
New Mills
Derbyshire
April 1999

1 and 2 *Grandville* (above): *'Everyone enjoys themselves in their own particular way.'* One of a series of lithographs for The Metamorphoses of the Day *(1829). Like Disney, Grandville is able to discern the animal in the human and vice versa, though his vision is more shocking.*

(right)*: 'Mama, are there really men with such faces?' Lithograph (1828). Grandville, whose real name was Jean-Ignace-Isidore Gérard, influenced many artists and illustrators from Griset and Doré in France to Tenniel and Rackham in England. His curious world anticipates that of the surrealists, and, like Disney, he caricatures man in animal guise.*

1

3 Ernest Griset: 'The Town Mouse and the Country Mouse.' Frontispiece for Aesop's Fables (1869). This charming illustration has its equivalent in Disney's Silly Symphony short cartoon of 1936 The Country Cousin.

ÆSOP'S FABLES

2781   McLOUGHLIN BROS., NEW YORK.

4 Ernest Griset: coloured lithograph for the American edition of Aesop's Fables (1869). The Tortoise and the Hare was also a Disney Silly Symphony of 1935.

5 (left) *Joe Grant: caricature of Greta Garbo (1933) for his friend Bill Cottrell's autograph book.*

6 (below left) *Emile Flohri: illustration for Bill Cottrell's autograph book. Flohri was a background artist for the early Disney films.*

7 (below right) *Sam Armstrong: illustration for Bill Cottrell's autograph book. Armstrong was senior background artist for* Snow White and the Seven Dwarfs *and later directed sequences for* Fantasia, Dumbo *and* Bambi.

JUST A BIT OF A MURAL FOR YOUR BREAKFAST NOOK!

8 *Still*: The Flying Mouse, *a Silly Symphony cartoon of 1935 which demonstrates the Disney ability to anthropomorphise, as well as to place the action within a convincing frame. The background of light cloud with the foreground of leaves, branches and toadstools echoes the English water-colour school of the eighteenth and nineteenth centuries. Disney characters © Disney Enterprises, Inc.*

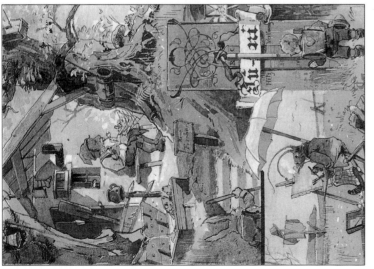

9 (above) Theodor O. M. Guggenberger:
illustration for a calendar. A back-packing rabbit,
a grasshopper artist, an old man and a rambler
share the same world of reality and fantasy.

10 (right) Arthur Rackham: illustration for
Mother Goose (1913). 'There was an old woman
lived under the hill.' The grotesque old woman
and the tree trunks are a striking contrast to the
children. Rackham's work was admired by the
Disney artists and there is an apocalyptic story
that he was invited by Walt Disney to go to the
studio as inspirational artist for Snow White and
the Seven Dwarfs. © Arthur Rackham family.

11 *Gustaf Tenggren: illustration for* Bland Tomtar och Troll *(1925). Tenggren followed in the tradition of his compatriot John Bauer who also influenced Rackham and, later, Kay Nielsen. Courtesy The Swedish National Art Museums, Stockholm.*

12 (above) *Theodor Kittelsen: illustration for* Peer Gynt. *This Norwegian artist with his powerful and frightening imagination, was a forerunner of Arthur Rackham in England and John Bauer in Sweden. Courtesy Scandinavian Film Group, Oslo.*

LITTLE GIRL TROLL

13 (left) *Ken Anderson: Troll design for a Danish film project (c. 1980). Anderson shows his debt to the dark but comic world of Scandinavian folklore. Anderson served Walt Disney faithfully for many years in different departments.*

14 *Still: the Queen in Snow White and the Seven Dwarfs. Walt Disney described her as 'a mixture of Lady Macbeth and the Big Bad Wolf'. Her fearful image, whether on the screen or off, is balefully present throughout the film. E. V. Lucas in* Punch *wrote that 'as the jealous stepmother she is of malignity compact, and as the Witch, an unholy terror.' © Disney Enterpises, Inc.*

15 (right) *Illustration for the story book edition of Disney's* Snow White and The Seven Dwarfs. *'Down the window-panes and off the roof, rain dripped like gentle tears.'* © *Disney Enterprises, Inc.*

16 (right) *Eighteeenth century marionette: few puppets from this period have survived, and this example from Linz, Austria, with its working mouth and head, anticipates some of the details of the Disney puppet. Courtesy Helga Schmidt-Glassner.*

17 (far right) *Gustaf Tenggren:* Death and the Maiden *(1936), a macabre sketch for Bill Cottrell's autograph album.*

18 (left) *Still: the opening sequence of Disney's Pinocchio. Jiminy Cricket invites us to enter his story book world.* © Disney Enterprises, Inc.

19 (above) *Rothenburg ob der Tauber: a gift shop with musical boxes. Albert Hurter drew many such toys for* Pinocchio.

20 (below left) *Rothenburg's Plönlein in a nineteenth-century engraving.*

21 (below right) *The Plönlein today.*

22 (above) *Gustaf Tenggren: inspirational painting for Disney's* Pinocchio. *The precise detailing (the stairs and the turret window for example) is based on Tenggren's observation of Rothenburg ob der Tauber.* © Disney Enterprises, Inc.

23 and 24 *Rothenburg ob der Tauber*
(below left) *The town wall and walk-ways, typical of the vernacular architecture of this area.*
(below right) *The Burg Tor, with its fierce mask to scare off hostile invaders. Tenggren illustrated this and there is a traditional puppet theatre just inside the archway.*

25 (facing page top) *Lee Blair: inspirational painting for 'Toccata and Fugue' from* Fantasia. *The frost-like trails in the sky echo Fischinger's abstract patterns.* © Disney Enterprises, Inc.

26 (facing page bottom left) *The Fox Cinema, Westwood, Los Angeles: typical art deco styling in a city where cinema expanded to adapt art deco in all its forms.*

27 (facing page bottom right) *Oskar Fischinger: Composition in Blue (1935). This film dazzled audiences with its comic and lyrical juxtaposition of square and rounded objects in abstract patterns.* © Fischinger Archives.

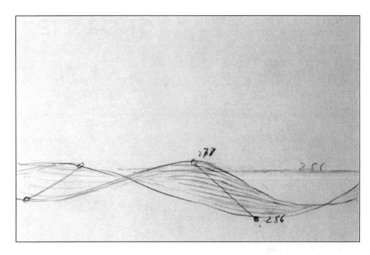

28 (right top) *Still: Bach's 'Toccata and Fugue' from Disney's* Fantasia. *The rolling wave designs that surge towards the audience have their origins in Fischinger's visual patterns.* © Disney Enterprises, Inc.

29 (right centre) *Oskar Fischinger: wave pattern design.* © Fischinger Archives.

30 (right bottom) *Oskar Fischinger: wave and pattern design. This is one of many exquisite poster-colour paintings designed for his own conception of how Bach could be interpreted visually.* © Fischinger Archives.

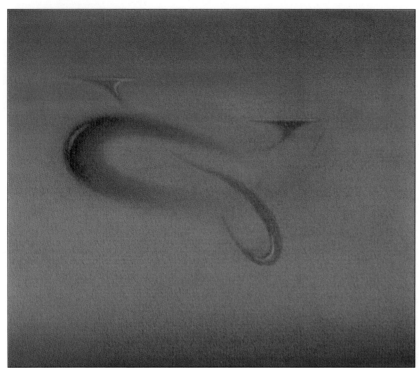

31 *Oskar Fischinger: an example of one of his swirling patterns for Bach.* © *Fischinger Archives.*

32 *(below) Oskar Fischinger:* Motion Painting One *(1947). This extraordinary film records 'the growth and evolution ... of many paintings, of the art of painting abstracted, and finally the art of cinema, of motion itself' (William Moritz).* © *Fischinger Archives.*

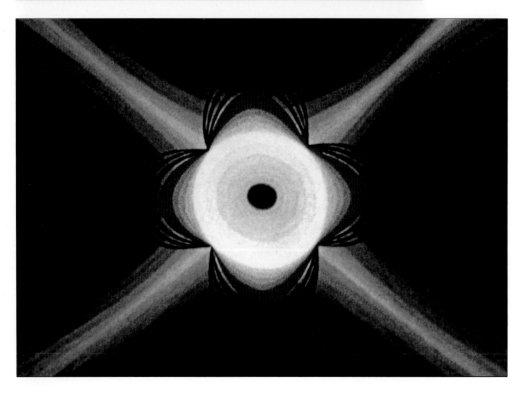

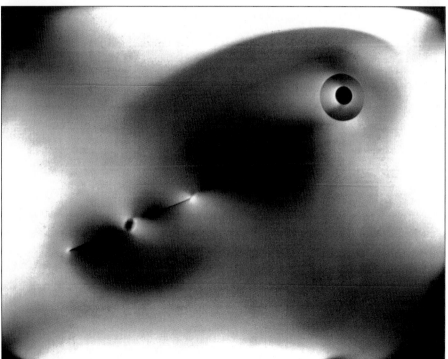

33A and 33B *Oskar Fischinger:
Demonstration of the
Lumigraph in the 1950s.   The
original instrument is now in the
Frankfurt Film Museum
© Fischinger Archives.*

34 and 35 *Richard Doyle:
illustrations (detail) for* In
Fairyland *(1870). Doyle's fairies
in a miniaturised natural world
foretell the Disney fairies of 'The
Nutcracker Suite'.*

36 *Arthur Rackham: illustration* 'Come now, a roundel' for A Midsummer Night's Dream *(1908). Rackham's world of fairy and nature combine in this picture of Titania the fairy queen and her servants. The Walt Disney Studio Library had many books illustrated by Rackham.* © Arthur Rackham family.

37 and 38 *Sylvia Moberly Holland:* (left) *two deer with ferns (c. 1935).*
This may be compared with Holland's rendering of horses, and it shows
that she possessed, like many Disney artists, great versatility.
(below) *Baby owls (1938): Holland showed this picture to Walt Disney*
as part of her portfolio before he hired her to work on Fantasia. *Both*
pictures courtesy Theo Halladay.

39 and 40 *Sylvia Moberly Holland:*
(right) *Illustration of horses. Courtesy
Theo Halladay.*
(below) *Storyboard by Holland for
'Waltz of the Flowers' from 'The
Nutcracker Suite' of* Fantasia.
© *Disney Enterprises, Inc.*

41 *Stan Spohn: inspirational painting for 'The Sorcerer's Apprentice' from Fantasia. Spohn's expressionistic painting suggests both the size and mystery of the cave.*
© Disney Enterprises, Inc.

42 *Still: 'The Sorcerer's Apprentice'; Mickey is overwhelmed by his own magic as the brooms continue their inexorable task.*
© Disney Enterprises, Inc.

·RIVERSIDE·BOOKSHELF·

WONDERBOOK · AND ·
TANGLEWOOD · TALES
NATHANIEL · HAWTHORNE ·

43 *Gustaf Tenggren:*
cover illustration for
Nathaniel Hawthorne's
Wonderbook and
Tanglewood Tales
(1923); Bellerophon
attacking the monster
Chimaera on the winged
horse Pegasus. The latter
appears in both Fantasia
and in Hercules *nearly*
sixty years later.

44 (above) *John Waterhouse:* Hylas and the Nymphs *(1896). This remains one of the most popular paintings in Manchester's City Art Gallery, which has outstanding nineteenth-century collections. Courtesy Manchester City Art Gallery.*

45 (left) *Inspirational painting influenced by Waterhouse, for the Beethoven section of Fantasia.* © Disney Enterprises, Inc.

46 *Freddy Moore: self-portrait (1935). Moore was one of the most gifted of Disney's early animators. His mastery of movement expressed in line is demonstrated in this quick sketch for Bill Cottrell's autograph album. Moore was senior animator for the Beethoven section.*

47 and 48 *Arnold Böcklin:* (above) The Island of Death *(1st version 1880). This was one of Böcklin's most popular pictures and he painted five versions of it, including one which is in the Metropolitan Museum of Art New York, painted in 1880 - the same year as this version in Basel. Böcklin's mixture of mystery, stillness and foreboding inspired paintings by Max Klinger, Dali and Ernst, as well as stage and opera settings.*

(below) *Böcklin's:* The Island of Life *(1888). This was intended to be the counterbalance to the* Island of Death *and is closer in its mood to Disney's Olympus than the earlier painting.*
Both pictures courtesy Öffentliche Kunstsammlung Basel, Kunstmuseum

49 Gordon Legg: illustration to demonstrate his mastery of air-brush painting. This was one of his portfolio pieces which impressed Walt Disney.

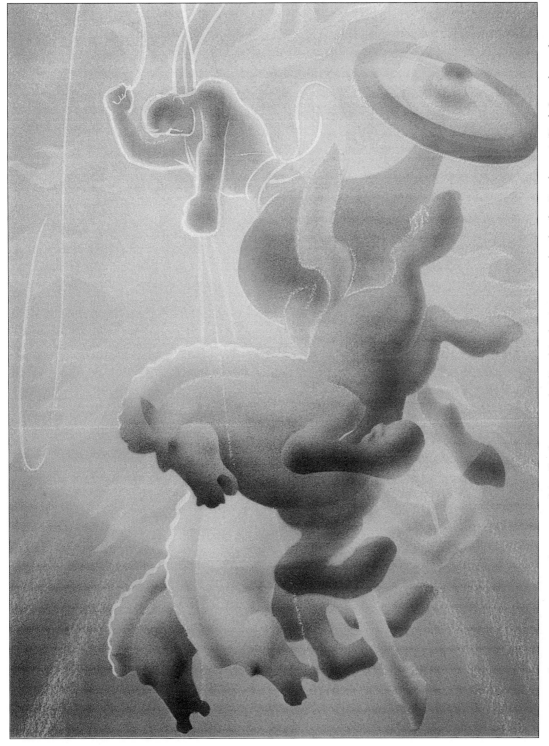

50 *Gordon Legg: inspirational painting of Apollo the sun god riding his chariot across the sky, for Beethoven's Sixth Symphony from Fantasia.* © *Disney Enterprises, Inc.*

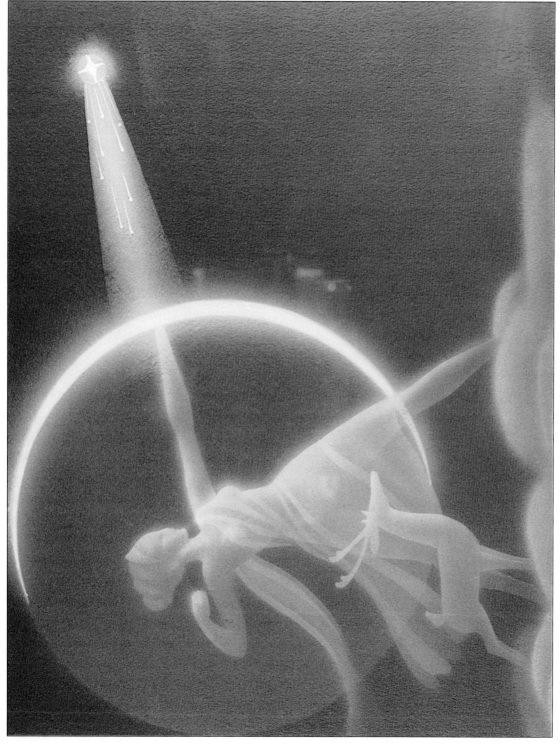

51 Gordon Legg: inspirational painting of Diana, goddess of hunting and of the moon, shooting out the evening stars with the moon as her bow; for the Beethoven section of Fantasia. © Disney Enterprises, Inc.

52 Gordon Legg: inspirational painting of the flying horse Pegasus for Beethoven's Sixth Symphony from Fantasia. The beauty of these preliminary pictures is conveyed in the final animation and backgrounds for the film. © Disney Enterprises, Inc.

53 (left) *Heinrich Kley: industrial scene (c.1909). Kley enjoyed inserting imaginary forces, such as the smoky devil here, into his industrial paintings. Courtesy Krupp Archives, Essen.*

54A and 54B (below) *Heinrich Kley: two studies of machinery for a large industrial painting (c.1942). Kley moved easily from the factual to the fanciful, at home equally with line or with colour. Both pictures courtesy MAN Historical Archives, Augsburg.*

55 (facing page) *Kay Nielsen: illustration for* In Powder and Crinoline *(1913). Nielsen looks back to Beardsley and to the Scandinavian illustrators, but possesses his own idiosyncratic art deco style. Reproduced by permission of Hodder and Stoughton Limited.*

56 (left) *Kay Nielsen: illustration for his most famous book* East of the Sun and West of the Moon *(1914). Nielsen is one of the great illustrators of the twentieth century and, on Joe Grant's recommendation, Disney was wise indeed to employ his talents on* Fantasia. *Reproduced by permission of Hodder and Stoughton Limited.*

58 (facing page) *Caspar David Friedrich:* The Tetschen Altarpiece *(1808). 'Friedrich's vision is echoed in Nielsen' paintings for the ending of the 'Ave Maria'. Courtesy Staatliche Kunstsammlungen Gemäldegalerie, Dresden.*

57 (below) *Kay Nielsen: inspirational painting for 'Night on Bald Mountain' from* Fantasia. © *Disney Enterprises, Inc.*

59 (above) *Illustration for the picture book version of 'Ave Maria' from* Fantasia. *The reference to Catholicism was dropped in the final version of the film.* © Disney Enterprises, Inc.

60 (facing page above) *Kay Nielsen: inspirational painting for 'Ave Maria' from* Fantasia. *Comparison may be made with Friedrich's painting alongside which also contains figures dwarfed in a landscape of trees and a ruined chapel.* © Disney Enterprises, Inc.

61 (facing page below) *Caspar David Friedrich:* Monastery Graveyard in the Snow *(1817-19). This painting was lost or destroyed in 1945. Courtesy National Gallery, Berlin.*

62 (above *Kay Nielsen:* The First Spring *(1942-5)* *This huge mural, 34 feet long by 19 feet high has been described as one of the most beautiful wall paintings in America.*

63 (left) *Kay Nielsen:* The First Spring. *Detail of the upper right hand side of the mural, with a stream of animals descending from heaven during the creation of the earth. Both pictures courtesy Sutter Junior High School, Canoga Park.*

64 *Kay Nielsen: detail of* The Canticle of the Sun *(1946). Another superb mural, with a landscape rich in detail.*

65 *Kay Nielsen: detail of* The Canticle of the Sun. *Both pictures courtesy Emerson Junior High School, Los Angeles.*

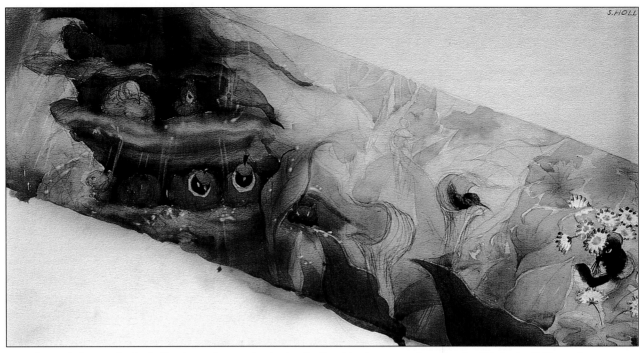

66 (above) *Sylvia Moberly Holland: inspirational painting for* Bambi. *A water-colour for the 'Little April Shower' sequence .*
© *Disney Enterprises, Inc.*

67 (below) *Still: 'Your mother
can't be with you any more'
from* Bambi.
© *Disney Enterprises, Inc.*

68 and 69 *Thomas Rowlandson: illustrations from* The Tour of Dr Syntax in Search of the Picturesque *(1812).* (above) *'Dr Syntax returned from his tour'*, and (below) *'Dr Syntax sketching after nature'. Rowlandson (1756-1827) caricatures domesticity. The Disney artists picked up on the line of wit from Gillray via Rowlandson to the twentieth century political cartoonists, and produced some of their most brilliant and savage animation in films like* Education for Death *(1943). The Disney short cartoons continued the tradition of the English water-colour school in films like* Cock of the Walk *(1935),* The Old Mill *(1937) and* Farmyard Symphony *(1938). Both pictures Courtesy Portico Library, Manchester.*

70 and 71 *Mary Blair: (above left) inspirational painting for* Song of the South *(1946). © Disney Enterprises, Inc. (above right) Blair's inspirational painting for 'Once Upon a Wintertime', one of the seven items that make up the 1948 package film* Melody Time. *The stylised backgrounds owe much to Blair's individual talents and are starkly expressionistic in mood. © Disney Enterprises, Inc.*

72 (left) *Illustration from a scrap-book of 1881. The nostalgia that pervades the Disney films* Melody Time (1948) *and* So Dear to My Heart (1949) *is shown in the Christmas card design that ends the 'Wintertime' item of the former film, and the animation of the latter.*

73 *Original Cel: The stepmother in
Disney's* Cinderella *(1950).*
© Disney Enterprises, Inc.

74 *Trade advertisement for Disney's
Cinderella (1950): **This charming
picture reveals an illustrative style,
based on Mary Blair's designs. The
look of the film itself is more
conventional, but there is still room for
expressionism.***
© Disney Enterprises, Inc.

75 (left) *Still: Cinderella's coach flees the palace at midnight. Expressionism is again the keynote in this dramatic scene from the film.* © Disney Enterprises, Inc.

76 (below) *Gordon Legg: inspirational painting for Disney's* Alice in Wonderland. *Legg's individualistic style was not followed in the film version of 1951.* © Disney Enterprises, Inc.

77 Stills: the Queen of Hearts chases Alice through a surrealistic landscape, reminiscent of Dali, at the end of Alice in Wonderland.
© *Disney Enterprises, Inc.*

78 Mary Blair: inspirational painting of the Mad Hatter's Tea Party scene for Disney's Alice in Wonderland. *Though following her own stylistic bent, Blair has paid attention to Tenniel in her rendering of character and background for the film.*
© *Disney Enterprises, Inc.*

79 (facing page above) *Gustaf Tenggren: inspirational painting for Pinocchio. This scene does not take place in the film, but the fox is pointing to Stromboli's marionette theatre, itself based on sketches by Albert Hurter. The design would later form the basis for the Pinocchio attraction in Disneyland.* © Disney Enterprises, Inc.

80 (facing page below left) *Disneyland Park: the Pinocchio attraction in Fantasyland. The design and detailed modelling match the marionette theatre painted by Tenggren for the film, even to the carved figure on the roof. Used by permission from Disney Enterprises, Inc.*

81 (facing page below right) *Eyvind Earle: inspirational painting for Disney's* Sleeping Beauty *(1959). Earle's individual style was a powerful influence, and he claimed to have been inspired by the patterning of Persian miniatures, as well as by medieval illustration.* © Disney Enterprises, Inc.

82 (right) *'September: harvesting grapes' by the Limbourg brothers, from the Duc de Berry's* Les Très Riches Heures *(early 15th C.). This is one of a series of miniatures which influenced Olivier's* Henry V *as well as* Sleeping Beauty. *Courtesy Victoria and Albert Museum / Bridgeman Art Library.*

83 (above left) *Villa D'Este, near Rome: the organ fountain, one of the most spectacular fountains in this stepped garden of water fantasies.*

84A and 84B (above centre and right) *Chatsworth House, Derbyshire: the Cascade (1696-1701) and the Maze (1962). The gardens at Chatsworth have many curious attractions, such as a squirting willow tree and a 'rocking stone' that would have delighted Walt Disney and his 'imagineers'.*

85 (below) *Still: detail of background for* The Jungle Book *(1967). There are reminders of Gauguin in the palette, but Doré again comes to mind with his sweeping landscapes filled with light and shadow.*
© Disney Enterprises, Inc.

86 (above) *Ken Anderson: atmosphere painting for a Danish film project   Anderson's water-colours show his knowledge and understanding of the Scandinavian world.*

87 (below) *Hans Bacher: inspirational painting for the Disney film* Beauty and the Beast *(1991). German expressionism and memories of the film* Frankenstein *(1931) come together for the villagers' march on Beast's castle.* © *Disney Enterprises, Inc.*

88 Frank Armitage: design for advertising Disneyland Paris. The debt to Eyvind Earle and the link back to Les Très Riches Heures is clear, and there are other European references in the trimmed landscape.
© Disney Enterpises, Inc.

89 Place des Vosges, Paris: Victor Hugo lived in this elegant older part of the city. The clipped, box-like trees and ornate fountains of France were picked up by the Disney designers for Disneyland Paris, both through the film Sleeping Beauty and through French architecture and landscape. The European theme park has strong French associations.

90 (right) *Design for Disneyland Paris, advertising the new theme park. Elements from the films are used in three-dimensional form, with galleons, a skull rock, swing bridges and the Swiss Family Treehouse as well as waterfalls and lagoons.*
© *Disney Enterprises, Inc.*

91 (below) *Albert Square, Manchester, 1992. A Disney plastic castle appeared overnight outside the town hall in this most Victorian Gothic city. It was difficult to decide which had the more cusps and crenellations.*

92 The Swan of Tuonela: *inspirational sketch by Sylvia Moberly Holland (1940) for the*
ongoing Fantasia *planned by Walt Disney.* © Disney Enterprises, Inc.

93 *Sylvia Moberly Holland: inspirational painting (c. 1946) for a Greek mythology project*
that was not developed, although the Disney company turned again to Greek mythology
many years later for Hercules *(1997).* © Disney Enterprises, Inc.

CHAPTER 1

Walt Disney:
the Man and the Studio

This chapter is a brief biography of Walt Disney and an account of the growth of his studio until his death in 1966; details will emerge later as the animated feature films are examined, with their debt to European sources and their absorption into the popular cultural mould which Disney embraced.

Until the mid-fifties Walt Disney remained personally involved in all stages of production, and in particular during the collectively creative period when stories and ideas were being thrashed out in committee; it can be said that he was if not the *auteur*, then the controlling editor of all his work. With the exception of his Latin American and war years, his sources were taken from Europe or from the small town rural community which he loved. These sources are examined in detail in the next chapter.

The success of the Disney empire is based on the ability to market the films that Walt Disney and his studio created. Excellence of product, both technical and artistic, drama and humour in story and believable characters with emotional appeal contributed to this success. It is an international phenomenon, transcending barriers of race, language and culture, and taken for granted by generations familiar with the images and iconography of the Disney studio. These range from Mickey Mouse to Mowgli and from Snow White to Sleeping Beauty; authorship, too, is taken over and books are entitled Walt Disney's *Peter Pan* and Walt Disney's *Alice in Wonderland*. The empire began with film and is still based on the familiarity of succeeding generations with situations, stories and characters made popular through film. Although both the man and the studio have received a great deal of attention (and the new criticism has belatedly discovered the films), the cultural and artistic forces which shaped the artists who worked for Disney, and indeed Walt Disney himself, have not been so carefully examined. The Disney product is indebted to an older cultural heritage; Disney absorbed and recreated that heritage for a new mass audience that was part of the popular culture of his own period.

Disney was a master of technological and cultural manipulation, taking stories and characters and style and mood and themes from Europe, and recreating them in animated form. An examination of his early life shows

The house on Tripp Avenue, Chicago, in 1994, where Walt Disney was born in 1901. Built by Elias Disney, Walt's father, the exterior of the house remains little altered.

how much Disney was himself a product of the mass culture of the twentieth century.

Walt Disney's life has been told over and over again[1] and the excuse for another retelling is to point out the background to his fierce independence and especially to the importance of the small town in Missouri where he spent a few happy years in his childhood. He was born in Chicago in 1901 of English, Irish and Canadian stock on his father's side, and his maternal grandmother was German.[2] He was poorly educated and deprived as a child, exploited by a father who believed in corporal punishment and whose tyranny caused two of his four sons to run away as boys from home. A fifth child, a daughter Ruth, completed the family. Elias Disney was a builder, businessman and farmer who moved five times before Walt was twenty-one, failing in all his enterprises. Walt's mother Flora remains a shadowy figure although we know that she was a schoolteacher who taught him to read. She was loyal both to her sons and to her husband throughout her life, and while Walt Disney retained a love/hate relationship with his father, he was always devoted to his mother. He formed a special relationship with his elder brother Roy who supported him as a child, protecting him from their aggressive father, and later becoming his business partner.

The young Disney's childhood was spent in cities, except for four crucial years from 1906 to 1910 when his father attempted farming in Marceline, Missouri. The boy Disney loved farm life, talking of it in later life over and over again. In 1933, after he became successful he and his brother Roy gave their parents an extended holiday back to Marceline. 'Don't leave Roy out of the picture', his mother told the *Marceline Press*. 'He has meant so much to Walt's success. While Walt is the creator, Roy is the promotor'.[3] Disney himself wrote to the town on its golden jubilee in 1938 and the authenticity is marked nearly thirty years later:

> More things of importance happened to me in Marceline than have happened since – or are likely to in the future. Things, I mean, like experiencing my first country life, seeing my first circus parade, attending my first school, seeing my first motion picture! ... One of my fondest childhood memories is of Doc Sherwood. He used to encourage me in my drawing, and give me little presents for my efforts ... My brother Roy reminds me of another flyer I took in the line of art at that time. I painted one side of our house with black pitch. The outcome must have been slightly frightening, to say the least, and I wasn't thanked for my efforts by the family ... Everything connected with Marceline was a thrill to us, coming as we did from a city the size of Chicago. I'm glad I'm a small town boy and I'm glad Marceline was my town. Thanks a lot for letting me write my impressions, and say hello to all the folks ... .[4]

Many years later the actor, Richard Todd stayed with Disney in Hollywood and recalled that the Marceline farm barn had been copied in California and had been re-built in the garden as a reminder of Disney's childhood. Marceline is a town created by the Atchison, Topeka and Santa Fe railway, and was only eighteen years old when the Disney family settled there. Many of Disney's interests were associated with Marceline. He would put his ear to the track to hear the trains coming and then go under the bridge, listening to their roar. The lane and bridge are still there, and the trains still roar through the town of Marceline today, little changed since Disney's childhood, though the family farm has been much altered. Disney's passion for trains can be seen in many of his films (*Dumbo* immediately springs to mind, and there are other instances, such as the Disneyland Railroad which circles the park). Later he made his own engine and model railway for his garden in Los Angeles, and Kathryn Beamont, the child actress who took the voice of Alice in *Alice in Wonderland* (1951) recalls that Disney took her on a ride in his train while he was testing it at the Studio.[5]

The boy Disney and his sister Ruth paid a clandestine visit to Marceline's first cinema. A kindly aunt sent him a set of paints, and the local doctor, as we have seen, encouraged his efforts. The ambience of small town America and the rural community that surrounded Midwestern settlements formed a visual accompaniment to many of his early cartoon films, and permeated the mood of later work; it is central to the small town life and farm community depicted in many of his short cartoons, from the *Alice* comedies of the early twenties to *Oswald the Lucky Rabbit* and the *Mickey Mouse* and *Silly Symphony* shorts. Its characteristically *naif* philosophy and moral conviction colours the animated feature films from *Snow White and the Seven Dwarfs* (1937) to *So Dear to My Heart* (1949) and forms part of the nostalgic Edwardiana of *Mary Poppins* (1964). It is the 'Main Street USA' heart of Disneyland.

A Marceline farm barn today. This is the traditional shape that Disney loved and which is seen in many of the shorts and features.

Kansas Avenue, Marceline, Missouri at the time when the Disney family lived just outside the town from 1906 to 1910. This was 'Main Street' for the young Walt Disney. Courtesy Kaye Malins.

Kansas Avenue, Marceline in 1994. The town has changed remarkably little in a hundred years and retains its charm.

Its importance, as the foundation upon which the veneer of European sources is overlaid in the Disney canon, cannot be overemphasised. Walt and Roy Disney returned to the town in 1956, by train of course, where Disney dedicated the Disney Park and opened the Walt Disney swimming pool. He returned in 1960 to open the new Walt Disney School. He dismissed his staff and retainers and told his host Rush Johnson, 'This is my home'. The entire Disney family returned to Marceline in 1968 when a special Walt Disney commemorative stamp was issued from the Marceline post office. Mercifully, the little town remains unspoilt and unexploited, proud of its famous boyhood inhabitant but fiercely protective of its own independent spirit.

The Disney Farmhouse, Marceline, 1994. The house is much altered but the surrounding countryside is little changed, including the unsurfaced road where the young Disney would go and listen to the trains.

Layout sketch for Mary Poppins *(1964). The English countryside is seen as a blend of the old world and the new. The Midwest-style barn has an English oast-house, with English garden gate and wall.* © Disney Enterprises, Inc.

Disney was nine when the farm failed, and Elias Disney moved to Kansas City where for six years young Walt delivered newspapers for his father in all weathers, rising at three thirty in the morning in order to complete a double round before school. That he was an indifferent scholar is not surprising, and 'he had a recurring dream in which he suffered torment because he had failed to deliver some newspapers'.[6]

One of Disney's school friends was Walt Pfeiffer whose jolly German father loved the theatre. Elias Disney, a congregationalist, did not approve and his son's visits to the cinema and vaudeville theatres were seldom mentioned at home. Encouraged by Mr Pfeiffer the two friends developed their own comedy routines based on acts they had seen on stage. Disney loved to imitate Chaplin. Another love was the circus, which he followed whenever a company visited town. When Elias Disney moved after the failure of his newspaper distribution business, Walt got a job selling refreshments on trains across the Midwest. Then he joined his family in Chicago where his father had invested in a jelly factory. This, too, failed though Elias agreed to pay for his son's correspondence course in art provided he continued to contribute to the family income. Walt Disney's caricatures and cartoons were published in his school magazine and he began collecting a jokes file based on theatre and cinema gags. Returning from service as an ambulance driver in France in 1919 he attempted unsuccessfully to obtain work as a cartoonist.

In 1920 Walt Disney's career as animator and film maker began, and his personal biography becomes bound up with the studio he developed. He worked briefly in Kansas City where he studied animation and made photostat copies of Eadweard Muybridge's books on human and animal locomotion, also studying E.G. Lutz's book on animated cartoons.[7]

Roy and Walt Disney on a return visit to Marceline (1957) at Yellow Creek with a young Marceline fisherman. Yellow Creek was a favourite fishing haunt for the young Walt Disney. Courtesy Rush Johnson.

Starting as a commercial artist he bought a film camera and, at the age of twenty, formed his own animation company in 1922 with a series of *Laugh-O-gram* films. Unscrupulous distributors led to the company's failure and Disney followed his elder brother Roy to California in August 1923, having poured all his resources into one film, *Alice's Wonderland*. Here, after trying unsuccessfully to get work in directing live action films, he developed the *Alice* Comedies, which mixed live action with cartoon. He formed the Disney Brothers' Studio with Roy as business manager. Roy remained his financial adviser and manager for the rest of his life; the relationship was a warm one in spite of acrimonious disputes over the younger brother's schemes. Roy Disney insisted that Disney World, which he opened after his brother's death, be renamed Walt Disney World 'so people will always know this was *Walt's* dream'. In 1926 the Studio moved to Hyperion Avenue and was renamed the Walt Disney Studio.

In 1925 Disney married Lillian Bounds, an ink and paint girl at the studio; their daughter Diane Marie was born in 1933; a second girl, Sharon, was adopted in 1936. In his private life Disney maintained a quiet and affectionately modest profile, refusing to allow his children to be exposed to the publicity associated with Hollywood. His elder daughter was surprised to discover that her own father was *the* Walt Disney.

The studio produced over fifty short films in three and a half years; and many of the ideas, gags, routines and technical skills so manifest in the later shorts were developed in these early years. Then, in 1927 Disney created a new character *Oswald the Lucky Rabbit*, drawn by his friend from Kansas City, Ub Iwerks. By this time Disney had stopped animating himself and was adopting the managerial and co-ordinating role that he assumed for the rest of his career. What happened next has been reported over and over again; the rights to Oswald were taken away from Disney by his distributor; this was not unusual at that time as most series belonged to the distributor rather than the creator of a cartoon series. What upset Disney most was that the distributor also stole all his staff except Ub. 'Never again will I work for somebody else', said Disney. Having lost Oswald, Disney created a new character, Mickey Mouse, drawn by Ub Iwerks,[8] and, aware of the potential that the sound revolution was causing in the cinema, he turned the third Mickey film into the first sound cartoon. *Steamboat Willie* (1928) caused a sensation. Once again an unscrupulous entrepreneur attempted to wrest the new series from Disney, but by this time the young film maker had learnt his lesson in a cut-throat business, and he held on to his new creation fiercely. From then on Disney made sure that that he owned all the rights to his characters. In 1929 he began a new series called *Silly Symphonies* opening with *The Skeleton Dance*.

In 1931 Disney suffered a nervous breakdown caused by overwork and stress, but after a short rest, he returned to the studio as energetic as ever. New technology fascinated him. He arranged an exclusive two year deal with Technicolor denying his rivals the full colour process. He produced the first successful colour cartoon *Flowers and Trees* (1932). This won the first Oscar for Best Cartoon Subject; in the same year he also received a special award for Mickey Mouse. The studio expanded rapidly during the thirties and took on staff from art schools and universities. Studio art classes were started in 1932. Donald Duck first appeared in *The Wise Little Hen* (1934), and soon overtook Mickey Mouse in popularity.

The shorts were popular and successful, but Disney's insistence on quality meant poor dividends. The double feature bill was crowding out short films and only feature-length films could offer sufficient financial return. Some time in 1934 Disney decided to make a feature length cartoon and *Snow White and the Seven Dwarfs* was released for Christmas 1937. Its world-wide success encouraged the production of more features and a move to purpose built premises at Burbank.

In 1938 the Disney brothers bought a house locally for their parents who had been living in Oregon; in November, less than a month after moving into the new home, Mrs Disney Senior died of asphyxiation; the accident was caused by a faulty furnace. This tragedy deeply affected all the Disneys and the father, Elias, never fully recovered, dying three years later in 1941.

Expansion in the thirties led to a huge increase of staff from a handful in 1930 to over a thousand a decade later. The Disney brothers and their families made an extensive visit to Europe in 1935. The two feature films that followed *Snow White and the Seven Dwarfs*, (*Pinocchio* and *Fantasia*), both released in 1940, were very expensive, and lost money.[9] War in Europe curtailed overseas markets, and in a bitter strike at home Disney lost some talented artists. In 1941 the US government asked Disney to make a goodwill tour of Latin America to counter possible Nazi influence. Disney took a group of senior artists with him and the visit was a great success, resulting in two feature films and a number of short subjects. When America entered the war the studio was used to make propaganda and training films. Compilation and package features followed until Disney returned to the classic story animated feature with *Cinderella* in 1950. Its success led to the production of other classics begun in the late thirties and then abandoned. Disney visited Europe again in 1949 and periodically until the year before he died, being especially fond of England and Switzerland. *Treasure Island* (1950) was the first of many live action feature films, the best of which were based on European classics or legends. His documentary films about wild life, beginning with *Seal Island* (1948), pioneered a whole range of subjects

Walt Disney and a young visitor at Selfridges store, London, for the opening of an exhibition of Sleeping Beauty *artwork (1959). Disney made many visits to the British Isles after the Second World War. Courtesy Richard Holliss.*

and were later developed as features, the most famous of which was *The Living Desert* (1953).

By this time Disney was planning his first theme park, Disneyland, which opened in 1955. In 1954 he launched his own TV programme, embracing the new media with typical confidence, utilising it to further the distribution of his product, and especially to sell Disneyland. He was not a creative presence in the production of his later animated features. His empire had expanded and he was bound up with the development of his second theme park at Florida, and more especially with the problems of pollution and environmental damage in large city conurbations. He had seen Los Angeles degenerate and was planning an experiment in urban development which he called an Experimental Prototype Community of Tomorrow. This, as well as a plan for a Walt Disney Boyhood Farm at Marceline,[10] was in embryonic form when he died of cancer in 1966, a few days after his sixty-fifth birthday.

Walt Disney was many men to many people; a devoted father and husband, he kept his private life strictly apart from the studio, and was loved by his family, friends and all those colleagues who were not his employees. To them he was generous in friendship, courteous in manner and considerate in association. They did not threaten him. He had been swindled three times as a very young man, and this accounts for his suppression of the egos of the men and women who worked directly for him. He was admired and feared, rather than loved at his studio, yet many of his associates remained loyal to him over a large number of years, his charismatic personality inspiring them to extend and expand their talents beyond their own expectations. Iconoclastic and hostile comment about the man has little substantiation; he deserves and will one day be honoured with a comprehensive biography.

Notes

1. See the bibliography for a complete list. Steven Watts *The Magic Kingdom: Walt Disney and the American Way of Life* (Boston/New York: Houghton Mifflin, 1997) is an excellent account of the man and his work, and the way they were shaped by and in turn influenced American society. Bob Thomas, *The Walt Disney Biography* (London: New English Library, 1977), though slim, still remains the only commissioned life, and the only book which quotes primary source material from the correspondence. Another biography approved by the family and based on oral histories and letters is Katherine & Richard Greene, *The Man Behind The Magic: The Story of Walt Disney* (New York: Viking Penguin, 1991). A number of books have been written describing the growth of the company after Walt Disney's death – see Alan Bryman, Ron Grover and John Taylor. The economic power of The Walt Disney Company lies beyond the scope of this study, but it should be noted that the operating revenue in 1991 was $6.2 bn., 'making it the third biggest leisure corporation in the world', Michael Durham, 'The Marketing of Mickey Mouse', *Independent on Sunday*, 5 April 1992, 3. By 1996 the Company had become 'the biggest entertainment company in the world and one of the 30 US stocks on which the Dow Jones index is based', Jonathan Glancey, 'Do we need Disney', *Independent*,

15 July 1996, 25. 'Disney, a $42-billion colossus after swallowing the ABC television network this year, has mastered the art of producing top-quality animation as well as mobilising the entire company to launch its films', James Bates and Patrice Apodaca, *Los Angeles Times*, 20 June 1996, A28.

2. The myths surrounding Disney's life and death remain unsubstantiated and the family has publicly disclaimed them. Like King Arthur, Robin Hood and Elvis Presley, Walt Disney has been born in more than one place and has died to be born again.

3. Quoted in Joan Gilbert, 'Disney's Marceline Memories', *Rural Missouri* January 1990, 5.

4. Walt Disney, 'The Marceline I Knew', *The Marceline News*, 2 September 1938.

5. In addition to the information in Thomas, 168, an ex-employee recalled: 'I saw a man in the machine shop drilling holes and he looked up and smiled. It was Walt Disney working on his train'. Tony Cierichetti, interview with author, Los Angeles, 12 June 1985. There are many instances of Disney's interest in the mechanical and intricate.

6. Quoted in Thomas, *The Walt Disney Biography*, 24.

7. There were many popular editions of Eadweard Muybridge's *Animals in Motion* and *The Human Figure in Motion*, first published in 1887. Disney also made use of a book on cartooning by E.G. Lutz, *Animated Cartoons: How They Are Made, Their Origin and Development* (New York: Scribner's, 1925). This has been pointed out in an excellent scholarly survey of Disney's early professional life: Russell Merritt and J.B. Kaufman, *Nel Paese delle Meraviglie: Walt Disney in Wonderland* (Pordenone: Edizione Biblioteca dell' Immagine, 1992).

8. The quotation is from Richard Holliss & Brian Sibley, *The Disney Studio Story* (London: Octopus, 1988), 14, which also gives a good account of the birth of Mickey Mouse. The origins are shrouded in mystery but we know that Walt Disney conceived the character and Ub Iwerks drew the master or 'key' animation drawings; the opening credits for the early *Mickey Mouse* cartoons contained the words 'A Walt Disney comic by Ub Iwerks'.

9. *Pinocchio* cost $2,600,000, *Fantasia* $2,280,000 and *Snow White* $1,488,000. Figures taken from Holliss and Sibley, *The Disney Studio Story*, 31 and 39.

10. See Chapter 10 for a description of Walt Disney Boyhood Farm.

CHAPTER 2

European influences before *Snow White and the Seven Dwarfs*

Vaudeville, the circus and early cinema

As an escape from the harshness of his childhood and early life, the young Walt Disney turned to popular culture. This naturally included the cinema which fascinated the boy, who was attracted to popular melodrama and to the comedies of Chaplin and Keaton. Chaplin himself and other English music hall artists had crossed the Atlantic to enrich the silent cinema. Vaudeville was another popular form of entertainment enjoyed by the young Disney. This American mixture of English music hall and European cabaret had become quite indigenous by the end of the 19th century and the height of its popularity in the United States was from about the turn of the century to the 1920s, an equally popular period for the British music hall. Both forms were largely superseded by the talkies and radio, but Disney grew up and enjoyed vaudeville at its height. Vaudeville was the relaxation of America, and, like the Disney cartoons that would come later 'it was a dig in the

A poster for Under the Gaslight, *an American melodrama of 1867. The exaggerated sentimentality and sensational aspects of melodrama were popularised by the silent cinema, and formed the cultural taste of the young Walt Disney.*

Circus and melodrama combine in The Corsican Brothers (1852) which was immensely popular on both sides of the Atlantic. It was filmed in 1915.

nation's ribs, its brassy assurance but a mask for an emotional simplicity, a beguiling sincerity, that was often as naive as a circus'.[1] We have seen how Disney loved vaudeville acts, and on one occasion he and his friend Walt Pfeiffer surprised Elias Disney who went on one of his rare visits to the vaudeville theatre and found that the youngster on top of a chair balancing act was his son Walt.

The circus was also an excitement for the boy who had come from the rural quiet of Marceline to the bustle of Kansas City. Parades and circuses would remain lifelong passions, and can be seen in many of his films, long or short, and remain part of the daily routine of the theme parks with their extravagant parades. The universality of the circus is well documented – it is an example of how Disney absorbed popular culture and then developed his own form, utilising both European and indigenous sources.

Popular music was another early influence – and here his father, who is generally regarded as a harsh parent, may be seen in a less formidable light. Elias Disney loved music and at Marceline he and his friend Will Rensemer 'played on their fiddles to the piano accompaniment of the Taylors' daughter. Walt sat on a straight-backed chair throughout the concert, enthralled by the music and astonished by this unexpected aspect of his father'.[2] Music was central to all Disney's work – even in the silent days, his characters dance and sing their way through the films;

Frontispiece to the 1850 edition of The Swiss Family Robinson *by J.R. Weiss. First published in 1812, it was translated into English in 1814 and has remained popular ever since. Disney loved adventure stories and he produced a live action film version of the Weiss novel in 1960; a Swiss Family Treehouse attraction based on the film was built at Disneyland.*

European influences before Snow White and the Seven Dwarfs

musical instruments, inanimate objects, and musical notes come alive, accompanied in the darkened auditorium at that time by live music, usually played on the piano. Not himself a musician, he would later employ composers and practitioners of the highest calibre to provide the music for his films.

The comic strip and adventure stories

Newspapers with their comic strips and adventure stories were readily available to the young Disney. According to his family and colleagues he was not a reader in later life, but there is evidence that as a boy he enjoyed reading some of the classic adventure stories that were available in the public library. He particularly liked the work of Mark Twain, Robert Louis Stevenson, Scott and Dickens, and it is worth noting that the first of his live-action feature films – and some of the best – are based on European classic adventure stories. They include *Treasure Island* (1950), *The Story of Robin Hood* (1952), *Rob Roy, 20,000 Leagues Under the Sea* (both 1954) and *Swiss Family Robinson* (1960). He was also interested in practical books on drawing or commercial art. In a letter written many years later Disney acknowledged his debt to the public library service. On 17 August 1937 he wrote to the American Library Association:

> It gives me great pleasure to tell you how much I regard services by the Public Libraries and especially that of the Kansas City Public Library. All during the early years of my youth, and a long time before I had given my career any thought, the Public Library has always held a tremendous interest for me.

... In Kansas City, when I became seriously interested in cartooning, I gained my first information on animation from a book written by H.C. [sic] Lutz which I procured from the Kansas City Public Library. I feel the Public Library has been a very definite help to me all through my career.

While we have established a sizeable library of our own, nevertheless we are constantly calling upon the local Public Library to supplement our needs ... [3]

Walt Disney's Laugh-O-grams *title card with a still from* Puss in Boots *(1922). The book and the castle were to be recurring images for Walt Disney.*
Used by permission from Disney Enterprises, Inc.

The book referred to here is *Animated Cartoons: How They Are Made, Their Origin and Development* by E.G. Lutz, first published in 1920. Popular with the animation industry, it strongly influenced the young Disney when he began his career as animator.[4]

Disney used the techniques suggested by Lutz to learn the craft of animation. At first he had to contend with a rough and ready form of entertainment which was not in very scrupulous hands, and the story of his early years is more a fight to maintain commercial stability and independence, using the popular cultural forms outlined here, than it is for seeking artistic expression. Later we shall see how European artistic influences were crafted onto the cartoons of the early and late thirties, and above all into the feature films which began with *Snow White*.

Early animation and Europe

Animation had flourished in Europe, along with live action film, before the first world war. Then Hollywood dominated the industry and Disney, by basing himself in Hollywood instead of in New York where most of the animation studios were established, allied himself to the centre of American popular film culture. As recent studies have shown, Disney's

The Four Musicians of Bremen. *A nineteenth-century illustration by Karl Offterdinger for the tale by Grimm. It was adapted by Walt Disney in 1922 for one of the early Laugh-O-grams.*

was one of many studios in the animation business; his early films were not very different from the output of his rivals, but quickly became technically and stylistically superior. He produced his *Laugh-O-gram* films in Kansas City with the help of his friend Ub Iwerks (1901–1971), the son of a Dutch immigrant. Kansas City was famous for its European immigrants[5] and some of the other young men that Disney employed in these early days were also the sons of immigrants.[6]

The cultural heritage of Europe, and in particular that of Germany, which the new Americans of the Midwest brought with them, cannot be over-emphasised. At the turn of the century more than twenty-seven per cent of Americans were of German stock, with at least one parent born in the old country. They came from all parts of Germany and settled in the Midwest. The majority were from humble farming, artisan and later on proletarian backgrounds. Many were illiterate.[7] They relied on popular cultural forms for entertainment and education, including the live theatre, comic strips, picture books and, increasingly towards the end of the 19th century, the cinema. The process of emigration was largely complete by 1917, though another influx took place in the late twenties and throughout the thirties, particularly by German Jews escaping from the Hitler regime, and this in turn affected Disney's work in the late thirties and forties.[8]

Seven out of Disney's first eight films are based on European fairy tales or folk tales. In 1922 he used the well-known German folk tale *The Four Musicians of Bremen* for the second in his early *Laugh-O-gram* series. The subtitle is 'a modernised version of that old fairy tale' by 'cartoonist Walt Disney'. The 'that' invites identification with the film maker; the implication here is of a new working, and a superior one, of an original which in some way is old fashioned or inferior. The taking over, and making afresh, material from the old world is demonstrated. The end is signalled by what was to become a standard conclusion to all Disney's films: 'and they lived happily ever after'. Though it has little in common with its original, the film reveals fluid animation and a series of meticulously plotted gags culminating in a chase and a battle; the Felix-like cat shows how animators were then, as now, borrowing from each other. The graphic line is vigorous, reminiscent of the comic strip; the situations rely on surprise and metamorphosis, staple ingredients of the animated films of that time. The running gag was constantly used; short climaxes with much repetition saved money and helped to divide labour so that animators could work on their own sections without the need to know what lay on either side of their sequences.

The graphic style of these films indicates the influence of newspaper cartoons and indeed many of the artists – for example Albert Hurter and Dick Huemer, both of whom would later work for Disney – worked on newspaper comic strips. At Hearst International the animators shared

Max und Moritz, gar nicht träge,
Sägen heimlich mit der Säge,
Ritzeratze! voller Tücke,
In die Brücke eine Lücke.

Als nun diese Tat vorbei,
Hört man plötzlich ein Geschrei:

„He, heraus! du Ziegen-Böck!
Schneider, Schneider, meck, meck, meck!" —
— Alles konnte Böck ertragen,
Ohne nur ein Wort zu sagen;
Aber, wenn er dies erfuhr,
Ging's ihm wider die Natur.

Schnelle springt er mit der Elle
Über seines Hauses Schwelle,

Denn schon wieder ihm zum Schreck
Tönt ein lautes: „Meck, meck, meck!"

Und schon ist er auf der Brücke,
Kracks! Die Brücke bricht in Stücke;

Wieder tönt es: „Meck, meck, meck!"
Plumps! Da ist der Schneider weg!

Grad als dieses vorgekommen,
Kommt ein Gänsepaar geschwommen.

Welches Böck in Todeshast
Krampfhaft bei den Beinen faßt.

Wilhelm Busch: Max and Moritz *(1865). The naughty boys play a prank on the tailor. The verses, also by Busch, form an integral part of his harsh comic world. His picture stories were published thirty years before the first successful comic strip. Courtesy Edith Wilson.*

Self portrait of Rudolph Dirks with his Katzenjammer Kids, created as a strip cartoon in 1897 and based on the Max and Moritz of Wilhelm Busch.
© Rudolph Dirks Estate.

The naughty Max and Moritz by Busch end up in the mill as corn fodder for ducks. The world of Busch is a rural one, like much of very early Disney.
Courtesy Edith Wilson.

floor space with the comic strip cartoonists, one of whom was George McManus of *Bringing up Father* fame. As early as 1913 the great European pioneer of animation Emil Cohl worked with McManus on a cartoon film series, now almost completely lost, of *The Newlyweds*.[9] Another of Hearst's animated cartoon series was *The Katzenjammer Kids* produced by Gregory la Cava and based on the comic strip drawn by Rudolph Dirks, a young artist of German descent. This had started in 1897 after Hearst, on a visit to Europe, had seen picture stories of the naughty boys Max and Moritz by the German artist Wilhelm Busch (1832–1908). The comic pictures and verses of this gifted artist were popular both in Germany and, to a lesser extent, in the United States. Working at Hearsts on *The Katzenjammer Kids* were George Stallings and I. Klein, who both later worked for Disney, Stallings on *Fantasia* and Klein on some of the *Silly Symphonies*.

Bold outlines characterise the animated films of the early Disney, in the tradition then of the comic strip, with a graphic fluidity of storyline laced with gags. Though there is no direct link between Disney and Wilhelm Busch there are many parallels; like Disney's, the world of Busch is a rural one, his characters and situations rooted in a popular tradition of peasant and lower bourgeois culture. The cruelty in Busch (Max and Moritz are ground up as corn and eaten for their naughtiness) is reflected in the ruthless *Schadenfreude* of the early Disney. Mickey makes a violin out of a cat in *Steamboat Willie* and hangs on a cow's udder when the latter becomes airborne in *Plane Crazy* (both 1928). The early Mickey Mouse and Donald Duck parallel Busch's harsh conflict between safe and repressive authority and the yearning for self-assertion. Before the mid 1930s these characters are like Busch's 'mar-peace, or troublemaker ... the dangerously vital, untrained, "unaccultivated" child, animal or rebel who challenges and ridicules the established order and the morality precariously constructed to sanctify it and uphold it'.[10] Heinrich Hoffmann (1809–1894) wrote *Struwwelpeter* in 1845 and it thus predates Busch by some twenty years; this famous example of picture stories depicting the cruel punishment meted out to miscreant children

„Her damit!" Und in den Trichter
Schüttelt er die Bösewichter. —

Rickeracke! Rickeracke!
Geht die Mühle mit Geknacke.

Hier kann man sie noch erblicken
Fein geschroten und in Stücken.

was enormously successful and acceptable, because the drawings were seen as grotesque caricatures.

Disney also showed concern for a continuous narrative which set him apart from his rivals. In this he reflected Busch's narrative drive and the editorial flair of men like Hearst which had led to the development of the comic strip. There is another link with Busch in that Disney's characters also inhabit a folktale world. Just as Disney looked back to a rural past in his films – and this applies throughout his work – so Busch and his contemporaries like Ludwig Richter (1803–1884) looked back to a sentimentalised golden age of pre-industrial rural Germany, exemplified in Romantic painting and decoration. This nostalgic movement, known as the Biedermeier tradition, is translated by The Oxford German Dictionary as a 'simple style of German interior decoration of about 1830' but the term includes realistic painting of the Romantic period, admired by the bourgeoisie at the turn of the century. Bourgeois *Gemütlichkeit* came to be seen as its keynote.[11] The word *gemütlich* is

Mickey Mouse has to resort to extreme measures to catch the plane in Plane Crazy *(1928).*
© Disney Enterprises, Inc.

Ludwig Richter: 'In the Meadow' from Fürs Haus *1859, a nostalgic look back to a rural past already disturbed by increasing industrialisation.*

Passagio chromatico.

Fuga del diavolo.

Forte vivace.

Capriccioso.

Wilhelm Busch: A New Year
Concert (1865). *The twisted legs
and multiple fingers anticipate the
distortions of the animated film.
Courtesy Edith Wilson.*

difficult to translate; cosy, pleasant, snug, warm, genial – adjectives applicable to much of Disney. Indeed Disney was a Biedermeier artist *par excellence*, since he used realism to promote nostalgia for a romanticised past.

There is a strong graphic line in the early films which reminds us of Busch and this extends to the grotesque. Busch also used the fluid distortion of people and objects that we associate with animation. This can be seen in the corkscrew legs of the listener and multiple arms and fingers of the performer in the story 'A New Year Concert'. Similarly Pete pulls Mickey's body till it collapses in a coil onto the ground, and Mickey has to pick it up in folds to tuck it back into his trousers (*Steamboat Willie* 1928). Disney's early work was ruthless but quickly became more Biedermeier than Busch. Just as in post-Romantic Germany naughty children were exorcised and transformed by the little angels of the children's magazines and journals, so Disney came to sanitise and sentimentalise his mouse in the post-Hays Code environment of Hollywood. A similar process took place in England. The robust illustrative tradition of Gillray and Rowlandson was continued by Cruikshank, Walter Crane and Randolph Caldecott in the 19th century, but sentimentalised by Mabel Lucie Attwell and her followers.

Anthropomorphism

Another European convention is the use of anthropomorphised animals for comic purposes, noticeable in most of the short cartoons of the period and in all Disney's early work. The *Alice* Comedies began in 1923 with the live action protagonist surrounded by cartoon animals but, by the end of the series in 1927, she is swamped by the animals who dominate the screen area. The debt to Carroll and Tenniel is slight, but the animals are, like many of their contemporaries, direct descendents of the European anthropomorphised creatures from stories, magazines and popular journals flourishing in the late nineteenth and early twentieth centuries.

As humanity has become less dependent on animals for its day-to-day life, this century has seen an increase in the anthropomorphic impulse, from Beatrix Potter in the nineteen hundreds to Kermit the Frog in the nineteen eighties. The impulse was, however, flourishing earlier; The French artist Honore Daumier (1808–1879) was acknowledged by the Disney artists as one of the painters they most admired. Daumier's ability to caricature society and to exaggerate with line and mass, appealed to the caricaturist in the Disney artists. His dancing line and visual commentary upon human behaviour was noted especially by the artists who were to work on the feature films.

Honoré Daumier: Emigration
(1856), from the series Actualitiés
in Le Charivari.
*Courtesy UCLA at the Armand
Hammer Museum of Art and
Cultural Center, Los Angeles.*

*Gustave Doré: illustration (detail)
for Orlando Furioso (1879). 'Never
did you set eyes on a more fantastic
throng.' This is typical of Dore's
fascination for the weird and
fantastic. He was one of the Disney
artists' favourite illustrators.*

European influences before Snow White and the Seven Dwarfs

The popularity of Gustave Doré (1832–1883) throughout Europe and the United States was immense. His work was particularly accessible through popular editions of his illustrations for Dante, Coleridge,

Ernest Griset: illustration for 'A Comical Picnic' from The Favorite Album of Fun and Fancy *(1880). Griset was influenced by Grandville and continued the anthropomorphic line.*

Cervantes and the Bible, which were dramatic, intense and theatrical. Although French and brought up in Strasbourg, his early life was spent close to Germany and the Black Forest, whose brooding darkness stimulated his imagination. A workaholic like Disney, his interest in the dramatic, macabre, comic and fantastic, expressed itself in over a hundred illustrated books and literally thousands of drawings. His charismatic personality and atelier attracted the fashionable and cognoscenti, just as Walt Disney and his studio would attract both artists and the world of fashion eighty years later. Doré's technically brilliant, often vulgar and melodramatic work appealed to Disney and his artists, for whom comedy, violence and the macabre were easily juxtaposed, though both Doré and Disney longed to be recognised for serious work rather than merely for 'cartoons'.[12]

The other striking example in France of anthropomorphic and grotesque illustration lay in the work of the tragically short-lived Grandville (1803–1847), whose real name was Jean-Ignace-Isadore Gérard (see Colour Plates 1 and 2). His fantastic drawings of animals and insects engaged in human activities influenced not only his fellow countryman Ernest Griset (1843–1907) (see Colour Plates 3 and 4), who spent most of his life in England, but also the English illustrators John Tenniel (1820–1914) and Edward Lear (1812–1888) and later still the Polish animator Ladislaw Starewicz (1882–1965) who worked in Moscow and Paris.[13]

European influences before Snow White and the Seven Dwarfs

American influences

There are, of course, many American influences on the early Disney, and we have seen how impressed he was by the silent cinema and in particular the work of Chaplin and Keaton. The American tradition of graphic anthropomorphism included artists like A.B. Frost who was the illustrator of *Uncle Remus*, and Harrison Cady, who invented a world of insects for his Beetleburgh. More important still as an influence was W.W. Denslow (1865–1915) who illustrated Frank Baum's *The Wonderful Wizard of Oz.* His strongly defined outlines, particularly the animals and characters of his illustrations, anticipated the clear outlines of the early animated cartoon. Mention should also be made of the comic artist T. S. Sullivant whose hippos, in particular, continue to endear.[14] As Lionel Lambourne points out, the anthropomorphic impulse is 'part of the recurrent mystery by which man, by his artistry, achieves the status of God, and remakes creation to his own fancy'.[15] Disney achieved this with his films and then three-dimensionally in the Magic Kingdoms. His first cartoon star was an animal, Oswald the Lucky Rabbit, a softer and more flexible Felix; his international success came with another animal, Mickey Mouse, revealing this impulse even more clearly; Mickey mirrors man.

Mickey Mouse and the *Silly Symphonies*

At first Mickey is the pioneer, pushing westwards and tackling the unknown by riverboat (*Steamboat Willie* 1928), triumphant in love over his feline rival, Pete, (*The Cactus Kid* 1930), rescuing Minnie from a

Walt Disney and Europe

fate worse than death or from a calamity (*The Fire Fighters* 1930). Though his playground is the world and Disney offers a universal background to Mickey's adventures, the environment is predominantly rural, small-town, the Midwest countryside close to Disney's heart and never far away from Africa or the South Seas or wherever the latest Mickey adventure takes place. The sense of improvised vaudeville permeates the early work; there is a constant reference to musical parades, pageants and theatricality in the silent work which is extended and repeated in the sound cartoons.[16] The distinctive narrative and editorial drive was Disney's personal contribution to the films since he was no longer having to do any of the drawing himself. His skills as raconteur and story teller began to flourish as he and his team developed the *Mickey Mouse* cartoons which continued their immense popularity. The confidence of the artists in Disney and in the character of Mickey is revealed in both the story development, the coarse good humour, and in the increasingly sophisticated black and white graphic skill of the animation.

Mickey Mouse goes to Minnie's rescue in The Fire Fighters *of 1930. The coarse humour and energy of the early Disney cartoons were appreciated by intellectuals and general public alike.*
© *Disney Enterpises, Inc.*

Illustrative art, and in particular the popular picture books and magazines of nineteenth and early twentieth century engravings become increasingly a visual source – one of many – for the *Silly Symphonies*. These followed closely on the success of Mickey Mouse, because Disney saw the need to expand his animation in a fiercely competitive field. Paul Terry, Walter Lantz and the Fleischer brothers were all bringing out cartoons with sound; Disney's able musical director Carl Stalling – who had also come from Kansas City – felt that the medium could be used purely to express music, without specific comic characters. Stalling said, 'I suggested not using the word "music" or "musical" ... but to use the word "symphony" together with a humorous word'. Walt asked me, 'How would "Silly Symphony" sound to you?' I said, 'Perfect!'.[17] The attitude towards high art is demonstrated by coupling the word 'symphony' with 'silly'; we are reminded of the 'that' in 'That old Fairy Tale'.

The first *Silly Symphony* was *The Skeleton Dance,* released in 1929, a few months after *Steamboat Willie.* Ub Iwerks animated almost the entire film; like Disney he was an instinctive artist without a conventional cultured background. The imagery of *The Skeleton Dance* is taken from nineteenth century gothic melodrama. The ghosts and ghouls of popular legend were staple literary and illustrative diet from Dickens and his early illustrator George Cruikshank (1792–1878), to Poe and his gothic illustrators. A howling dog, cats, bats and dancing skeletons are in a graveyard with a chapel, tombstones, the moon and waving branches. The film uses imagery of the ghost train or spook house of the fairground, where skeletons rise from tombs and cobwebs brush the visitor. Stalling also recalled a vaudeville act of skeleton dancers that he had seen as a boy. There are reminders of the comic-gothic in the silent cinema.[18] Here is a making over into film of various forms of popular art and

An illustration for The Skeleton Dance (1929): *the first of the* Silly Symphonies *it combines comic melodrama with skilful manipulation of sound and vision. The same adroit handling of popular attitudes to death can be seen the Haunted Mansion attraction at Disneyland Park.*
© *Disney Enterprises, Inc.*

George Cruikshank: illustration *'Ghosts'* (1841) reprinted in his 1870 *George Cruikshank's Omnibus*. Gothic melodrama has its comical side in Cruikshank's work, just as Disney's animated films a hundred years later would combine the comic and the macabre.

culture. The Disney 'Imagineers' were to exploit the same genre in the 'Haunted Mansion' attraction at Disneyland many years later. What gives the film its distinction is not only the comic effrontery with which it treats death and the convention of horror – one skeleton makes a xylophone of his fellow's ribs – but the graphic fluidity and conviction of its animation.

The fairy tale and European folk tale had been used in some of the *Mickey Mouse* shorts; (*Ye Olden Days* (1933) and *Gulliver Mickey* (1934) are examples), but the exploitation of European sources developed with the *Sillies*. In *The Clock Store* (1931) for instance, the ticking clocks and dancing figures are antecedents for those in *Snow White and the Seven Dwarfs* and more particularly in Geppetto's workshop in *Pinocchio*; another variation on the same theme is *The China Shop* (1934). The references to European popular illustration and entertainment are numerous; the wicked behaviour of the villain gloating over the lady shepherdess is out of Victorian melodrama via the Hollywood silent film. The behaviour of the wicked crow in *Bugs in Love* (1932) is similar. *Three Little Pigs* (1933) develops individual character and uses both music hall and melodrama in a comic mixture of both.

Satire was taken from the world of newspapers and used in both the *Mickeys* and the *Sillies* in such films as *Mickey's Gala Première* (1933), *Who Killed Cock Robin?* (1935) and *Mother Goose Goes Hollywood*

Some of Albert Hurter's sketches from He Drew as He Pleased *(1948). Hurter's fertile imagination inspired Walt Disney and his colleagues for more than ten years between 1931 and 1942.*
© Disney Enterprises, Inc.

(1938). The artists responsible for *Who Killed Cock Robin?* were Bill Cottrell and Joe Grant. The former (1906–1995) was of English parentage, and was engaged by Disney in 1929 on the strength of work that he had done for the George Herriman comic strip *Krazy Kat*.[19] Joe Grant (b. 1908) came from a newspaper background and his satirical cartoons in the *Los Angeles Record* caught Disney's eye (see Colour Plate 5).[20]

As the studio developed, and as more staff were employed from universities and art schools, the films became more sophisticated, the style more realistic. In 1932 art classes were begun by Don Graham, art teacher at the Chouinard Art Institute in Los Angeles. The Disney veterans

Walt Disney and Europe

Still: The Night Before Christmas *(1933). This opening scene is typical of the rich backgrounds for many of the* Silly Symphonies *of the 1930s.*
© Disney Enterprises, Inc.

found him an inspiring teacher with his 'action analysis' classes, and insistence on the observation of the movement and repose of the living model, following the European tradition. As well as using live action film footage, and the artists' own animation, Graham conducted classes at the nearby Griffith Park Zoo where the artists could observe and sketch living animals. There was some resistence to Graham at first, particularly from the older artists and animators from New York, but both sides learnt from each other.

The inspiration, for example, of the Swiss born Albert Hurter (1883–1942) is acknowledged by the Disney artists.[21] He joined Disney in 1931 after working in animation on the East Coast and he was given complete freedom to offer his own idiosyncratic sketches as ideas for film; he humanised inanimate objects in bizarre and surreal ways; flowers, plants, furniture and utensils took on strange and sometimes alarming life under his pen. He introduced the studio to the work of Busch, Hermann Vogel and Heinrich Kley. (The two latter German artists influenced the early feature films.) Hurter had a great knowledge of European art and a photographic memory. Bill Cottrell remembered that he could identify errors of architectural design or a period costume detail without recourse to reference books or photographs. 'He could look at a cartoon character, say a military man, and he'd say, "That uniform needs six buttons, not five". "How do you know?" we asked.

European influences before Snow White and the Seven Dwarfs

Arthur Rackham(above): illustration for Aesop's Fables (1912). Rackham's work was popular in the United States and admired by the Disney artists. © Arthur Rackham estate.

Model Sheet (right): Flowers and Trees (1932), Disney's first cartoon in colour. The wicked old tree, who lusts after the heroine, is a reminder of Arthur Rackham's anthropomorphised trees. © Disney Enterprises, Inc.

"Because I saw it in a museum in Zurich" he said'. In a generous tribute after Hurter's death Ted Sears of the studio story department collected 700 of his drawings for publication. Walt Disney, who rarely praised and who suppressed the individuality of those who worked for him,[22] wrote:

> Albert Hurter was a master creator of fantasy. In his whimsical imagination all things were possible. The sketches in this book testify not only to his rare sense of humour but also to his genuine ability as an artist.[23]

Hurter had a profound influence on the work of the studio; of the seventy-five *Sillies* produced between 1929 and 1939 – when they ceased – fifty-two are based on European stories or ideas. *Babes in the Woods* and *Santa's Workshop* (both 1932) show the influence of Hurter's gothic fantasy and love of the droll. His influence pervades *Lullaby Land*, *The Pied Piper* and *The Night Before Christmas* of 1933 and *The Flying Mouse*, *Goddess of Spring*, and *Peculiar Penguins* of 1934. The list continues in 1935 but by 1936 he was working on *Snow White and the Seven Dwarfs*, and his inspiration on more feature films such as *Pinocchio*, *Fantasia*, *The Reluctant Dragon* and *Peter Pan* was felt into the 1940s and early

Walt Disney and Europe

1950s. He had no idea of the value of his work, which was taken away by the other artists. When Ted Sears began his compilation, Bill Cottrell remembered that '[Hurter's] pictures were stolen from the studio. When the book came out it was not even his best work because ... a lot of the stuff had disappeared'. In the catalogue for the last major exhibition of Disney art in Britain in 1976, John Russell Taylor wrote:

> His influence is visible in many of Disney's shorts and features up to (his) death at the time of *Pinocchio*, particularly those aspects of the gothic and the grotesque which relate most closely to European book illustration of the period and look back towards art nouveau and symbolism. Hurter indeed seems to have been responsible almost single handed for grafting this strain on to Disney's original home-grown American.[24]

European visit 1935

Increasing strain and fear of another breakdown (he had suffered from nervous exhaustion in 1931) led Disney to take an extended holiday with his brother Roy in the summer of 1935. With their wives, the brothers visited England, France, the Low Countries, Italy and Switzerland. Disney discovered sources in Europe for model making, picking up feathers and fabrics which could be used later in the model department. 'He brought back automata – he admired a mechanical man that whistled and model birds that sang' recalled Bill Cottrell who had also accompanied Disney on his European tour. The seeds for Disney's obsession with the mechanical simulation of reality can be traced to this European visit. The European forests of *Snow White and the Seven Dwarfs* and the little town of *Pinocchio* led on to the miniature Europe of Disneyland. The mechanical man who whistled led him on the Audio-Animatronics figures which populate his fantasy worlds.

After eleven weeks he returned refreshed, and full of new ideas. While in Europe he had ordered a large quantity of books. Some he brought with him, and the Disney Studio Library received a further consignment from 5 July to 24 September 1935 with 90 titles from France, 81 from England, 149 from Germany and 15 from Italy.[25] They included many standard illustrated classics. In a memorandum dated 23 December 1935 Disney outlined his ideas to Ted Sears and the story department:

> Some of these little books which I brought back with me from Europe have very fascinating illustrations of little peoples, bees and small insects who live in mushrooms, pumpkins, etc. This quaint atmosphere fascinates me and I was trying to think how we could build some little story that would incorporate all of these cute little characters ...

Hermann Vogel: illustration for his Album (1896). Vogel's picture albums were in the Disney Studio Library and influenced Albert Hurter, Ken Anderson and others.

Disney's enthusiasm is captured in the dictated memorandum as he went on to suggest ideas incorporating Mickey and the gang into the world of European nursery rhyme and fable:

... Maybe to make these things more individual so they would stand out from the mob type of cartoons, we could incorporate Mickey or Minnie or the Duck into the fantastic settings they suggest. Mickey and Minnie might take a ride on a magic carpet and arrive in a weird land or forest, meet little elves of the forest, or be captured by an old witch or giants and ogres. They could eat some fruit that makes them grow very tall or small – or get into a forest of wild trees and flowers and grotesque mirror pools with reflections and images. They might be trapped by three enormous spiders. Might get into a land of shadows ...

This memorandum affords a rare opportunity to 'see' Walt Disney at work, surrounded by his staff, his charismatic personality infecting them with his enthusiasm. He mentioned *The Big Frog and the Little Frog* and *The Frog Who Would A'Wooing Go*. 'We might use something on this order where we could bring in frogs, crickets, bugs and insects around ponds and marshes, etc'. This idea was used in *The Old Mill* (1937) which opens at dusk in a long shot. We see a pond with reeds and a cobweb in the foreground, and an old mill in the distance. Cows move slowly home across the landscape. The colours are muted, the outlines soft, a sense of dampness, mist and impending darkness is obtained through light and shade, a chiaroscuro which reminds us of Dutch landscape painting. Frogs, crickets and fireflies begin a twilight chorus. This is a late, complex example of a *Silly Symphony* (it won the Academy Award for 1937) and it shows how the studio was able to present a short subject with great subtlety, when its resources were being fully stretched on the first feature film. The staff had grown from a handful to over a hundred in the early thirties to 750 by the time Disney was making *Snow White and the Seven Dwarfs*. His artists had a cultural background and an understanding of European influences which he utilised and made anew in the popular American form of cinema (see Colour Plates 6 and 7). The energy of the technician and the perfectionist were not the only qualities which he added, however. He brought a gift of storytelling, a restating in visual terms of an old popular form. This quality began to show itself in the shorts and was developed, along with complex associations, resonances and tensions in *Snow White and the Seven Dwarfs*. It was a period of intense creativity which is summed up by a comment of Joe Grant, one of Disney's closest associates: 'I was enthusiastic as hell about that business. I thought it was the greatest thing; I couldn't think of anything beyond it ... I had fallen in love with the *idea*, particularly the idea and then him later because, God, he was – he *was* the idea' (see Colour Plates 8 and 9).

Notes

1. Phyllis Hartnoll, *The Oxford Companion to the Theatre* (London: Oxford University Press, 1951), 823.

2. Thomas, *The Walt Disney Biography*, 21.

3. Quoted by Paul Anderson in *Persistence of Vision* 5 (1993), 8.

4. Merritt and Kaufman, *Nel Paese delle Meraviglie*, 56.

5. H.W. Gatzke, *Germany and the United States* (Cambridge, Mass: Harvard University Press, 1980), 30.

6. Hugh Harman, Rudolf Ising, Carman Maxwell, Lorey Tague, Otto Waldman. Some of these young men were later to make distinguished careers for themselves in animation.

7. Gatzke, *Germany and the United States*, 39.

8. German expressionism would have an effect on the first three feature films; Oskar Fischinger was to work briefly for Disney on *Fantasia*. See Chapter 6.

9. Donald Crafton, *Before Mickey: the Animated Film 1898–1928* (Cambridge, Mass: MIT Press, 1982), 83. One film of the series has been discovered. See Donald Carfton, *Emile Cohl, Caricature and Film* (Princeton: University Press, 1990), 164.

10. Walter Arndt, *The Genius of Wilhelm Busch* (Berkeley: University of California Press, 1982), 16.

11. Geraldine Norman, *Biedermeyer Painting* (London: Thames & Hudson, 1987).

12. After seeing the film *To Kill a Mockingbird* (1962) Disney said 'Why can't I make films like that?' Interview with Diane Disney Miller, 5 August 1986.

13. See the Bibliography for references to Grandville, Griset and Starewicz.

14. I am indebted to Russell Merritt and Will Ryan for drawing my attention to the work of Denslow and Sullivant.

15. Lionel Lambourne, *Ernest Griset* (London: Thames & Hudson, 1979), 4.

16. Merritt and Kaufman, 25.

17. Quoted in Holliss and Sibley, *The Disney Studio Story*, 18.

18. The English pantomime tradition of an interlude with skeletons dancing continues to this day.

19. William Cottrell was born in South Bend, Indiana in 1906, of English parents. His maternal grandfather Benjamin Davis was a Shakespearean actor; his paternal grandfather was Thomas Cottrell a theatrical scene painter. Cottrell *père* was a graduate of Birmingham University and emigrated in 1901. Young Bill Cottrell himself graduated in English and Journalism from Occidental College California. On the strength of work that he had done for George Herriman's *Krazy Kat* comic strip, he was engaged by Walt Disney in 1929, staying with the company for 53 years apart from a short break with Paramount. He worked as inker and painter, then on camera, and later in the story department. He brought gentleness and good taste to all his work, a foil to the satirical sharpness of his colleague Joe Grant with whom he worked happily in the late 1930s until Disney split the partnership. He moved over to work at WED, the planning and design department for the Magic Kingdoms. A Sherlock Holmes admirer, Bill Cottrell's idea of a story about a dog detective was taken up many years later by the company for its animated feature *The Great Mouse Detective* (1986). Bill Cottrell died in 1995.

20. Born in 1908 and son of the Art Editor of *The New York Journal*, the young Joe Grant grew up in a newspaper atmosphere. His cartoons and caricatures of film stars for *The Los Angeles Record* caught the eye of Walt Disney, who personally telephoned him and offered him a job. Well read, Grant brought articulate erudition and visual sophistication to the studio; he was familiar with the work of Busch, Daumier, Doré and other artists and illustrators such as Hermann Vogel. He liked reading and knew the work of popular classical writers like Carroll, Dickens and Jane Austen. He was aware of the astringent literary tradition of New York epitomised by *The New Yorker* and was familiar with the cartoons in *Punch* and the German *Simplicissimus*. He worked with and admired Albert Hurter and was instrumental in acquiring copies of illustrated books for the newly opened (1934) Disney Studio Library. He worked with Bill Cottrell in the story department until Disney made him head of the new model department in 1938. Here he exercised great power and influence. With Dick Huemer he was co-story director of *Fantasia* and co-writer of *Dumbo*. He was production supervisor of *Make Mine Music* but left the studio a disillusioned man in 1949. An outstanding calligrapher and graphic artist, Joe Grant who at the time of writing (1998) is ninety, is again working for the studio to which he once contributed so much. He has been senior story advisor on the animated feature films *Pocahontas* (1994), *The Hunchback of Notre Dame* (1995) and *Hercules* (1996), and is the Grand Old Man of the Disney Studio. See John Canemaker, *Before the Animation Begins* (New York: Hyperion, 1996), 50–63.

21. Swiss born, Albert Hurter (1883–1942) studied academic art in Switzerland and France, where he also taught painting. After emigrating to the United States, he joined Raoul Barré's Studio as cartoonist and animator. The studio was famous for its *Mutt and Jeff* (1916) series. He was passionately attached to the desert so he moved to the West Coast and set up a small commercial art studio in Los Angeles. He joined Disney in 1931 and designed the characters, costumes and homes for *Three Little Pigs* (1933) which was one of the studio's early successes. The Disney Studio Library accessions at this time attest to his contribution of large numbers of illustrated European books. Given complete freedom to produce drawings of startling and bizarre originality, his influence on the shorts and early features was profound. Shy and unassuming, he spent his time in the desert or with his valuable stamp collection when he was not at the studio. He continued to draw right up till the end of his life, making fun to the last, even of his hospital surroundings. See Canemaker, *Before the Animation Begins* 8–25.

22. Disney's determination to assert his name is linked with his obsession with control and quality of product. It has often been noted and the following comment is typical: 'When I first joined the studio, Walt took me on one side and said, "If you have any idea about making a name for yourself, get out. I'm the only star here".' Ken Anderson, interview with author, 10 May 1985.

23. Albert Hurter, *He Drew as he Pleased*, Intr. Ted Sears (New York: Simon & Schuster, 1948).

24. *The Artists of Disney*, Intr. John Russell Taylor, (London: Victoria & Albert Museum, 1976).

25. Records of Walt Disney Studio Library.

CHAPTER 3

'I believe in Fairy Tales': *Snow White and the Seven Dwarfs*

Producing an animated feature film

Disney worked in conference with his staff, accepting material from all departments and paying bonuses for ideas or gags that were used. The outline of a film was discussed in the story department, the heart of the entire creative process, where the artists' collaborative drawings and 'inspirational' sketches were examined at every stage by Disney and his senior associates. These sketches were intended to inspire and stimulate; they were presented in sequences of forty-eight or more drawings on large storyboards. All the details were finalised and approved by Disney before being photographed and circulated to all departments. Characterisation was then developed by the animators. Scripts were written, but the storyboards were the creative centre. As an actor fleshes out a role, so the animators gave life and personality to their characters. The main actions were drawn by the senior animators, the remainder by their assistants. These were again previewed on test reels by Disney and the senior artists and directors. By this time the sound track had been recorded, to which the animation was matched by a precise set of instructions to the animators on exposure sheets. This stage of animation may be likened to the actual stage performance of actors, the animators using pencil and paint instead of voice and body movement to bring life to characters that had been designed over a long period of trial and error. It is not surprising that the senior animators have received most of the studio publicity; Disney called some of them his 'nine old men'. The 'inspirational' and story artists, layout men and women and background painters have recently begun to receive the attention due to them.[1]

Before the invention of the Xerox process in 1959, allowing the direct transfer of drawings from paper to transparent celluloid (cel), the animators' outline drawings were carefully cleaned up by another assistant and sent to the all-female inking and painting department. The drawings were traced onto cels in various coloured inks; as many as four or five coloured inks might be used on one character (see Colour Plate 73). When the Xerox process was first used, outlines were all in black, though recent technological advances now allow a variety of coloured outlines. Modern Disney animation is still initially an artistic process with the final work produced by computer, dispensing (except for promotional and spurious 'special edition' cels) with the laborious skills of inking and painting, but our concern is with the traditional inked cel, the reverse side of which was then painted and the cel photographed against its appropriate background. The layout and background departments ensured that character and background worked together. The backgrounds were essential environments in which the characters lived and moved. There might also be the need for elaborate special effects, and a separate department was evolved.

Thousands of drawings were needed for a Disney short, and up to a million or more for a feature. The whole elaborate, painstaking and expensive process was controlled and managed on strict factory production lines, with one department knowing little about another. At the height of production at the end of 1938 Disney employed 1,200 artists.

The development of *Snow White and the Seven Dwarfs*

The studio's work on the *Silly Symphonies* served as artistic and technical preparation for *Snow White and the Seven Dwarfs*, and recruitment from art schools and universities ensured an academic dimension to the creative input. In spite of the studio's popular success, especially with *Mickey Mouse*, the cinema industry's distribution system was squeezing out shorts with its new double feature packages. To survive, like Chaplin and Laurel and Hardy, Disney had to make features; his shorts, no matter how successful, did not pay well enough. The full length possibilities of *Alice in Wonderland* and *Rip Van Winkle* had been considered but the projects fell through, despite the enthusiasm of Mary Pickford who wished to star as Alice;[2] and Disney was refused permission to make *Babes in Toyland* since it was earmarked for Laurel and Hardy by RKO. After considering *Snow White and the Seven Dwarfs* as a short subject, he decided to make it his first feature. Disney remembered his grandmother reading him the tales of Grimm and Hans Andersen. 'It was the best time of day for me', he said, 'and the stories and characters in them seemed quite as real as my schoolmates and our games. Of all the characters in the Fairy Tales, I loved *Snow White and the Seven Dwarfs* the best'.[3] Disney's enthusiasm for the story of *Snow White and the Seven Dwarfs* is recalled in many accounts. Ken Anderson, one of the film's art directors remembered:

> We went to the sound stage where there was a tier of seats and Walt told us the story of *Snow White and the Seven Dwarfs* ... We were spellbound. The lights were all on and they were on us, not on him. He was all by himself and he acted out this fantastic story. He would

become the Queen, he would *become* the dwarfs. He was an incredible actor, a born mime.

In a magazine article for *Photoplay Studies* Disney gave his reasons for choosing *Snow White and the Seven Dwarfs*; he remembered seeing it 'as a play [sic] when I was a small boy. I saved some of the money I made from my newspaper round to go and see it, and I was so impressed that I could have seen it over and over again'. The story also had universal appeal, he said, and the dwarfs would be interesting characters to animate. He could introduce attractive 'little animals and birds of the type with which we had success in the past'.[4]

Disney had in fact seen a film, not a 'play', in 1916, starring Marguerite Clark who looked like Mary Pickford. He attended a free showing, simultaneously projected on four screens to sixteen thousand children, some squeezed two to a seat in the twelve thousand seater Kansas City Convention Centre. The Director of the film J. Searle Dawly wrote:

> Seated in one of the top galleries was ... Walt Disney. Years afterwards at a Special Diner [sic] given to Marguerite Clark at the Disney Studios in Hollywood he told Miss Clark that Snow White picture he saw in Kansas City – from a loft gallery seat – was the inspiration that caused him to create the first long cartoon picture.[5]

Thus out of popular culture Disney made another product of the same culture, reflecting his own, but imbuing the new version with complexities which revived and have subsequently sustained its popularity. The film has been re-released many times. This popularity is due as much to the European origins of the story and the way Disney utilised these origins, as to the responses that he and his staff brought to bear upon it. The Marguerite Clark version has recently been found and it may not have been available when Disney's film was in production. There is no mention of it in the story conference notes in the Walt Disney Archives. These meetings began in 1934 and continued until the film's release in December 1937.

From Grimm to Disney

The Grimm story was considerably altered. Disney removed two attempts by the Queen to kill Snow White, first with a poisoned comb and then with a bodice. He replaced the traditional repetitive narrative element with running gag and comic repetitions, both visual and verbal; these include Doc's spoonerisms, Grumpy's misogyny and the slow tortoise joke. In Grimm the Queen dances to death in red hot shoes at the wedding; in Disney she falls off a precipice. Grimm's line 'the wild beasts roared about her, but none did her any harm' is expanded into the scene where the animals and birds help Snow White and take her to the dwarfs'

Ludwig Richter: illustration for 'Snow White' in Grimms' Fairy Tales (1838–46). The disguised queen meets Snow White at the dwarfs' cottage; the Disney version has a similar scene.

cottage. At her death in the story the 'birds came too and wept for Snow White'; this is elaborated into the mourning of all nature round the coffin which is central to the film. The Disney Studio Library contained copies of illustrated versions of Grimm by artists such as Richter, Von Schwind and the Dutch illustrator Rie Cramer.[6]

Disney based his scenario on Winthrop Ames's successful play. This was produced on Broadway in 1912, adapted from a German play *Schneevittchen* by the nineteenth century writer Karl August Goerner. Ames drew upon European theatrical tradition, English pantomime, and especially *Cinderella*. He also made use of *Peter Pan*.

Disney used the stage convention of disguise when the Queen becomes the Witch; it is a transformation convention taken from stage to screen. His Snow White, like Cinderella, is dressed in rags and made to clean the palace – this is not in Grimm. Animals and birds (in the play a bird) help her to find the dwarfs' cottage. The affinities to Barrie's play are striking. *Peter Pan* was a great success in America, opening on Broadway on 6 November 1905 with Maud Adams in the title role; dressed in a costume of leaves she looked like Cinderella, and Marguerite Clark's 1916 Snow White costume is similar. Clark had played Peter Pan in St Louis before opening in *Snow White and the Seven Dwarfs* on Broadway. Peter and the six Lost Boys need a mother and Snow White acts as mother to the seven dwarfs; Peter wants Wendy to act as mother, cook and housekeeper as well as to play games, and Snow White cooks, cleans, dances and sings with the dwarfs.

Another link with the theatre, especially English pantomime, is the asexuality of the heroine. Disney issued a circular to the effect that 'she is a Janet Gaynor type – 14 years old'.[7] Grimm's seven year old child has become the idealised silent screen heroine epitomised by Mary Pickford, whom Disney admired. Janet Gaynor had been a childlike actress of the silent twenties, and presented an ambiguous sexuality

Layout drawing of Disney's Snow White in the woods being conducted to the dwarfs' cottage by the animals.
© Disney Enterprises, Inc.

which became more complex in the thirties. The attitude towards Snow White is ambiguous because although she is seen as a child – running away, at play, saying the dwarfs' cottage is 'just like a dolls' house', she also has sexually romantic longings for the Prince. This is emphasised by the Queen's jealousy when she sees the first meeting between the Prince with Snow White.

The artists were told to stress Snow White's isolation. On 27 June 1936 Disney suggested that when she talked to the lost bird, what she said 'should have a double meaning – such as "Are you a little orphan?" In other words, have the conversation with more contact to her present predicament ... It should be a little baby bird to parallel her own situation'. The flight through the forest projects the imaginative fear experienced in childhood which the adult remembers. Disney also likened Snow White's rider to her prayer 'and please make Grumpy like me' to a child's sudden afterthought.

Starting with the Ames play, Disney tried to develop the relationship between the Queen, the Prince and Snow White. The Prince trespasses upon the Queen's domain when he hears Snow White singing. His love for Snow White is jealously watched by the Queen, and on 15 October 1934 Disney suggested:

> ... that the Queen captures Prince to keep him in her power. Queen wants to marry Prince but he refuses to acknowledge that she is 'the fairest in the land' since he has seen Snow White ... He has been dragged away to think it over, [so] that he will not interfere with her diabolical plans on Snow White. Heh! Heh! Heh! Is *she* a witch!

In this early version the Prince escapes with the help of the birds and rides off to the rescue of Snow White. The scene was dropped, but the idea was used later in the 1959 Disney version of *Sleeping Beauty*, in which the prince is captured by the evil fairy Maleficent and then rescued by the good fairies.

Ludwig Richter: Snow White. *This shows Snow White with blond hair, and the Disney heroine was also blond in some early sketches. Richter emphasises, as does Disney, the sympathy between Snow White and the animal world.*

Snow White and the Seven Dwarfs: *Layout drawing of the Prince and Snow White. Like Juliet, Snow White is wooed from below. Though out of sight, the wicked queen looks on.*
© *Disney Enterprises, Inc.*

Ludwig Richter: illustration for Beschaulischen und Erbaulischen *(1851–1855). The conventional romantic hero's costume, with jerkin, short sword and feathered cap, can also be seen in the Disney version. Richter, like Disney, has doves and an older woman looking on. In Disney a dove acts as a messenger from Snow White to the Prince.*

The Ames play then is the foundation upon which Disney worked. We know that he saw a version of the play acted locally in Pasadena in February 1935, at a girls' school, the Flintridge Sacred Heart Academy. He wrote to the Principal, Miss Lillian Fitch on 9 February:

> Thank you very much for the tickets to the presentation of Winthrop Ame's [sic] *Snow White and the Seven Dwarfs*.
>
> Mrs Disney and I enjoyed the performance very much and we wish to compliment you on your clever staging of the production. We should also like to congratulate the members of the cast who handled their parts in a manner that would do justice to professionals.

The use of music in the film demonstrates a further link with the theatre, acting as an interlude to the dramatic action as well as furthering the plot. Disney wanted the music 'to set a new pattern – a new way to use music – weave it into the story so somebody doesn't just burst into song'.[8]

On 31 October 1935 he was clear about what he wanted from the composer, Frank Churchill, '... Dialogue and music work together and use dialogue to lead into songs naturally ... Out in the woods she picks up words from the birds and it suggests song to her.'

Frank Churchill (1902–1942) was steeped in popular classical and light music, and had composed the music for fifty Disney shorts before his work on *Snow White and the Seven Dwarfs*. He sensed just how to pitch the musical level between operetta and popular ballad, seeking for ways to let the music spring from the dramatic action.

The conventions of operetta, the theatre, even Shakespeare – and *Romeo and Juliet* in particular – are evident in the scene at the wishing well between the Prince and Snow White. Operetta was used by Hollywood in the early thirties in its voracious search for absorbing sound into entertainment; *The Vagabond King* (1930) and *The Merry Widow* (1934) are two examples, and the ornate *Romeo and Juliet*, partly designed by the Englishman Oliver Messel and premièred on 20 August 1936, was one of the 'art' films on release during *Snow White and the Seven Dwarfs*'s creative period.[9] The *mise-en-scène* of Gothic balcony, flowers in blossom, courtyard and wall, and the protagonists separated by height are similar in both, the sense of danger dramatised by Shakespeare with the arrival of day, and by Disney with the jealous Queen looking on from her curtained window. Disney also chose an operatic voice for the heroine. Many voices were tested including that of Deanna Durbin, whose voice Disney rejected as too mature. He chose instead the voice of Adriana Caselotti, the eighteen year old daughter of an Italian singing teacher. Caselotti made her coloraturo soprano voice sound younger than it really was. 'I knew I had to be the little fourteen year old,' she said, 'so I imitated that voice that I thought a fourteen year old would sound like ... but I never told Disney that. He never knew it.' The importance of diction was stressed, but Caselotti found the spoken lines difficult and the screen Snow White has, in consequence, a robust American idiomatic quality which was an unintentional contribution from the actress/singer.

One of the lines was, 'Grumpy, I didn't know you cared'. Instead of that I couldn't get the DNT at the end: *didn't* ... I would say 'din''. We rehearsed this thing over and over again and Walt said, 'Listen, you're going to have to put this thing in there'. So I tried again – fine in rehearsal and came the take. I still got it wrong and Walt said, 'Oh, the hell with ...' And it's still there.

The theatrically based adaptation via stage and screen, with its roots in Grimm, gave Disney a strong story structure. The difficulties began in attempting to develop the straight human element, and the limitations of animation pushed the story away from popular romantic convention towards caricature, with anthropomorphic animals and birds. The attempt to develop the straight human element failed because the artists

Still: Romeo and Juliet *(1936) directed by George Cukor, with Leslie Howard and Norma Shearer. There are several visual parallels between this and* Snow White and the Seven Dwarfs. *© Time Warner. Courtesy British Film Institute.*

Publicity illustration for The Goddess of Spring *a Silly Symphony of 1934, in which Pluto the god of the underworld captures Persephone, the goddess of spring. © Disney Enterprises, Inc.*

'I believe in Fairy Tales': Snow White and the Seven Dwarfs   41

were not capable of animating human beings convincingly. An experiment was made with a *Silly Symphony*, *The Goddess of Spring* in 1934 and the struggle to master the human form continues until this day. There was also a failure in style; the resort of the artists, when unable to exaggerate or caricature, was to cliché, to an accepted convention of the period which was not imaginatively realised in the animated form. One example of this failure was the Prince, who was to have appeared in a romantic dream sequence in the middle of the film during Snow White's song 'Some Day My Prince Will Come'. The scene was to include a wedding in the clouds, with Snow White and the Prince being escorted by a troupe of baby stars pulling or blowing a love boat through the sky. On 8 December 1936 Disney suggested:

You take some of those European story books and you see little baby stars. Like some holding sheets of music and all singing ...

I felt this sequence would be for the women. After all 80 per cent of our audience are women. If we get something they loved it would

Story sketch for Snow White and the Seven Dwarfs: *Snow White and the Prince are drawn by stars through the sky in a love boat, in a proposed dream sequence to accompany the song 'Some Day my Prince will Come'. The sequence was dropped before it reached the animation stage.*
© *Disney Enterprises, Inc.*

Walt Disney and Europe

help because there is a lot of slapstick stuff that women don't like so well. If our characters are cute they'll like them.

We don't cater to the child but to the child in the adult – what we all imagined as kids is what we'd like to see pictured.

This comment by Disney on the audience he and his colleagues was addressing is important. Again and again he referred to 'the audience', and at this stage in the history of the studio, there was never any reference in all the story conference discussions, except by implication, to children. He saw his audience as adults *and* children. Indeed, there had been no audience research for the animated feature film because there had been no precedents for *Snow White and the Seven Dwarfs*, and the concept of discrete audiences of adults, teenagers or children had not yet been formulated. Disney conducted audience research among studio personnel and later by more sophisticated means, through ARI research.[10] He was always aware of popular response to his work, and the comment here about the proportion of women in the audience is evidence of his awareness. The appeal to women, as understood by Disney and his colleagues (women were seldom present at the story conferences), can be seen in the story sketches of the dream sequence showing the stars lining up, Busby Berkeley style. They reappear in the *Silly Symphony Wynken, Blynken and Nod* (1938) as 'star-fish' captured by the babies in their wooden shoe ship. Baby imagery continued until the plethora

Illustration: Water Babies, *a* Silly Symphony *of 1935.*
© *Disney Enterprises, Inc.*

of fauns and cupids in *Fantasia* (1940), which reinforced the accent on sentimentality and baby appeal in Disney. The majority of cinemagoers were women who were also the main target for advertising.[11] A sentimental appeal aimed at women thus forms part of the complex make-up of the film.

By early 1937 Disney had, however, abandoned the dream sequence. Instead, as Snow White sings to the dwarfs, the camera allows close shots of all the characters, emphasising the romantic mother/child relationship between them. Also abandoned for reasons of length were a comic soup-drinking sequence and one where the dwarfs made Snow White a four poster bed. The dream sequence was again adapted for *Sleeping Beauty* (1959) as a fantasy ending to the film with the hero and heroine dancing up into the clouds.

Hollywood reiterated the same stories in different ways over and over again 'with minor variations on recurring themes. By far the most persistent story element was romantic love'.[12] In Disney's *Snow White and the Seven Dwarfs* much of this element was attempted and then abandoned. The scenes between the Queen and the Prince were deleted and the latter is seen only at the beginning and end of the film. It is as if Disney, wanting to make his film more acceptable, to fit the cartoon into the pattern of popular cinema, was frustrated from doing so by what he saw as technical incompetence. He realised that the Prince lacked robustness and credibility as a character, and cut back on his scenes; these still exist in comic strip form and are evidence of how the studio returned to its own sources for the much later film *Sleeping Beauty*.

Deny story, deny the need for narrative and we deny imagination and what Laurens van der Post calls 'the wisdom of the dark ... the night in which we have our being, the base degrees by which we ascend into the day'.[13] Disney's mind was uncluttered by formal education or direction, and he absorbed stories orally from his grandmother's readings or from the storytelling medium of popular film. James Algar, who worked closely with him on *Snow White and the Seven Dwarfs* repeated what has been said of him by many of his associates: 'He was an intuitive person ... he had more ideas going in the back of his head than any two men alive and he was something of an enigma'. Disney's control of the narrative can be demonstrated in the extracts given from the story meetings. In 1934, before the main work had even begun on *Snow White and the Seven Dwarfs*, he grasped both story and presentation. As early as 16 November 1934 the structure, montage and grammar of the film were all clear in his mind as can be seen when he discussed the continuity of the story in the dwarfs' cottage, after the Queen's transformation scene.

> Outside of the house seen all lit up when we come back to it after the Queen sequence. Cross dissolve to entertainment in full swing.

The final version precisely parallels the instructions given here. The film relies on direct visual narration without recourse to an off-screen narrator (unlike *Cinderella* and still more *Sleeping Beauty*). Disney is here a story teller in the oral tradition, using the medium of film. Steeped in film himself Disney encouraged his artists to see films and not merely the popular Hollywood product. Marc Davis, one of Disney's 'nine old men' recalled that they

> ... saw every ballet, every film. If a film was good we would go and see it five times ... Walt rented a studio up in North Hollywood and ... we would see a selection of films – anything from Charlie Chaplin to unusual subjects. Anything that might produce growth, that might be stimulating – the cutting of the scenes, the staging, how a group of scenes was put together ... *The Cabinet of Dr Caligari, Nosferatu* were things that we saw. I remember *Metropolis* ... I would never want to see this film again because it had a very strong impact on me. I have built it up in my mind and I want to leave it that way.[14]

Europe and the silent cinema, and German expressionism in particular, is the background to the powerful scenes of Snow White's flight through the forest and the Queen's transformation scene. For the nightmare flight, the artists Frank Thomas and Ollie Johnston remembered the use of sound to support montage in narrative in *Private Worlds* (1935), an unusually adult film about a mental hospital.[15] Gothic elements echo F.W. Murnau's *Nosferatu* (1922) and Fritz Lang's *Metropolis* (1926) where Rotwang's house looks like an early model for the dwarfs' cottage. Jonathan Rosenbaum also cites Leni Riefenstahl's *The Blue Light* (1932) as an influence indicating its striking resemblance to Disney:

> It begins with the framing device of a luxurious leather bound volume being opened to lead into the story proper; even in Riefenstahl's gleaming blacks and whites, the book cover appears to shine with the regal splendour of inlaid gold. The intense pantheism, the poetic innocence and purity of the heroine, the telepathy and empathy shown to animals ... the sheer terror of the flight ... the misty idealism ... all are recognisable features of the Disney kingdom.[16]

The image of awe attached to the large close shot of the leather bound book which opens the film had connotations of magic, learning, power and secrecy. A real book was made by Gordon Legg who had joined the studio in 1936. He did all the titling for the film including the decorative narrative titles at the end, when the apparently dead Snow White is mourned by the animals and dwarfs. On 7 December 1936 Disney gave exact instructions for these which are minutely observed in the film itself:

Inspirational sketch for Snow White and the Seven Dwarfs: *exterior of the dwarfs' cottage at night before the party., an image precisley matching Walt Disney's description.*

Production still: Metropolis *(1927). The medieval cottage of the evil scientist Rotwang who lures the heroine into his clutches and creates a false Maria.*

Ludwig Richter: Illustration for Ehrenpreis *(1853). Richter's pictures anticipate the old world charm that Disney searched for and achieved.*

When we fade out on the animals in the rain the music comes in very pretty and very sad under these poetic titles. All I see under them is a clear background with nothing but the branch of a tree up behind the title. As the verse changes, the background changes, and snow falls, snow on the same limb. Then, as we express hope, the third title, four lines – is the same tree covered with buds.

Books of black magic dominate the early part of the Queen's transformation where she scans her shelves passing over Alchemy, Astrology, Black Arts and Witchcraft to find her book of Poisons. The opened page of gothic script is an ironic mockery of the opening story book title.

References to both sides of the Atlantic were used by the Disney artists in developing their atmosphere and characterisation. The forest scenes are both European *and* North American where chipmunks and raccoons mingle comfortably with creatures of the older world. Albert Hurter was the inspiration for much of the detailing of the film. He was frequently referred to in story meetings and publicly praised by Disney. The supervising director, David Hand, pointed out his importance at a background meeting with the layout artists, at which some of the most gifted painters were present. Hurter was given responsibility by Disney and by Hand for continuity of style and character. This 'keying' process was outlined by David Hand in a studio directive of 25 January 1937:

When you layout men get the rough well built, give it to Albert before the animator gets it. Then before it goes to Sam [Armstrong, in charge of backgrounds] Albert gets it once more ... Albert can make suggestions if they don't destroy gags. He dresses them up – we take them back and shoot them in for the animators. Before final colouring Albert gets them again. That keeps the key of the picture and the characters.

Hurter's influence is seen in the interior of the dwarfs' cottage and in all the exteriors – woods, sunlight, dark moonlight shots. 'It would be necessary' said David Hand, 'for each layout man to work with Albert ... He is to control the keying of the character throughout the picture – is that clear?' Disney had objected to the rocks and trees in a background that had not been keyed by Hurter. 'They are not at all like he [Disney] sees them', added Hand at an earlier meeting on 1 December 1936. 'They are not fairyland type of stuff ... Albert knows the character of the picture better than anyone'. Hurter, with his encyclopedic knowledge of detail and his European background gave the film its confidence of locale. He introduced the work of illustrative artists like Rackham, Busch and Hermann Vogel (1854–1921) into the Walt Disney Studio Library.[17]

In *Snow White and the Seven Dwarfs*, animation blends with illustration and caricature with painterly assurance. The emphasis on a soft palette throughout the film is well known; it was felt that bright colours would exhaust audiences for the length of a feature. At a background meeting on 23 November 1936, Disney said:

> We want to imagine it as rich as we can without splashing colour all over the place. I saw Harman-Ising's cartoon about spring (*To Spring 1936*, MGM) at the Four Star last night. They got colours everywhere and it looks cheap. There is nothing subtle about it at all ... I think we can achieve something different here. We are not after the comic supplement colouring.

Segovia Castle, Spain: *alleged to be one of the places to have inspired the Queen's castle in* Snow White and the Seven Dwarfs. *Other associated places include Bavaria, the Rhineland and Cyprus.*

An example of this delicacy in colouring may be observed in the first sequence of the film. The Queen's castle is seen in the distance in early morning sunlight. This is a multiplane shot, with layers of the foreground painted onto glass of different planes to give the illusion of depth. The scene is framed by trees and the sky patterned with clouds, with toadstools and bushes in the foreground, a moat beyond and hills in the distance. The castle is half in shadow half in sunlight, symbolic of the good and evil within in Snow White and the Queen. The camera tracks into the castle and due to the multiplane effect it seems we are entering a moving painting. The Queen as Witch paddling her canoe through the mist into the dawn is another example of pictorial elaboration supporting the dramatic atmosphere, and one that echoes the canoeist on another evil lake – Doré's Charon in Dante's *Inferno*. Benign nature is asleep while the forces of evil are awake and at work. Only two vultures follow the Witch through a bleak landscape whose dead trees and parched terrain echo the sterility of the Queen herself. Disney indicated the contrast with Snow White:

> There would be the vultures landing on a tree ... The tree should be dead – you see the ashen colour of it ... Everything about her is ugly, scrawny and angular; nothing graceful as with Snow White (story meetings 15 December 1936 and 5 March 1937).

The other European artists associated with Hurter were Gustaf Tenggren (1896–1970) and Ferdinand Horvath (1891–1973).[18] Tenggren was Swedish and was influenced by his fellow Swede, John Bauer (1882–1918) and by the Norwegian artist Theodor Kittelsen (1857–1914). The English illustrator, Arthur Rackham (1867–1939) was also an influence (see Colour Plates 10, 11 and 12). Tenggren had emigrated to the United States where he became a successful illustrator and commercial artist. In 1936 Disney appointed him to *Snow White and the Seven Dwarfs* as art director. He stayed for three years. The forests of his homeland appear in the outdoor scenes, the woodcarving remembered from his grandfather's house in Sweden alongside Hurter's Germanic style, in the dwarfs' cottage. He designed the famous poster

Ilustration for Burgenromantik: *the castle as an icon of romance, mystery and adventure. There are castles in many of the Disney animated feature films, and three-dimensional versions in all the theme parks.*

Stygian gloom: the Queen as Witch sets out from the castle in this illustration for Snow White and the Seven Dwarfs.
© *Disney Enterprises, Inc.*

which advertised the film, and which was also used for the published music sheets and decorated gramophone record labels. His designs were 'inspirational' rather than detailed and he did not have Hurter's overall responsibility for 'keying' the whole film. At a story meeting on 2 October 1936, David Hand outlined his work as 'more or less working on preliminary story and working with the different units for mood and keying of that particular sequence ... I think Tenggren has a great deal of ability along certain lines and we should use it'.

Ferdinand Horvath also emigrated about the same time as Tenggren; he joined the studio as animator and story artist and then, for *Snow White and the Seven Dwarfs*, as inspirational sketch artist. His character designs and cartoons for many of the shorts reveal an artist of considerable comic ability, though lacking Hurter's flourish. Carl Barks, the comic strip artist of Donald Duck, remembered Horvath as 'one of the two finest illustrators to have worked for Disney during the thirties' and Grim Natwick remembered him as 'Hungary's gift to animation'.[19] Horvath provided sketches of Snow White's flight through the forest, dwarf studies and the Huntsman.

The darkness of the wood that Horvath so skilfully sketched presents again the question of what kind of audience is being addressed by Disney and his colleagues. By this time Mickey Mouse clubs had been established, with a successful merchandising campaign that appealed to adults as well as to children, with the cartoon characters of Mickey and the gang

One of Gustave Doré's illustrations (1861) for Dante's Inferno. 'Charon, demonaic form, with eyes of burning coal ...' Canto III l. 103 in Carey's translation.

Ferdinand Horvath: Atmosphere sketch of Snow White's flight through the forest. Fear of being lost in a dark wood is an archetypal nightmare.
© Disney Enterprises, Inc.

being made over for children.[20] Disney himself however saw *Snow White and the Seven Dwarfs* extending his medium, as an appeal to adults. There is a genuine wish to aspire towards maturity, to adulthood, to take the cartoon medium as Disney called it, into a new realm. Bob Thomas in his biography quotes Disney remembering a conversation he had had on his way out to Los Angeles; the idiomatic turn of phrase gives the quotation a stamp of authenticity:

> I met a guy on the train when I was comin' out. It was one of those things that kind of made you mad ... 'What do you do?' (he asked.) I said 'I make animated cartoons.' 'Oh.' It was like saying, 'I sweep up latrines.' ... I thought of that guy on the back platform when we

Gustave Doré: Illustration (1861)
for Dante's Inferno, *canto XIII. l.3.*
  '...Not verdant there
The foliage, but of dusky hue;
  not light
The boughs and tapering, but with
  knares deform'd
And matted thick...'

had the première of *Snow White and the Seven Dwarfs*. And the darn thing went out and grossed eight million dollars around the world.[21]

The film contains scenes of terror which link it not only to the popular cinema in general and to the horror film in particular, but also to European melodrama and stage gothic tradition. Disney is addressing an audience of both adults and children which makes the texture of the film particularly dense. In his attempt to extend his resources, Disney's imagination shaped the scene where Snow White flees from the Huntsman into the wood. In story meetings on 27 June and 18 December 1936 he said:

> It would be good for her to be caught in the bushes showing these grotesque hands, then the wind and all the things that frighten her. Have it lead to things that make her think things are alive, but at the same time the audience should have a feeling that it is all in her mind ... her imagination goes wild.

And:

> I like the background behind her going right into blackness. *That's the thing they don't do in cartoons* [author's italics] ... Maybe we'll have no sound effects on the sequence. Do the wind and water and

everything with music ... If you don't keep these things in the depth and in the darkness we will have a comical effect instead of a dramatic effect.

These scenes still disturb children. I can remember the furore that the film created on its first release and my anger at not being allowed, at four years old, to accompany my older brother when it came out in England in 1938. Subsequent viewings over the years induce tears and terror in the darkened auditorium at Snow White's flight and particularly at the Queen's transformation scene, where the gothic element, the melodramatic, the grotesque – for the Queen as Witch is a comically ghoulish figure as well as being a figure of terror – are all powerfully represented. In story meetings and discussions, Disney made constant reference to the 'audience', which he instinctively identified with and appealed to. This address is part of the early Disney feature films' layered texture; it disappeared when the Disney studio later identified itself with a distinctly younger audience in the post-war era. At this early stage Disney was taking on the role of complete story teller, absorbing the gothic tradition from Europe via the German expressionist cinema as well as the rise in popularity of the horror film in the early days of sound. The terror induced by the Queen is directly proportionate to the identification we feel for the predicament of Snow White. Here is further evidence of Disney's confidence with his sources. Grimm, Germanic and

Nordic backgrounds, operetta, German expressionism, the grammar of the popular film all lie behind the *mise-en-scène* of *Snow White and the Seven Dwarfs*. The theatre, pantomime, melodrama and the American children's Christmas play are also foundations upon which the film is built, providing a framework within which the characters can move. One of the art directors was Ken Anderson, himself steeped in the European tradition of illustrative art (see Colour Plate 13). There is also a unity of time and plot which echoes two out of Aristotle's three unities; excluding the epilogue, the whole story takes place within the space of 36 hours, beginning in the morning when Snow White cleans the palace steps and the Queen consults her mirror, and ending the following day with the storm and the Witch's death. There is unity of action too, with subsidiary plots set aside or abandoned. Compare this with both *Cinderella* (1950) and *Sleeping Beauty* (1959) where subordinate plot and character vie with the main story.

Characterisation

Disney closely linked narrative and characterisation. A story outline of 9 October 1934 stressed the terrifying elements of the Queen in her laboratory:

> When the Queen gets angry, her face grows menacing – eyes big – fearful, hideous and distorted features ... Queen is in her laboratory ... Cauldron bubbling and change of colour in the flames. Dungeon far below – stairs leading down – go limit in building up shadows, dank and dripping wet – cobwebby musty effect, skeletons in chains.

The macabre and ghoulish had always been part of animation's imagery. The *femme fatale* figure in a position of power in exotic or alarming surroundings was familiar to Disney and his artists, through the silent screen. Disney said he wanted the Queen to be a mixture of Lady Macbeth and the Big Bad Wolf, and here lies the key to the conviction with which the artists invested the boldness of her character. Her animator, Art Babbitt, said that she was 'all of the women I've known'. Following in the tradition of the great European witches from Circe onwards, including Morgan le Fey, she controls not only men, but also the elements, with storm, wind and lightning at her command. She is the contrast to Snow White, her power extending beyond the castle walls, a representative of woman feared by the male in a male dominated society. She is both learned and beautiful, traits feared and desired by the male and she is a good example of the tensions in Disney's work. Europe and its traditions, its learning and its venerability have to be combined with American ruthlessness and determination. Her face is the Hollywood mask, Joan Crawford indeed, with age held at bay by

cosmetics. Her character and surroundings, however, inhabit a more ancient world. She is both female and American/European. For Hollywood's American audiences in the 1930s Europe 'represented a half-admired, yet half-condemned sophistication. Europeans were daring but decadent, sensual but self-destructive, charming, but dangerous and even evil'.[22]

The artists relished the sequences involving the Queen. She sweeps down her stone staircase, with Frank Churchill's music complementing her movement on a descending brass scale. Her cloak billows out in rage and rats scuttle for shelter. The camera follows her down from floor to floor, with a visual reminder of Piranesi's architectural fantasies. Fascination for and fear of science explain Hollywood's obsession with laboratories and white coated experimenters with power; the sensational success of *Dracula* and *Frankenstein* at the beginning of the decade had led to a series of horror films. Transformation scenes were also popular in the thirties, and the first sound version of *Dr Jekyll and Mr Hyde* was released in 1932. Reference was made by Disney specifically to this film in the story conferences; here was a terrifyingly familiar basis for the dramatic action. Another immediate parallel was *The Devil Doll* (1936) in which Lionel Barrymore's villain disguised himself, like Disney's witch, as an old woman with cloak and basket.[23] In a story treatment

suggestion of 30 October 1934 Disney wanted the Queen 'to be drawn along the lines of the Benda mask type ... as a high collar stately beauty'. The veteran Disney artists, including Babbitt, denied any parallel between the costume of the Queen and that of Helen Gahagan in *She* (1935), but there is an interesting resemblance between the appearance of Disney's character and that of the medieval statue of Uta outside Naumberg Cathedral.

In the same story treatment suggestion, the Queen could have been 'a fat cartoon type; sort of vain – batty – self-satisfied comedy type'. Joe

Grant's doodles, which decorated his personal copy of the Outline of Characters of 22 October 1934, show a variety of Queens from the sinister to the comic and ugly. The short Fleisher cartoon *Snow White* of 1933 also has a fat ugly Queen; Disney directed his artists to view Fleisher's work and it is reasonable to suppose that they were familiar with this anarchic Betty Boop short. Suggestions noted on this date were used in the final version. The Queen's beauty was described as 'sinister, mature, plenty of curves. She becomes ugly and menacing when scheming and mixing her potions'. Grant worked closely on the Queen-into-Witch transformation scene. His knowledge of literary and illustrative sources included Busch and Piranesi. With Bill Cottrell he made use of the skull and crow (from Busch) as macabre comic contrasts to the Queen.

We first see the Queen invoking her magic mirror. As she gesticulates melodramatically her cloak flares up in the wind like the batlike cloak of Dracula, whose name is mentioned by Disney in a general continuity conference of 22 December 1936:

> This mirror is draped with curtains – like Dracula ... We go into the action of the story and open up with Queen who is very majestic, cold tiger woman type ... When the Queen is making her transformation you see a lot of shadows, and from the shadows you see the Queen emerging – like Dr Jekyll and Mr Hyde.

Because the Queen is drawn, her character and movement have been distilled until she is the epitome of evil; this overcomes the sense of period. Other evil figures depicted on screen at this time suffer from their live action limitations; limitations of costume, acting style, lighting and all the rest of the contemporary *mise-en-scène* which serve to emphasise their use as product, as fashionable entertainment of the day. The drawing in this section of the Disney product raises the work from the dismissable to the valuable, from the obsolescent to the permanent. The Queen is both a thirties *femme fatale* and a genuinely disturbing figure from an older world. Her menace is established in a series of quick cuts between her and the mirror when it reveals that Snow White is 'the fairest in the land'. In a gesture of alarm and despair the Queen puts her hand to her thoat and spreads out her arm in fury on her words 'Snow White'! Ludicrous, melodramatic, exaggerated, this gesture invites ridicule. In live action, a studio set, unimaginative lighting, make-up, acting style of the period and the rest would produce such an effect. Animation transcends it. The caricature of the Queen, controlled by line, is signified in make-up and costume; the Joan Crawford lips, lidded eyes and white face framed by a wimple that is a mockery of a heart; the heart echoed as decoration on the box in which she believes the Huntsman has placed Snow White's heart; the blood red fingernails; the black dress and purple cloak which are always in motion, all add life to the animation; all signify

Statue of the medieval Lady Uta, consort of Count Ekhart, exterior of Naumberg Cathedral (c.1245). This statue predates Disney's queen by seven hundred years, but the women have striking similarities in costume and in expression. Courtesy Helga Schmidt-Glassner.

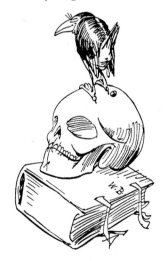

Wilhelm Busch: Gorglos 1894. Courtesy Edith Wilson.

Story sketch for Snow White and the Seven Dwarfs: *Joe Grant knew Busch's work well and made darkly comic use of the raven and the skull in the Queen's transformation scene.* © Disney Enterprises, Inc.

evil (see Colour Plate 14). In animation, nothing that we see is not intended. Animation requires movement and movement expresses character. Marc Davis, the animator of a later Disney villainess, Maleficent, in *Sleeping Beauty* (1959) complained that:

> Maleficent was a very difficult character because she always raised her arms and gave a speech. This is a very difficult thing to make come off. When one character is working with another, you get the contact, you feel the reaction. Once you have two characters that work together, then they come to life.[24]

The Queen is always seen with another character – with her mirror, her Huntsman, her raven, even a skeleton – and this adds conviction to her character. Her early scenes are quite crudely drawn but their lack of technical fluidity adds to their interest.

Her part was filmed in live action and then rotoscoped, a device for tracing live action footage to catch human movement in animated form. This misguided copying of photographed movement lacked the interpretive freedom to represent or caricature human movement by the elision or emphasis that animation might provide. The more the Disney artists attempted to match human reality the greater the artistic and aesthetic failure. The success of the human beings in *Snow White and the Seven Dwarfs* depends upon the the artists' ability to avoid merely copying. In later feature films their technical facility was much greater, but their human figures became dead products of the photographs that they so slavishly copied. At the time of *Snow White and the Seven Dwarfs* it was still possible to caricature the character without losing its conviction. The animation went beyond rotoscoping into imaginative expression. Art Babbitt explained:

> Every time they did this rotoscoping they vitiated it ... They couldn't do it any more than a good poem copies life. You *caricature* life [author's italics], your stories, your characters, your action ... They forgot ... to invent. The idea is not to copy life in appearance but to invent something that no human being can possibly do, and that I think is one of the functions of animation.

Lucille La Verne (1869–1945) took the voice of both Queen and Witch, although she was at first asked only to provide the voice of the witch. She read in for both parts and when no one more suitable was found for the Queen, she undertook both roles and also acted as the rotoscope model for some of the latter's scenes.[25] An experienced character actress, her deeply modulated, clearly articulated words take the character out of the nineteen thirties:

Slave in the Magic Mirror – come from the farthest space
Through wind and darkness I summon thee;
Speak! Let me see thy face!

There was criticism at the studio that her voice was too deep, but David Hand defended Disney's choice. He said that La Verne knew 'how to deliver lines ... especially down here with the mummy dust section where it needs to be delivered with a great deal of feeling' (layout meeting, 3 May 1937). The actress also brought relish to her reading of the Witch and Joe Grant remembered her 'taking her teeth out to help the change'.

The Witch also has a long history of literary, artistic and theatrical presentation; stage transformation scenes where the hag is transformed into a beautiful fairy godmother were popular in the nineteenth century and are still seen in pantomime today. The expressionistic *Frankenstein* was indebted to German cinema and affected Hollywood's treatment of the subject for the next two decades. Rotwang's laboratory in Lang's *Metropolis* (1926) is another example of the German influence, though not without promptings from Walt Disney himself.

I felt terrifically disappointed in your transition here (from Queen to Witch). It should be a Jekyll and Hyde thing ... It didn't punch me strong. (Concerning the potion that the Queen drinks) I think it's better to have imaginative things – like the scream of a man who died of fright (story metting, 10 March 1937).

Theodor Kittelsen (1857–1914): Illustration (detail, left) for 'The Pixie' from Norwegian troll tales. Kittelsen's elves and dwarves are typical of the rich illustrative north European tradition.

An early model sheet of the dwarfs for Snow White and the Seven Dwarfs *(right). The sharper and more grotesque elements were smoothed out before the final characters were animated.*
© Disney Enterpises, Inc.

Reference was made to the scene in *Macbeth* where the witches brew their potion. Disney commented, 'The main thing is to get things that picture', and the final result which is a mixture of expressionistic imagery and sound, reflected his concern – at this comparatively late stage – in the making of the film; it was now March 1937 and great efforts were made to complete work in time for a Christmas release.

The Disney artists also photographed real dwarfs as models, though early designs show that the more grotesque aspects, akin to the trolls and dwarfs of Theodor Kittelsen, John Bauer and Arthur Rackham, were exchanged for softer, rounder characters. The comic gags which enlivened the shorts were now given to the dwarfs, and the threatening, sinister quality of Horvath's drawings was exchanged for a childlike representation. Other European artists who drew early dwarf pictures for Disney were the Italian, Ugo D'Orsi, and, of course, Hurter. The dwarfs emerged physically and sexually safer than the grotesque adults which appeared in illustrations and which threatened the heroine. In this respect Disney moved away from Grimm who increasingly emphasised, through subsequent editions, the isolation of his heroines.[26] Disney's dwarfs were more like the children who played the dwarfs in Ames's play. Voices were chosen from vaudeville and radio shows to give them a comforting familiarity to the audience, with mime and the silent cinema particular references for Dopey.

Disney was not the first, as studio publicity claimed, to give the dwarfs names, but he greatly improved on Ames's Blick, Flick, Plick, Whick, Snick, Click and Quee (the smallest). Much effort was made to develop the dwarfs' individuality. David Hand complained in a story conference that 'the dwarfs can't be distinguished – can't tell Doc from Sleepy' (17 November 1936). There is a link with the European morality play, each Disney dwarf having a universal trait. We are reminded that there were also seven deadly sins.

There are local references to popular culture in the use of Ray Atwell for Doc's voice. Atwell was famous for his stutter and spoonerisms and these are characteristics of Doc, but the jokes wear badly and jolt the film, on review, back to its period. Disney was conscious of too much local reference. He welcomed yodelling but qualified the use of 'hot' jazz:

Walt: Yodelling has so much pep.

Jaxon (Wilfred Jackson): What about getting hot on the end?

Walt: Just some of it could be good if you could work it in. I don't like the Cab Calloway idea or too much Oh-de-oh-do. Audiences have a lot of hot stuff. If we can keep this quaint it will appeal more than the hot stuff. (entertainment conference 18 January 1936)

Walt Disney and Europe

The Fleischer studio used Cab Calloway the singer and band leader for their Betty Boop cartoons. Yodelling was popular and fashionable; in 1938 a professional yodeller Raynard Faunfelder attempted unsuccessfully to sue the Disney Studio for stealing his material.[27]

The dwarfs remain an object lesson in economy and ingenuity; caricature gives them easily identifiable characteristics, skilful animators provide their robust movement, professionals their voices. Popular culture is drawn upon and utilised. Supporting this is the reference, through the theatre, to Europe.

And what of Snow White herself, so criticised by contemporary and later reviewers? An extreme comment is by John Canady who described her as 'That mawkish, vapid, gooey voiced, rubber bodied specimen of animated vanilla custard'.[28] She appears in thirteen of the film's twenty scenes, and holds the film together. Because of the difficulties in handling rotoscope, the naivety in rendering gives the character an interesting historical perspective. Grim Natwick (1890–1990), an experienced animator who had developed Betty Boop for Fleischer, worked with Norman Ferguson on Snow White.[29] He recalled that they extended the character beyond rotoscoping, and invented the rest, reconstructing the entire body. Natwick had studied art in Europe and commented that when he arrived at the studio, 'nine tenths of the animators could not even draw Snow White. I was very lucky; they were beginning to take the better artists from the art schools, and I had them for assistants. They didn't know how to animate but they drew very well'.

Caselotti's voice supports the presentation of the little girl/woman. Apparent simplicity and naivety however cloak complex attitudes and responses. The art deco plasticity, yellow dress, puffed sleeves and bright red hair ribbon match the round baby-face and wide-eyed look of the all-American child innocent. She comes from a long line of idealised heroines, in a masculine dominated society that was sexually repressive and guilt ridden. The pictorial references are to Pickford and Gaynor, but Shirley Temple should also be borne in mind. Snow White's ribbon, gestures, voice, echo Temple, presexual, yet guided by adults to be consciously imitative of sex. There is a confusion here between the European heroine and the popular heroine as represented in Temple, though Snow White does not disturb as much as Temple, because she is not a living child. Comparable examples of the child-adult Hollywood heroine may be cited in Judy Garland and Deanna Durbin, whose film careers began in 1936 at the ages of 14 and 15 respectively. Her rotoscope model was played by the dancer, Marjorie Belcher.

The graphic heritage of the heroine in illustration goes back at least to Rowlandson and Gillray but her individuality is lost in mid-Victorian illustration. Snow White's forbears come from the Pre-Raphaelites and the late nineteenth century Romantic vision in England and in Germany,

Moritz Retzsch: illustration for Schiller's Song of the Bell *(1834). Another idealisation of the nineteenth-century hero and heroine. The line continued with Richter, Vogel and Rackham. The rounded rendering of leaves and landscape foretells the Disney convention.*
Courtesy Theo Halladay.

Hermann Vogel (1854–1921): illustration for 'The Sick Hermit' in his Vogel Album *of 1894. Vogel's detailed pictures of animals and humans, blending the realistic with the fantastic had an especial charm for the Disney artists.*

popularised through illustration. Burne Jones's Beggar Maid and the medieval ladies portrayed by Millais and then by the Robinson brothers and by Arthur Rackham were vulgarised into Mabel Lucie Attwell's cherubic little monsters. In Germany there were Ludwig Richter's and Moritz Retsch's illustrations. Later Hermann Vogel's fairy tales became popular; they were in the studio library. The genre was continued in America by illustrators such as N.C. Wyeth and Jessie Willcox Smith.

The Disney Snow White is both child and mother figure, protecting birds and herself protected by animals and dwarfs. Part of her continuing success lies in the Disney artists' ability to create an idealised figure in contrast with her surroundings; although we only see her in one scene with the Queen, the contrast between them is implicit throughout – where Queen is not, Snow White is and vice versa. It is Snow White's association with the dwarfs and with animals and with nature in general, that adds conviction to her scenes. There is however, an ambivalence, for the dwarfs are sometimes children to her as adult, sometimes adults to her as child. William Paul indicates how the animation underlines the alliance between human and animal appealing to an older world than Disney's.[30] The dwarfs have animal characteristics and Snow White is able to communicate with the animals in a childlike way. Abandoned in the forest, nature comes to her rescue, a typical wish fulfilment on the part of a wronged person. Ludwig Richter's Snow White is also surrounded by animals in the forest. In his *Genoveva in Waldeinsamkeit* the heroine is seated on the ground with deer by her side. In Disney the dwarfs kneel weeping, believing Snow White to be dead, and a candle drips, echoing, as Paul says 'the dwarfs' tears in both shape and movement as the tears conversely echo the wax drop. Character, whether human or animal, and setting are here alike, all made from the same material (see Colour Plate 15). All things are literally animated by the same spirit.' Disney commented:

> There's not much light except around her. She's got to be beautiful as she lays there. Sort of like Juliet ... When someone good dies there is always that question why. So many bad things in the world that go on ... Remember *Romeo and Juliet*? How pretty Juliet looked? They had her so she looked very beautiful there ...
> *Dick Creedon* (story adapter): When it's over (the Queen's death) the rain drops like tears (mourning Snow White).
> *Walt*: Sad – yes – sort of steady. You could work that in like the rain symbolises tears ... I believe any fairy tale can have wishing things ... I believe in fairy tales (story meeting 7 December 1936).

The character of Snow White involves the audience – not yet a discrete audience of different ages or interests – and we experience a distinct sense of loss, especially at the bier, but there is a more complex response at the end of the film when we adults as children or children as adults to be, 'lose' Snow White out of our lives. We identify with the dwarfs, while she goes on to marriage and sexual fulfilment in a Maxfield Parrish landscape of trees, sunset and castle in the air, all images derived from Romanticism and specifically developed in the Hollywood musical of the thirties. We and the dwarfs are left behind to grow old and die; Snow White, resurrected, moves towards everlasting life. The complexity of her appeal lies not only in the imaginative and graceful delineation of her movement – the house cleaning and dancing sequences are good

Rie Cramer: illustration for a Dutch edition of Snow White and the Seven Dwarfs *that was in the Walt Disney Studio Library.*

examples – not only in the piping of her childlike voice, not only in her ambiguous role as sister, playmate, child, mother or sweetheart, but also in an appeal that stretches back through the previous century and through the illustrated heroine of the European fairy tale. Ritualistically she also functions as a young woman enjoying a degree of premarital freedom with an opportunity of meeting the opposite sex. She expresses courage and independence. She has romantic yearnings. Magically, she survives death. She offers an elixir to the audience – a pure heart and intense longing can build a love that transcends stasis and pain. The complexity of response to the character of Snow White echoes the complexity of responses to the film, and to its continuing appeal. The story discussions show how there is also, on the part of Disney and his colleagues, a naivety which is neither self-conscious nor effete. The new world builds confidently on the old: 'I believe in fairy tales'.

Snow White and the Seven Dwarfs, released in the States just before Christmas 1937, was a critical and popular success that exceeded all expectations. The reviews were favourable, though there were reservations about the animation of the human beings and, in particular, Snow White herself and the Prince. Concern was also expressed about the element of terror and its effect upon young cinemagoers. In the UK the film was issued with an A certificate, and when it received a U certificate after the Second World War, two scenes were cut (Snow White falling into a swamp and the witch in her lower dungeon). The film was an instant popular success all over the world, and there were a number of foreign language versions. The revenue allowed Disney to proceed with plans for a move from the overcrowded Hyperion Avenue Studios to new premises in the San Fernando Valley. It also gave him the confidence to produce more full-length films and by the spring of 1938 he had decided to make the story of *Pinocchio* his next animated feature.

Notes

1. See John Canemaker, *Before the Animation Begins* (New York: Hyperion, 1996) for an excellent account of these neglected artists. One of the best and fullest descriptions of the production process is in Frank Thomas and Ollie Johnston, *Disney Animation: the Illusion of Life* (New York: Abbeville, 1981).

2. J.B. Kaufman, 'Before Snow White', *Film History* Vol. 5, No. 2, 158.

3. Quoted in Rudy Behlmer, *America's Favourite Movies: Behind the Scenes* (New York: Ungar, 1982), 49. It is important to distinguish between the Walt Disney who speaks directly in the story meetings to his own colleagues, the Disney who writes or dictates his own words, and the public Disney reported in the press, generally in ghosted accounts.

4. Walt Disney, 'Why I chose *Snow White and the Seven Dwarfs*', *Photoplay Studies*, Vol. 3, Part 10, 7–8. See note three above.

5. Karen Merritt, 'The Little Girl/Little Mother Transformation: The American Evolution of Snow White', *Storytelling in Animation: The Art of the Animated*

Image, Vol. 2, ed. John Canemaker (Los Angeles: American Film Institute, 1988), 111 and 119.

6. There have been many versions of Grimm, both in the original and in translation. The version quoted is from Jacob and Wilhelm Grimm, *Fairy Tales* (1813–1816); trans. Margaret Hunt (New York: Pantheon, 1944), 291. For the publishing history of Grimm see Ruth R. Bottigheimer, *Grimms' Bad Girls and Bold Boys: The Moral and Social Vision of the Tales* (New Haven: Yale, 1987), 98 and 102; and David Blamires, 'The Early Reception of the Grimms' *Kinder und Hausmärchen* in England', *Bulletin of the John Rylands Library of Manchester*, 1989.

7. Story outline, 27 October 1934, Walt Disney Archives. All subsequent quotations from story meetings, conferences or correspondence are by Walt Disney or his colleagues and come from the Walt Disney Archives unless otherwise stated.

8. Behlmer, *America's Favourite Movies*, 49.

9. Charles Castle, *Oliver Messel* (London: Thames and Hudson, 1986), 102.

10. Susan Ohmer, 'Plenty of Action and Just Enough Romance: Debates around Disney's Adaptation of Peter Pan', unpublished paper for 3rd Annual Conference of Society for Animation Studies, Rochester, New York, 4 October 1991.

Marc Davis: 'A good golfer is a smart golfer! Be sure to select the right club!' This cartoon, one of a series, is characteristic of Davis's vivacious graphic style.
Courtesy Marc Davis.

A good Golfer is a Smart Golfer! Be sure to select the right club!

11. *Dreams for Sale: Popular Culture in the 20th Century*, ed. Richard Maltby (London: Harrap, 1989), 59. See also Margaret Farrand Thorp, *America at the Movies* (London: Faber, 1946), 17.

12. *Dreams for Sale*, ed. Maltby, 111.

13. Laurens van der Post, *Venture to the Interior* (London: Hogarth Press, 1952), 228.

14. Marc Davis, interview in *Crimmer's Journal*, Winter 1975, 40. Marc Davis was born in 1913 in Bakersfield, California, the son of an itinerant watchmaker and jeweller. Of mixed European parentage, he has Russian and Polish blood on his father's side and Scottish-Irish blood on his mother's. When he was a child the family moved constantly – he attended 32 schools and four art schools – and he drew from an early age to amuse himself. He enjoyed adventure stories and illustrative art, in particular the work of Howard Pyle and N.C. Wyeth. He joined Disney in 1935 and became one of the Nine Old Men after working as an animator on all the major features. His graphic ability and mastery of line and colour is remarkable and it is not surprising that he was invited by Don Graham to take over his drawing classes in 1947 for the Chouinard Art Institute. He has maintained close contact with Chouinard's successor, the California Institute of the Arts. Davis has illustrated two beautiful books, so far alas unpublished, one on the native peoples of New Guinea and one on human locomotion. His vigorous sketches of Chanticleer are published in Fulton Roberts, *Chanticleer and the Fox* (New York: Disney Press, 1991).

15. Thomas and Johnston, *Disney Animation: The Illusion of Life*, 381.

16. Jonathon Rosenbaum, 'Walt Disney', *Film Comment*, Jan/Feb 1975, 65.

17. The catalogue of the Walt Disney Library contained a list of additions, donations and purchases, discovered by the author on two visits, 3 and 12 July 1985. The library was richly stocked with many European illustrated classics and was widely used. Though disbanded in 1986, part of it has been preserved at Walt Disney Imagineering.

18. See Canemaker, *Before the Animation Begins* for detailed biographies of both these artists. After leaving Disney in 1939 Tenggren continued his distinguished career as illustrator and commercial artist. Some of his most successful work was published by the Golden Press, of which his *Golden Tales from the Arabian Nights* (1957) and *The Canterbury Tales* (1961) are fine examples, though his inspirational paintings for the Disney *Pinocchio* remain unmatched. It is still not clear why he received no credit for his seminal work on this film.

19. Grim Natwick, quoted by Mark Mayerson in letter to author 21 October 1991. Carl Barks is quoted in an undated letter by Bruce Hamilton in *Catalogue of Horvath Art* (West Plains, Mo.: Russ Cochrane, n.d., c.1985).

20. A new ambulance, decorated with characters from Disney's shorts, was presented to the Royal Manchester Children's Hospital in 1936. '1936 was the year *Mickey Mouse Weekly* first appeared here, and the Disney merchandising office in London was associated with it ... The ambulance was one of the sights on the streets of Manchester and it was still in service well after the war.' Tony Glyn, letter to author, n.d. 1991.

21. Bob Thomas, *The Walt Disney Biography*, 108.

22. *Dreams for Sale*, ed. Maltby, 83.

23. I am grateful to Brian Sibley for drawing my attention to this film.

24. Davis, *Crimmers Journal*, 40.

25. Lucille La Verne (1869–1945) began her stage career at the age of fourteen. She toured widely in Europe, and later owned her own theatre on Broadway. She was

the first female Shylock in a production that ran for seven months in London. She appeared in many films, her first role as crone in Griffiths' *Orphans of the Storm* (1922). The Queen in *Snow White and the Seven Dwarfs* was her last performance.

26. Bottigheimer, *Grimms' Bad Girls and Bold Boys*, 110.

27. Unsuccessful lawsuit brought by Faunfelder, n.d. c.1938. RKO Radio Pictures Archives.

28. John Canady, 'The Art So to Speak of Walt Disney', *New York Times*, 28 October 1973.

29. Grim Natwick (1890–1990) was the grand old man of animation. Born and raised in Wisconsin, Myron H. Natwick studied art in Chicago, New York and at the Vienna National Academy. 'I spent about four years in Europe,' he said, 'covered all the galleries. So about the time I returned from Europe, all the people you might call illustrators, Doré, Delacroix among them, I admired their work; I copied their work; I studied their work.' (Interview with author, 2 July 1985.) He began his animating and cartooning career at the age of sixteen and worked for all the major studios. He specialised in the development of female characters, creating Betty Boop in 1932 for Fleischer and the heroines of the Disney *Silly Symphony* films *The Cookie Carnival*, *Broken Toys* and *Music Land* (all 1935). In addition to Snow White, he animated the heroine Princess Glory in the Fleischer feature *Gulliver's Travels* (1939) and he gave Nelly Bly her curves and seductive line in the UPA classic *Rooty Toot Toot* (1952). His last work as animator was for the feature *Raggedy Ann and Andy* (1976) when he was 86. A few weeks before his death he celebrated his centenary with 400 old and new friends at a party in Hollywood. In a tribute John Canemaker said 'He was a great animator, who created important work. But to live for a century and to have never made an enemy is an equally remarkable achievement'. (*The Art of Grim Natwick* Catalogue, Burbank: Howard Lowery, 1991.)

30. William Paul, 'Pantheon Pantheist', *Village Voice* 2 August 1973.

CHAPTER 4

The Dark World of *Pinocchio*

Background to the film

Pinocchio is a complex film, drawing upon sources both European and indigenous. Conventional references to popular culture in general and to Hollywood in particular – such as a romantic plot and the use of musical comedy formulae, which supported *Snow White and the Seven Dwarfs* – are largely ignored. This may partly explain its disappointing performance at the box office. In spite of enthusiastic reviews, it did not quite meet public expectation. There is a darkness which Disney brings to the film that is his own, replacing the homiletic Victorian values of the Collodi story, but not offering a sentimental alternative. Surrounding and supporting the loneliness of the puppet hero are grotesque Dickensian characters, presented with a technical virtuosity that shows the studio's progress beyond the simple story book adventure of *Snow White and the Seven Dwarfs*. Indeed, the technical skill of *Pinocchio* underlines the conviction with which the story of bleakness and despair is told; odd terms to apply to a Disney film. This chapter shows how Disney strove to accommodate his original European material, and how his absorption of its sources was only partial. The uneasy response by audiences (and its initial lack of success at the box office) was due partly to its dark issues, partly to the conflict between origin and presentation, and partly to historical circumstance. The technical ease and confidence, the delight in mechanical virtuosity, the relish in characterisation and in comic incident, cannot mask the darkness at the centre.

European influences are profound, from the original Italian story, to the design, *mise-en-scène*, decoration and musical score. The American elements, in particular the hobo-like character of the chorus-narrator Jiminy Cricket and the Jean Harlow look-alike Blue Fairy, do not appear to be integrated into the European framework.

The film is based on the didactic tale by Carlo Collodi (1826–1890), but whereas much of Collodi's story takes place in daylight and in the open air, the Disney version occurs at night or indoors. The film is dark in content and in presentation, with seventy-six of its eighty-eight minutes taking place at night or under water. Cold moonlight scenes which open the film contrast with the warmth of Geppetto's workshop. Light is magical in the Blue Fairy scenes, or lurid in the marionette theatre scenes

*Gustaf Tenggren: Atmosphere
sketch for* Pinocchio *which shows
the dark* mise-en-scène *of the film.
The living puppet is locked up in
Stromboli's caravan with the other
lifeless marionettes.
© Disney Enterprises, Inc.*

or on Pleasure Island, where there is also a sense of claustrophobia;
although it is in the open air, darkness overhangs the fun-fairs, a foretaste
of the prison which encloses Geppetto inside the whale. Pinocchio is
locked up in Stromboli's caravan on a stormy night. It is foggy and
mysterious when the Fox and Cat conspire with the Coachman at the
Red Lobster Inn; the darkness is terrifying when the boys are turned
into donkeys. When Pinocchio and Geppetto escape from the whale,
the sky is almost as grey as the sea and the whale itself; all nature is here
threatening. Geppetto lays the dead Pinocchio out on his bed at night
in his own dark little house. The upbeat ending is too short to mitigate
the darkness and despair, and we are thrust out into the cold moonlight
with Jiminy Cricket.

Only one scene takes place in sunlight, the morning of Pinocchio's
first day as a live puppet on his venture into life. On looking at paintings

for this scene Disney complained that it was too dark. He wanted it bright and sunny, 'a beautiful day for him to start his adventures in the world' (colour test meeting, 19 January 1939). This is one of the few scenes where the screen is filled with life (apart from the crowded scenes under water which make an ironic contrast with the bleakness on the surface). It is this bleakness which makes the response to *Pinocchio*, for all its technical accomplishment, so uncertain for both child and adult. The feeling of loss, emptiness and betrayal transcends boundaries of age and experience.

Story sketch: Pleasure Island in Pinocchio. *The crowds are seen at the edge of the frame.* © *Disney Enterprises, Inc.*

The wandering traveller, Jiminy Cricket, comes upon the apparent security of Geppetto's house and, an American searching for his identity, he attains a sense of purpose as Pinocchio's conscience, but he is thrown out of the warmth of Geppetto's house at the end, doomed to begin his travelling again. Jiminy represents the American overlay upon a European framework of quest. The quest for identity extends to Pinocchio, but the film's theme is loss; loss of the father and loss of the son, with both father and son setting out on picaresque adventures which take them away from the certainty of home to brave the unknown. The loneliness of the protagonists is echoed by the emptiness of space on the screen. The characters are largely held in spotlight or streetlight or firelight while darkness surrounds them. Crowds – children going to school, spectators at the puppet show and the delinquent boys on the rampage at Pleasure Island – are seen only briefly, at a distance, on the periphery or in silhouette. This does not mean an empty screen. Rather it is filled with a rich texture of artificial or alien life; the clockwork toys, marionettes and fish simulate but cannot replace living reality; Pinocchio and Jiminy run through empty streets, down echoing alleys, into dark abysses. Geppetto, a latter-day Jonah, is lost in the murk inside the whale. The image of light surrounded by darkness is paramount from the opening shot of the diminutive cricket in a spotlight on a shelf of books, to the final shot of the magic wishing star shining out of a black sky.

The moral complexity of the film matches its rich texture. While *Snow White* is an innocent victim of injustice and deprived of her place in society, the issues here are more complicated. The search for identity extends to all three of the main characters, forcing them to face dilemmas from which they learn, but which do not result in a victory over evil. Nor is happiness easy to attain.[1] Geppetto's moral choice is to send his new 'son' into the world unaccompanied, alone; he does not go with him, suffers for his decision and only later, under stress, does he venture out himself to search for the puppet, to be swallowed up by a greater menace than he could have imagined, Monstro the whale.

Jiminy Cricket fails as the official conscience of Pinocchio. He gets up 'Late the first day', and is unable to prevent Pinocchio from falling into the hands of the wicked Fox and Cat. He abandons his role as

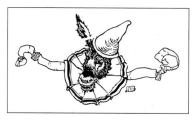

Charles Folkard: Illustration (1911) for Collodi's story. In the original, Pinocchio is turned into a complete donkey, but in the Disney version, he sprouts only ears and a tail. Courtesy Orion Publishing Group Ltd.

Conscience and turns away when he sees Pinocchio's success with Stromboli's marionette show, the puppet's attainment of 'the easy road to success'. 'What does an actor want with a conscience anyway?' mutters Jiminy as he turns into the darkness leaving the crowd roaring approval in the distance. He is unable to help when Pinocchio is locked up by Stromboli.

As the film continues, moral transgression leads to physical regression; wicked boys are turned into donkeys. Pinocchio reverses this tendency when he rescues Geppetto, literally taking the human out of the animal and asserting his own humanity. He attains his wish to become a real boy, achieved through moral choice and difficulty resulting, albeit precariously, in strengthening the bonds between parent and child. The villains' self-gratification is the obverse of this moral education. They exploit and corrupt but, unlike those in other Disney films, they are not destroyed. They simply vanish. The Fox and Cat, Stromboli, the Coachman and Monstro all continue to prey on others. In this respect *Pinocchio* is unique in the Disney canon. Evil remains lurking on the edge of and beyond the screen in both narrative and visual terms. The overlay of American virtues of self-sufficiency, wish fulfilment – 'When You Wish Upon a Star' – and the attainment of a materialist happiness, sits uneasily upon a much older European moral tradition. Indeed, the medieval morality play can be seen as an analogy for the main protagonists of the film, with Pinocchio as Innocence or Everyman, Jiminy Cricket as Knowledge, Geppetto as Good Deeds and the Blue Fairy as God or an Angel. The bad characters represent some of the Seven Deadly Sins, Sloth, Cunning, Greed and Pride. This is only one analogy; the complexity of the characterisation within the narrative structure adds to the layers of meaning within the film.

There is also a relationship between art and artifice explored by Russell Merritt who suggests that Stromboli is:

> ... selfish and devoted more to money than to art. He is the crowd pleaser *par excellence*, cruelly exploiting the talents of others. By contrast Geppetto is selflessly obsessed with his art; like the public image of Disney, he is preoccupied by creating illusions of life, indifferent to payment.[2]

The dwarfs' cottage in *Snow White and the Seven Dwarfs* was a place in which to work, dance and sing. Although Geppetto's house is also a warm, attractive home for singing and dancing as well as for work, it is a lonely house. In it, Pinocchio and Jiminy meet only Geppetto and the magical Fairy, or inanimate objects, or Geppetto's pets Figaro the kitten and Cleo the goldfish. The latter is all artifice, a parody of a flirt, with large eyelashes and pouting lips, but her sexuality is confined behind glass. The other female presence is the Blue Fairy, apart from some

Walt Disney and Europe

marionettes who make the briefest of appearances and who are inanimate. No older woman of wisdom or virtue obtrudes.[3] The Blue Fairy sets off the adventures of the hero, activating his body's mechanism, as Geppetto activates his toys. She is an alien presence, her allure seen by Jiminy as both glamorous and threatening. She represents the mysterious in the feminine which the American male felt was to be reckoned with and if necessary overcome.

Collodi and Disney

Collodi, whose real name was Carlo Lorenzini, was a journalist and educator. His *Le avventure di Pinocchio* was published in serial form in *Giornale per i bambini* in 1881 and this may explain the picaresque quality of the story. It appeared in book form two years later. The book was popular and was quickly translated into English, appearing in America in 1892, and in the Everyman edition in 1911.[4] It is unclear whether its initial popularity was with children or with adults and the author is not alone in recalling the difficulty encountered as a child with the complete text. This may help to explain the marked difference between the adulatory press reception given to the film and its failure to perform well at the box office.[5] Jacqueline Rose has shown in her pioneer work on *Peter Pan* that much needs to be done in connection with the social issues that are raised by works of literature and/or drama that purport to be for and about children but which involve and manipulate a much wider readership.[6] Like *Peter Pan*, *Pinocchio* was altered and adapted almost as soon as it was published in English and Disney was not original in making his changes. With Grimm, Disney had to expand a short tale, but *Pinocchio* was long and episodic, requiring considerable modification. As has been noted with *Snow White and the Seven Dwarfs* Disney worked on tried and tested material. Though not published until April 1939, Yasha Frank's play of *Pinocchio* was performed in Los Angeles at least as early as June 1937.[7] Collodi's Pinocchio was a delinquent forced by suffering and terror into a state of grace while Frank's was an innocent, incapable of promoting mischief. The play followed earlier bowdlerished versions which cut out much of the didacticism and violence. The earliest revised translation was in 1904 and the first dramatised version, also bowdlerised, and 'arranged as a dramatic reader' by Emily Gray, was published in 1911. The Collodi original was obviously not thought suitable for children's reading. Collodi assumed a nineteenth century view of children, and:

> ... while it purports to be a children's tale (it) is actually a didactic fable designed to indoctrinate chidren into conforming to the existing adult world while presenting them with the inevitable punishments for those that resist.[8]

In the book, shortly before the puppet kills him with a hammer, the cricket admonishes:

> Woe to those boys who rebel against their parents, and run away capriciously from home. They will never come to any good in the world, and sooner or later they will repent bitterly.[9]

Later The Blue Fairy gives the puppet this advice:

> 'It is never too late (she said) to learn and instruct ourselves.'
> 'But I do not wish to follow either an art or a trade.'
> 'Why?'
> 'Because it tires me to work.'
> 'My boy,' said the Fairy, 'those who talk in that way end almost always either in prison or in the hospital...Woe to those who lead slothful lives. Sloth is a dreadful illness and must be cured at once, in childhood.'

The Victorians assumed that children were uncivilised and must have the devil forced out of them; fear of hell and eternal punishment was part of literary fare in nineteenth century fiction. Like Tom in Kingsley's *The Water Babies* and like the child Jane in *Jane Eyre*, Pinocchio is threatened with damnation, though Frank, and earlier adaptors, removed the threat.

Collodi also relishes the anarchic activity of childhood, its cruelty and uncontrolled emotional behaviour, especially in boys. Here he describes the Land of the Boobies, a scene which occurs late in the book (which becomes Pleasure Island in the film):

> It was a country unlike any other country in the world. The population was composed entirely of boys. The oldest were fourteen, and the youngest scarcely eight years old. In the streets there was such merriment, noise, and shouting, that it was enough to turn anybody's head. There were troops of boys everywhere. Some were playing with nuts, some with battledores, some with balls. Some rode velocipedes, others wooden horses. A party were playing at hide and seek, a few were chasing each other ...

And so it goes breathlessly on, imbuing the text with an exuberance which counterbalances the didacticism. Collodi describes sadism, cruelty, death and attempted murder in the same manner; when the Fox and Cat, disguised as assassins, capture Pinocchio they attempt, unsuccessfully, to stab him to death – 'the puppet luckily was made of hard wood' – and then they try to hang him – 'At the end of three hours the puppet's eyes were still open, his mouth closed, and he was kicking more than ever ...'.

The villains are eventually exposed and scorned:

The Cat had so long feigned blindness that she had become blind in reality, and the Fox, old, mangy, and with one side paralysed, had not even his tail left.

'Oh, Pinocchio!' cried the Fox, 'Give a little in charity to two poor infirm people.'

'Infirm people', repeated the cat.

'Begone, impostors!' answered the puppet ...

The book is Chaucerian in embracing many aspects of life, the cruel and the kind, the energetic and the violent, the gentle and submissive as well as the didactic and homiletic. Death and death bed scenes abound; Pinocchio also gets caught in a man trap and chained up as a watch dog. Disney replaces all this with an innocent hero trying to make his way in a complex and frightening world; the darkness of that world forms the central bleakness of the film and this is, for all its adaptation, the strongest link between Disney and Collodi.

Disney acquired the Italian version and different translated editions; he also contracted a member of his staff, Bianca Majolie, who worked in the story department, to make a new translation (1937). In an internal memo. of 9 June 1937 the Disney artists were asked to see Frank's play 'since he (Walt) feels that this might be possible feature material, he is anxious to have all who can attend.' Conference notes from February of the same year show that Disney was open-minded about the next feature film after *Snow White and the Seven Dwarfs* and the studio was also working on *Bambi*. The title *Pinocchio* had been registered as a feature as early as May 1934, though the first story conference notes seem to be for 24 March 1938. The pressure to complete *Snow White and the Seven Dwarfs* in time for Christmas 1937 accounts for the delay. There is no evidence, however, that Disney felt a personal commitment to make the film, as was the case with *Snow White and the Seven Dwarfs*. Ken Anderson recalled that Ben Sharpsteen, who was the supervising co-director, drew it to Disney's attention. There is also evidence that Disney knew of the book earlier. A family friend, Mrs K. Evers wrote to Walt Disney on 8 April 1935 suggesting it, though not at that time as a feature, and the Italian journalist and author Lo Duca, who had met Disney on the latter's European tour of that year, wrote that he was delighted to hear of Disney's plans for making *Pinocchio*. In a letter of 4 July in the same year he wrote, 'I take the liberty of calling your attention again to the use of the language and the pronunciation ... It is a masterwork full of episodes and fit to be developed'. The Disney version followed Frank and the other adaptations. It was close to what parents preferred to believe about their children and what they in turn felt was appropriate for their children to know. Disney modified the sadism and violence, concentrating on developing Pinocchio as child hero.

Marionettes

The fascination for marionettes dates back to ancient Greece and Etruria, with references in English and European literature from Chaucer onwards. The puppet theatre became the most truly popular form of dramatic entertainment when, in the seventeenth and eighteenth centuries, live theatre was less all-encompassing in its appeal and in its accessibility. Large marionette troupes travelled throughout Europe and though few puppets have survived this period one example from Linz in the Austrian Tyrol is still extant. The figure has remarkably realistic detailing, with the eyes and jaw mobile, and it wears a Tyrolean hat similar to that worn by Disney's hero (see Colour Plate 16).[10]

In Italy marionettes were associated with the popular theatre form of Commedia dell'Arte, illustrated by the braggartly behaviour of Collodi's Pinocchio and in his meeting with the other puppets including Harlequin and Punchinello, who recognise him as one of themselves. Disney replaced this European element with American variety or vaudeville influences predominating in Pinocchio's encounter with Stromboli's puppet theatre. With the puppets Pinocchio is the innocent American abroad with the older and wiser cultures of Europe. He dances with Dutch, French and then Russian dolls and though he causes chaos, he is an immense success, triumphing over the 'dead' dolls of the older cultures and generating wealth for Stromboli. Also, an ethnic reference during the marionette show was deleted: 'The final act is a jungle scene in which the music is treated in an unusual, modern manner, building up to a strong climax of dancing Ubangi puppets'.[11]

These were replaced by Russian marionettes because once again Disney was anxious to avoid topicality, and Ubangi dancers from Africa were a temporary sensation at the time in the United States.

When Disney visited Europe he became fascinated by the miniature and the mechanical, and by the turning of illusion into reality. Marionettes were one way of achieving a transformation, and he realised this later through actual moving figures, the grotesque Audio-Animatronics figures which are central to the Magic Kingdoms, the new life-size (and larger than life-size) puppets portending a future of terror rather than delight. He and his 'imagineers' used puppets to create images of horror on the attractions in Disneyland which link back to the dark sources which he drew upon for *Snow White and the Seven Dwarfs* and *Pinocchio*. In Pleasure Island, for example, there is a complex response which leads to real terror when we discover, with Jiminy, that the island is a façade to attract naughty boys for sale as donkeys. At first the island is inviting, with helter skelters, ferris wheel, roller coasters, circus tents and pleasure domes lit up against a dark and menacing sky. Here Pinocchio's vice is to smoke a cigar, pick a fight, drink beer and play billiards, activities associated with adolescence, but not necessarily with delinquency. In the Magic Kingdom, created among the orange groves at Anaheim in California, the cartoon king would fifteen years later create his own Pleasure Island of fantasy, which denies adolescence. Disneyland looks like Pleasure Island, and the identical artefacts and props can be located there; it is a three-dimensionalising of the two dimensional cartoons. *The Pirates of the Caribbean* attraction, with its animated rapists, arsonists and murderers (though in its turn bowdlerised for political correctness in the late 1990s), perhaps most invokes the darker side of Pleasure Island. The concern for the mechanical, for the seductively elaborate toys that crowd Geppetto's shop also indicates Disney's desire to be seen as a grand toy manufacturer or puppet master. The 'attraction' at Disneyland with which he was personally most involved was the 'Enchanted Tiki Room', a presentation of mechanical singing birds. Like Geppetto he wanted to be recognised as a benevolent creator; like a puppeteer however, his magic was kept out of sight; animation was seen as sleight of hand.

As the grand master of illusion, Disney made *Pinocchio* his most elaborate work. Costing $2,600,000 it was also his most expensive. There was ebullience and confidence in all departments of the studio after the international success of *Snow White and the Seven Dwarfs*. Determined to create illusion, Disney wrote:

> We've tried in various ways to give the characters the feeling of more depth and roundness – or more of a third-dimensional quality ... We're able to make you see even [the whale's] muscles rippling underneath his shiny, menacing, dark exterior.[12]

Once again Disney's control of narrative does not allow the technical virtuosity to take over, although it does mask the bleakness of the theme. The narrative is at first entrusted to Jiminy Cricket who is seen spotlit on a bookshelf, surrounded by artefacts of an older period and culture, with *Alice in Wonderland* and *Peter Pan* (both to be adapted later by Disney) on a shelf behind him. Another book lies on its side against which the *Pinocchio* volume leans, its value as book-object enhanced by the clasps that bind it, an anachronism that adds weight to the historical context of the *mise-en-scène*. A manuscript wrapped up with a seal is glimpsed to the left. Spectacles, inkwell and quill add cultural weight, and a fat tobacco jar, pipe, matches and tobacco box lend associations of masculine comfort (see Colour Plate 18).

A candlestick is used by the cricket to prop open the book *Pinocchio*, a page of which starts to fall back when he begins his narration. 'Pardon

Layout sketch for Pinocchio: *This scene involved a number of multiplane levels and was extremely complex and expensive to shoot. The final version of the Alpine town was considerably more elaborate.*
© *Disney Enterprises, Inc.*

me,' he says. 'Wait till I fix this thing.' The incident adds nothing to the story, which has not yet begun, but it establishes the character of Jiminy Cricket, emphasising his size and resourcefulness. It indicates his relaxed modernity and his superiority amongst old world objects. The colloquial reference to the candlestick as 'this thing', and the verb 'fix' establish Jiminy as one of the boys, a Yankee at the court of Europe, practical and ingenious when confronted with the detritus of the past. He is also a link with a storytelling past, in a line of minstrels and wandering story tellers that stretch back to Homer, so he is both European and American. When opened by Jiminy the book reveals a beautiful picture but no text. Jiminy leads us into the magic as chorus narrator, whereas with *Snow White and the Seven Dwarfs* the book opened of itself and revealed gilded words before a dissolve to the Queen's castle. Jiminy Cricket also sings the opening song behind the credits and then addresses the audience directly. 'Pretty, huh?' he says. 'I bet a lot of you folks don't believe that, about a wish coming true, do you? Well, I didn't either. Of course,

I'm just a cricket singing my way from hearth to hearth ...'.[13] The colloquial tone is established at the beginning and Jiminy is used as chorus narrator until the film can sustain its own momentum and his narration is dropped completely. Disney commented favourably on this opening at a story meeting on 16 January 1939:

> I kind of like that where he starts to tell a story in this little prologue affair someway. We have this beautiful line in it 'that quaint little village' – I would not even say 'Alpine'.

Disney went on to say that a suggestion for the opening (not cited) was too American, but the meetings were generally positive, with great care taken over mood and atmosphere. An example of this is the early morning scene already mentioned, which is one continuous take lasting several seconds, opening on the belfry tower of a little church, with the Alpine village below and the mountains behind. As the bells peal, pigeons fly out from the belfry, the camera pans right, and down through several planes until it comes to rest overlooking a little square. Women are at work cleaning, dusting, herding a flock of geese, sending children to school. It is an elaborate shot involving at least seven levels for the multiplane camera, and it cost either $25,000 or $48,000 depending on which source is consulted.[14] Detail is piled upon detail so that the spectator is reduced to a condition of wonderment and acceptance of the spectacle, of fantasy made flesh.

The film's music is also complex, ranging from ballads to a fully orchestrated symphonic score. One song, 'Three Cheers for Anything' sung by the boys on their way to Pleasure Island, was dropped, leaving all the songs in the first part of the film, accentuating the alienation and menace towards the end as Pinocchio adventures into the unknown to rescue Geppetto. The titles of the themes written by Leigh Harline for the second part of the film include 'Sinister Stromboli', 'Sad Reunion', 'Fog Music', 'Tragic Happenings', 'Deep Ripples', 'The Terror', 'Desolation Theme' and 'Hopeless'. There is, it is true, a reprise of 'When You Wish Upon a Star' at the very end but it only acts as a coda to the final part, and offers a perfunctory conclusion. The music was one of the few elements – another was the character of the Blue Fairy – to receive criticism from contemporary reviewers. Richard Mallett of *Punch* (27 March 1940) was a lone dissenter: 'I will not follow the others in making remarks about the alleged regrettable inferiority of the tunes in *Pinocchio* to those in *Snow White and the Seven Dwarfs ...*' The uncertain response from his contemporaries to the music of the film, which is now regarded as one of the finest Disney scores, suggests that Disney miscalculated his address to the public, in his search for perfection. Harline did not work for Disney again.

Ludwig Richter: Illustration 'In the Street' from Furs Haus *(1859). The activity of the street has parallels with the morning scene in Disney's film, with children playing and housewives at the door. There is a village well in both scenes.*

Tenggren and Bavaria

An important difference between the book and the film lies in its geographical location; the book is demonstrably Italian, both in locale and mood, redolent of sunshine and storm, with sudden and volatile changes in atmosphere. The film is North European in look and specifically German in detailing. This is due not only to the influence of Albert Hurter who designed many of the props, and to the success of *Snow White and the Seven Dwarfs*'s old world look from which it borrowed, but more specifically to Gustaf Tenggren. Tenggren joined the studio in 1936 and began work on *Snow White and the Seven Dwarfs* before concentrating on a series of important inspirational paintings for *Pinocchio*. He received no credit for his contribution to the latter film, though Disney admired his work and referred to it in story meeetings. Ken Anderson remembered that Tenggren was brought in at an early stage and another art director, Charlie Philippi, discussed his work at a colour test meeting with Disney on 19 January 1939:

> *Charlie*: This is a Tenggren ...
>
> *Walt*: I like the general tone of things here. [Later, in the same meeting and looking at atmosphere pictures of Geppetto's room] That is good ... I love that lighting there ... and the moonlight scenes. Is that one of Tenggren's drawings? An original?
>
> *Charlie*: Yes.
>
> *Walt*: It looks good.

Tenggren was responsible for the design of the Alpine town in the shadow of the mountains, and it is specifically German in spite of Disney's wish to universalise the setting and to remove the word 'Alpine' from the dialogue. The Germanic influences are many from the architectural detail of the village streets to the carved interior of Geppetto's workshop. Disney insisted on developing 'all this carved stuff because you never see it any place else – you never see it in another picture ... the mantel on the fireplace should be different, not plain like this one. All our interior should be carved' (story meeting 27 September 1838). The precisely modelled toys, clocks and music boxes – those sections of the film which so ravish the child – are German, most of them based on designs by Albert Hurter (see Colour Plate 19). Geppetto is German and voiced by an expatriate German actor Christian Rub. Tenggren himself, though not German, was eclectic and absorbed a variety of styles.

The film was in progress before and during the outbreak of war in Europe. Despite the strong Germanic overtones, contemporary reviews in England made no objection; at the same time there were political tensions within the studio.[15] Tenggren had emigrated from Sweden in 1920 and by the time he joined Disney in 1936 he had been influenced

Hermann Vogel: Illustration for his poem 'Fairy Tales' (1891). Vogel's detailed designs have a richness of texture that Tenggren and the Disney artists would emulate in the film of Pinocchio.

by the work of Rackham, Dulac and Bauer as well as by the painters of Victorian academic art. American illustrators like N.C. Wyeth and Jessie Willcox Smith were also well known to him, themselves owing a debt to Europe. Tenggren brought with him the confidence of his European background coupled with an enthusiasm for his new cultural environment, adapting and adopting disparate visual styles and combining Europe and America with ease (see Colour Plate 17).

Throughout his life he drew upon visual memories of his grandfather's home in Magra, a small village in Vastergotland, a province in the

southern part of Sweden where he lived after his father had emigrated to America, and where he watched his grandfather carve wooden figures for neighbours and for church restoration projects.[16] Germany and Sweden come together in the three-dimensionalising of Geppetto's workshop interior. Tenggren was a meticulous researcher and kept files and cuttings, noting the cinematic influence of Hollywood upon commercial art, with its suggestion of camera angles and vividness of movement. The heightened perspectives of his street scenes are reminiscent of the angled perspectives of the paintings of Thomas Hart Benton – a painter of the rural scene like Disney – and his crisp rendering of details is a reminder of the toylike landscapes of Grant Wood. Magazine illustrations of work by both these artists were collected by Tenggren. His contribution to *Pinocchio* cannot be over-estimated as his mark is on many of the major scenes even though only some ten paintings remain extant at the Disney studio archives. These are large works, tempera on board, and from comments made at a number of story conferences, there were others which are now in private collections or which have not survived.[17] Geppetto's shop, the arrival of the Blue Fairy, street exteriors, architectural detailing including weather vanes, rooftops and drain pipes, Stromboli and his caravan, the exterior of the Red Lobster Inn, scenes under the sea and the interior of the whale, were all painted by Tenggren and then elaborated and blended by background artists. Many of these exquisite paintings are reproduced in Pierre Lambert's book on *Pinocchio* (1995).

Tenggren also made a number of model drawings and atmosphere sketches, architectural studies of the town, which help to place it so strongly in northern Europe. He sketched doorways, streets, clock-towers, roofs, signs and steps. The town he studied can be identified as Rothenburg ob der Tauber, an almost perfectly preserved medieval town in Bavaria, its towers and city walls lovingly restored. Entering its walls is a curious experience, as it resembles precisely the town in *Pinocchio* as well as the entrance to the Fantasyland section of Disneyland, which was to draw in turn for its inspiration upon Hurter and Tenggren's work for the film (see Colour Plates 20 and 21). Like Disneyland, Rothenburg is crowded with tourists. Tenggren made sketches in particular of the Plönlein and Siebersturm and the Hotel Altfrankische Weinstube. The backgrounds in the film are generalised, though Geppetto's house and surroundings bear a close resemblance to Tenggren's Rothenburg sketches and especially to the Plönlein area (see Colour Plates 22, 23 and 24).

Tenggren left the Disney Studio in 1939, before the film was completed. He received no credit for his contribution and yet no single artist, except perhaps Mary Blair, and certainly no single European artist would so stamp their signature on the Disney *œuvre* in quite the same way again.

The artificial light that shines on the characters and which illuminates the story is, like the spotlight which focuses on Jiminy in the first shot, theatrical. The film has elements which echo European theatrical conventions absorbed into American popular culture. The complexity of reference between European theatre, English music hall and American vaudeville are all brought into play at this point and audiences on both sides of the Atlantic would make easy identification of the Fox and the Cat as presenting a 'turn' on the stage. There are references to vaudeville in Disney's discussion on the scene when Pinocchio tells lies:

> I've seen it done in the old days on the stage ... I've seen some of those comics walk all round the stage and keep looking at the orchestra leader and the musicians – so it feels sort of suspended (story conference, 16 September 1938).

The theatre is central to the marionette scenes, and the mechanical toys and clocks foretell the deadness of the puppets which we see later hanging lifeless in Stromboli's caravan or abandoned in a corner waiting to be split up for firewood. In a scene reminiscent of Victorian melodrama

Nineteenth-century illustration of a hotel in Rothenburg (courtesy Charlotte Alexander), above Gustaf Tenggren's atmosphere sketch of the same building for Pinocchio. *© Disney Enterprises, Inc.*

the evil Coachman, dressed as a Dickensian character in full surcoat and top hat and with a Cockney accent to match, tempts the Fox and Cat over a pint at the Red Lobster inn. The film indicates theatrical convention throughout, with accented entrances and exits, leaving the screen clear for the next scene.

The insistence on the creation of convincing three dimensional settings echoes another element of the theatre, the suspension of disbelief. Here the master puppeteer Disney manipulates his artists to create a convincing illusion. The insistence on this element can be seen in connection with Geppetto's toys. These were first of all made as working models to the artist's designs, and then redrawn for animation. Albert Hurter and his colleagues in the character model department designed many toys with European and especially Bavarian motifs. These were turned into scale models by Bob Jones (1913–1990) an engineer and puppeteer, who made working models not only of the toys and clocks, but also of Stromboli's caravans, complete with miniature props such as pots and pans, the birdcage where Pinocchio is imprisoned, the coach that takes the bad boys to Pleasure Island, Geppetto's boat and the skeleton of the whale.[18] Three dimensional models such as these were of great help when it came to animating complex scenes with different kinds of movement within the scene. Reference to the theatre, its illusion, lighting and form, lies behind much of the film.

Characterisation

The Commedia clown of the Italian illustrations of Chiostri and Mussino formed the basis for the early Disney sketches of Pinocchio by Hurter, and this was developed into a coy pixie figure similar to the elf that was materialising in the later *Silly Symphonies* like *The Moth and the Flame* (1938). Disney abandoned six months' animation on the character until the childlike Pinocchio that we know was developed in relationship with the worldly wise cricket, also expanded after the film had gone into production. The final solution was, as Russell Merritt has pointed out 'maddeningly simple. By enlarging and softening Pinocchio's forelock, and broadening and puffing up the cheeks, the pixie-clown was transformed into a bashful wide-eyed child'. The forelock too is an Americanism, belonging to an older boy, and it plays against the European, Tyrolean costume. The cowlick has been the signature for American rural heroes from Tom Sawyer to Will Rogers and on to Elvis Presley, and Disney uses it 'to accentuate Pinocchio's shyness and boyish enthusiasm'. In *Pinocchio* some of the difficulties between the wooden stolidity of the original character and the need to bring it to life in animation, are resolved by the Disney artists in these Americanisms. The whole of the new character – even the nose when the puppet tells lies –

can be animated, from the feather on the hat down to the floppy collar and bow tie. The principles of 'squash and stretch' to bring life to the character are realised[19] and Pinocchio, by being made more childlike and less elfin has a degree of realism needed for the purpose of audience identification with him as hero. There are other references to the cartoon; the large eyes, the dimples and the wide mouth remind us of Mickey Mouse, and there is also the cartoon convention of the three fingered glove hand.

Pinocchio is thus recognisably American without losing our identification with his European source. We forget that he is a puppet, and this is emphasised at the end of the film when he does become a real boy. The only thing that changes is his nose – the face remains the same, but the animated real child is a disappointment. This is just another American kid. The wooden nose, the icon of difference, has vanished and sympathy for the hero is lost. There is also an awareness of Pinocchio's mortality; he will grow old and die like the rest of us, and the brief happy ending leaves us, and Jiminy, shut out from the warmth and happiness within Geppetto's house. We must travel again, like the rootless cricket narrator. Critics have stressed Disney's optimism, his American belief in happy endings and successful conclusions. This film provides a more complicated set of responses generated both by Disney and his artists and by us as viewers, particularly as we move towards the end of our darkening century. The child hero, Pinocchio-Candide, cannot remain in the Geppetto warmth for ever. He must venture beyond, like Voltaire's naive hero, into an altogether unstable and threatening world. Once again, the darkness of the film overrides the brevity of happiness.

The phrase 'Jiminy Cricket' is an American slang expletive, a euphemism for 'Jesus Christ'. The character is a mixture of W. C. Fields and Charlie Chaplin, of the New World by definition of his looks and voice, explaining away magic and art to the *reductio ad absurdum* of the commonplace and every day. The swagger and self-consciousness have the look of Fields, while the tramp figure eliciting sympathy derives from Chaplin. The voice of Cliff Edwards, a vaudeville singer and professional actor known as 'Ukulele Ike', helped Disney and his artists to flesh out the character. 'Cliff was somewhat responsible for changing Jiminy's character', said Disney.[20] 'Cliff's voice had so much life and fun in it that we altered the character to conform with the voice'. Moving as always from the tried and tested, Disney based the character at first upon the studio's Grasshopper in *The Grasshopper and the Ants* (1934). Jiminy then became more like a beetle, rounder, shorter, softer, a genteel tramp (animated by Ward Kimball) which in itself absorbed some of the picaresque qualities of the original story. Once his character had been firmly established, production quickly picked up momentum, developing a dramatic relationship between the puppet and the cricket which had hardly existed at all in the book and in the early versions of the film. Jiminy guides our responses at the beginning, and we see much of the magic from his point of view, for example his reaction to the Blue Fairy; 'As I live and breathe,' he says, 'a fairy!' When she brings Pinocchio to life he comments, 'What they can't do these days!' There is collusion here, a self-consciousness in narration which elicits a complex response, since we identify with Jiminy as adults and his appeal is often deliberately made to us as adults. As chorus figure he is dropped as the film progresses, though his colloquialisms serve throughout to remind us that he is the common man on our side in the adventure. His slang expressions and contemporary allusions mean less as the years go by. References to the lift-man in department stores, an all but defunct office today ('Going up,' says Jiminy as he climbs up one of Pinocchio's strings), and a popular song of the thirties which Jiminy deliberately misquotes ('Little man you've had a busy *night*') place him firmly in his own period, addressing a contemporary adult audience and in his own hemisphere. His size offers an opportunity for the artists to present contrasts; the carved details of Geppetto's workshop and toys can be examined and the huge size of the whale is shown compared with the tiny cricket.

There is little romantic interest in the film and the appearance of the Blue Fairy is a deliberate attempt to offer a feminine presence. She was modelled by Marge Belcher (who had also taken the part of Snow White) and her voice was taken by Evelyn Venable, an actress experienced in demure parts. The attempt at idealisation is based on the popular acceptance of the glamour girl as an ideal, engineered for some thirty years via Hollywood, fashion design, advertising and the cosmetics

Layout drawing of Jiminy Cricket and Geppetto's pipes, based on Albert Hurter's drawings. Part of the comedy lies in the difference in size between the cricket and the objects he encounters.
© Disney Enterprises, Inc.

industry. At a story meeting on 12 January 1939, Disney insisted that 'although she should give the appearance of loveliness, she was not to look like a glamour girl.' This is exactly what she does look like, and some of the changes that occurred between Tenggren's model suggestions and the finished character demonstrate how the artists were locked into their own time as well as their own technology when attempting to realise an ideal. Tenggren's first painting shows a smaller, more ethereal spirit than the blond who eventually emerged. His fairy has a costume similar to the final version with jewel brooch at breast and waist to emphasise her femininity. She has a star on her head, but in the film she is given a blue hairgrip placing her firmly in the late 1930s. Tenggren's illustration shows she has fair hair; it is loose and unkempt (she has, after all, literally, just flown in); the Disney fairy has yellow peroxide hair which has just left the hairdresser. The Tenggren fairy has a plain dress with a pale aura around it, whereas Disney's fairy has a dress sparkling with what came to be known as Disneydust. The Disney version is larger, cruder, heavier. America coarsens Europe, yet Disney once again woos the spectator with transatlantic wizardry by introducing her in a dazzle of white light which comes out of the wishing star, and which surrounds her at all times, forcing us to accept her as a magical presence. The sparkle of her wand was created by another European artist Oskar Fischinger, the German abstract filmmaker who was now also working for Disney on *Fantasia* (1940).[21]

The Tenggren fairy is poised from flight, her clothing billowing out to emphasise her weightlessness; the Disney version, patiently copied

Charles Folkard: Illustration of the the Blue Fairy for the 1911 English edition of Pinocchio, in the convention of idealised women that began in the nineteenth century with Dickens in literature and the Pre-Raphaelites in art.
Courtesy Orion Publishing Group, Ltd.

by rotoscope, is conventionally human. This is a solid woman walking across a room with clichéd movement unable to express the lightness of a fairy. The opening of the hands in a gesture of pleasure at seeing the puppet, the hunching of the shoulders and crouching benevolence of the mother to child stance that she adopts towards Jiminy are examples. There are complex sexual attitudes present also in the Disney fairy which are absent in Tenggren's picture. She is seen both as feminine and desirable by the cricket but also as a remote and powerful female presence. She is huge and alarming yet alluring and provocative. She flirts with Jiminy, bats her eyelids at him and causes him to blush. In spite of Disney's desire for her 'not to look like a glamour girl' he was clearly pleased when this became the end result:

> ... The first time we ever showed a colour test of her to some of the boys, as she flashed on the screen a whistle went up all over the room and the gang shouted: 'Oh, Walt! Have you got her phone number?'[22]

There is a reminder of the Hollywood star in general and of Jean Harlow in particular. The Blue Fairy is sexy – her voice has a fruitiness absent from Snow White, and her body language refers to the sex goddess of the thirties who had died in 1937. The fairy's make up is emphasised in a huge close up with Jiminy Cricket, allowing us to observe the popularly established Hollywood face as idealised mask. Here is a transatlantic overlay of an older European idealisation of femininity. The technical effects associated with her arrival are, literally, dazzling, and take away from the disappointment of her actual presence, where the New World reduces magic to allure, mystery to glamour, and femininity to sexual signification.

The other sympathetic characters remain somewhat on the periphery of the central narrative. Geppetto's personality was altered from one resembling Doc the dwarf in *Snow White and the Seven Dwarfs*, to one based on the German actor Christian Rub who voiced the part. He is stolid in movement due to the rotoscope technique and is ungainly when seen in association with his pets. He is an adult innocent shut off from the world, the last to understand a situation, double taking on at least three occasions. The intention is to represent in him old world grace but he emerges as a pedant whose habitat is to be enjoyed and occupied by the new world in the shape of Jiminy, who literally enters the old and makes it his own, accommodating himself to the richly carved interior and making music out of Geppetto's musical boxes. Of Geppetto's pets, Figaro is the more interesting; painted with a delicacy that extended to using airbrush stippling on his ears, he is both child and kitten, a caricature based on the movements of the nephew of the animator Eric Larson (1905–1988).[23] Cleo as stereotype leads on to the goldfish in *Fantasia*. Only Pinocchio and Jiminy Cricket were thoroughly promoted in the advertising campaign attached to the film's release and the other characters largely ignored. The *Pinocchio* attraction at Disneyland was added only when the park was refurbished in 1983.

The other characters are either grotesque or disturbing. Honest John is a latter day Volpone, preying on the unsuspecting in an almost rural community. There are references here to quack doctors in the Commedia tradition (in Ben Jonson and in Molière's interludes in *The Hypochondriac* and in Voltaire's *Candide* for example) but the same tradition is retold in Mark Twain's confidence tricksters the Duke and King who make unscrupulous prey on the innocent communities along the Mississippi in *Huckleberry Finn*. The Fox is histrionic and affects to examine Pinocchio as doctor; he and the Cat Gideon, a silent mime of ineptitude, belong to an ancient literary and visual tradition and the characters are enriched by references to both Europe and America. The appeal is a sophisticated one and depends upon parody and satire which the child in the audience would not be able to comprehend.

More alarming than these confidence tricksters is Stromboli, who was animated by Bill Tytla (1904–1968).[24] The ethnic reference with its implicit anti-Semitism cannot be ignored. The Jewish-Gypsy link is present in Stromboli's caravans and artefacts, though there are Italian artefacts too, a bottle of chianti and garlic sausage for example. The over-exaggerated movement of Stromboli is striking, his attitude and threatening gestures towards Pinocchio alarming. W.C. Fields commented at the première that 'he moves too much'.[25] The Jewishness is marked in facial expression and in conventional views of character; Stromboli is obsessed with wealth. The parallel with Disney the 'good' artist and the Jewish Hollywood moguls, the 'bad' artists who exploited the talents of others has been drawn by William Paul:

> It is not too difficult to regard Stromboli as burlesque of a Hollywood studio boss, complete with foreign accent. Disney's own relationship to the Hollywood power structure was always a difficult one, and his distrust of the moguls was well justified by his earliest experiences in the industry.[26]

The charge of anti-Semitism was first brought by Richard Schickel but in fairness to Disney, some of his closest associates and colleagues were Jewish and unaware of any prejudice.[27] In Collodi's story Fire-eater is not the monster that characterises Disney's version. In the book he relents and kisses Pinocchio, though he does have a black beard that 'covered his chest and legs like an apron'. Disney's Stromboli is also bearded like the 'Jew with the long goat's beard (*ein Jude mit langen Ziegenbart*)' which links him both to the devil, according to hallowed iconographic traditions, and to scapegoat figures.[28]

Illustration for Disney's Pinocchio: *Stromboli is handling puppets that do not appear in the film.*
© *Disney Enterprises, Inc.*

Charles Folkard: Illustration of Fireater for the 1911 English edition. Fireater is more sympathetic in Collodi than Stromboli in Disney.
Courtesy Orion Publishing Group Ltd.

As for the Coachman and Lampwick, they are grotesque Dickensian characters, the former's cruelty made explicit at the Red Lobster Inn, so that he frightens even the Fox and Cat. Lampwick is a petty hoodlum, voiced by Frankie Darro who had played similar roles in films since the twenties. Scenes of violence on Pleasure Island associated with vandalism were reduced, and though we see windows smashed and an old master vandalised, early sketches also show Lampwick and other boys breaking up houses, destroying lamposts, carving names on furniture, breaking effigies of their teacher and of the teacher's pet and even shooting down police. The film only touches upon such scenes, which seem prophetic in their appellation not only to the United States but also to Europe. Lampwick suffers a complete transformation into donkey form; the fears of change and sexual development are shown as he grows ears, a tail and hairy hooves before turning into a complete donkey with bass bray. Pinocchio maintains some innocence under the guardianship of Jiminy who helps him to escape with only donkey ears and tail. Lampwick dies in the book as a worn out donkey but in the film he simply disappears, presumably to the mines. There is a brooding atmosphere in his scenes, made up of a dark palette and chiaroscuro, which reminds us of Doré in general and of the *Inferno* in particular. The high rocks that shut in Dante and Virgil and which are present throughout Doré's vision of Hell, are echoed in the rocky barriers of Pleasure Island.

The comparative failure of *Pinocchio* at the box office has been partly explained by its content; it did not offer comfortable viewing at a time of global instability, nor did it fit into a mode with which audiences were familiar. It did not meet with expectation, and the reviewers' ecstatic notices did not send the public into the cinemas. Word of mouth publicity, so prominent in the case of *Snow White and the Seven Dwarfs*, was unenthusiastic; war in Europe, unforeseen when Disney began work in the euphoric spring of 1938, closed off European markets – perhaps those same markets that would have responded to the film. All this was a bitter disappointment to Disney. Joe Grant recalled that 'he went upstate for a short holiday to lick his wounds'. But he was a man who did not remain disappointed for long and he was back at the studio shortly afterwards to continue superintending his next feature film, as deeply rooted in Europe as *Pinocchio*, which was already in production. This was *Fantasia*.

Notes

1. Mark Mayerson, 'Right and Wrong: Morality and the Story Construction of *Pinocchio*', unpublished paper presented at the proceedings of the first annual conference of The Society for Animation Studies, University of California at Los Angeles, October 1989, 1.

2. Russell Merritt, 'Analysis of *Pinocchio*', unpublished paper at the proceedings of first annual conference of *Society for Animation Studies*, University of California at Los Angeles, October 1989, 10.

3. American stories have mother figures, for example Aunt Polly in *Tom Sawyer* and Aunt Em in *The Wizard of Oz*, but these are hardly magical beings. In *Cinderella* (1950) Disney created a motherly godmother because he already had an idealised heroine. Three motherly fairies continue this line in *Sleeping Beauty* (1959) and there is Nanny in *101 Dalmatians* (1961).

4. Carlo Collodi, *The Story of a Puppet or the Adventures of Pinocchio*, trans. M. A. Murray, illus. C. Mazzantini (New York: Cassell, 1892). Carlo Collodi, *Pinocchio The Story of a Puppet*, trans. anon., illus. Charles Folkard (London: Dent, 1911). Subsequent quotations from the text are taken from this edition. I am indebted to Susan Hill, Lecturer in Italian, University of Salford, for her translations and information on Collodi.

5. 'It befits us to take *Pinocchio* to our hearts with gratitude and pleasure,' *New Yorker*, 10 February 1940: 62. 'It is easily Mr Disney's masterpiece ... Is it better than *Snow White and the Seven Dwarfs*? I think it is, much better, not *in spite of* (as at least one reviewer said) but partly *because* of the absence of so much conscious sentiment and charm.' Richard Mallett, *Punch*, 27 March 1940: 340. '*Pinocchio* is a triumph ... absolutely real but also absolutely fantastic. It is, in fact, genuinely imbued with the atmosphere of a dream.' Basil Wright, *The Spectator*, 22 March 1940: 412. '... The most perfect example of cartoon work ever seen on the screen, and ... a great advance on *Snow White and the Seven Dwarfs*.' *Monthly Film Bulletin*, March 1940: 41.

6. Jacqueline Rose, *The Case of Peter Pan: or the Impossibility of Chidren's Fiction* (London: Macmillan, 1984).

7. Information in this paragraph comes from R. Wunderlich and P. Morrissey, 'The Desecration of *Pinocchio* in the United States', paper presented at the annual conference of The Children's Literature Association, Minneapolis, 27–29 March 1981, 11. Jack Kinney, *Walt Disney and Assorted Characters* (New York: Harmony Books, 1988), 110, also relates how members of the story department attended the play, and how it was disrupted by paper darts flung from the balcony by the young Roy E. Disney, Roy Disney's son.

8. Wunderlich and Morrissey, 14.

9. Quotations from *Pinocchio* are taken from the Everyman edition of 1911.

10. Margarete Baur-Heinhold, *Baroque Theatre*, trans. Mary Wittall (London: Thames and Hudson, 1967), 8 and 23.

11. *Walt Disney's Pinocchio: Overall Continuity Outline* (London: Collins, 1939), 5

12. Walt Disney, 'The Inside Story of the Filming of Pinocchio', *News of the World*, 21 March 1940. Articles in the press purporting to be by Walt Disney decreased throughout the forties, and the authentic voice is muffled by ghost writing.

13. The reference is to a line from Milton's *Il Penseroso*:
    Far from all resort of mirth,
    Save the cricket on the hearth.

    This was picked up Dickens for his 'The Cricket on the Hearth', and Jiminy Cricket is actually seen as a cricket on Geppetto's hearth. (Brian Sibley, letter to author, June 1996.)

14. John Grant, *The Encyclopedia of Walt Disney's Animated Characters* (London: Hamlyn, 1987), 146 or Holliss and Sibley, *The Disney Studio Story*, 35. Canemaker quotes the latter's $48,000 in his 'Secrets of Disney's Visual Effects: The Shultheis Notebooks', *Print* Mar/Apr 1996, 73.

15. Milt Kahl, one of the animators on *Pinocchio*, recalled that Christian Rub was a Nazi sympathiser and while filming his live action scenes on the raft, the animators tipped him up into the studio tank.

16. Mary Swanson, *From Swedish Fairy Tales to American Fantasy: Gustaf Tenggren's Illustrations 1920–1970* (Minneapolis: University of Minnesota, 1987), 6. Information on Tenggren comes from this source, and see also John Canemaker, *Before the Animation Begins* for a detailed biography of Tenggren.

17. Tenggren's paintings, all signed, are reproduced in a number of books on Disney and some of his work came up for auction in 1997. See *Christie's Animation Art* (Los Angeles: Christies Catalogue, 7 June 1997).

18. Information on atmosphere sketches by Tenggren is taken from Bob Jones's collection, and from *Walt Disney's Pinocchio*, which also contains many Tenggren sketches. Bob Jones also wrote of his model making in 'Three Dimensional Models in *Pinocchio*' (unpublished paper, 10 April 1989), Bob Jones collection. There is an account of the models made by the model department in Howard Lowery and Paula Sigman Lowery, 'Walt Disney Studio Character Model Statues' *Film Animation Art* (Los Angeles: Lowery catalogue, 3 December 1990), 17 and 51.

    Information on Rothenburg comes from *Rothenburg ob der Tauber: Worth Seeing, Worth Knowing* (Rothenburg: Tourist Information Office, 1990), from Manfred Balbach, *Rothenburg ob der Tauber* (Starnberg: Joseph Keller, 1989) and from a visit made by the author 4–5 July 1996.

19. 'Squash and Stretch' are terms used to describe extreme movements when drawing objects in animation. The obvious example is the rubber ball which is squashed flat on impact and stretched at its extreme movement. The process is well described and illustrated in Thomas and Johnston, *Disney Animation: The Illusion of Life*, 47–51.

20. Disney, 'The Inside Story of the Filming of *Pinocchio*'.

21. William Moritz, 'Fischinger at Disney', *Millimetre* February 1977, 65.

22. Disney, 'The Inside Story of the Filming of *Pinocchio*'.

23. Eric Larson (1905–1988) was the son of a Dane, who changed the family name from Larsen. Eric was brought up in the Midwest, his father by turns a cattle rancher and the manager of a co-operative store. The boy became addicted to the comic strips collected by Larson *père* and he also enjoyed the comic humour of magazines like *Punch* and *Judge*. He joined the Walt Disney Studio in 1933 and remained there all his working life, becoming one of Disney's Nine Old Men and contributing his animation skills to all the major features. Generous in praise for others and modest in accepting it for himself, he was an inspiration to the young artists who worked through the difficult period after Disney's death. 'What a pity,' said his colleague Mike Gabriel, 'that he did not live to see the renaissance of animation at the end of the eighties'. (Interview with Mike Gabriel, co-director of *The Rescuers Down Under*, Burbank California, 21 October 1992). Eric Larson's testament is the charming *The Great Mouse Detective* (1986) for which he was the animation consultant. Other young artists at that time, like Glen Keane and Andreas Deja, who became senior animators in the late 1990s, testify to Larson's contribution to the Disney œuvre.

24. See Canemaker, *Before the Animation Begins* for a full biography of Tytla.

25. Quoted in Finch, *The Art of Walt Disney*, 214.

26. William Paul, 'Art, Music, Nature and Walt Disney', *Movie*, No. 24, 1977, 50.

27. When asked about the charge, Joe Grant said 'As a practising Jew I was unaware of this'. Disney employed a number of Jews in senior positions, for instance, the musicians Robert and Richard Sherman and Marty Sklar, a senior advisor for the Magic Kingdoms. He supported Jewish charities and contributed funds regularly to a Hebrew orphanage (Walt Disney correspondence, 1935).

28. Bottigheimer, *Grimms' Bad Girls and Bold Boys*, 139.

CHAPTER 5

Introduction to *Fantasia*

Although made up of eight sections *Fantasia* has sufficient thematic and stylistic unity to be considered first as a whole, and later as separate items. The way the film's European sources are absorbed and recreated for essentially American mass audiences is expressed in a wide variety of styles from the academic to art nouveau to almost pure abstraction, but art deco is the predominant style, detectible in four and perhaps five of the eight sections. This stylistic variety shows a continuing willingness to absorb, experiment and explore, and is evidence of Disney's continuing optimism in the medium. The film was in production, like *Pinocchio,* throughout the expansive and self-confident period that followed *Snow White and the Seven Dwarfs* in 1938 and 1939. Disney was like the sorcerer or Zeus controlling the elements. He saw himself, Joe Grant recalled, as a benign paternalistic boss with a wholly devoted work force. Six months later he was like Mickey with machinery out of control; the element of which he thought himself the master threatened to overwhelm him, and the history of animation changed direction.

Disney's insistence on technical excellence (an insistence that pervaded all the major studios in Hollywood) was part of his belief in selling his films as products, and this concern extended to all the planning of and attitudes towards the film. It uses American technology and skills for a 'quality' product. Its impact on cinema-goers unfamiliar with classical music has often been noted, and was specifically commented on in later years by the conductor Stokowski.[1] Its educational value was considerable when only the cinema, radio and the comparatively expensive and cumbersome 78 rpm gramophone record, were available as purveyors of music to mass audiences. Concert halls were widely scattered and available only to city dwellers; they were also regarded as élitist and remote. Disney saw the film as a conscious effort to make classical music acceptable to a popular audience.

The music is all European, and so is much of the imagery and style of the design. Like *Pinocchio,* which was in production at the same time, there is technical mastery of both animation and special effects, but the film is more self-conscious and the European elements less well assimilated.

Both *Snow White and the Seven Dwarfs* and *Pinocchio* reflected the absorption of academic painting in the style of picture book illustration, through the work of artists like Hurter and Tenggren. The style of *Fantasia* is more disparate and eclectic. This diverse and complex approach by Disney and his artists to their sources is reflected in the response to the film by music and film critics. The former derided it. Writing in *Musical Opinion*, Richard Capell commented that '*Fantasia* will be dead before this summer's fashion in women's hats. But that the thing should have been possible – that is the fearful symptom.' In *The Nation*, B.H. Haggin said:

> There is ... in short no vulgarity or indignity perpetrated on music that is not accompanied by its defiant recommendation to the public to pay no attention to the 'purists' who will disapprove of what real, healthy, normal music-lovers will enjoy.[2]

If music critics ignored the visual impact of the film, film reviewers were puzzled. Bosley Crowther of *The New York Times* wrote 'to match his (Disney's) cartoon concepts with the music of eight masters ... what a perilous thing to do!' The *Punch* critic, Richard Mallett found the film 'extraordinarily difficult to say anything useful about ... But of course the whole affair is an interesting patchwork'.[3] In these comments there is an element of qualification, as if the film should not be praised for its overtly popular appeal, yet it is the symbiosis of old and new which gives the work its density, and which was neglected in its dismissal by contemporary music critics.

The film was a development from the *Silly Symphonies* which explored music and image without the need for specific characterisation or story gags. Classical music had already been adapted and amplified by Disney's resident team of composers, Frank Churchill, Oliver Wallace and Leigh Harline. Synchronised sound and music had given Disney the edge over his rivals in 1928 when he had produced *Steamboat Willie*. Roald Dahl, who worked with Disney for a short time during the Second World War, emphasised that '... The whole thing was his animators and his composers. I still feel the music was half of it; the other half was very talented animators ... It's the combination of music and animation'.

By the late thirties Disney was seeking for ways to expand the *Sillies*' repertoire. The music for *Farmyard Symphony* (1938) was adapted from Beethoven, Liszt, Rossini and Wagner among others and the *Mickey Mouse* shorts also contained classical music, notably *The Band Concert* (1935) in which Mickey conducts the *William Tell* Overture.

Disney began work on Dukas' *The Sorcerer's Apprentice* in 1937, using a Toscanini recording. This special short would star Mickey Mouse and combine the qualities of the *Mickey Mouse* and *Silly Symphony* cartoons – technical virtuosity with a witty, character oriented, story line. An account of the early stages is given by the Disney Studio archivist, David R. Smith.[4] Disney met Leopold Stokowski (1882–1977) by chance in Hollywood where the latter was making a film. After Stokowski had agreed to conduct the score, Disney wrote to his New York representative on 26 October 1937:

> I am all steamed up over the idea of Stokowski working with us on *The Sorcerer's Apprentice* ... and believe that the union of Stokowski and his music, together with the best of our medium, would be the means of a great success and should lead to a new style of motion picture presentation.

Stokowski replied formally to Disney's invitation and said, 'I am thrilled with the idea of recording *The Sorcerer's Apprentice* with you, because you have no more enthusiastic admirer in the world than I am'. He suggested replacing Mickey Mouse with a new character which '... could represent you and me'.[5] He was unaware of the extent to which the film-going public identified Disney with Mickey Mouse, and Disney did not follow up the idea.

It soon became clear that the film would be too expensive and too long for an ordinary short, which would make it hard to distribute. Disney saw this as an opportunity, not as a difficulty. With Stokowski an eager collaborator, he decided to expand the film to feature length with a number of animated classical music items. This was known, to begin with, as *The Concert Feature*.

The collaboration between Disney and Stokowski was a happy one, a meeting between two showmen with equally powerful egos, but with their own identified spheres of influence. Stokowski's contribution to the film, at least in its early stages, was considerable, and he was fascinated by the technology of the studio.

> *Stokowski*: Do you mind if I go into the colour departments some time?
> *Walt*: Any place you want to go.
> *Stoki*: Where are they mixing the pigment? I would like to study that in particular.
> *Walt*: Feel free to go anywhere you want (story meeting, 7 October 1938).

Disney respected Stokowski's technical achievements and musical knowledge. Both men were confident that their collaboration would have popular appeal, combining showmanship with grandeur. Both men were naïve, with a childlike enthusiasm for technology. They collaborated in an elaborate attempt to create stereophonic sound for *Fantasia*. Stokowski, a Pole born in England, lacked formal education; his admiration for Disney explained his patience and lack of critical comment at the story meetings. His enthusiasm for the new medium, and his passion for technological development especially in sound reproduction, led to his experiments with acoustics and the relationship between light and sound. He patiently informed and extended the Disney artists' musical horizons. He shared with Disney an optimism for the American way of life:

> When Americans are gradually approaching their ideal of a good life for everybody in which a privileged few have ceased to retain for themselves all the benefits of wealth and leisure, and culture is no longer an esoteric religion guarded by a few high priests, *Fantasia* may be a quickening influence.[6]

Many years later he added in an interview with the Royal College of Music in 1971:

> I often receive letters from people to say 'Thank you for doing it (*Fantasia*) because I was always afraid to go to a concert hall. I don't know why I was afraid but I was. When I went to *Fantasia* I heard the great masters' music and realised it was not at all painful. On the contrary I enjoyed it'.[7]

Stokowski was also an artistic pioneer. In 1916 he conducted the first US performance of Mahler's 8th Symphony with its 1068 performers, and the first ballet performance of Stravinsky's *Rite of Spring*, though Stravinsky was severely critical, even then, of Stokowski's liberties with his scores.[8] He pioneered work by Schoenberg and Berg when their music, like that of Stravinsky, was not familiar to American audiences. The first American performance of Schoenberg's Violin Concerto was hissed; Stokowski interrupted the performance and spoke sternly to the audience:

> Shall we forever make the same foolish, narrow-minded unsportsman-like blunders, upon only hearing a thing once? (silence from the audience) Certainly Schoenberg is one of the greatest musicians alive today. His music is extremely difficult to understand. We do not ask you to like or dislike it, but to give it a fair chance. That is America.[9]

He promoted American composers with emphasis on the new and experimental and he made well publicised tours away from Philadelphia and its orchestra. This lost him the support of the orchestra's management committee in the mid thirties, when he was guest conducting elsewhere and was a household name on radio programmes and on gramophone records. The loss of record sales in the depression led to the establishment, through improved radio technology, of a new mass listening audience. Classical music, as well as the 'sweet' popular music of swing, was therefore made more accessible. European classical performers were heard, and Stokowski both followed and participated in the absorption by radio, and later by Hollywood, of popular trends. *Dreams for Sale* showed that by 1930 classical music took twenty six per cent of air time;

'the balance between popular and classical music shows radio's desire to live up to its requirements as a public service, while giving the public what they wanted'.[10]

Like Disney, Stokowski saw opportunity for self-expansion by exploiting such popular trends. Hollywood used classical music in different forms from operetta to review to biopics. Refugees from Europe during the thirties brought musical knowledge and appreciation. Richard Tauber, Jascha Heifetz, Lily Pons and Kirsten Flagstad made films. Stokowski made his first film for Paramount in 1937, when he conducted the Philadelphia Orchestra in his own arrangements of Bach's Chorale 'Ein Feste Burg' and the 'Little G Minor Fugue' for *The Big Broadcast of 1937*. The film was a great success. Preben Opperby noted that several critics:

> ... referred to the lighting which played upon his face and hands, and then revealed in turn the different sections of the orchestra, and said that his appearance was theatrical, but they altogether missed his intention to show people who had never attended a concert how an orchestra and its conductor work.[11]

This description is similar to the opening live action footage of *Fantasia*, and the sequence is almost identical to the 'Toccata' as it emerged in the Disney film.

Other performers on film of classical music included Grace Moore, Lawrence Tibbett and Deanna Durbin. The latter's popularity saved Universal Studios from bankruptcy in 1936 and she starred in Stokowski's next film *One Hundred Men and a Girl* (1937). The film was immensely successful; its enjoyment and understanding of the social importance of classical music was infectious. Stokowski made a flamboyant figure as conductor, though as actor he was lamentable.

As with *Snow White and the Seven Dwarfs* and *Pinocchio*, Disney took care to work upon ground that had already been tested. Stokowski gave him the confidence to expand one special short into a feature, and it was Stokowski who helped him to choose some of the music. Disney also used an interpreter and mediator between the world of high art personified by the maestro, and the public. He selected a then famous though now largely forgotten musical personality, Deems Taylor. As a composer, Taylor had had two successful operas produced at the Metropolitan Opera House, New York – *The King's Henchman* (1927) and *Peter Ibbetson* (1934) – and he had also written extensively on classical music as well as introducing early Metropolitan Opera radio broadcasts. He was a familiar commentator on the New York Symphony broadcasts. He wrote and spoke the introductions to *Fantasia* and was an eager collaborator. 'If you get it into correct French, German and

Dick Huemer: Self-portrait, for Bill Cottrell, with a reference to his work on the Koko-the-Clown *series for the Fleisher Studios. He worked closely with Joe Grant on* Fantasia, Dumbo *and other animated features.*

Italian, I guarantee to read it', he said to Disney at a story meeting on 30 September 1938.

By this time *The Sorcerer's Apprentice* had been previewed to studio employees and to equally enthusiastic visitors. *Snow White and the Seven Dwarfs* was breaking box office records all round the world. *Bambi* and *Pinocchio* were both in production. All the famous wanted to meet the great Walt Disney. The excitement and the euphoria is recalled by those who have gone on record to describe the period. Bob Jones, who assisted in the model department under Joe Grant and Albert Hurter remembered that:

> It was like a college campus. It was like a narcotic. I couldn't wait to go back to work. I guess you heard about the Disney widows – we were so wrapped up in it. There was a minimum of jealousy, and I had no training. If you thought you could do it, you ran with it. I would go home and I was so high on it. I would grab a sandwich and go straight back (at night) and three quarters of the animation building was lit up ...

In this heady atmosphere in 1938, Disney, Stokowski, Deems Taylor and two of the studio's top story directors, Joe Grant and Dick Huemer selected the music. On 10 September 1938 *The Firebird* and *Petrouchka* were discussed, and Deems Taylor commented that *The Firebird* 'would be a perfect closing number. It is dynamic, dramatic and pictorial'. Disney did not contribute much to these early discussions, admitting that his knowledge of music was instinctive and untrained. The studio publicity department was, however, selling his image as an artist. In 1938 he was awarded honorary degrees by the Universities of Harvard, Yale and Southern California. The following year, artwork from *Snow White and the Seven Dwarfs* was displayed in the Metropolitan Museum of Art, and photographs of 'Walt' with pencil in hand began to be issued. In interviews and on radio, he maintained his self-effacing modesty and conscious naivety. 'Not Art Says Disney' was a typical headline, emphasising his appeal to a mass audience.

By 20 September, the items selected were – in addition to the Dukas music – Tchaikovsky's *Nutcracker Suite*, *The Witches' Revel* (Moussorgsky's *Night on Bald Mountain*), Schubert's *Ave Maria*, 'An encore with singer and chorus', Pierné's *Cydalese* (later dropped and replaced by Beethoven's *Sixth Symphony*), Bach's *Toccata and Fugue in D Minor*, Debussy's *Clair de Lune*, *The Animal Ballet* (Ponchielli's *Dance of the Hours*), 'an interval with a pianist' and Stravinsky's *Rite of Spring*.

Intense discussion continued till the end of the month. On 26 September Stokowski considered Beethoven's Ninth Symphony but he added, 'I don't think it is for this picture'. The group discussed the lack of American composers in the programme, and accepted Stokowski's view of the international stature of the music chosen. 'This picture is for the world,' he said, 'I like this picture because it is new; this will come to the whole world like an explosion ... We mustn't call it a concert ... we mustn't make it seem like a lecture'.

On 29 September 1938 proposals for *The Concert Feature* were circulated and suggestions invited. Some items were discarded, including Paganini's *Moto Perpetuo* with its 'shots of dynamos, cogs, pistons, whirling wheels, the feeling of blind titanic forces obeying the will of man ... The pay-off is when man holds up the finished product – a collar button!'. Other deletions included Rachmaninoff's *Prelude in G Minor* and *Troika*, and a rendering of 'The Song of the Flea' to be sung by Lawrence Tibbett. Debussy's *Clair de Lune* was chosen and later animated to Stokowski's orchestral recording, but dropped for the time being. It was issued later, with different music, as part of the package film *Make Mine Music* (1946). Disney's contributions to the musical discussion, though infrequent, are interesting. On 30 September 1938, he asked if there was anything suitable in *Don Quixote* (the composer Richard Strauss is not mentioned), as 'he was a comical character'. On hearing *The Rite of Spring* at the same meeting, he commented, 'This is marvellous. It would be perfect for prehistoric animals'. The instinctive response by an uneducated ear to a piece of difficult modern music, cut through the trained responses that would have been an obstacle to a more sophisticated listener. He wanted the *Rite of Spring* to conclude the film, but the final running order became:

Bach's *Toccata and Fugue in D minor* in Stokowski's orchestral version
Tchaikovsky's *Nutcracker Suite*
Dukas' *Sorcerer's Apprentice*
Stravinsky's *Rite of Spring*
Beethoven's *Sixth (Pastoral) Symphony*
Ponchielli's *Dance of the Hours*
Moussorgsky's *Night on Bald Mountain* combined with Schubert's *Ave Maria*.

There are two major themes running through the film; the first is a cyclical theme of natural order that stresses growth, rebirth, development and ultimate harmony. The second theme is allied to this and concerns power, with natural forces dominated and opposed by authoritarian figures reasserting order after chaos or confusion; sometimes the forces of nature are allowed free rein and the film celebrates a natural order and energy, but in many instances this freedom from restraint is curtailed and bounded.

The image of water, cascading, running, flowing is in every section. There are also many images of power, podia, mountains, pillars, and authority figures such as the conductor and the sorcerer. Flowing, like the water images, in and out of the film, are musical and visual references, generated by Europe, creating an uneasy mixture of reverence for and rejection of the film's sources in the Old World.

The images of power can also be given an historical context; as Disney imposed his authority on his artists, so Stokowski imposed his authority on the musicians of the Philadelphia Orchestra. In the middle of the production of *Fantasia* Disney supervised the move to a new purpose-built factory in the San Fernando Valley. The new studio, though designed with great care for comfort and for humanitarian concerns and still a model of studio design, was resented by many of Disney's colleagues, who felt the machinery was taking over from the man. Disney's office was, for instance, less accessible to his staff.[12] Within six months of the release of *Fantasia* the studio would enter upon a strike which profoundly affected both Disney and his product. In the same year Stokowski resigned as conductor of the Philadelphia Orchestra. He lived a peripatetic life until he returned to Europe, and worked, like Disney, till the end of his life.

This is the first Disney film to use live action since the early *Alice* Comedies, though special effects had already been used in the *Silly Symphonies* and in *Snow White and the Seven Dwarfs*. In *Fantasia* the opening section, and all the links between the musical numbers, are in live action and are the tenuous reality which holds the 'real' film together. The animated sequences are more compelling than the silhouettes of the musicians and the conductor, for all the backlighting and colouring of individual instruments. These links represent the confined high European art bases on which the free American animation can play.

The *mise-en-scène* supports this. All the players are in full evening dress, and once settled they are locked into immobility, almost as stiff as the dummies used in some of the live action sequences.[13] The only time the musicians relax is in the interval when Stokowski is presumed absent, and they indulge in some light musical improvisation. Authority is superseded by democratic informality, high art by popular. Nevertheless, animation only is alive. Deems Taylor, also formally dressed, imposes his own authority, but he is uncomfortable. He stands stiffly in the presence of the high art form of classical music, but then puts a hand into his pocket as if to deny the formality. Pose, stance, phraseolgy and intonation, betray uneasiness and tension. Taylor starts by saying, 'How do you do? Er ... my name is Deems Taylor'. Later he says, 'These are not going to be the interpretations of trained musicians which (chuckle) I think is all to the good'. We soon tire of Taylor and his introductions in our desire to be taken on a Disney dream ride via the popular art form, an American art form, of animation.

This is the reality for us as audience, the Disney artists' response to the music, not the high academic musical art form of the concert imposed on us in the live action filming of the conductor and interpreter, and indeed the players. Colouring their instruments with spotlights which glow and vibrate in synchronisation with the music can do nothing to mitigate the alienation between them and us, between the exponents of high art, the mysterious practitioners and us, the receiving and passive public.

Taylor's authority is asserted from the start; he is shot from below so that he looks down on us; he fiddles with a music stand, presenting himself in his familiar role as music commentator. The second figure of authority is Stokowski who climbs the podium and who is seen repeatedly, backlit, sometimes lit from the sides, haloed and deified. The third figure is never seen; it is Disney, ironically represented by Mickey Mouse who breaks the division between fantasy and reality by running onto the podium to shake the Maestro's hand. It is a famous moment, and adorns the cover and endpapers of John Culhane's book on *Fantasia*. The two meet, the magician masked, though Disney is present in Mickey in the voice; and Mickey is still performing, in costume and breathless after his escape from his cartoon controller, the Sorcerer Yen Sid (Disney spelled backwards). The tall conductor leans down to shake hands with the childlike Mickey. The child and the adult come together. High art meets popular art.

In the Bach section art deco style and a demonstration of the flux of natural forms are counteracted by forces of power and dominance in the vertical thrusting colours and shapes. Images of power and dominance are contrasted with softer images of yielding and withdrawal. Water and underwater scenes alternate with pale blue skies, stars and clouds, through which are thrust waves, mountains and pinnacles. These images of natural forces and of power recur throughout *Fantasia*. The tensions within this first piece are reflected in Disney's own uncertainty for he considered deleting it after a special preview at the studio.[14] His hesitancy is expressed visually in the film itself, with its homage to high art in the shots of the formally clad members of the orchestra arriving to take up their places; the mixture of solemnity and camaraderie of Deems Taylor; the live action rendering of the *Toccata*; the technical disparity between animation and special effects in the *Fugue*. In spite of the latter's double exposures and distortions, the *Fugue* suffers from the lack of technological sophistication that Disney wanted; three D and stereophonic sound. Three dimensionality, with the use of special glasses was not fully explored, but the expensive stereophonic sound system 'Fantasound' was used for the film's first release. For economic reasons it was soon abandoned.

Disney's uncertainty about this section was shared later by his colleagues. Joe Grant recalled: 'The clumsiest thing we did in *Fantasia* was the *Toccata*. We flung in all sorts of cubism and it misfired. It was clumsy.

Still: The sorcerer restores order from chaos; the parting of the waters at the end of 'The Sorcerer's Apprentice' from Fantasia. *Water in all its forms is a constantly recurring image throughout the film.* © Disney Enterprises, Inc.

It was like someone trying to do a Jewish accent'. The debt to Europe was only partly absorbed and Disney's concern about the film's effect on his audience was expressed in his reliance on technology. At the same time he recognised the skill of artists like Oskar Fischinger, the abstract artist and filmmaker, making over their talents and exploiting their resources. Stokowski, European himself, was already popularising music for a wide, mass audience. In fact, the Bach section shows widely differing aesthetic responses, from the lone individual like Fischinger via the cheerfully exploitative European Stokowski, to the receptive but uncertain Disney.

Authority exerting itself upon the freedom of natural forces is expressed throughout the film in images of male dominance; the podium, rocks, mountains, pillars, trees. Mickey, wearing the sorcerer's phallic hat of power, conducts the elements from his mountain top. The magician high on his staircase quells the flood in a Biblical division of the waters. Mountains erupt, rocks burst up from earthquakes, a mountain peak opens to reveal the devil. Trees form a natural Gothic cathedral; organ pipes become mountains, then Gothic windows. Benevolent figures such as Stokowski, the Sorcerer and Zeus, are contrasted with primitive images, the carnivorous Tyrannosaurus Rex which destroys the herbivore Stegosaurus, and the army of brooms out of control at their automatic task in *The Sorcerer's Apprentice*. The devil himself lures spirits and lesser devils into the furnace at the base of his loins. Authority is represented in moral terms in the last two items, with the European images of good and evil 'the sacred and profane' (as Deems Taylor puts it in his commentary) combined as devil and holy procession. Stokowski, to whom we return again and again, is seen as the dominant figure:

> Seemingly neutral, the figure of the conductor is the film's consummate image of domination. It welds the notion of artistic creation to the necessity for centralised production. His hands, like those of the sorcerer and Satan, give shape to art by bringing order to an orchestra whose music is first perceived as the formless, discordant tones of many separate musicians 'tuning up'.[15]

Natural forces also imply order; the profusion of nature that the film depicts is a cyclical climate of change, variety, decay and rebirth characteristic of a temperate climate and alien to the desert landscape of Los Angeles. The sun and water images combine to create and destroy life. The first animated sequence, Bach's *Toccata and Fugue*, presages the visual content of the rest of the film, with sun, water and cloud imagery. In the *Rite of Spring* the sun brings life and death to prehistoric life on the planet. Its presence is accepted in the seasonal celebration of variety in *The Nutcracker Suite* and it informs the tone of *The Dance of the Hours*. The sun god Apollo drives his horses across the sky after the chaos of storm in the *Sixth Symphony*, and the sun orders the beatifying peace in the *Ave Maria* that closes the film.

Nature is also present in *The Nutcracker Suite*, which examines miniature shapes such as seeds and snowflakes, and celebrates natural order through the seasonal cycle. The fairies dictate nature's laws – early morning sunrise, dewdrops, seasonal change from autumn to winter – and energy is expressed through dance. Ballet and dance forms are used throughout the Tchaikovsky piece and in the whole of *Fantasia*; the most famous example is the mushroom dance, but there are many others, and the dance patterns are European. This is not surprising since European music provides the inspiration, with European visual influences deriving from a variety of sources. In *The Nutcracker Suite* the marked seasonal changes and rich vegetation place it in the Romantic tradition which is essentially European.

Water is seen constantly; as dewdrops, river, lake, waterfall, bubbles, as an element in itself under water, and as ice. Susan Willis comments: 'Churning, bubbling, flowing, cascading, congealing, splintering – water is everywhere, challenging the animators with its many forms'.[16] Flowers and leaves dance on water and fish glide in it, water engulfs Mickey as it engulfs and endows life in the *Rite of Spring*. It is played with and feared in the Beethoven piece, and enjoyed as a comic element in the Ponchielli; dark and sinister in *The Night on Bald Mountain* it reflects calm and peace in the Schubert. Susan Willis has emphasised the allegory of water in the film and its association with the importance of water for Los Angeles. The Disney Studio was built in a desert landscape. Los Angeles has no natural water supply and the magical element of water is brought in by mysterious forces. The magician Disney creates the seasons by magic, and water especially, giving back to a people without a seasonal structure a heritage which engulfs them in a nostalgia for their histiographical past. It is a new Romanticism,[17] but only one contemporary critic noted the proliferation of liquid and bubble imagery and commented: 'Maybe living in the luscious surroundings of Hollywood has given both Walt and the Associates a champagne fixation'.[18] Lava, too, is liquid, bubbling and cascading down a mountainside like a river; wine bursts its bounds and pours down and into river water; in *The Rite of Spring* life is created in water and the first amphibian comes out of water.

The flow of water, sometimes natural, sometimes controlled, links the other connecting themes which bind *Fantasia*, the representation of cyclical spontaneity with order and control. It is symbolic of countries enriched with a variable climate that is lacking in southern California. It is an allegory of the confidence and optimism of the studio, demonstrating its achievement in animation and special effects. For Disney order and control meant a perfection of his medium, animation, but he used European art forms, music, dance, art, design, to demonstrate his completeness, his finalisation, his 'arriving' by the use of instant imagery, undigested by assimilation, adaptation or the simply historic absorption of these forms by time. Where there is direct, instinctive response to music which leads to control by narrative animation, the imagery is confident and convincing, as in *The Nutcracker Suite*, *The Sorcerer's Apprentice* and *The Dance of the Hours*. When the music is not immediately assimilable there is uncertainty in treatment. This is Disney's uncertainty of response, based on his sense of the audience's response. There is an earnest attempt to reach out and absorb high culture. The process of adaptation is both simple and complex. On the one hand Disney saw his audience in terms of himself – 'You can't have a motion

picture audience asking too many questions'; on the other hand he was striving to extend his own and his audience's horizons – 'We want to go beyond those obvious things we've done'.[19] The taking over and remaking of European art and music is part of the complicated process which *Fantasia* exemplifies. Throughout all his discussions, Disney considered his response and that of the audience; *Fantasia* struggles to expand horizons while respecting limitations in those responses.

Before examining European influences upon the eight items, it should be noted that they have a stylistic cohesion partly based on art deco. North America adopted art deco enthusiastically. Los Angeles today, despite massive rebuilding, still contains evidence of that influence in its public buildings and domestic architecture. Hollywood used it in its architecture, sculpture, painting, fashion and design (see Colour Plate 26). Disney, fascinated by the technical, and picking up on fashions when they had become popularised, was no exception. Art deco 'fostered collaboration between the arts and industry, and relied as well on the mass production of its designs'.[20] This essentially eclectic style, based as it was on decoration and plant motifs, suited Disney art and pervades four or five of the eight sections of *Fantasia*, from the semi-abstract shapes of the *Toccata and Fugue* to the patterns and landscapes of the *Nutcracker Suite* and *Pastoral Symphony*, from the theatrical design of *The Dance of the Hours* to the plastique of the final item, the *Ave Maria*.

Another influence is European illustrative art, adopted in *Snow White and the Seven Dwarfs* and *Pinocchio*, and this also helps to unite the disparate items, especially in *The Nutcracker Suite*, *The Pastoral*, the Moussorgsky and the Schubert. German expressionism is present in *The Sorcerer's Apprentice* and in *The Night on Bald Mountain*. Nineteenth century academic art also exerted an influence. Precise references are given in the next two chapters which outline in detail the separate items that go to make up the film.

Disney intended that the film should be be treated as a concert, with items replaced or exchanged during later releases. Soon after the film's limited release in November 1940, Stokowski wrote to him in December: 'From all the talk I hear in and around New York about *Fantasia*, I think if we put in one new number, almost everyone would go to *hear* [author's italics] the whole picture again'.[21] It is worth commenting on the verb used by the conductor who responds to the film as a listener. Disney was still optimistic at the end of the year, and still believed that his special release intentions for the film would result in an ultimately popular success. In an article in the *Journal for the Society of Motion Picture Engineers* in January 1941 he said: 'It is our intention to make a new version of *Fantasia* every year. It's [sic] pattern is very flexible and fun to work with – not really a concert, not vaudeville or revue, but a grand mixture of comedy, fantasy, ballet, drama, impressionism, colour, sound, and epic fury'. *The Hollywood Citizen News* announced on 20 January 1941 that:

> Debussy's *Clair de Lune* is to be added, and remarkable sound effects are being worked out for a new dimensional treatment of Rimsky-Korsakov's *The Flight of the Bumble Bee*. A cinematic streamlining of *The Ride of the Valkyries* is being perfected and new recordings of Stravinsky's *The Firebird* and Sibelius's *Swan of Tuonela* are keeping the Disney experts busy.

In addition, preliminary work was under way on Weber's *Invitation to the Dance*, and *The Minute Waltz* by Chopin, known in the Studio as *The Dragonflies Ballet*. This, and a *Mosquito Dance* (the composer is given only as White), Grieg's *Butterflies* and the Rimsky-Korsakov piece were to form *The Insect Suite*. A *Baby Ballet* with music by Mozart, Brahms and Handel was also being considered and so was *Adventures of a Perambulator* by John Alden Carpenter (1876–1951), the only American composer in the list. (See Appendix A for details of the items planned for continuing *Fantasia*.)

These plans were abandoned as the studio's financial troubles increased throughout 1941. The strike, loss of foreign markets and America's own entry into the war at the end of the year meant a jettisoning of all ideas connected with *Fantasia*. These included the intended road showing of the film at special prices, although it was first released in a few towns with theatres that had installed the expensive Fantasound equipment. The critical reception was muddled and the public puzzled by the film. The distributors RKO wanted quick returns and did not allow the film time to make its effect. It was cut from two hours to eighty minutes and released as a double bill with a Western. According to his daughter, Disney was deeply upset at this decision,[22] and he abandoned his attempt to come to terms with the inheritance of a culture that was now a part of the Americanisation of Europe. The creative period of the late thirties had led to a buying up of many European classics, and these would be drawn upon in the years that lay ahead. They would be made, with some exceptions, to formulae, and Disney himself turned away from animation to other forms of popular cultural expression. *Fantasia* remained unique. 'Oh, *Fantasia*!' said Disney in retrospect. 'Well, we made it and I don't regret it. But if we had to do it all over again, I don't think we'd do it'.[23]

Notes

1. The most comprehensive account is in John Culhane, *Walt Disney's Fantasia* (New York: Abrams, 1983). Reappraisals of the film include Philip French, 'Return of *Fantasia*', *Observer*, 1 April 1979; Robin Allan, 'The Real *Fantasia*, At Length At Last', *The Times*, 25 August 1990, and Bernard Levin, 'A Wondrous Journey', *The Times*, 16 February 1991.

2. Richard Capell, '*Fantasia*: or the New Barbarism', *Musical Opinion*, November 1943, 41. B. H. Haggin, 'Music', *The Nation*, 10 May 1941, 566.

3. Bosley Crowther, 'Yes, But is it Art?', *New York Times*, 17 November 1940. Richard Mallett, *Punch*, 6 August 1941.

4. The relationship between Disney and Stokowski is discussed by David R. Smith, 'The Sorcerer's Apprentice: Birthplace of *Fantasia*', *Millimetre*, Vol. 4, No. 2 (February 1976), 18–24, 64–67.

5. Information on Stokowski in this chapter comes largely from two sources: Preben Opperby, *Leopold Stokowski* (Speldhurst: Midas, 1982) and Abram Chasins, *Leopold Stokowski: A Profile* (New York: Hawthorn, 1979).

6. Leopold Stokowski quoted in 'Stokowski Has His Say', *New York Times*, 5 January 1941.

7. Leopold Stokowski, '*Fantasia* Impromptu: Interview with the Editor', *Royal College of Music Magazine*, Vol. LXVII, No. 1, Easter 1971, 15.

8. Chasins, *Leopold Stokowski: A Profile*, 101.

9. Opperby, *Leopold Stokowski*, 45.

10. *Dreams for Sale: Popular Culture in the 20th Century*, ed. Maltby, 102.

11. Opperby, 65.

12. Bob Thomas, *The Walt Disney Biography*, 129.

13. Finch, *The Art of Walt Disney*, 229.

14. Thornton Delahanty, 'A Curious Bystander at *Fantasia*', *New York Herald Tribune*, 20 October 1940.

15. The water element in the film has been analysed by Susan Willis in her unpublished paper 'Fantasia: Walt Disney's Los Angeles Suite', University of California, Santa Cruz: History of Consciousness, (n.d. c. 1985), 5.

16. Ibid., 10.

17. As Disney gives fecundity by magic to the film, so Los Angeles acquires its water by feats which seem, to the outsider, magical. It is one of the most astonishing features of the city. For someone like the author who has lived for many years in similar desert climates where spring is brief and grass and leaves quickly become parched and withered, the faucet-induced green of Los Angeles is an extraordinary phenomenon. It is also part of the reconstitution of stories and dreams still continuing to be manufactured by the dream factories. The creation of its water supply (see *Los Angeles 1900–1961* [Los Angeles: History Division of the Los Angeles County Museum, 1961]) continues to exercise the attention of Los Angeles and there are important sociological and political issues involved which go beyond the scope of this study; reference may be made to the film *Chinatown* (1974), and to Mark Reisner, *Cadillac Desert: The American West and its Disappearing Water* (New York: Viking, 1986).

18. Ralph Denton, review in *Picturegoer*, 29 November 1941.

19. Walt Disney, quoted in Robert D. Feild, *The Art of Walt Disney* (London: Collins, 1944) 124.

20. Eva Weber, *Art Deco in North America* (London: Bison, 1985), 11.

21. Leopold Stokowski, letter to Walt Disney, December 1940. Quoted by John Canemaker, 'The *Fantasia* that Never Was', *Print*, Vol. XLII, Jan/Feb 1988, 77.

22. Diane Disney Miller, *Walt Disney* (London: Odhams, 1958), 157.

23. Walt Disney quoted in Schickel, *Walt Disney* (London: Weidenfeld and Nicolson, 1968) 238.

CHAPTER 6

Fantasia: from Bach to Stravinsky

Disney designed *Fantasia* like a concert with the musicians arriving and tuning up. Deems Taylor makes his introduction before Stokowski mounts the podium and begins conducting. Then we move from live action to animation, returning for the intermission from animation to the live action orchestra, with the conductor absent. The players indulge in some light-hearted jazz improvisation and Deems Taylor introduces us to the sound track, shown in animation. Stokowski returns to his podium and we are led into animation as soon as the music begins for the second half. This chapter deals with the first four items only, up to the intermission.

Bach's *Toccata and Fugue in D Minor*

The *Toccata* is presented as an impression of the orchestra. Groups of instruments are picked out in silhouette with different coloured backgrounds, and with coloured spotlights on individual instruments. As the Fugue begins the conductor vanishes into cloud giving way to animation and special effects. 'It's like I almost went to sleep on this music', said Disney at a meeting on 3 August 1939, 'and then suddenly woke up. Then I become conscious of it. That's sort of the way I take in music. This is more or less picturing subconscious things for you ... It's the nearest I can come to giving a reason for abstract things'.

Recognisable violin bows and strings cross and recross the screen in front of a pale sky with cloud shapes in the background. These are followed by birdlike metronomes which dance and flutter and then fall before a background of sky and cloud. Violin bridges flash by. Red shapes with black shadows flow over translucent and shimmering hills with a hint of the aurora borealis behind. Star bursts and flat buttonlike discs float as if in three dimensions across the screen and we tilt down to a dark mass where bright yellow spangles spread across a red sea of ripples. The aurora suggestion is expanded with clouds and frostlike vapour trails making arcs which end in shooting stars creating Gothic arches against the sky (see Colour Plate 25).

Next, five waves roll towards us from alternate sides of the screen and we tilt up following vertical art deco shapes like organ pipes and mountains, which in turn become Gothic arches and streams of light. Multi-coloured stars fall in a cascade, before two blurred skybursts open up the screen to coloured vortices. A large tomblike stone lumbers away down a tunnel before three streams of light shine down to form a golden screen. There is a reference here to an altar. Stars leap up and searchlights cross and recross a sunset, like klieg lights in the sky at a Hollywood première. Gothic windows flying up on each side of a huge central sun are conjured up by the conductor, who is revealed in silhouette. Art deco stained glass effects are in the sky behind him as the Fugue ends, and the live action camera shows Stokowski lowering his arms.

This brief description of the *Toccata and Fugue* shows its struggle towards abstraction and its reliance on art deco patterning. Disney wanted to extend the studio's repertoire, but felt that the way to make abstraction more palatable as popular art was through his technical resources and not through artistic expression. There is little animation in the piece; it relies on the skilful use of special effects, lap dissolves and superimposition. Disney wanted further technological sophistication; the programme outline of 29 September 1938 makes particular mention of stereophonic sound and the use of 3D (with special glasses):

> To abstract and mathematical music of grandeur we give an abstract interpretation – abstractions, geometrical and colour patterns.

> A fugue is the weaving together of several themes, and this has given Walt the idea for a very novel effect. All about the theatre will be concealed loud speakers. Thus, for example, we can get the music marching about the theatre ... We are also considering third dimensional effects for this number.

The phrase 'very novel effect' is telling. Disney was unable to register appreciation of the non-literal in art, and was using the difficulty of the music as a challenge to his artists, a technical challenge which he turned into a virtue through sound and light. Later screenings of *Fantasia* underline the complexity of this item, and its three dimensional effect without the use of special glasses. Disney's struggle to come to terms with anything other than the directly popular in art is clear from the long discussions over the *Toccata and Fugue*. He tried over and over again to appreciate abstraction, but the concept eluded him.

Bach's music for organ had already been adapted by Stokowski for orchestra for his wide-ranging tours with the Philadelphia. The decision to use abstraction in some form was also not new; once again Disney used European sources. He later wrote:

> They (abstractions) were something we had nursed along for several years, but we never had a chance of trying due to the fact that the type of pictures being made up to that time did not allow us to

incorporate any of this type of material in them. Actually, it was an outgrowth of our Effects Department which we organised long before we had any contact with Stokowski. The idea of colour and music is very old. The colour organ is really the key to it all and that goes way back. I remember seeing such a demonstration in 1928.[1]

Disney added that 'there was an Englishman named Len Lye who did colour and movement to music'.[2] Colour harmony, the synesthesia or fusing of the perceptions of discrete sensory awareness, has been a dream dating back to antiquity, with the desire of creating a colour music for the eye comparable with auditory music for the ear. William Moritz has shown that the loss of instruments and paucity of information hinders detailed discussion of early colour music practitioners.[3] Colour organs varied in size and scope; they were usually console instruments with keyboards for projecting coloured light patterns onto screens or light boxes. Stokowski had made use of such an instrument, the Clavilux, in Rimsky Korsakov's *Scheherazade* and in Scriabin's *Prometheus*. The latter's score contained 'a complete twelve note part for colour organ to be played together with the music in a gigantic work of total art'.[4] The Clavilux was an invention of Thomas Wilfred (1889–1968), a Danish scientist and theosophist. He toured America and demonstrated his machines at the Art Deco Exhibition in Paris in 1925. He presented his colour organ at The Neighborhood Playhouse in Los Angeles in the 1920s and perhaps it was Wilfred's machine that Disney claimed to have seen in 1928.[5] One thing is certain; both Disney and Stokowski knew about the colour organ and both saw its possibilities as an extension of sensory awareness.

Another European used colour music in the cinema, and claimed to have influenced Disney's interpretation of Bach. This was a Swiss, Charles

Charles Blanc-Gatti:
Chromophonie *(1939). The
alignment of musical instruments is
similar to the opening of Disney's*
Fantasia.
Courtesy Cinematheque Suisse.

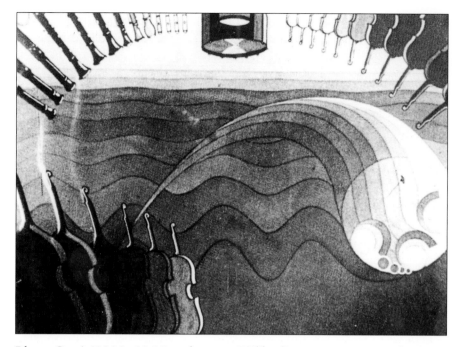

Blanc-Gatti (1890–1966), who saw Wilfred's experiments at the Paris exhibition in 1925.[6] Blanc-Gatti was an abstract artist and colour music performer; his paintings were praised at the first Artistes Musicalistes show in Paris in December 1932, and then toured Europe and Japan. He gave performances of a colour organ system in Paris in the same year and showed it in Hamburg the following year. When Disney visited Paris in 1935 Blanc-Gatti approached him about making an abstract film together. On 27 June Disney replied that 'his principle was only to use his own ideas or those of his immediate collaborators'.[7] On hearing that Disney was making *Fantasia*, Blanc-Gatti wrote and told him in 1939 that he had made his abstract film *Chromophonie* which was premièred in Switzerland on 24 November of that year. Disney did not reply to his letter but Moritz notes that 'the sensibility of *Fantasia* is certainly closer to the Romantic abstraction (tied to the representation of instruments and programme imagery) of the Artistes Musicalistes than to Fischinger's non-objective geometry'.

When *Fantasia* was first released in Europe in 1946, critics pointed out the debt to Blanc-Gatti and the Artistes Musicalistes. On 1 Novembewr 1946 D. Chevalier wrote 'For the most part, the ideas, forms and characters of *Fantasia* have been taken from a catalogue of an exhibition of musical painters in Paris in 1932. Blanc-Gatti's orchestra has been reconstructed in *Fantasia* during the presentation of the orchestral section. There is the same grouping of instruments, the same identification by colour ... It is right that since Walt Disney receives the praise for his successes, so he should take the blame for his daubs'.[8] And again, 'We are simply unravelling the sources of the inspiration of Walt Disney, demonstrating his lack of imagination'. Lo Duca (whom Disney also met in Europe in 1935) noted in his book *Le Dessin Animé* that 'an indisputable contribution to the plastic inventions of *Fantasia* comes from Charles Blanc-Gatti'.[9] Blanc-Gatti himself commented wryly in the second edition of his book *Sons et Couleurs* that 'visitors, on viewing my work said, "Yes, yes, of course I see what it is – you've been inspired by *Fantasia* ..." They must be forgiven for their ignorance'.[10] Whatever is the inspirational truth behind the film, this all points to a fascination with the concept of film abstraction on both sides of the Atlantic.

Disney also knew the work of Oskar Fischinger (1900–1967), whose abstract films were then internationally renowned. Fischinger signed a contract with Disney on 30 November 1938. Like Gustaf Tenggren, he was a distinguished European artist brought into the Disney Studio for a specific purpose. Unlike Tenggren, however, his tenure at the studio only lasted a year and he left disillusioned.[11]

Fischinger had aquired a distinguished reputation as an original abstract film maker and he won the Grand Prix at the Venice Film Festival in 1935 for his film *Composition in Blue*. This also won a special and unexpected prize at the Brussels Film Festival in the same year (see Colour Plate 27). Despite world-wide fame, he was thought subversive to the Nazi government as a 'degenerate' abstract artist, and although not Jewish he thought it wise to leave Germany in 1936 when Paramount offered him a Hollywood contract. He met Stokowski when they were both working at the Paramount Studio. Stokowski sponsored Fischinger in his application for American citizenship recommending him 'as one of high aptitude and distinguished originality'.[12] Fischinger enquired about the use of some of Stokowski's arrangements, in particular of Bach's *Toccata and Fugue in D Minor*. In a letter to Fischinger from Philadelphia on 9 October 1936, Stokowski wrote, 'I should be very happy if we could work together – you doing what is seen, I doing what is heard. If Paramount does not wish to make shorts of this kind, there is a company in New York that is asking me to make shorts ...' In his reply of 15 November, Fischinger suggested:

> I'd like to make a full-length shot of you in such a way that the visual part of the film could begin with you conducting the first few bars of the music, and then the eyes of the viewer would glide with a movement of your hands off into endless space where the rest of the visuals would unfold.

This has an affinity, in *Fantasia*, to the presentation of Stokowski in the link between the *Toccata* and the *Fugue*. After several discussions, Stokowski decided that the project would be too expensive and complex for Fischinger to handle alone and suggested that a major studio, perhaps Disney, might be helpful. After an uneasy time at Paramount, and then at MGM, Fischinger was wary of the studio system and instead drove across the States to Detroit and New York, seeking backing for a feature length animated film of Dvořák's *New World Symphony*. Nothing came of this project, though he found the atmosphere of New York, where he was treated as a major artist, more sympathetic than that of the West Coast. He was called back to Hollywood by his agent who had procured him a contract with Walt Disney to work on *Fantasia*.

Fischinger's return was not auspicious. While he had been away, Stokowski and Disney had met and begun work on the film. Fischinger was employed as 'special effects animator' at $60 a week (he had been paid $250 by Paramount) and not, as he had hoped, as director or visual designer. With work scarce and a wife and four children to support, he had little choice. 'It was I who urged him to take the job,' Elfriede Fischinger recalled, 'because it offered us security. Later we were so poor that we ate the garbage from other people's bins'.

Oskar Fischinger began his new work happily enough; his films were screened for the Disney personnel and were received enthusiastically. Disney commented at a story conference on 28 February 1939: 'It has been fascinating. From the experience we have had here with our crowd – they went crazy about it. If we can go a little further here and get some clever designs, the thing will be a great hit ...' However, at meeting after meeting, Disney worked away at the notion of making abstraction acceptable through the introduction not only of identifiable images but also of a structural simplicity of presentation. Only one idea or image at a time, with a slight overlap of the previous image, was acceptable. The word 'abstract' was treated with a diffidence bordering on the contemptuous which remained constant throughout the long months of discussion.

> You should give them something realistic. I don't think the average audience will appreciate the abstract, but I may be all wrong (24 January 1939). If we can get a little connection to this the public will take to it. It would be better than some wild abstraction ... I would like to see it sort of near abstract, as they call it – not pure ... Do you think we ought to have pictures in mind through this thing? Then we don't get a conglomerate mess – an abstraction (28 February 1939). There's a theory I go on that an audience is always thrilled with something new, but fire too many things at them and they become restless. (5 June 1939)

Brought up in the Midwest, and absorbing the popular cultural influences of his environment, Disney struggled to accommodate this culture and the individual talent of Fischinger, radical but steeped in an older, established aesthetic. Disney's views were anathema to Fischinger; the latter's work was pure abstraction, uncompromising, distinct, mystical, and moreover it was visually complex, its patterns and images not only overlapping but interlocking and counterbalancing each other in a structurally complex way which Disney could not comprehend. Fischinger, too, had always made his own decisions, performing most of the production details himself, designing and making his own equipment, and creating all the artwork from the early sketches through to the final drawings and set-ups as well as the actual camera work. Now he was subject to committee decisions and the regulations of a large factory organisation. Nevertheless, Fischinger was a naif, seduced by the Disney aura like so many others. After his experiences at Paramount and at MGM, Fischinger hoped things would be different; he hoped 'with the incredible technical resources of the [Disney] studio and its personnel to be able to create a magnificent film, more complex, richer, more astounding than anything seen before'.[13]

Besides the difficulties experienced by Oskar Fischinger who spoke little English, there were personality clashes, especially with the senior animator Cy Young, a Chinese with limited English himself, whose strength lay in special effects and meticulous attention to detail. Gordon Legg, who worked on *Fantasia*, remembered that 'Oskar had difficulty in understanding Cy Young. Oskar had such great ideas and Cy wouldn't let him do it. Walt had got hold of his (Oskar's) avant garde stuff and shown it anyhow. Cy told him how to do it ... Oskar was very shy and unsure of himself ... it was just pathetic to see this poor talented guy sweating away in there, trying to put over an idea and Cy saying, 'Oh no, we don't work that way. Better do over. Mus' have more ...' whatever. Nothing he did ever got on the screen ...'.[14] Mrs Fischinger was more succinct. She described Cy Young as 'a no good boot licker'.

Oskar Fischinger terminated his contract with Disney on 31 October 1939. He was by nature a withdrawn man, though capable of lively and stimulating conversation. He did not speak about his experiences at the studio and his name does not appear on the credits. There is only one letter extant in which he expressed his disappointment:

> ... The film *Toccata and Fugue by Bach* is really not my work, though my work may be present at some points; rather it is the most inartistic product of a factory. Many people worked on it, and whenever I put out an idea or suggestion for this film, it was immediately cut to pieces and killed.[15]

Despite his disclaimer, there is something of Fischinger in the Bach section; it is clear from the story conference notes that Disney often referred to Fischinger's sketches and the clarity and freshness of his colour is noticeable. The rolling waves are a direct result of Fischinger's wave patterns which he broke down into numbered sections, though he envisaged four complex movements of swirling shapes (see Colour Plates 28 and 29). His abstract sketches become semi-recognisable forms; motion-phase breakdown sketches are turned into violin bows and metronomes, and some of his arcs and patterns can be seen in the frost shapes and shooting stars that become Gothic frosted arches in the film. The animated sections can be attributed at least to Fischinger in spirit. They have a sharpness of outline, (in addition to the colour clarity) which gives them a linear sturdiness lacking in the surrounding areas which depend upon effects. It is as if Fischinger has given the Disney artists a confidence that is aesthetically proved through the use of animation, the individual European artist marking the texture of an American product (see Colour Plates 30 and 31). Fischinger's liberating vision is also noticeable later on in the film during the interlude when the sound track gives out colour patterns which are more purely abstract than the Bach section.

Many of Fischinger's sketches and paintings for the Bach sequence survive; there are exquisite pastels, poster colour drawings, inspirational sketches and some sixty pencil drawings. Filtered through his work are other abstract European influences – Kandinsky and Klee are palely reflected in his drawings, and then diluted through the popularising art deco of Disney. Fischinger himself knew 'that the non-objective world had always existed even though European art was just rediscovering it. He felt comfortable in its absolute landscape of geometric colour fields, organic auroras and mathematical trajectories'.[16]

Though Oskar Fischinger lived for another twenty seven years, he made only one more major film, *Motion Painting One* (1947), which is both painting and film and deserves a book to itself (see Colour Plate 32). Although he turned to painting, he still considered himself as a film maker, and he influenced the work of Len Lye, Norman McLaren and other modernists of whom Jordan Belson (b.1926) is a contemporary example.

There is another link between Europe, Fischinger and Disney. When he left Disney, Fischinger invented a colour organ called the Lumigraph (see Colour Plate 33). Elfriede Fischinger recalled that 'the instrument could be played with the greatest of ease, and I was thrilled to feel the tremendous joy of being able to improvise, to see music take form and colour instantly on the screen, responding to each subtle or strenuous dancelike gesture of the player'.[17] Mrs Fischinger returned to Germany in 1993 and played her husband's Lumigraph at a triumphant exhibition of Fischinger's work at Frankfurt's Deutsches Filmmuseum.[18] Germany in America returned to Germany.

Back in 1939 Disney was struggling to present his own form of colour music, with animation as his colour organ and a factory to assemble it.

The Bach section is an extraordinary visual hybrid, repaying attention and attaining layered textures of meaning and resonance as the years go by. It deserves to be seen again and again and only the big screen does justice to its swirling shapes and colours. As has been discussed in the previous chapter, it contains within it all the themes and styles of the rest of the film.

Tchaikovsky's *The Nutcracker Suite*

Music critics who objected to the changes to Bach, Beethoven and Stravinsky, made no comment on the alteration to Tchaikovsky's score, nor on the deletion of two sections; the film opens with the Dance of the Sugar Plum Fairy and omits the Miniature Overture and the March. Writers on music did not consider Tchaikovsky's work as important as other compositions. This emphasises the difference between the attitude of the élite and that of the ordinary cinemagoer.

The Disney artists offer confidence in every detail, from the animation of natural forms like flowers and leaves, to the exaggerated and caricatured forms of fish, mushrooms and thistles, from the delicacy of backgrounds to the incorporation of special effects. This confidence stems partly from story telling through music which characterised the *Silly Symphonies*; it is noticeable in an unidentified story conference:

> *Norman (Wright)*: After the flowers fall down and hit the water, too, we use these with scintillation to establish the water.
> *Walt*: That's fine.
> *Sam (Armstrong)*: It comes in very handy as the excitement grows. We build up that scintillation in the distance.
> *Walt*: It seems there should be some sort of finish to this.
> *Cy (Young)*: A quick fade.
> *Walt*: Yes, a quick fade, and leave nothing but that scintillating effect. Then that comes right into those bubbles and you are right there.

The piece was originally conceived in 1935 as a *Silly Symphony* called *Ballet des Fleurs*. Anthropomorphised flowers, plants and fairies were to join in and dance. In *Flowers and Trees* (1932), for instance, flowers brush their teeth and mushrooms perform early morning exercises. *The Nutcracker Suite* has a more naturalistic style, with the balance of nature ordered by the fairies who conduct nature's dance, as part of that natural world; at one point their wings only are seen and they look like dragon-flies. The two sections in which flowers and mushrooms initiate the dance begin from a naturalistic premise, a still picture, to which we return when the dance is over. Order is maintained through natural form.

Indirectly, Europe is present in the vegetation, in the dance movements which have their ethnic associations and especially in the fairies. Diminutive fairies were popularised in nineteenth-century illustrations, androgynised and reduced in size from the robust rural figures which Shakespeare brought to life in *A Midsummer Night's Dream*. The Disney artists admired and were influenced by the Pre-Raphaelites, especially in their rendering of detail in the natural world. Minutely observed grasses and flowers were characteristic of William Henry Hunt (1790–1864), whose bird's nest paintings are good examples. Richard Dadd (1817–1877) mixed paintings of fairies and flowers with the

Richard Doyle: illustration of fairies in a chapter heading for The Chimes *by Charles Dickens (1844). Fairy pictures became increasingly popular throughout the nineteenth century.*

Gustave Doré: Illustration (1866) for Dante's Paradiso, *'The sparkling circles of the heavenly host', canto XXVIII in the translation by Lawrence Grant White. The fairies in Disney's 'The Nutcracker Suite' also create glittering light patterns.*

Walt Disney and Europe

intensity of schizophrenic vision. The interpretation is childlike, with a lurking feeling of dread that colours much of the nineteenth-century obsession with fantasy and dream. Disney's perception is allied to the bright clarity of the child; and there is a dark sense of foreboding. Disney, too, was obsessed by the perfection and control of the miniature, which led to the Magic Kingdoms.

Another English artist, who drew and painted fairies was Richard Doyle (1824–1883) (see Colour Plates 34 and 35). His enchanted worlds were revisited in the early twentieth century by Rackham and Dulac, and Disney's fairies come from this tradition. The Disney library contained books illustrated by Rackham and Dulac as well as by Doyle, and it was Disney we may recall who said, while discussing *Snow White and the Seven Dwarfs*, 'I believe in fairy tales.' Sir Arthur Conan Doyle, the nephew of Dickie Doyle, and the creator of the world's most famous detective, was also a believer in fairies (see Colour Plate 36).

Gustave Doré (1832–1883) drew fairies too, although they looked rather like his angels; his illustrations were known by all the Disney artists, and his fairies and angels had been made popular through many editions of Dante and Milton. There were a number of copies of both *The Divine Comedy* and *Paradise Lost* in The Disney Studio Library. His pictures were used by Anton Grot, the designer of the Warner Brothers' film of Shakespeare's *A Midsummer Night's Dream* (1935). Grot was a Polish emigre who had been art director for the cinema since 1913, and whose designs made use of Doré's woodland settings with fairies rising like mist into the sky. The film was directed by two *émigrés* from Europe, Max Reinhardt and William Dieterle.[19]

Although the orchestra of insects that was to have performed the miniature overture was abandoned, the detail of the natural world and the magical properties of nature are quickly established at the opening of the sequence. Dancing coloured lights like glow-worms are superimposed on the upper left-hand side of the screen during the live action, with a medium close shot of Stokowski. The coloured lights take over and we lose the conductor and the live action; the lights are fairies, bringing dew and early light to flower, leaf, dandelion and cobweb. The emphasis is on detail; dew on a cobweb, a flower petal opening, seeds falling, a leaf caught in ice. The seasons are presented robustly – the delicacy is feminine but not effeminate – from the opening on a spring morning to high summer and on to autumn and winter. The cycle is represented as the dance of life and the dance of death; milkweed seeds billow out like ballerinas, their heads like dancers', to fall lifeless as they reach the ground and are covered with leaves. The exuberance of the *mise-en-scène* reflects the exuberance of the dances. *The Nutcracker Suite* has a feminine element absent from the rest of the film. Power imagery (podia, rocks, mountains, trees) is lacking and camera movement is predominantly lateral and horizontal, not vertical. The animation is circular, oval, elliptical. Three women (and eighteen men) are credited with *The Nutcracker Suite*; Sylvia Holland, an Englishwoman, was in charge of story development. With Bianca Majolie and Ethel Kulsar, she contributed much to the delicacy of the musical interpretation.[20] Dick Huemer recalled these women in interviews of 1968 and 1969.

> They would pick flowers and weeds in the outside lots and bring them in ... They would use them for designs and for some of the little characters like the thistles. Surprisingly interesting. They were a very dedicated group. People who work on story boards are generally fine artists.[21]

Sylvia Holland (1900–1974), an Englishwoman born Sylvia Moberly in rural Hampshire, knew and loved English flora and fauna, and combined graphic ability with colour sense (see Colour Plate 37). She was a trained musician and architect and an admirer of late nineteenth and early twentieth-century illustrators, particularly Arthur Rackham. Her daughter Theo Halladay recalled that Holland was one of the few musically trained artists at Disney and her colleagues 'kept coming to her because she knew all the answers, drew pictures and made wonderful suggestions. She knew music backwards and forwards and could relate to the musicians'. She saw *Snow White and the Seven Dwarfs* and fell in love with it, exclaiming, 'I've got to do that. When I saw the vulture sequence, I beat on the doors of Walt Disney Productions' (see Colour Plate 38).

On joining Disney she worked in the story department on Pierné's *Cydelise*, which was later replaced by Beethoven's music. Her daughter said that one of her mother's first recollections was of 'Walt Disney striding down the hall saying, "Anybody know how to draw a horse?" And she jumped up and said "I do!" because she was an expert artist at drawing horses and she ran into the hall beside Walt Disney, drawing a horse as she walked along ... and he liked it' (see Colour Plate 39). By December 1938 she was in charge of the story department unit for *The Nutcracker Suite* and 'ideas, character designs, continuity, colour, rough layouts and suggestions for animation poured from Holland. Disney admired her sketches of balletic leaf dances and said, 'I love the autumn colours – I think they'll be a relief after the flower colours all the way through".[22] Some of the artists were unhappy at taking orders from a woman and felt that working on the *Nutcracker* was not sufficiently macho but Holland encouraged them to enjoy the aesthetic element in their work, emphasising that they were not being too effeminate. She worked on other sections that Disney intended to add to *Fantasia* as part of its concert repertoire, and her contribution to the unfinished *Fantasia* is acknowledged in Appendix A.

She was made redundant at the time of the Disney strike in 1941, though her relationship with Disney always remained cordial. She told her daughter that Disney

> ... had excellent judgement, that he especially had a feel of how an audience was going to react. And for timing – how long they could carry a sequence on before people would be bored ... He was very supportive of her.

Here is the response of the cultured European artist to the American entrepreneur. There is no clash between the self-educated man and the academically trained woman. The tensions between the source and the interpretation are mutually beneficial; Disney admired Holland for her talent and her ability to command the respect of her fellow, male, artists. As John Canemaker points out, she got as close as any woman ever has to the position of Film Director at the studio. When she left, Walt Disney wrote an open letter saying that she was 'A highly talented artist with a marvellous sense of decoration and colour.' She had contributed 'immensely to the good taste and beauty of our pictures, particularly *The Nutcracker Suite* where she played an enormously vital and important part in its production'.[23] Ed Plumb, the Musical Director of *Fantasia*, after praising her contribution to *The Nutcracker Suite* added:

> She proved to possess a great genius for expression of music in colour and design. It is unusual for the profound feeling for sight and sound to be combined so successfully. In the many informal discussions with Stokowski and Deems Taylor ... she was one of the few people able to stay 'on the beam' with other musicians and artists.[24]

One short extract from *The Nutcracker Suite* shows the delicacy of the work; two autumn leaves dance against a background of dark green foliage – they dance within the frame and are also whirled by the autumn fairies before they are joined by many different kinds of leaves which whirl down and up and around them as Tchaikovsky's main waltz theme is expressed (see Colour Plate 40). The camera pans to the right throughout the scene defining a three-dimensional foreground and background of twigs and foliage. It finally tilts down following one leaf on its journey to the ground. The sequence lasts thirty nine seconds and contains only two cuts.

Other European contributors to *The Nutcracker Suite* include John Walbridge and Jules Engel. Walbridge was an Englishman who, with Ethel Kulsar and Elmer Plummer is credited with Character Designs for *The Nutcracker Suite*. Little is known about him but Sylvia Holland remembered he had 'a nice sense of humour ... A gentle, sexless gnome'. He worked on *Pinocchio*, *Dumbo*, *Make Mine Music* and *Alice in Wonderland*. The original idea for the mushrooms as little Chinamen

was his, with their mandarin hats and suggested moustaches and pigtails. Disney was impressed. 'I like these models', he said. 'Johnny worked on them a year or so ago and then came back with these new ones that I think are very good'.[25]

The second European is the Hungarian born Jules Engel (b. 1918) who was employed on *Fantasia* as a consultant on choreography. His name does not appear in the credits, though he is listed in a Disney House Journal featuring *Fantasia*.[26] Engel produced assured preliminary work reflecting his study of dance and classical ballet – he had earlier supplied photographs for a book on dancers. For *The Nutcracker Suite* he made many rough choreographic sketches, and he also contributed to the dance parody in *The Dance of the Hours*. He recalled:

> I drew out exacting choreography sketches for both sequences – up to 50 pictures for a one minute movement – which were then passed on through countless hands (background artists, character animators, in-betweeners, cel-painters etc. etc.) before the finished film was able to be seen. Miraculously, many of my original conceptions – for example, the pure black backgrounds on the low-angle perspectives on the twirling Russian flowers – and the choreography on the Chinese and Russian Dance actually survived into the finished product.[27]

When interviewed, Engel also paid tribute to the French artist Honoré Daumier (1808–1879), who indirectly inspired his own work and those of his colleagues at the studio. 'Daumier's gestures have had an enormous influence', he said. 'Although his drawings didn't move, you can *see* movement'. Daumier's caricatures were famous, and his nervous, sensitive line has a striking affinity with some of the finest of the Disney artists's animation drawings before they are cleaned up and inked.

Engel mentioned the pastel quality of the Tchaikovsky piece. This was promoted by Joe Grant who recalled that Disney wanted this quality to appear on the screen; we owe, then, some of the initial ideas which characterise *The Nutcracker Suite* to Jules Engel. He is now a distinguished teacher and director of international repute, and remains supportive of Disney:

> Walt had fantastic talent. He had carte-blanche for storyboard ... he was a man who loved film, who was also a good actor of a kind; intuitive. Nothing was intellectualised. It [*The Nutcracker Suite*] was a massive piece of illustration. If you run that section by itself it shows some of the best art of the industry.

Dukas' *The Sorcerer's Apprentice*

This is the most famous piece of the eight *Fantasia* concert items and stars the Disney icon of success, Mickey Mouse. It has affinities with *The Band Concert* (1935) in which Mickey does not speak, wears a robe that is too big for him, and conducts. There is a reminder too of the speechless innocent Dopey, from *Snow White and the Seven Dwarfs*, suggested at one stage for the apprentice; the child is evoked. But this is a child with power, power that extends beyond the confines of the film, with complex forces exploiting the image both as innocence and childhood for commercial consumption. The image of Mickey wearing the Sorcerer's hat continues to sell the film on its various re-releases, and is an icon throughout the Disney empire, on posters, buttons, badges and merchandising in general.[28]

The film is now associated with Mickey Mouse as a child's property, and current audiences, judging by the author's experience, consist of families with very small children who form a restive crowd throughout the two hours of *Fantasia*. Disney, however, did not make it primarily for children. The studio's inability to handle the film as a property ever since the failure of its first limited release, emphasises the tensions between Disney's striving to produce a film that would attract a large public and his desire to create a new form of film based on an older cultural heritage; and in 1937 the Mouse had not been made over completely to children nor had the company exploited the 'family' audience as such. *The Sorcerer's Apprentice* was conceived as an extension for Mickey Mouse into a special film as a tribute to the mouse that made the man. There were no difficulties in the creative process; the music has a strongly defined linear and dramatic pattern and the Disney artists responded sympathetically to its narrative pattern.

Goethe's poem *Der Zauberlehrling* of 1797 was based on a story by Lucian (c. 115 – 200 AD), and has maintained its popularity in Germany. It was first published in English as 'The Apprentice to Magic' in 1830. The Scherzo, *The Sorcerer's Apprentice*, first performed in 1897, and based on Goethe's poem, was one of Dukas' most famous compositions. Disney obtained the music rights in July 1937, several months before the release of *Snow White and the Seven Dwarfs* in December.[29] The film narrative follows Goethe closely, although the apprentice in Goethe's version, who tells the tale, splits the broom into two parts, not into the many that overwhelm Mickey:

Krachend trifft die glatte Schärfe.
Wahrlich! brav getroffen!
Seht, er ist entzwei!
Und nun kann ich hoffen,
Und ich atme frei!

The polished blade hits
And the sharp axe splits!
The broom is cleft in twain.
Now's my chance to breathe again![30]

Disney wrote to his New York representative on 26 October 1937 that he had already put 'the finest men in the plant from colormen down to animators' on the piece.[31] *Snow White and the Seven Dwarfs* was being completed against the clock in time for Christmas 1937. At the same time the studio was also working on the shorts, and about to begin production on *Pinocchio* and *Bambi*. It was under ten years since the release of the first *Mickey Mouse* cartoon. Disney was so enthusiastic about his new *Mickey Mouse* Special that 'he called in anyone he could lay his hands on to view test reels and give their reaction. He was pleased that everyone shared his enthusiasm ...' On 10 June 1938 Roy Disney remarked in a letter that 'The picture is practically completed; it looks grand and I am sure will be a credit to everybody concerned'. The involvement of Stokowski and the idea of a Concert Feature grew from the animation of Dukas' work.

The theme of the master magician exercising his male, paternalistic power, is evident throughout. Disney is both Mickey and Yen Sid the Sorcerer, who raises a characteristic Disney eyebrow at the end of the section. Authority is usurped by Mickey, Disney's alter-ego, who, like his vocal creator, stands on a pinnacle alone in a position of authority. However, when he can no longer control the magic broom, he attempts to destroy it, unleashing an army of brooms in its stead. He cannot handle the adult male power invested in him; his phallic Sorcerer's hat is dented at the end. Disney, like Mickey, created an army – of artists.

Walt Disney and Europe

He told Joe Grant that artists were 'a dime a dozen'. His ability to handle talented individuals and to unite them to create works such as *Fantasia*, was part of his entrepreneural genius, but, like Mickey, it unleashed forces which he could not control. Joe Grant recalled that 'the artists forgot one thing, they could never see it beyond ... They were disillusioned because they really didn't play a part in it'.

Snow White and the Seven Dwarfs was not yet completed, and it is the distancing of history which allows us to see the irony of subsequent events; the over-expansion and frustration which led to the strike of 1941 and to a change of direction. Like Mickey, Disney released great power; he is both the childlike Mickey at play with the forces he unleashes, and also the remote father figure of authority in the person of Yen Sid who dominates and controls chaotic creativity; unlike Yen Sid, however, Disney was not able to dominate or contain the events of 1940 and 1941 which led to loss of revenue (because the war in Europe prevented distribution) and loss of confidence (which led to the strike of 1941). Like Mickey, he is a child who has unleashed forbidden forces. The story of Pandora's box is painfully retold.

In this piece and elsewhere in *Fantasia* there are images of authority, power and magic expressed through hands. We see Stokowski release the power of music through his hands alone; the Sorcerer's hands release images of a bat transformed into a butterfly; Mickey, wearing the magic hat, conjures the broom with his fluttering fingers, coaxing life into the wood; in his dream he conducts a symphony of the spheres. The dream becomes nightmare when the broom continues to fill the pool and the apprentice has not the means to reverse his magic. As Susan Willis points out:

> This terrifying image out of control reverses the pleasure associated with the moments when Mickey first brought the broom to life. The multiplication of the single animatory event transforms the original master/slave relationship into a horrifying image of modern factory production where a robotoid proletariat threatens to destroy the entire operation.[32]

The image of the hand also has special connotations with animation; the animator's hand is seen in early cartoon films controlling the paint brush or pencil which creates a cartoon character. The hand in close up has power to create and to destroy. The absolute power of the artist/animator is shown with the artist's pencil creating or rubbing out the animated character on the screen, from the very earliest days of animation up to the present time. In *Duck Amuck* (1953; a Chuck Jones film for Warner Bros), for example, Daffy Duck is subjected by the artist's brush to a number of graphic humiliations. In *The Sorcerer's Apprentice* the artist-magician is akin to the scientist-creator. The hand, which can

release primeval forces is a theme runing through European mythology and literature from Pandora's box to Bluebeard. Such forces were expressed through film particularly in the aftermath of the First World War. The creation of a robot or living creature from inanimate objects appears in Mary Shelley's novel *Frankenstein* (1818) in the middle of the first great Romantic period; German expressionism in the cinema used the imagery of mindless energy in films made after the First World War. It is worth recalling the comments of Marc Davis who has pointed out the Disney artists' debt to German expressionism (see Chapter 3: *Snow White and the Seven Dwarfs*, above).

Cesare, in *The Cabinet of Dr Caligari* (1919) is the first of many helpless figures in the hands of magicians who create to destroy. The workers in *Metropolis* (1926) move mechanically to destroy the machinery of the city, lured on by the robot version of Maria, created by an evil scientist Rotwang. (Rotwang looks like Yen Sid, though the latter is benign.) The movement of the workers in *Metropolis* is, like the movement of the brooms in *The Sorcerer's Apprentice*, inexorable, highlighted by shadows, remorseless.

The irregular shaping of the Sorcerer's cave is similar to the distorted caverns below the surface in *Metropolis*, where Rotwang drags the real Maria. Empty staircases, their blankness a source of fear, loom in both films, and are swiftly filled with advancing brooms, workers, water. The expressionism of the film (more than the attempt at abstraction in the

Bach *Fugue*) has come about through the absorption of European expressionism via the cinema and through the impact of the expatriate, largely German influx of artists and craftsmen into Hollywood from the twenties onwards. The distorted sets and abrupt changes in scale and lighting in the films of the nineteen thirties reflect its influence.

Shadows in this film are a reminder of German cinema. 'In German films shadow becomes an image of Destiny' says Lotte Eisner in her book *The Haunted Screen*,[33] which mentions Reinhardt's realisation of the power of shadow on stage. The links between Reinhardt's Doré-inspired *Midsummer Night's Dream* and Disney's *Nutcracker Suite* have been noted. In Ibsen's *Ghosts*, when the mother runs after her delirious son, Eisner describes how Reinhardt got the actors to pass in front of the light 'and immense shadows shot around the walls of the stage like a pack of demons'. The use of shadow is remarkable in the American adoption of expressionism; *Frankenstein* (1931) is a good example, and the convention would extend into the *genre* of *film noire*. Near the beginning of *The Sorcerer's Apprentice*, Mickey's shadow stretches across the cave towards the retreating Sorcerer, who goes upstairs to take a nap (see Colour Plate 41); the shadows of Mickey's hands stretch out to animate the broom, and the broom with its new master is shadowed against the wall; Mickey in his abandon dances into shadow and is seen in silhouette; the shadow of the broom crosses Mickey's face as a symbol of the tyranny it will exercise later; while conducting on his rock/podium the apprentice is by turns in bright light or in deep shadow; the attack by Mickey with the axe on the broom is seen as a shadow play, and the colour red splashes across the screen. Colour drains from the screen and the following seconds of monochrome add to the expressionistic effect. Then comes a complex sequence of images, shadows, reflections and silhouettes as the broom army continues to pour water into the trough (see Colour Plate 42). The dream turns into nightmare, power deranged, unleashed and relentless. There is a reminder of the images of mass power presented in Leni Riefenstahl's *Triumph of the Will* (1936). The visual effect of this scene is built up by a series of quick cuts which echo the remorseless repetition in the music. James Algar (1913–1998), the director of *The Sorcerer's Apprentice*, commented: 'It became almost abstract with the brooms coming down the stairs. I do think that the rhythmic pounding of the music was a litle bit like *Bolero*; it worked on you and there did come a point when you panicked as much as Mickey.'[34]

The special water effects for *The Sorcerer's Apprentice* were in the hands of an Italian artist, Ugo D'Orsi. Gordon Legg remembered that D'Orsi dealt with all the really intricate and tedious work, 'with transparent oils, right on the cels, painting all the cels himself'.[35] We see through a waterfall to the courtyard beyond, which has expanded expressionistically to a vast stage taking in the army of brooms that move

Adolphe Appia: Design for a stage setting for Tristan und Isolde *(1923). Disney's setting for 'The Sorcerer's Apprentice' echoes the theatrical designs of Appia and Edward Gordon Craig. Courtesy Schweizerische Landesbibliothek, Berne.*

in different directions and at many levels. After Mickey has chopped the broom into pieces and the splinters rise up to become a hundred brooms each with a pair of arms and two buckets, we enter Mickey's nightmare, and the scene enlarges to become a wide hall with raised stage from which the brooms advance in ranks and empty their water; the staircase grows wider and higher; the stark theatrical settings and unnatural lighting add to the terror. The scene relies on expressionistic use of space and light; it is reminiscent of the sparse stage designs of Adolphe Appia and Edward Gordon Craig which had revitalised theatrical sets at the turn of the century. James Algar recalled that the film 'was going to be *almost like an opera set* (author's italics)'.

At the climax there are twenty-four shots in one minute and twenty seconds, before the Sorcerer descends to quell the flood. There is little camera movement and the sense of nightmare is generated by the relentless rhythm of the music, the movements of the brooms, the flow of water, the expanding settings contrasted with the insignificant Mickey who vainly attempts to counteract the ravages of the brooms, first with his bucket at the window and then with the sorcerer's book of spells. He is sucked into a whirlpool which is like Poe's 'Descent into the Maelstrom'. Only the superpower of the sorcerer can save him.

The spectator is able to respond in two ways; by being caught up in the narrative and yet distanced enough by the persona of Mickey, in a Brechtian way, through the iconographical power of the protagonist. There are links between Brecht's *verfremdungseffekt* and expressionism.

The *mise-en-scène* is also based on the studio's own history, leading out of the tradition of the shorts from the late 1920s. It draws its strengths from both sides of the Atlantic and the tensions are well contained. The nightmare is mitigated for us because Mickey Mouse extends his normal comic role to become the archetypal survivor of the thirties. His face and body language are minutely observed; he is universalised and is without the androgynous voice supplied by Disney which gave a Midwestern colouring to the character. Here he is in the tradition of the great cinematic mimes, encompassing the comedy of Chaplin and the pathos of Keaton, surrounded by the chiaroscuro of Europe, and in particular the cinema of Germany.

Stravinsky's *The Rite of Spring*

Europe is, in this piece, taken over by America, and the Disney Studio turns difficult music into an identifiably popular work. Disney gives *The Rite of Spring* a narrative and visual structure, via the cinema and scientific journalism. The visual style echoes the fantasy films of Willis O'Brien (1886–1962), particularly *The Lost World* (1925) and *King Kong* (1933). The famous dinosaur in Winsor McCay's animated classic, *Gertie the Dinosaur* (1915), was familiar to Disney and his artists[36] and Disney himself loved dinosaurs. The child in him responded to their mixture of charm and terror.

Disney takes European music and transforms it for the New World. The images match the sound, harsh, rhythmic, relentless. According to Culhane, it was Deems Taylor, supported by Stokowski, who suggested the music.[37] Disney issued an outline on 29 September 1938 in which he saw the ballet as 'The story of evolution; Part 1 Volcanoes, cooling earth, first life bacteria, dinosaurs. Part 2 Age of mammals and first man. Part 3 Fire and the triumph of man'. The second and third parts were abandoned because fundamentalists might have objected to the evolutionary element.[38]

Disney and Stravinsky: The Disney version was very different from Stravinsky's controversial ballet which had been greeted with uproar and riot at its first performance in Paris in 1913. Disney changed the order and omitted one of the sections. In his book on Walt Disney, Richard Schickel implies that Disney abused Stravinsky and that since the work was not copyright under the Berne Convention, Disney could make any changes that he wished despite the composer's objections. The record should be set straight. Schickel is a stimulating commentator on Disney, but now admits his hostility was partly based on pique; he is also inaccurate.

On 12 April 1938 Disney's agent asked Stravinsky's publisher for permission to use *The Firebird* though nothing further at the time came of the enquiry.[39] After the selection process in September 1938 between Disney, Taylor, Stokowski, Dick Huemer and Joe Grant, the decision to use *The Rite of Spring* was taken. Stravinsky signed a contract on 4 January 1939 giving Disney 'the irrevocable right, licence, privilege and authority to record in any manner, medium or form *Rites* [sic] *of Spring* for use in the film *Fantasia*'.

Stravinsky made at least two visits to the studio. Just before Christmas 1939 he saw *The Sorcerer's Apprentice* and work in progress on some of the other sections including *The Dance of the Hours*. Bill Roberts, the co-director of *The Rite of Spring* showed him inspirational sketches. He allowed himself to be photographed studying his score with Disney, and he signed a photograph for Disney with the words 'from an admirer of your great achievements'. Woolie Reitherman, who animated the battle of the dinosaurs, recalled that as it was nearly Christmas, there was an office party in progress. 'After a few drinks,' he said, 'I started running the sound track backwards ... Suddenly the door opened and there was Walt with Igor Stravinsky. Stravinsky was very nice about it. He said, "Sounds good backwards too".'

Joe Grant, co-story director for *Fantasia* remembered:

> Stravinsky was present at one of what we call the 'sweat box' (pencil test) showings of *The Rite of Spring* sequence and he was accompanied by one of his associates. We ran it off and at the end Stravinsky remained silent. Finally his companion said 'Well, that isn't at all what Mr. Stravinsky had in mind.' Then, all of a sudden, out of the darkness, we heard Stravinsky say, 'Oh, yes it is'.[40]

Disney showed Stravinsky a preview on 12 October 1940. Eleven days later, on 23 October, two of Disney's colleagues called on Stravinsky and discussed the possibility of animating his musical fable *Renard*. He sold them the option and also for *The Firebird* and for *Fireworks*. This was before the film opened, at a time when Disney was still confident of adding to its repertoire.

The première of the film was in New York on 13 November 1940. It had a mixed critical reception, did not achieve the special kind of release that Disney had hoped for, and became a commercial failure. By 1949 when Disney's films were dismissed in one or two lines at the bottom of reviewers' columns, Stravinsky had second thoughts about his admiration for the former cartoon king. In an interview he complained that Disney's treatment of his work was 'terrible' and that he 'saw part of it and walked out'.[41] Twenty years later he was more splenetic. He attacked both Stokowski and Disney, calling the former's performance 'execrable' and Disney's interpretation 'an unresisting imbecility'.[42] No doubt time distorted Stravinsky's and Disney's accounts, but Stravinsky did sell three more of his works before *Fantasia* was released and made no complaint until years later. He was an inaccurate observer, constantly altered his scores and, despite adjuncts to others, rarely conducted at the same speed. Like Disney, his personality was subject to reinterpretation and in his autobiography he adjusted the facts to suit the public image that he moulded.[43]

The story of the birth of our planet and the rise and fall of prehistoric life, lent itself to animation. It was a new theme, in part, for the cinema and one which could not easily be expressed in live action except through trick photography and special effects. Culhane quotes Pare Lorentz, the critic and documentary film director of *The Plough that Broke the Plains* (1936) and *The River* (1937), who felt that *The Rite of Spring* was the most successful part of *Fantasia*.[44]

Disney felt that Stravinsky's powerful music should form the last section of the film. He said at a story meeting on 30 September 1938:

> I feel there is a an awful lot that we have wanted to do for a long time and have never had an opportunity or excuse, but when you take pieces of music like this, you really have reason to do what you want to do. If we put *Rite of Spring* anywhere else (except at the end) everything else would be dead following it.

He added, 'The things we show will be beautiful pictures to look at. Get the earth belching smoke and fire. We can draw that kind of stuff so it's better than a photograph'. Disney's approach combined the aesthetic with the realistic in his search for expression; much publicity was given to the project and to its educational value. Experts on geology and paleontology were consulted and photographed at the studio. The printed programme for the film boasted that:

> In picturing a primitive world Disney has let science write the scenario. Such world famous authorities as Roy Chapman Andrews, Julian Huxley, Barnum Brown and Edwin P. Hubbell volunteered helpful data and became enthusiastic followers of the picture's progress.[45]

Those who worked closely with Disney were sceptical of the contribution these famous scientists made. They certainly visited the studio – there are publicity photographs of eminent men like Edwin Hubbell and Julian Huxley – but the life breathed into the dinosaurs was from the artists and not from the scientists. Dick Huemer, co-story director on the film, claimed that the artists' inspiration came from books. 'We were influenced', Huemer wrote later, 'by a fellow named Knight who illustrated booklets that were issued by the Union Oil Company ... and a guy named Major as well as Elmer Plummer'. Charles Robert Knight (1874–1953) was a distinguished American scientific artist, who made countless drawings, paintings and models of prehistory and who published a popular book on the subject.[46] When asked about the contribution of scientists like Andrews or Huxley, Huemer was firm. 'They never came to the studio if that's what you mean ... I didn't see them ... If the programme says that, I never read it'.[47] Joe Grant who was Huemer's other co-story director on the whole film, confirmed that the artists worked from reference material supplied by the Walt Disney Studio Library.

In America there is a need to make over and recreate the past; here the prehistoric past is the model, and Disney recreated it in animation. Ray Bradbury, the science fiction writer who became a friend of Walt Disney, stressed Disney's intuitive response and the scientific accuracy of *The Rite of Spring*. He went on to say:

> He [Disney] wasn't trained in any of those things but his love caused him to go out searching around and come back and build the trains and keep them there at Disneyland, and give us back the Dinosaurs – really give them back to us – in *Fantasia* and then in various exhibits.

An interest in prehistory and magic had been a characteristic of the cinema from its early days; dinosaurs and dragons are not far removed from each other. Disney paid tribute to Winsor McCay, the creator of the animated *Gertie the Dinosaur* (1914) in a Disneyland Television programme written by Dick Huemer. Georges Méliès showed monsters of all sizes in his films, and Willis O'Brien's prehistoric monsters fought each other in *The Ghost of Slumber Mountain* (1919). In O'Brien's more famous films *The Lost World* (1925) and *King Kong* (1933) dinosaurs battle and devour each other; there is a similar battle in Disney's *The Rite of Spring*. O'Brien's pupil Ray Harryhausen uses the same stop-frame animation technique with models for his fantasy films. Astonishing as some of these effects are, with computerisation and advances in electronic puppetry, McCay's Gertie and Disney's monsters still retain their conviction. The dinosaur battle was used by Disney again in three dimensional model form for the New York World's Fair of 1964–1965 in the Ford pavilion; the model was rebuilt as part of the Disneyland Railroad attraction, and a more sophisticated version may be seen today in the Universe of Energy pavilion at Epcot in Florida. The Disney artists discussed their creations at a story conference of 8 October 1938:

> *Walt*: (looking at a sketch of a dinosaur) Here's one that has a tail on him with a club – a club tail; now, if you have a couple of them fighting, how would he come around? – BONG! At the other guy.
>
> *Bill Martin* (Co-director): Here's one with spikes. He could get these caught in trees.
>
> *Joe (Grant)*: I think we can go as screwy as we want on backgrounds.
>
> *Walt*: Fantastic backgrounds.

The Conference notes show how humorous elements were almost completely deleted. An early outline continuity of 18 October suggested that one monster should have 'vaguely the manners and appearance of a modern puppy, wakes and stretches, rolls in the grass and rubs itself against the trees ... Soon it catches sight of the awkward looking 'Ostriches' and chases them out of the scene the way a dog chases chickens'. This was dropped and Disney's obsession with the miniature is only glimpsed in a shot of some baby monsters following their mother in a line, a favourite image which occurs again and again in the films.[48] Another of Disney's obsessions, the posterior, is also missing, since, without humour there are no excuses for 'fanny' jokes.[49]

The themes of *Fantasia* are continued in *The Rite of Spring*. Cataclysmic natural forces follow upon each other in a succession of visual and aural explosions, after the slow initial movement 'Trip Through Space'. Erupting volcanoes are followed by tidal waves, storms and whirlwinds. Under the water, molecular marine life develops into a fish with legs which leads us back to the surface. In a primeval world of water and mist, pterodactyls and giant prehistoric creatures feed and prey on each other till their order is subverted by the flesh eating *Tyrannosaurus Rex*. He destroys his vegetarian rival Stegasaurus, but his reign is brief, for drought leads the dinosaurs to death and extinction. There is no water – that element so relished in this film which chronicles water in all its forms – and there are painful images of the beasts dropping dead of thirst in the desert, as dust storms blow around them. Animation invests these prehistoric creatures with tragic dignity as they lift parched heads to the sun, eyes glazed, tongues lolling.

Chaos follows, with earthquake and inundation leading to a new order. Movement to music is extended to embrace the whole earth. Dance, in some form or other is characteristic of *Fantasia*, and here it is a male dance, aggressive and restless. 'It's fascinating,' said Disney on listening to the music. 'We have always wanted to do something like this in a symphony where we could let Nature be something ... the whole earth is full of rhythm'.[50] The rawness of the landscape is emphasised with colour; red is used to underline brute force, the force of volcanoes, lava, the brutality of the dinosaur's eyes, his mouth and tongue. Brown is the palette of the earth, of bodies and of mud, black that of space, the depths of the sea. Yellow is harsh, a burning sun, desert, sand, bones. Greens and blues are dark, misty, rain swept, although there is a gentler range of colour in the underwater scenes. The colours echo the raw quality of the film, its geographical location in America's West. *The National Geographic Magazine* is the visual reference here, and the artist who comes to mind is not the great American visual poet of the desert, Georgia O'Keeffe (1887–1986), but the observer of the American urban desert, Edward Hopper (1882–1967). O'Keeffe's bright colours and clear compositions are removed from the violence of Disney's landscapes. Hopper is closer to the tragedy of decay, isolation and death that is portrayed so savagely in *The Rite of Spring*. The Disney artists drew upon the harshness of their own continent; nothing in European illustrative art approaches the horror of its self-destructive power.

Notes

1. Quote in Culhane, *Walt Disney's Fantasia*, 37.
2. Len Lye (1901–1980) was a New Zealander whose most famous abstract films were made for the British Post Office in the 1930s and received wide circulation.
3. William Moritz, 'Abstract Film and Colour Music', *The Spiritual in Art: Abstract Painting*, ed. Edward Weisberger (New York: Abbeville, 1986), 297–312.
4. Opperby, *Leopold Stokowski*, 22.
5. Thornton Delahanty, 'A Curious Bystander at *Fantasia*', *New York Herald Tribune*, 20 October 1940.
6. Information on Blanc Gatti comes from Wiliam Moritz, 'Towards a Visual Music', *Cantrill's Film Notes*, Melbourne, Summer 1985, 6.
7. Quoted by Bruno Edera in *Histoire du Cinema Suisse d'animation*, trans. author, (Yverdon et Geneva: Cinematheque-Travelling, 1978), 74.
8. D. Chevalier, 'Les Sources d'inspiration de Walt Disney', trans author, *Arts, Beaux Arts*, 1 November 1946, quoted in Edera, 75.
9. Lo Duca, *Le Dessin Animé*, trans. author (Paris: Prisma, 1948), 91.
10. Quoted in Edera, 76.
11. In this chapter reference is made to information supplied in interviews with Fischinger's biographer William Moritz and with his widow Elfriede Fischinger, and in particular to the following biographical and critical studies by William Moritz: 'The Films of Oskar Fschinger', *Film Culture*, No. 58–59–60, 1974, 37–189; 'Fischinger at Disney: or Oskar in the Mousetrap', *Millimetre*, Vol. 5, No. 2, February 1977, 25–28 and 65–67; *The Private World of Oskar Fischinger* (Los Angeles: LaserDisc, Visual Pathfinders, 1989). The letters quoted are from the Fischinger Archives.
12. Leopold Stokowski, letter to American Consul, Mexicali, Mexico, 23 January 1937. Fischinger Archives.
13. Quoted in Moritz, 'Fischinger at Disney', 18.
14. Gordon Legg, interview with author, 21 June 1989 and unpublished interview with Milton Gray, 31 March 1976, 47. Courtesy Gordon Legg.
15. Quoted in Moritz, 'Fischinger at Disney', 65.
16. Moritz, *The Private World of Oskar Fischinger*, n. pag.
17. Elfriede Fischinger, 'Writing Light', *Relay* Vol 2. No. 3, May 1984, 3.
18. *Optische Poesie: Oskar Fischinger Leben und Werk* (Frankfurt, Deutsches Film-museum, 1993).
19. John Hambley and Patrick Downing, *Thames Television's The Art of Hollywood: Fifty Years of Art Direction* (London: Thames Television, 1979), 33.
20. For a detailed biography of Sylvia Holland see the author's 'Sylvia Holland: Disney Artist', *Animation Journal* Vol. 2, No. 2, Spring 1994, 32–41, and Canemaker, *Before the Animation Begins*, 106–113; Canemaker, 'The *Fantasia* That Never Was', *Print* Jan/Feb 1988, Vol XLII.I, 85–86 and 139; Canemaker, 'Sylvia Moberly

Holland, *Animation Art Catalogue* (Burbank: Howard Lowery, 1990). I am indebted to Theodora Halladay, daughter of Sylvia Holland, for granting a number of interviews as well as allowing access to her mother's archives. Unless otherwise cited, the information and letters in this section come from this source.

Ethel Kulsar contributed beautiful inspirational paintings for the *Nutcracker*. Her artwork is reproduced in Deems Taylor, *Fantasia*, 38–39. Bianca Majolie was an old school friend of Walt Disney's. She translated *Pinocchio* and worked in the story department on *Fantasia* and other early ideas for feature films. Her biography is in Canemaker, *Before the Animation Begins*, 96–105.

21. Dick Huemer, 'With Disney on Olympus: An Interview with Dick Huemer', *Funnyworld* No. 17, 42.

22. Canemaker, 'Sylvia Moberly Holland', 50.

23. Walt Disney, letter of recommendation, 11 August 1941. Courtesy Theo Halladay.

24. Ed Plumb, letter of recommendation, October 1941. Courtesy Theo Halladay.

25. Culhane, *Walt Disney's Fantasia*, 47.

26. 'Fantasia Edition', *Disney Bulletin*, Vol. 3, No. 5, 15 November 1940:2. The *Disney Bulletin* was an occasional house journal for employees of the Disney Studio. Information here is taken from interviews with the author unless otherwise cited.

27. Jules Engel, 'Teaching Animation', *Millimetre*, Vol. 14, No. 2, February 1976, 30. After a distinguished career at the UPA Studios, and as independent film maker, Engel accepted the post of Director in charge of experimental animation at the Californian Institute of the Arts, originally founded by Walt Disney. See Janeann Dill 'Jules Engel: Film Artist A Painterly Aesthetic', *Animation Journal*, Vol 1, No. 2, Spring 1993, 51–73.

28 Mickey Mouse as Apprentice was the main image for a Disney retrospective of all the animated feature films at the Los Angeles County Museum of Art in the summer of 1986. It formed the letterhead of the company for the film's re-release in 1990 and was the recurrent image for the sales promotion of the video in 1991. It was prominently advertised in connection with selling Euro Disney (now Disneyland Paris) in 1992, with sales of a model of Mickey 'meticulously crafted in fine pewter and hand-painted ... atop a wondrous wave of lead crystal'. Buyers were invited to 'join in this spectacular tribute' at £145 for the model. The mouse as apprentice was also the corporate logo for The Walt Disney Company's theme parks creative branch, WED Enterprises (now Walt Disney Imagineering).

29. David R. Smith, 'The Sorcerer's Apprentice: Birthplace of *Fantasia*', *Millimetre*, Vol. 4, No. 2, February 1976, 19.

30. Adapted by the author from the unpublished translation of Uwe Kothenschulte, 1996.

31. Quoted by Smith 'The Sorcerer's Apprentice', 20.

32. Susan Willis, '*Fantasia*: Walt Disney's Los Angeles Suite', unpublished paper for University of California, Santa Cruz, n.d., c. 1985, 6.

33. Lotte H. Eisner, *The Haunted Screen* (London: Secker and Warburg, 1973), 130.

34. James Algar, interview with author, 1985. Algar (1913–1998) studied at Stanford University before joining Walt Disney as an animator in 1934. He directed *The Sorcerer's Apprentice* and other Disney films of the 1940s including sections of *The Adventures of Ichabod and Mr. Toad* (1949). He then went on to direct many of the *True-Life Adventure* series, which won a number of awards. He struggled courageously after a massive stroke in 1989.

35. Legg, unpublished interview with Grey, 49.

36. John Canemaker, *Winsor McCay: His Life and Art* (New York: Abbeville, 1987), 309.

37. Culhane, *Walt Disney's Fantasia*, 126.

38. Ibid.

39. Ibid.

40. Joe Grant, '*Fantasia* Revisited', Disney News, Vol. 25, No. 4, 1990, 31.

41. Igor Stravinsky, interview in *Champaign-Urbana Illinois Courier*, 3 March 1949.

42. Igor Stravinsky and Robert Craft, *Expositions and Developments* (Garden City: Doubleday, 1962), 159ff.

43. Peter Paul Nash, 'Music Weekly', *Radio Three*, BBC, 2 April 1991.

44. Culhane, 126.

45. Programme, *Walt Disney's Fantasia* (New York: Walt Disney Productions, n.d. 1940).

46. Charles Robert Knight (1874–1953), illustrator and scientist, painted pictures and lectured on prehistory; two of his best known books are *Life Through the Ages* (New York: Knopf, 1946) and *Prehistoric Man* (New York?: Appleton, 1949). This information comes from Henry C. Pitz, *200 Years of American Illustration* (New York: Random House, 1977), 424 and from selections of Knight's work *Life Through the Ages* (Orlando: Natural History Prints, 1991). I have been unable to discover anything further about the artist referred to as Major. Elmer Plummer was story artist and designer for the studio throughout the 1940s. His work was strikingly beautiful. In a letter to the author John Canemaker writes that some of the most beautiful sketches were by an artist called Robert Sterner, about whom little is known. He was born in 1899, studied two years at Otis Art Institute, worked in advertising art and did freelance jobs for magazines. He worked at Disney from 1938 to 1940.

47. Huemer, 'With Disney on Olympus: an Interview with Dick Huemer', *Funnyworld*, No. 17: 42.

48. Some examples of baby animals following their mothers are: the Quail family in *Snow White and the Seven Dwarfs*, the Flying Horse family in *The Pastoral Symphony* of *Fantasia*, Quail families in *Bambi* and again in *Melody Time*.

49. Disney's penchant for 'outhouse' humour, and in particular his anal fixation has been well documented. One comment made during a story conference of 3 October 1938 on the Rite of Spring is worth noting in full:

    Walt Disney: 'Even the guy who isn't interested in fact should be able to come in and enjoy this – and there's nobody left but the blind people and even they will come in to hear the music. You may not believe it but there will be a story written to the music of *The Rites of Spring* for the blind; they will listen to that music and read the story of our interpretation of it. That's a fact – like *The Three Little Pigs*. They played the music and they take the scores which is on a record, and they have a book which tells the story (written in Braille), as the music plays – here comes the wolf! Every once in a while they have a picture – pictures drawn out of the three pigs, suckling the mother – which the blind can feel with their fingers – and at the very end was the rear end of the pig. They could actually feel the rear end as they listened to the music ... so you can even reach the blind.'

50. Transcript of Story conference, 3 October 1938.

CHAPTER 7

Fantasia: from Beethoven to Schubert

There is a short live action intermission after *The Rite of Spring* while we assume Stokowski has left the stage. The orchestra improvises with a jazz piece *Mr Bach Goes to Town* and we are invited to relax with some home grown music after all that high art stuff. There is also an interview with the sound track which creates abstract shapes reflecting the sounds of various instruments. This item is more purely abstract than any imagery in the Bach section and is a reminder, in colour and design, of the influence of Fischinger's films. The colours are primary and bright, bursting from a vertical key line which runs down the middle of the screen, so that the shapes extend laterally across it in a mirror image of colour. It is a stimulating surprise in spite of Taylor's self-conscious commentary, which leads us at first to think that we are to meet Walt Disney himself:

> I'd like to introduce somebody to you. Somebody who is very important to *Fantasia*. He's very shy, and very retiring. I just happened to run across him one day at the Disney Studios. But when I did, I realised that he was not only an indispensible member of the organisation, but a screen personality whose possibilitiies nobody around the place had ever noticed. And so, I am very happy to have this opportunity to introduce to you [pause] the sound track.

Animated experiments with sound and colour similar to this interlude can be seen later in *The Three Caballeros* (1945), in which Donald Duck's Mexican gift turns into musical instruments which develop their own abstract shapes and colours, finally enveloping the hapless Donald who becomes a colour symphony himself until popped like a balloon. In *Make Mine Music* (1946) also, there is a colour/sound introduction of the various instruments which play key narrative and musical roles in the 'Peter and the Wolf' section. Fischinger had long gone from the Disney Studio, but his influence can still be felt in later work.

Beethoven's *Sixth Symphony* – *The Pastoral*

The uneven quality of *The Pastoral Symphony*,[1] both aesthetically and technically, still perplexes today. It is a complex piece; forty-six people are given credit for it in the programme and a hundred and ten are mentioned in the studio house bulletin.[2] This is at least twice as many as almost all the other pieces, the biggest production crew otherwise being on *The Rite of Spring* which credits twenty-six in the programme and sixty-four in the bulletin. Audience response ranges from admiration to outrage. The lapses in taste are remembered by the first generation of filmgoers who saw *Fantasia* in the 1940s and who have difficulty in remembering other sections, or at least have difficulty in identifying the images connected with them. It dominated not only its first audience's reception, but has continued to exercise the attention of The Walt Disney Company in later releases, being edited or altered in some scenes which are not considered politically correct for contemporary audiences.[3]

The section had a long and difficult gestation. It was first designed for Pierné's short ballet *Cydalise* and the aesthetic problem lies in the fact that imagery for a light, brief piece of music composed for the stage was transposed to Beethoven's much more complex work, and pictures conceived to accompany lightweight music suitable for *The Silly Symphonies* cannot match the kind of imagery required – if any is required – to accompany *The Pastoral Symphony*. It also relies on the animation conventions of the previous decade, and especially the formulae of the *Silly Symphonies*. These, too, had used classical music for lyrical or comic effect, but not within a larger structure. Their success lay in their very brevity. This new work is a *Silly Symphony* stretched and distended beyond a seven minute short cartoon. It has the qualities which characterise the later films in that series; naivety, archness, self-consciousness and a straining for effect coupled with technical accomplishment and delicacy in rendering. These are all present in the Beethoven film. Characters and gags, too, are carried over from the shorts. *Wynken, Blynken & Nod* (1938) is a miniature *Pastoral*; the babies are forerunners of the cupids and fauns, and they float through an art deco sky similar to that in *The Pastoral*. In *Little Hiawatha* (1937) there is a similar child/baby and there are many babies in *Merbabies* (1938), to mention only two late *Silly Symphonies*. Babies also appeared in profusion in the MGM and Warner Brothers cartoons of the time.

There are many reasons for this, one being the phenomenal success of Shirley Temple who was a top box office star in the 1930s and who won a special Academy Award in 1934 when she was six. Also, the Disney artists were more or less of the same age, many born in the late 1900s or between 1905 and 1915. They were producing offspring of their own at more or less the same time (Disney himself was somewhat older than his staff, and his first eagerly awaited child, his daughter Diane was born in 1933. The adopted Sharon joined the Disney family in 1936.) Baby imagery is scattered throughout the shorts and this section of *Fantasia*. Disney was also considering a complete 'Baby Ballet' as part

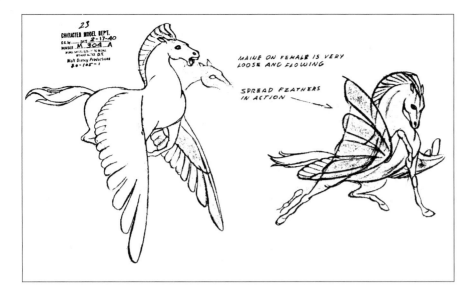

Model sheet (detail): Female Pegasus for the Beethoven section of Fantasia. *The flying horses feature in the first movement and are some of the most successfully animated classical creatures.*
© Disney Enterprises, Inc.

of the ongoing *Fantasia* of the 1940s (See Appendix A). Finally, Disney was aware that women comprised a large proportion of cinemagoers, and he was always conscious of audience appeal. This section of *Fantasia* is not, therefore, breaking new ground with regard to some of its characterisation, situations and backgrounds.

(Henri Constant) Gabriel Pierné (1863–1937) was a French composer of serious organ music – his teacher had been Franck – and he also composed sensual, popular music which related to his studies under Massenet. His light and pretty *Cydalise* (1923)[4] was chosen as one of the items for inclusion for *The Concert Feature* in September 1938. Work began immediately. The first outline, dated 29 September, stressed that 'We play for comedy ... Improving on the Greek, we show the winged horse Pegasus, nesting in a tree, and in the nest are winged colts ...'. On 13 October, George Stallings presented a story outline which developed these ideas and introduced burlesque. 'The Fauns come upon a herd of grazing Unicorns which they mount and ride them [sic] like cowboys and pursue the Girls'. The outline ends with the centaurs returning from the hunt, spanking and routing the fauns. The ballet by Pierné links the mythological with the real worlds, and there is a romantic love affair between a faun and a mortal, but the Disney film remains entirely within the confines of an American idea of comic mythology; there is no link between reality and fantasy except in comic allusion to the contemporary in mores or in fashion.

The reference to flying horses in the September outline is taken up and developed. A later conference of 17 October 1938 states: 'They finally light on the lake, fold their wings back and swim like swans.' This enchanting image is preserved in the film, a lyricism taken over from the original Pierné interpretation, matched later by the first movement of Beethoven's music (see Colour Plate 43). 'Don't get too complicated with story, George,' said Disney at the same meeting, 'because the music ...' The Disney voice of authority trails off, the sentence remains unfinished. His famous inability to articulate is demonstrated; his colleagues had to guess what he wanted. He went on to stress a comic strip element which he would later retract: 'The old man is hunting for them (the Fauns). Show him chasing ... He has a club there don't you think? Like calling the Katzenjammer boys.' By 2 November, however, Disney felt that Pierné's music was 'wrong for the story. We should find music to fit the things we have in mind here – but good music.' The discussion then turned to *Petrouchka* (*Patricia* in typescript) which Disney rejected, and the meeting closed with his comment:

> Let's do some exploring first. Let's see if we can't put together the right stuff ... if the music hasn't the right class, we will have to hold it up – we can always come back. Of course Pierné doesn't mean anything.

Disney's final comment is significant; it shows his concern for the value of the music as product for mass consumption since Pierné had no recognisable status in popular appeal. The quality of the artwork that was being produced also caused him to shift focus and on 23 December 1938 he was aware of a cultural change:

> We've taken good music and bastardised it and it's served our purpose and nobody kicked. This is something different we're selling the public, though, and we've got to stay in line. I know it's not right yet ... It could be done a little differently. I hate this Katzenjammer Kid angle entirely. You feel there's something good in all this stuff and we don't seem to get it.

Beethoven was mentioned early in November, though no specific work was cited. The decision to use the *Pastoral* was taken after story, design and continuity had been worked on for several months, and had been approved by Disney. The quality of his artists' work was impressive. Not a man to praise often, he said, 'The material is so damn good here!'

By the middle of 1939 work was being done to accompany the Beethoven music and at a meeting in August Disney was explaining to Stokowski that he did not want 'to get too serious'. He was also aware of the quality of the music and the discussion shows the tensions between the cartoon film maker and the conductor:

> *Walt*: ... We're not going to be slapstick. We'll go for the beautiful, rather than the slapstick ... I thought maybe you felt we were going overboard and make a Donald Duck of it.

Stokowski: The thing I want is to be loyal to you and the picture, and to be sure that we don't offend the kind of worship there is all over the world for Beethoven.

Walt: I think this thing will make Beethoven.

Stokowski: That's true. In a certain sense it will. Some who have never heard his name will see this.

Walt: It creates a whole new feeling, a whole new sympathy for this music ...(Meeting on the sound stage, 8 August 1939).

These extracts emphasise the struggle Disney had in encompassing material that was not immediately seen by him as popular. He was trying to extend his craft as product, through the heritage of Europe and its mythology, and at the same time he was caught up in the desire to create work that transcended the current, the acceptable face of 'Disney'. His artists were providing an extended comic strip version with gags appealing to his naive sense of humour, and at the same time they were offering the lyrical quality of the flying horses which so touched his aesthetic sense that he wanted this to be matched by appropriate music. Such ambiguities emphasise the difficulty that Disney had both in claiming classical music as his provenance for reinterpretation, and denying at the same time any claim to artistic pretension or status. These ambiguities explain the studio's difficulty in selling *Fantasia* to the American public after its première and limited release. The difficulty is still evident today.[5]

Another telling phrase in these discussions is Disney's defensive remark; 'We've taken good music and bastardised it and it's served our purpose and nobody kicked. This is something different we're selling the public ...' The struggle to deal with art from the old world, European art that has a certain 'class' – another of Disney's phrases – is central to an understanding of the work and of its complexity of content, and of the continuing complexity of audience response.

The narrative was handled by Dick Huemer and Joe Grant who worked with four different units, until they were ready for Disney's comments. Beethoven's music was slightly shortened but otherwise presented in the right order. The 'nymphs' of the original outline of 29 September 1938 have become centaurettes in Stallings' outline of 13 October:

Luxuriating, primping by a pool, are centaurettes ... beautiful faces and voluptuous breasts atop the body of a horse, come-hither eyes and the seductively switching rump of a truck horse. You've seen the type ... In short, the Golden Age of Greece reborn.

The Golden Age of Greece reborn! The centaurs of Greek mythology possessed both wisdom and sexual licence. They were depicted as mature, robust, bearded, and Robert Graves claims that they 'were not differentiated from satyrs in early Greek vase paintings'.[6] The Disney centaurs

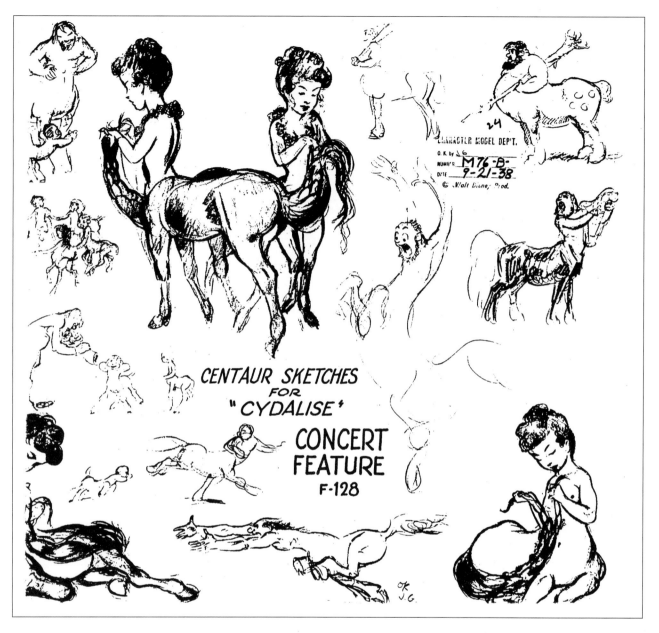

Inside the image:
CENTAUR SKETCHES
FOR
"CYDALISE"

CONCERT
FEATURE
F-128

CHARACTER MODEL DEP'T.
O.K. by J.G.
NUMBER M 76 -B-
DATE 9-21-38
© Walt Disney Prod.

Model sheet (detail): Centaurs by Albert Hurter for Beethoven's Sixth Symphony in Fantasia. There is a direct link between Hurter's centaur in full chase, and that painted by Stuck.
© *Disney Enterprises, Inc.*

lack age, wisdom or sexual prowess; they are emasculated idealisations of the contemporary all-American clean-cut college boy, Nordic rather than Latin. The idealisation of the purely Germanic in Nazi art is a parallel that is worth making historically; the war with Germany was still three years away, and the influence of nineteenth century academic art, in particular from Germany, is, as was the case with *Snow White and the Seven Dwarfs*, demonstrable.

Albert Hurter inspired the early studies of centaurs and centaurettes. He looked at both academic and illustrative sources, searching for the comic and the bizarre. His doodles show that he had seen the work of Franz von Stuck (1863–1928), who was one of the few artists to depict female centaurs. The symbolism of Stuck, who admired Böcklin, is picked up in the film at moments of voluptuousness, such as the parade of the centaurettes before the centaurs, but the dangerous eroticism that informed Stuck (and Arnold Böcklin) is missing in Disney. Stuck however does present, like Böcklin and Disney, a wholly created mythological world. His centaurs and fauns cavort in friezes and panels in the Villa Stuck he designed for himself in Munich, and which stands today, like Leighton House in London, as a monument to the successful academic artist of the late nineteenth century. Stuck has some comic classical creations, such as his *Battling Fauns* (1889), *Going for a Stroll* (1903) where three ladies, naked but for flowers in their hair, take a ride on the back of a bearded centaur, and *Dissonance* (1910) which looks as if it has been painted by a Disney 'inspirational' artist. A baby boy is attempting to play the pan pipes, while the neighboring faun blocks his ears at the resulting cacophany. The picture is both vulgar and robust, qualities which appealed to Hurter and in turn to Disney. It is clear from an examination of Hurter's model sheets for centaurs that he had seen Stuck's *The Chase* where a surprisingly modern looking female centaur is being pursued by a male. However, the robust humour which Hurter picked up from Stuck and Böcklin is missing by the time the work has

Franz von Stuck: The Chase *(1890). Stuck's cheerfully vulgar mythological creatures have an affinity with the Disney oeuvre and it is clear that Hurter knew and studied Stuck's work. It is a pity that the energy of Hurter and Stuck was lost in the animation process. Private collection.*

Arnold Böcklin: Play of the Waves
*(1883). Like Stuck, Böcklin
combined great delicacy with
vulgarity, qualities which epitomise
Disney's work.
Courtesy Neue Pinakothek, Munich.*

reached the animation stage, replaced by a nervous prurience in Disney. The staff bulletin devoted to *Fantasia* stated:

> If you scan mythology books from Gayley to Fraser, you'll find no saucily stepping Centaurettes. The word and character originated in story meetings, stepped down off Fred Moore's walls onto film. They put brassières and garlands on the gals, but aside from that, they're much the same as when they hung photostated in scattered rooms throughout the Studio.

The mention of brassières and garlands refers to the problem of what should be done about the nipples on the centaurettes – to show or not to show. Fear of the Hays Code led to the decision outlined here, though nipples were painted in on women depicted as witches and evil spirits in the Moussorgsky piece and Hays blushed not. There was also a technical problem, as one of the animation supervisors for the sequence, Ward Kimball, explained: 'There was a big argument over whether we should put nipples on the breasts or not, or at what point should you use a couple of dots. As they walked away should you stop using the dots so they wouldn't wiggle and jump around.[7] The sexism of the scenes which feature the centaurettes, especially when they parade in front of the males as if they were offering themselves for sale in a bordello, is blatant, as is the racism which has now been removed. In the carefully restored print for release in 1990, references to Sunflower and Otika the black centaurettes who groom and serve the others, have been skilfully omitted. The image has been enlarged to exclude them; an earlier release of the film in the 1980s reorchestrated these sections to cover the cuts.[8] A 1996 screening of the film with all the original footage intact, only confirms that the removal of one currently offensive part emphasises the sexism of another. Perhaps in the twenty-first century our descendents will replace those areas which we find unacceptable, just as we have put back those parts of classical literature which our Victorian forebears bowdlerised for their sexuality.

Heinrich Kley: Centaur, illustration from his Sketchbook *(1909).*

Another artist who depicted centaurs and female centaurs was the German Heinrich Kley, an important influence on *The Dance of the Hours*. His female centaurs are women of determination in a world of ribald licence. Centaurs and centaurettes had also appeared in earlier animated films. *The Centaurs* (1916) by Winsor McCay, (the creator of *Little Nemo* and *Gertie the Dinosaur*) only survives as a fragment, and has never been issued commercially. The Swedish animator Victor Bergdahl saw McCay's *Little Nemo* in Sweden, however, and made his own animated films as a result, directly influenced by McCay.[9] In Bergdahl's *Kapten Grogg bland andra konstiga kroppa* (*Captain Grogg Among Strange Creatures* 1920), the Captain gets into trouble with a centaur when he is found making amorous advances to the centaur's wife. The animation is fluid and confident, and appears to be based on some form of rotoscoping; the centaurs and lady centaurs are convincing and vigorous. The *Captain Grogg* series was widely distributed and we can assume was seen by the Disney artists. Model sheets for Disney centaurettes show hair styles which date to the early part of the century and look anachronistic; they are based on either McCay or Bergdahl. John Culhane quotes Bill Tytla, the Disney animator, who regretted that he did not work on the *Pastoral* sequence. He thought the Centaurs in both the McCay and Bergdahl films were superior in design, draughtsmanship and animation to those in the *Pastoral*. 'They should have been big stallions with dark Mediterranean faces on them. Instead they were castrated horsies [sic] with a type of Anglo-Saxon head ...' James Bodrero (1900–1980) who was born in Belgium and who

. . . och han kan lyfta av inkräktaren Grogg.

Ett mycket energiskt skakande för att skrämma offret.

Men skakandet framkallar ett egendomligt ljud.

Hon som egentligen startade det hela ser oroligt på.

Victor Bergdahl: Stills from his Captain Grogg *film of 1920.* Courtesy Swedish Film Institute, Stockholm.

emigrated as a youngster to the United States, also painted some vigorous studies of centaurs, but his work was dissipated through the production process and in animation.[10]

Nobody was willing to take the blame for the centaurs and centaurettes, though Eric Larson felt that the decline of Freddy Moore's career as animator began at this time, and that Moore received the blame (see Colour Plate 46). It is difficult to assign responsibility, and it must ultimately rest upon Disney's shoulders. His staff were delivering what he wanted – Joe Grant, widely read and with a large library of his own, was familiar with Böcklin and Kley, and his model department developed the models; he gave his signature of approval to the model sheets. Dick Huemer, also well read, was Grant's co-story director for *Fantasia*. On being asked in interview if *The Pastoral Symphony* was his idea, replied, 'No, you can't blame me'. Later in the same interview he added that he and Grant had presented the Beethoven to Disney who agreed to use the music. 'But Stokowski didn't like it at all. Not a damn bit!'[11] Stokowski's dislike for the mythological approach is confirmed in the transcript for a story conference on 14 July 1939 at which Disney was not present. 'I don't want to come out of my own field', he said. 'I'm only a musician, but think what you have there, the idea of great mythology, is not quite my idea of what this symphony is about. This is a nature symphony.' Eric Larson recalled not only his own contribution to the sequence, but also his distress at the result:

> It was such an asinine approach ... This is a block on my life. We didn't do proper research. It was my *job* and I did it [animating the centaurs and centaurettes] the easy way, like humans do it, consequently they were not humans *or* animals.

Herb Ryman (1908–1989), one of the six art directors for this item commented: 'Nobody knew what the hell to do with it'. The error was to attempt to copy human movement. The Bulletin also mentions the rotoscoping of 'chubby Erwin Verity, who served with distinction in the matter of acting as hind-quarters of a dainty centaurette'. Bob Jones remembered that he had the task of finding props and costumes for the live action filming that was used for rotoscope. He recalled one of Disney's sudden whims:

> Three o'clock on a Thursday Walt called me. 'What if Deems [Taylor] comes up to the mike after the *Pastoral* and he was half a man and half a horse? Get me a costume.' I called Western Costume and I said I would be over in an hour. They had nothing. I was frantic. We went to United and found a pony costume which I could *just* get into. Went home, put up mirrors and tried it on with my brother. I knew it wouldn't work. So next morning I took it to the sound stage. Walt said, 'Let's see it,' so I put on the back part and Taylor took the front. 'Bob,' said Walt, 'You know, if someone told me that you'd end up being Deems Taylor's ass ...'

Disney usually avoided direct appeals to the contemporary by eschewing localising references; we have noted this in connection with both *Snow White and the Seven Dwarfs* and *Pinocchio*. In the Pastoral section, current appeal is overt, linking the film to marketing and merchandise. The centaurettes' hair is deliberately dressed in late thirties fashion, and contemporary hats are styled for them by the cupids. This was a point taken up by the Disney merchandising department, and the house bulletin noted that 'Hat designers and manufacturers eyed with interest the flower hats from the Centaurette fashion show in the *Pastoral* sequence'.

Ward Kimball: Animator's drawing of Bacchus and his unicorn-donkey Jacchus, for the Beethoven section of Fantasia.
© *Disney Enterprises, Inc.*

Wilhelm Busch: Silenus (1878).
Courtesy Edith Wilson.

The first movement of the music invites us into a mythological world, enchanting and fantastic. At the meeting on the sound stage of 8 August 1939 Stokowski had urged Disney to create 'the more fantasy the better'. By the second movement we are invited to laugh at this world, because Disney has relied on the burlesque element of the *Silly Symphonies* to make the Beethoven music more acceptable to American audiences. The high seriousness of art, the cultural heritage of Europe expressed in Beethoven's music has to be made over, in a consciously popular form, through comedy and burlesque. Rick Altman has also pointed out the romance and courtship element of Hollywood during this period and the coupling of the centaurs and centaurettes is another example of the appeal to a mass audience.[12] The centaurettes are reduced to stereotypical objects of desire by cardboard cavaliers.

The character of Bacchus or Silenus on his diminutive and dim-witted steed, the unicorn/donkey Jacchus, is animated with assurance by Ward Kimball. The antecedents for this comic strip god come from academic art, a favourite subject from Titian to Rubens. Also, Böcklin's leering mermen in his aquatic fantasies are close cousins to Bacchus. One of Wilhelm Busch's picture stories is about Silenus and his drunken encounter first with a nymph and then with Cupid. There is, too, Dickie Doyle's Punch/Bacchus figure which was on the cover of *Punch* from 1849 to 1956. There is ample illustrative background to the comic god, and this reference and familiarity imbues the Disney Bacchus with an energy which sits unhappily with the contemporary 1940s account of the centaurs and centaurettes. The same ambivalence applies to the greater deities which are seen in close association with the backgrounds.

Early inspirational paintings show a symbolist influence,[13] and we have noted the work of Franz von Stuck in this connection, but the influence of art deco is more pronounced. The backgrounds are a blending of the old world and the new. High academic Victorian art is borrowed for the sylvan settings; John Waterhouse (1849–1917) painted classical scenes with Romantic overtones. His *Hylas and the Water Nymphs* (1896) is one of the most popular paintings in Manchester's City Art Gallery (see Colour Plates 44 and 45). It was adapted for an early inspirational painting of the centaurettes in the water. The fondness of nineteenth century academic painting for children frolicking in the countryside is reflected in Disney; fauns, baby unicorns and cherubs cavort in a landscape of bright stylisation. Philipp Otto Runge (1777–1810) painted allegorical landscapes with children; one German reviewer commented that *Fantasia* 'was as natural as a department store or petrol station. Disney's artists were collaborators of Dalí, Grandville and Runge'.[14] The Beethoven item is an example of Victorian ideals set in an art deco landscape. The old world meets the new; women are seen as alternately desirable and seductive objects (centaurettes) or deified

(Diana, Iris). Though manifestly sexual as they primp and parade, the centaurettes lack sexual markings. In this respect they are like the soft pornographic delineations of women in sculpture and painting that adorned the wealthy, *nouveau riche* Victorian home. Waterhouse, Lord Leighton, Burne Jones and Herbert Draper were among artists made popular when photography revolutionised printing processes, enabling the wide distribution of the art print into ordinary homes.[15]

Edward Poynter's (1836–1919) girls in *A Visit to Aesculapius* (1880) stand before the physician in the same way as the Disney centaurettes parade before their beaux. The High Academic art of England is as emasculated as the worst of Disney; its influence alone cannot explain the boisterousness of the film, the mixture of rudeness and reverence that is its special characteristic. We must turn to the Continent for an explanation; the European influence here is Germanic and in particular the German speaking part of Switzerland, where Arnold Böcklin (1827–1901) was born.

Böcklin studied art at Dusseldorf, and then later, after touring Europe, lived in various parts of Germany before retiring to Florence. His paintings are little known in Britain, and our galleries contain none of his works, though there are 50 in Switzerland and 24 in Munich, as well as several others scattered in various German collections. The first and only (minor) exhibition of his work in this country was held in London at the Hayward Gallery in 1971.[16] Many of his pictures were lost or destroyed in the second World War but five are in the United States, four publicly owned. One of these paintings, the *Island of the Dead* (1880) is in the Metropolitan Museum of Art, New York, where it achieved, and has maintained, immense popularity, and it was frequently reproduced. Böcklin painted five versions of the same subject, one of which was purchased by Hitler and hung in the Chancellery, Berlin.

Böcklin, speaking of the first version of the *Island of the Dead*, said explicitly that this was a picture for dreaming about. His paintings exerted their influence even in reproductions and helped the painter achieve a dubious popularity.[17]

Böcklin was well known to the Disney artists (see Colour Plates 47 and 48). Joe Grant and Albert Hurter were familiar with his work, and the model departmant based studies of the centaurs on his paintings. Ken Anderson (1909–1993), an art director for the sequence, and John Hench (b. 1908) who painted some of the backgrounds also knew his work. Disney's attention was drawn by Dick Huemer and Joe Grant to Böcklin's combination of mysticism and vulgarity which was attractive to the artists working on this sequence. Böcklin's friend Floerke spoke of his tough grotesque realism which cut across the dreamy idealism, and mentioned his 'kitchen oceanids' and 'errand boys' of the sea. His Teutonic kitsch and dark eroticism also disturbed contemporary reviewers. Claude Phillips' comment in 1885 might apply to Disney:

> [Böcklin] succeeds so thoroughly in giving form and life to the mythical beings in a sense created anew for him, that the effect produced is often a startling one – so strong is the contrast between the theme and its treatment; nay, the boundaries which separate art from the purely grotesque are often reached and well-nigh transgressed.[18]

Two of the art directors for the sequence were Ken Anderson and Gordon Legg. Ken Anderson was a Disney artist for more than forty years. He used Böcklin as reference for the backgrounds that he designed for the *Pastoral*. 'I was inspired by Böcklin's *Isle of the Dead*,' he said, 'and also by The Isola Bella in Italy. Walt said, "Read up on Beethoven and get some style". So I read up on the ribald and the classical.' 'Ribald' and 'classical' are terms eminently applicable to Böcklin and explain the mixture of these elements in Disney's film.

The only consistency in the Beethoven piece is the art deco background for which Anderson and his colleagues Gordon Legg, Herb Ryman and others were responsible. The rounded landscapes and stylisation in the backgrounds can be partly attributed to Gordon Legg (b. 1909) (see Colour Plate 49) who told Milton Grey:

> They wanted Classical backgrounds ... and they didn't care too much how accurate it was. I kind of followed Grant Wood and Rockwell Kent[19] – you know, cleaned up the trees, so that everything was neat and clean and precise. It was like Forest Lawn. I wanted to keep the colours rich and subtle – olive greens and maroons – played down colours like you see in the backgrounds of portraits that were painted in the Italian School ... I worked with Ken Anderson; he was the final layout director [for the *Pastoral*], and a very talented artist. But I guess Disney got in there someplace and said 'Let's brighten this thing up.' That's where we got into the peppermint candy. It bothered me; I didn't want it that way. It was too sticky, too sweet.[20]

Some of Gordon Legg's inspirational sketches are reproduced in the first book on *Fantasia* by Deems Taylor. The beauty of the opening landscape survives on film, though the work was painted over by another artist. Legg's delicate paintings formed part of an exhibition of Disney art at the Portico Library, Manchester in 1990,[21] and included Pegasus at night on his tree, Apollo in his sun chariot, and Diana shooting the stars out with the crescent moon (see Colour Plates 50, 51 and 52).

Throughout this section there is reverence for and misunderstanding of sources. Confidence is expressed in the rendering of the flying horses in the first movement, and crassness in the account of the centaurs, centaurettes and *putti* in the second. This reflects the inability to distinguish between the calibre of Pierné's music and that of Beethoven; the studio struggled to accommodate Beethoven by a mixture of reliance on the graphic conventions of *The Silly Symphonies* and by an appeal to a mass audience that would identify the contemporary references to fashion and to sexual stereotyping in the centaurs and centaurettes, while at the same time attempting to match the lyricism of the music in the landscapes. These moments give this section its mixture of, as one reviewer put it, 'Kunst und kitsch'[22] and are expressed in the closing scene of the film; there is vigour in the delineation of Bacchus and the storm while the flying horses, Apollo and Diana are animated with great beauty and based on the inspirational paintings of Gordon Legg. Iris and Morpheus are unconvincing deities, larger versions of Snow White. The viewer is lurched from beauty to bathos within the same frame and at the same time in a complicated, layered struggle to present visually, 'to create a whole new feeling' for the audience, one of the most sublime pieces of music in the western world.

Ponchielli's *The Dance of the Hours*

The story conference notes show that there was no difficulty in approaching Ponchielli's music. It was understood from the start in the outline of 29 September 1938 to be 'very trite and typical ballet music' and the pejorative tone exemplified here gave Disney the confidence to parody ballet. His strength lay in caricature, and this section of the film has a consistency of style which is lacking in the treatment of *The Pastoral Symphony*. There was no problem in assimilating the European sources, and, by parody and burlesque, reinterpreting those same sources for mass appeal. Film itself and ballet, particularly as interpreted by Hollywood, was another way of accommodating the sources, and one particular film, *The Goldwyn Follies* (1938) bears especial study in this connection.

Thematically, *The Dance of the Hours* echoes several motifs that have presented themselves in earlier sections of *Fantasia*. Cyclical order and balance through rhythm and dance is subverted and destroyed by male

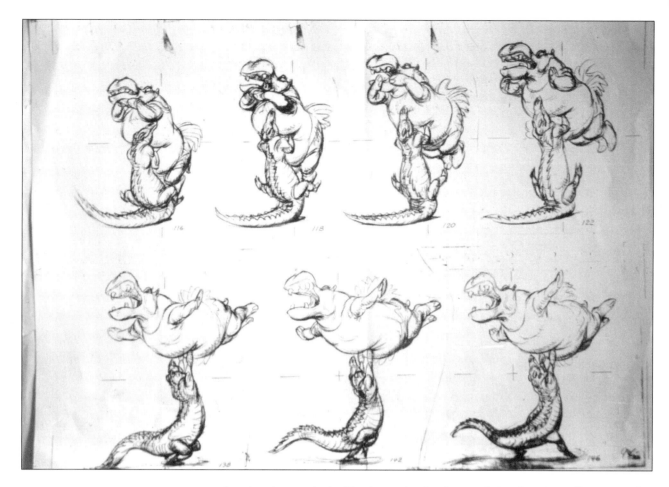

Animator's drawings: Ben Ali Gator and Hyacinth Hippo in their pas de deux *for 'The Dance of the Hours' from* Fantasia.
© *Disney Enterprises, Inc.*

domination and phallic thrust in the form of the dancing alligators who take over the other animals and who finally cause total destruction. Time and the order of time, as day gives way to night and then to chaos, is in direct contrast to the order of the Olympian day celebrated in Beethoven's *Pastoral Symphony*. The artificial world of the theatre is stressed through design and *mise-en-scène* and the presentation of movement as dance gains its most explicit and direct expression through animation. There are also recurring water images, particularly in the dance of the elephants, which remind us of similar imagery in earlier sections.

The European influences can be seen in two areas; firstly there is the debt to the theatre, to formal dance and classical ballet, and to the classical shape of the theatre with its open staging and Greek design; Ionic columns surround the action once the dance has moved away from the art deco auditorium. Secondly there is homage, via classical dance, to the art of caricature; here the late nineteenth century from Grandville to Tenniel and on to Busch and Heinrich Kley may be cited. Unlike the development of the Beethoven section, there is no hesitancy, no diversion from Disney's main intention, as can be seen from the crucial outline of proposals circulated on 29 September 1938. 'Strictly burlesque. Interpreting this very trite and typical ballet will be a troupe of elephants, hippos, giraffes and other dainty jungle ballerinas.'

The caricature of the animals is contrasted with the extreme formality of the setting, flat, austere and empty. This adds to the incongruity of animals taking part in Ponchielli's ballet. *The Dance of the Hours* was part of his opera *La Gioconda* (1876), the ballet forming a pageant celebrating the hours of the day. This form is followed in the Disney film, with the day divided into four parts. Part one, 'Morning' is danced by ostriches in a huge art deco theatre; they dance into the open air and vanish over the horizon, followed by 'Afternoon' danced by Hyacinth Hippo and her *corps de ballet*. 'Evening' is danced by elephants, literally blown away by time, as the wind might blow leaves. The stage is clear for 'Night' danced by alligators, who have replaced the giraffes suggested in the early outline. Ben Ali Gator is their leader and after an impassioned *pas de deux* with Hyacinth Hippo he and his colleagues conduct a frenzied dance involving all the different groups of animals, leading to a conclusion that shakes the theatre doors off their hinges.

The theatrical setting is emphasised at the beginning, but it quickly becomes apparent that this is too large a stage to be contained within the bounds of a proscenium arch and within an ordinary theatre. Here is a reminder of the Hollywood tradition of the musical number extending beyond the theatre or cabaret setting in which it is placed. 'The setting in a way,' said Disney, 'should be like a Warner Brothers Musical on a stage 500 feet long and 2000 feet wide – at least it looks that way' (story conference 17 October 1938).

Other theatrical elements are the wings, and the shadows of the curtains, which enter the scene momentarily as reminders that *The Dance of the Hours* is still bound by the theatre even though we have gone well beyond its confines. A story man Jack Caldwell outlined the need for variety of mood as well as of design within the sequence, appealing to the audience 'in those ways recommended by such stage designers as Gordon Craig and Robert Edmond Jones'.[23] Provided the source could be related to 'audience appeal', Disney was able to accede to the suggestions of his collaborators. It is difficult, otherwise, to understand his acceptance of the blank, flat, theatrical settings for *The Dance of the Hours*. Here we are thrown back yet again on his instinctive reactions; he took Caldwell's tip, for the theatrical shape and look of the sequence is indeed indebted to the spare European stage settings of men like Appia, Craig and the American designer Robert Edward Jones.[24]

A scale model was made of the set, with models of the characters. Bob Jones, who worked in the Character Model Department under Joe

Grant and with Albert Hurter, designed a special lighting rig that matched the passing of the daylight hours. He calibrated the sun by light on a tracer which gave meticulous detailing of the shadows cast throughout the day. The clarity of lighting and design with the art deco spareness of background gives the sequence its cohesion and emphasises the bizarre dancing of the animals. The layout director Ken O'Connor, an Australian who had worked with Disney from *Snow White and the Seven Dwarfs* onwards, commented on the symmetry of the design:

> We concealed the arts from almost a graphic league of nations. We concealed the art of France in the form of flat pattern a la Matisse and Picassinine color ... America and Greece contributed when a rash of dynamic symmetry broke out in the layout room.[25]

A linear motif was adopted for each time of the day; the 'Morning' section was vertical and horizontal which 'tied in with the vertical necks and legs of the ostriches, and as far as possible the birds were kept moving horizontally and vertically'. The static calm of the early morning hours was expressed by 'cool greyed colours in the background and neutrals in the characters'. The sunny afternoon that followed was interpreted with an ellipse motif, emphasised by the round pool which fills the screen at the opening of 'Afternoon'. There is rather more action in this scene and the ellipse design fitted in well with the hippos' shapes and with their circular ballet movements. The serpentine movement of the elephants' trunks suggested the motif for the short 'Evening' scene, and in 'Night' the artists introduced a violent zig-zag motif related to the angular reptilian construction of the alligators. When the dance becomes climactic and all the animals are involved, the ellipse and the zig-zag combine in a single image; Ben Ali forms a diagonal pattern on the body of his lady love as he embraces her, while she whirls in ecstacy round her pool.

The clowning, comedy routines and caricature in *The Dance of the Hours* are based upon vaudeville which flowered in the United States at almost the same time as English variety and music hall. It was at its height in the United States during Disney's childhood and adolescence, from the end of the nineteenth century till the advent of sound in the cinema and the growing popularity of radio during the 1920s.[26] *The Dance of the Hours*, therefore, has familiar references, from its immediate homage to the film musical back to its theatrical and circus background. The circus reference occurs in the dance of the elephants – themselves circus animals – who at one moment dance in a line behind each other, holding each other's tails with their trunks.

The Goldwyn Follies (1938) contains a ballet sequence choreographed by Balanchine and danced by the Norwegian Zorina and the American Ballet from the Metropolitan Opera. It is intended as a homage to high

art, and at a climactic moment there is a close shot of Zorina's head rising from a circular pool. In an almost identical shot Hyacinth Hippo rises from a similar pool, and the scene, as Alastair Macauley points out, 'is a tease directed at the 1938 movie'.[27] Goldwyn's film shows a background of Greek columns and bare stage, in a semi-circular shape which is almost identical to that presented in the Disney layout. The colours too, blues and yellowish white are similar and there is a play between two dancers behind the columns which is picked up by the Disney artists and retold in parodic form.

Disney's histrionic ability is noted once more, at a meeting on 17 October 1938, in his visualisation of the alligators for the 'Night' hours: 'When the music goes DI-DUMP, they open their mouths slowly – here's the funny part where the guys go ...' (Walt bares his teeth, snarls, prances)'. At the very first meeting on 29 September, he stressed the importance of conviction in comedy. 'I think the main thing we must

Still: The Goldwyn Follies *(1938), parodied in Disney's 'The Dance of the Hours' in* Fantasia. *The sensational underwater arrival of a leading dancer was continued by the* Folies-Bergère *at least until the 1960s, and in Hollywood by Esther Williams.*
Courtesy Goldwyn, still British Film Institute

keep in mind is that the animals are serious. They are not clowning, otherwise they would only be a bunch of smartalecks'. He was anxious that his artists observe real dancers in action, and real animals in movement at Griffith Park Zoo.

Jules Engel who had contributed to the dance choreography of *The Nutcracker Suite* (see Chapter 6), was also employed on *The Dance of the Hours* and comparison between his sketches and the film show how his suggestions were used in the ostrich dance. His focus on camera angles and layout adds to the visual wit. Two huge ostrich feet take up the foreground of the screen and it is through them that we see the other dancers lining up. This was a late addition and shows how Disney was willing to introduce new ideas at an advanced stage in the production process. He had pulled out scenes that he felt were holding up the narrative of *Snow White and the Seven Dwarfs*, though they had been fully animated, and had cost a great deal in terms of labour and money. Here, his authority operated in the reverse direction, by the input of Engel at a late stage in the design and layout of this sequence. Engel recalled that *The Dance of the Hours* was nearly complete when he was sent in to assist.

> I made two little sketches with two ostrich legs in the front, close-up, on a toe. Up. Then two sketches both down and then one up. Walt saw it and sent it into layout immediately. I felt that it needed to be more filmic, a little more mobile and boom! It went into production. Those animators didn't put feeling into it – that was Walt.

John Hench (b. 1908) was a background artist sceptical about ballet. When Disney learnt this he arranged for Hench to sketch the Ballets Russes, and the experience changed Hench's attitude to dance altogether.

Jules Engel: Story sketches for the 'Morning' section of 'The Dance of the Hours'.
© Disney Enterprises, Inc.

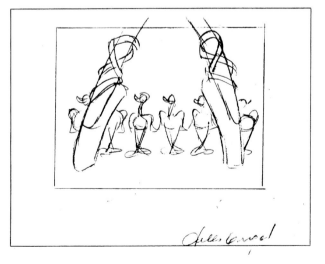

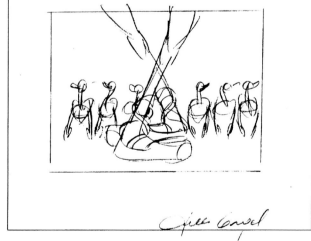

Walt Disney and Europe

Disney and his studio had been anthropomorphising animals since the early days, and before him there was a tradition in animation of animals-as-humans. The use of rotoscope, too, was designed to assist the artists in their study of the actual dance steps, and not as a means of recreating reality through animation. Art Babbitt commented on the fact that rotoscope was used with imagination for *The Dance of the Hours*. 'You caricature life, your stories, your characters, your action,' he said. 'When they (the artists) left the humans, the animal characters came to life'.

The graphic influences are both European and American. Albert Hurter once again provided inspirational sketches which he had in turn taken from T.S. Sullivant's families of hippopotami and from Heinrich Kley's animal drawings. T.S. Sullivant (1854–1926) loved drawing hippos – and alligators – which appear again and again in his cartoons. His influence on the Disney artists can be seen in some of the drawings in Joe Grant's collection. Grant's own inspirational drawings may also be taken into account in the process of development towards the final hippo caricature that would emerge as the prima ballerina Hyacinth Hippo. Another Disney artist who admired Sullivant's work was Walt Kelly, himself to become famous as the creator of the animal comic strip *Pogo*.

The French artist Ernest Griset (1843–1907), who spent most of his working life in England, also drew dancing animals, and the famous Guiness advertisements artist John Gilroy claimed that Disney was interested in his cavorting ostriches and alligators.[28] However, the major

T.S. Sullivant: Cartoon, 'A plunge before breakfast is a great thing to sharpen one's appetite'. Courtesy Will Ryan.

Heinrich Kley: 'Elephants skating', from his Sketchbook II *(1910).*

artistic influence on *The Dance of the Hours* was provided by a German artist, Heinrich Kley.

Kley (1863–1945) was admired by Disney who owned a large number of Kley drawings and sketches. He was born in Karlsruhe and spent most of his working life in Munich, developing his career as an industrial artist and his paintings for the great giants of industrial Germany reveal meticulous detail and acute observation, not only of the workings of machinery which he clearly loved, but also of the men who laboured in the factory workshops of Krupp, MAN and Bilfinger (see Colour Plates 53 and 54). He then developed his skills as a satirist and caricaturist, his

Heinrich Kley: 'Gout' from his Picture Album (1923). Walt Disney collected Kley's work.

observation of human beings brilliantly highlighted in anthropomorphic guise for comic illustrations in the magazines *Simplicissimus* and *Die Jugend*. He owes much to Daumier in style, and something to Doré in wit. Kley's harsh depiction of our foibles was softened in the animation processes, but he was referred to again and again in the story conferences, not only on *The Dance of the Hours* but also, in passing, during discussion on the Pierné/Beethoven section and on the Moussorgsky piece. There are references to his work in later films like *Dumbo* (1941) and *The Jungle Book* (1967). Disney's purpose was a particular one, whereas Kley 'made fun of the seriousness of the times ... the whole moth-proof box of classicism and German romanticism flew open'.[29] Disney observed the seriousness of Kley's comedy:

> *Walt*: If we start clowning too much, don't you think it's going to take away from the comedy? Don't you think some of the stuff we get out of the Kley book is good because they are always more or less serious? We should make it to the point of being ridiculous.

Dick [Huemer]: Heinrich Kley was the keynote for that type of thing.
Walt: He gets the anatomy of whatever he has, but it looks human. Have we Kley's stuff here? It's marvellous.
Joe [Grant]: He simply takes the clothes off human beings to show their inner workings.
Walt (scans Kley's drawings): There's an elephant sitting in that chair, but by God! He looks like an old man. (Looks at Kley sketches): He went nuts, didn't he? (Story meeting 29 September 1938).

Discussion then centred on Kley's life and the difficulty of obtaining any information about him.[30] Jack Caldwell added, 'I was wondering if Kley's treatment could be used all the way through. It is sharp satire of definite human types which is seen in each animal'. Many years later, Disney made reference to Kley on his TV programme. He said, 'Without the wonderful drawings of Heinrich Kley I could not conduct my art school classes for my animators'.[31] Publicity issued in 1965 stated that the studio continued to refer to Kley for its drawings on animals in general and elephants in particular (work was being undertaken on *The Jungle Book* released two years later). Kley's acerbity modified the easy accessability of Ponchielli, and the Disney artists' technical skill provided the catalyst. *The Dance of the Hours* celebrates 'the pure art of metamorphosis' which Paul Valery describes as the true essence of dance.[32]

Moussorgsky's *Night on Bald Mountain*

There are forces in Moussorgsky's music which Disney could not comprehend or easily identify, though it is clear from the gestation of the piece, and from the discussions he held with his staff, that he was attempting to come to terms with the complexities of the European element in the work, or at least to make it comprehensible to himself and to his mass audience. He had optimism and technical confidence, those still formidable transatlantic characteristics, and was attempting to go further aesthetically, using his resources to interpret an older, European culture. As with the Beethoven section, we can see the conflict between the European source and its American interpretation, which creates a layered and complex piece of animation, unravelled by continued re-readings.

Power is shown in the evil of the devil and in the forces of good, as the pilgrims wend their way, presumably to church, in the *Ave Maria* that follows. First there is a demonstration of male, thrusting power, the movement within the frame being vertical, the imagery also vertical: the devil, the mountain and its peaks, the Gothic towers and roofs of the town, the vertical shadows. The circular movements are of dance, wind and flames, but these are subject to the dominance of the male devil. In the *Ave Maria* that follows, the Gothic imagery is continued, where celestial light filters through the cathedral shaped trees thrusting up into the sky towards Heaven. The cyclical theme shows order following chaos, after the eruption of satanic force, which, like the eruption of lava in *The Rite of Spring*, has threatened to overwhelm the natural order. Then mystical power overcomes evil; light is stronger than darkness, day stronger than night.

The music was first written for solo piano and orchestra in 1870. Modest Moussorgsky (1839–1881) modified it and it was reorchestrated and conducted by his friend Rimsky-Korsakov for the first successful performance in 1886, after the composer's death. This was the score used by Stokowski. Moussorgky said of his music: 'What I project is the melody of life, not of classicism ... I do not intend to debase music to the level of mere amusement'.[33] These programme notes were attached to Moussorgsky's score:

> Appearance of the Spirit of Darkness, followed by that of Chernobog (literally The Black God). Glorification of the Black God. The Black Mass. The revelry of the Witches' Sabbath, interrupted from afar by the bell of a little church, whereupon the spirits of evil disperse. Dawn breaks.[34]

Story sketches of the black god Chernobog in 'Night on Bald Mountain' from Fantasia. *© Disney Enterprises, Inc.*

Disney follows this narrative and shows the Black God on the mountain top unfolding his wings and conjuring up the dead from the little town at the foot of the mountain. There is a reminder here of *The Sorcerer's Apprentice* where Mickey similarly conjures the broom to do his will. Like the shadow of Mickey's hands stretching out to the broom, so the shadow of the devil's hands slides down the mountain to conjure spirits from their graves. The Black God plays with demons who dance on his outstretched hand and in the flaming pit of his loins, before the church bell and the oncoming dawn force him to relinquish his power.

Moussorgsky's contrast of despair and hope is not conveyed in the Disney version, though the interpretation of the story caused considerable difficulty. Disney struggled to absorb the complexity of the music and to delineate it in pictorial terms other than those with which he was already familiar. A basic linear narrative was not satisfactory. At first he wanted a satirical element which he understood – *The Dance of the Hours* is an example – and again he turned to Kley for inspiration as he had done with Ponchielli. At the first story conference on 29 September 1938 he said 'If we could get some mischievous pranks in there like that Kley drawings [sic] blowing smoke down the chimney and the people running out coughing. They are really doing mean stunts'. Disney referred to the Devil as 'a huge Gulliver' and searched for ways to present him as a prankster rather than a monster, and something of the contrast in size between the Black God and his victims is maintained in the final version. At a story conference, quoted by Robert Feild,[35] we can observe

Disney struggling to go beyond the literal: 'We want to go beyond those obvious things we've done (cartoon and comic bats and cats and graves and spooks). We're getting all mixed up here and nothing is coming out of it. It's just an attempt to do something big but it's falling flat'. He had faced the same difficulty when interpreting Bach's music for a mass audience, and continued:

> You can't have a motion picture audience asking too many questions. They are not that patient. We can't have a certain select group that likes to make something out of nothing. They are the absolute minority. Your house would be half empty if you got much of that stuff.

The result is a struggle to escape from the bats and graves and spooks that Disney had tried to avoid; there are references to European sources which show his difficulties. The late medieval obsession with death in German art is continued into the 19th century and both Böcklin and his colleague Hans Thoma (1839–1924) painted self-portraits with death in the shape of a skull at their shoulder. Böcklin's *Die Pest* (1898) depicts

Heinrich Kley (left): 'What a devilish stench!' from his Sketchbook (1909). Disney sought ways of introducing humour to the Moussorgsky piece after he had seen Kley's drawings.

Heinrich Kley (right): 'Sabotage', another drawing from his Sketchbook (1909).

Still: Faust (1926) *directed by F.W. Murnau. The* mise-en-scène *has an affinity with Disney's* Night on Bald Mountain.
Courtesy Murnau Stifftung.
Still, Daniel Kothenschulte.

Francisco de Goya: Modo de volar *(A way of flying, c. 1816) from his* Los Proverbios.
Courtesy Manchester City Art Gallery.

Fantasia: *from Beethoven to Schubert*

death riding on a dragon through a plague ridden street. In Disney we have skeletons on horseback rising from their graves

Disney also attempted to satirise the witches's sabbath theme; the Kley drawings suggested this and Hurter once again provided inspirational sketches. Many artists including Goya and Doré had created the devil and his followers; the German cinema was an immediate inspiration, in particular the *Faust* (1926) of F.W. Murnau, who emigrated to Hollywood the following year. Emil Jannings as Mephisto resembles Disney's devil Chernobog in physical appearance and in movement within the frame. The *mise-en-scène* is similar. In Murnau's *Faust* 'the entire town seems to be covered by the vast folds of a demon's cloak (or is it a gigantic lowering cloud?) as the demoniac forces of darkness prepare to devour the powers of light'.[36] In the Disney version the shadow of Chernobog's hands falls across the roofs of the sleeping town and the buildings lean towards the source of power as the shadow falls across them. The town has the Gothic detailing of German expressionist cinema. In the first crucial discussions on 29 September 1938 Disney mentioned Faust in passing while he talked of Kley's work.

The studio used Bela Lugosi as a model for publicity but Wilfred Jackson, one of the Disney directors, was used for the rotoscope photography. A three-dimensional winged model was also made, complete with wire wings. There are reminders of Goya in the flying devils and spirits; Diane Disney Miller recalled that her father particularly admired Goya's work and the Prado was one of his favourite galleries. Bosch is present in the grotesques conjured by the devil, and these are given a stylisation which is expressionist in colour and rendering, sometimes reminiscent of German expressionist woodcuts. These echoes and influences are articulated through the art direction of Kay Nielsen.

Nielsen (1886–1957) was the son of the director of the Dagmartheatre in Copenhagen. His mother was a distinguished actress and singer and the Nielsen household was full of artists, writers and singers. The boy Nielsen remembered meeting Grieg, Bjornson and Ibsen. After a distinguished career as book illustrator (see Colour Plates 55 and 56), Nielsen was invited to Hollywood in 1936 as the designer of von Hoffmannsthal's version of Reinhardt's *Everyman* which was staged at the Hollywood Bowl. In 1938 Disney asked him to be art director for *Night on Bald Mountain* and *Ave Maria* and he stayed on to design a version of *The Little Mermaid*[37] as well as to contribute sketches for the extended sections of *Fantasia* that Disney wanted to include in its later repertoire. He made some pastel drawings of great power for *The Ride of the Valkyries*, but this project was shelved after the failure of *Fantasia*. Like Fischinger, he was unhappy working with Disney, but unlike Fischinger, considerably more of his work is identifiable in the final result. He was proud and introspective and though he was able to speak excellent

English – unlike the unfortunate Fischinger – he was not able to adapt to the rough and tumble of the cartoon factory. He was also considerably older than most of the staff. After leaving Disney in 1941, absolute poverty was avoided through his obtaining the commissions for three mural paintings in the Los Angeles area. These remain as testimonials, apart from his book illustrations, to his genius. They are astonishing, radiant works.[38] After the second world war Nielsen returned to Denmark, endeavouring to obtain work again as book illustrator or stage designer, but without success; his style was too rigidly locked into the precise art deco mould which had originally brought him fame. It was too soon for a revival of interest. He returned to California where he died destitute in 1957. His wife Ulla died a year later. Forty years later his original artwork was fetching tens of thousands of dollars at auction.

Jules Engel remembered him as an artist of great taste, aloof, remote. Jack and Camille Cutting also remembered him as a gentle presence at the Disney Studio. Joe Grant was emphatic about Nielsen's importance as contributor to the style of the Moussorgsky section. 'Kay Nielsen did almost the identical pastels as appear in the film' (see Colour Plate 57), he said, and Joe's wife Jennie remembered him as 'gallant, very old worldly ... You couldn't get him into arguments'. Joe Grant added, 'I tried desperately to keep [Nielsen] in a job; being a story man was not his forte. He had such a distinct visualisation. Of course Walt knew the value of Kay as product – the way it could be transformed'.

Disney manipulated artists as source material for the marketing of his work for an audience which he understood as being, like himself, unsophisticated, naive and yet complex and uncertain as human beings. Artists were dispensible in this search for making culture palliative. They were, as he told Joe Grant on more than one occasion 'a dime a dozen'.

Nielsen produced many paintings and sketches; designs for Chernobog, details of ghosts and demons and atmospheric sketches of graves, ruins and landscapes. His illustrations were directly influenced by art deco styling, the designs of Persian miniatures and Japanese painting. His love of oriental art is captured in the opening and closing shots of the sequence which show the sharply etched mountain placed in a landscape reminiscent of Hokusai or Hiroshige. This is in contrast to the lyrical picture of Mount Olympus seen at the opening and closing of the Beethoven section. The detailing of buildings, gravestones, memorials and the grotesque creatures conjured up by the Black God have precise origins in sketches by Nielsen. However, much is lost in the transference from still painting to animated film, and it is perhaps this loss that Nielsen found disturbing. He 'did not care for the dogmatic Disney who insisted on simplifying his designs',[39] and his style, remote, cool, detached, for all the ferocity of his subject, does not lend itself easily to animation. He fails to convey the evil at the beginning of the

Still: The Night on Bald Mountain (1934) *by Alexander Alexeiff and Claire Parker, made with a pin-screen device. Pins of varying length were pushed through an upright screen to achieve a tonal effect.*
Courtesy Cecile Starr.

Inspirational sketch: 'Night on Bald Mountain' from Disney's Fantasia. *The dancing figures in the flames resemble expressionistic woodcuts, and are reminders of the German school of inter-war artists.*
© Disney Enterprises, Inc.

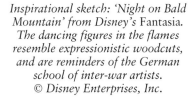

sequence. Instead of the terror and darkness of legend Chernobog unfolds his wings rather jerkily on the top of his mountain. This may be deliberate, emulating a bat, but I am not able to share the general enthusiasm for Bill Tytla's animation of the devil. The figure is like a cardboard cut-out and the element of surprise is removed; there is no opportunity for the workings of the imagination. The subtlety of delay, so cleverly narrated in *Snow White and the Seven Dwarfs* is abandoned. Horror is presented head on, as on a fairground ghost train. Disney is in fact giving us a ride.

An animated version of *The Night on Bald Mountain* had been made in 1934 by Alexander Alexeieff, a Russian, working with Claire Parker, an American, using a pin-screen device, called 'l'écran d'épingles'. The film was a critical success but a commercial failure.[40] Its strength lies in its inference of evil rather than in the direct portrayal of evil itself; menace is suggested, hinted at, surmised, allowing the viewer freedom to use imagination. This is partly due to the animation technique which produces shadowy, tonal pictures of great beauty, instead of the sharp clarity of line of Disney cel animation. While the Disney version is technically brilliant in rendering the ghosts rising up from their graves and gliding round the mountain, there is no *frisson*, and the jump cuts and lunging close-ups of skulls and harpies rely on sensation for effect.

In *Snow White and the Seven Dwarfs* there is more creative control of the medium; the simulated camera work withholds revelation of the witch until the last moment. Expectation and fear are aroused by the

Queen's transformation; the moment of truth is delayed and the camera lingers on the hooded shadow of the Witch before it tilts down to the Witch herself and the final revelation is delayed by an arm raised to hide the complete face. In *Pinocchio* the fear of evil and the unknown are hinted at and then sketched in rapidly. There are elements of character and identification in those films which are, by nature of the subject matter, missing in the Moussorgsky. This leads to a mixture of stylistic presentation which adds academic interest but takes away from the cohesion that full identification with Nielsen's style might have brought to the visual form.

The figures round Bald Mountain resemble some of Goya's drawings, many of which expressed his disturbed vision after he became deaf, and include terrifying and obscene etchings of witches and monsters. There is a reminder of Bosch, too, in the demons that dance around the burning pit at the belly of Chernobog, but it is German expressionism which once again dominates the central section of the piece, in the stylised delineation of fire and smoke. Dancing female forms made of flame are depicted in the rough style of the woodcut or the poster; there are reminders of Emil Nolde (1867–1956) and of Ernst Ludwik (1880–1938) here, and also of Doré who is never far away in Disney's work, particularly in the scenes where minute devils dance or crouch in the bleakness of the rocky landscape of hell. There are reminders also of the German silent cinema in the flight of the ghosts around the mountain.

At the end the style changes; the camera tracks back to show the early morning mist around the mountain, no longer menacing, with trees in the foreground and tranquillity in the music. Nielsen is again the inspiration for this shot, his oriental interest explicit, and the imagery matches the music, the art deco clouds blending with the oriental landscape. This is a poised moment before the *Ave Maria* takes over.

Schubert's *Ave Maria*

This follows the end of *Night on Bald Mountain* without any intervening live-action footage. Deems Taylor introduces the two pieces together. 'Musically and dramatically,' he says, 'we have here a picture of the struggle between the profane and the sacred'. The *Ave Maria* was originally a setting for a song from Scott's 'The Lady of the Lake' and was secular in form if not in mood. It is not surprising that Scott's work affected Schubert. Scott was one of the great literary figures of the Romantic period, influencing music, painting and literature in Britain and on the Continent. Franz Peter Schubert (1797–1828), living at the height of the first great Romantic period, was a close friend of the painter Moritz von Schwind (1804–1871) who in turn influenced Biedermeier painters like Spitzweg and Ludwig Richter; the latter, as has been noted, was an influence on Disney's *Snow White and the Seven Dwarfs*. For Disney, faith is combined with the mysterious power of nature, in turn linked to the sun, the last image in the whole film. Faith, with light and life, is opposed to the dark forces of evil and night. There is a return to order and calm after the madness of darkness and despair; a suggestion of spring, with trees in early leaf after the bleakness of winter. In addition to the Catholicism expressed in the lyrics and imagery, pantheism is also suggested, with nature and humanity literally moving together in praise and worship. We are denied a close view to determine the sex or individuality of the pilgrims as they progress through a wood in the early morning.[41] The natural forms are seen at first as hills and river banks and groups of trees which become more Gothic in shape until the pilgrims vanish within their shade as worshippers might vanish inside a cathedral. The symbolism is explicit.

In the Moussorgsky section, fire is the element with which the devils are created and in which they dance for Chernobog. In the *Ave Maria*, water is the natural element balancing and reflecting the procession of the pilgrims. It appears in three out of the four shots that comprise this item. The editing of the two pieces also emphasises their contrasting contents; the Moussorgksy (fire) is all varied tempi, with slow pans followed by jump cuts and fast tracks, huge close-ups alternating with long shots, while the Schubert (water) is entirely in long shot connected only by slow dissolves.

The difficulty for Disney arises once again in the interpretation of sources for a mass audience, between the aesthetic individual response of early nineteenth century Romantic artists and that of an American producer of popular culture over a century later. The intensity of subjective vision inherent in the Romantic period of which Schubert was representative is converted into an objective demonstration of emotion. Awe is seen as a stage spectacle. 'You should have more of a procession' insisted Disney at a story conference of 12 January 1940, 'more staged'. Feeling becomes convention. Religion becomes religiosity.

We can see Disney and his colleagues struggling to produce a climax to the whole film. The lack of visual focus, the determination to stay in long shot, to present slow dissolves on misty landscapes, is part of an uncertainty of intent which is central to this section. 'Pretty scenes' Disney continued, 'aren't going to carry this'. The end result is an attempt to stretch a popular art form beyond the expected and the secure. 'This is not the cartoon medium' Disney insisted. 'It should not be limited to cartoons' (story conference 8 December 1938).

The art director for Disney's *Ave Maria* was again Kay Nielsen, his mannered landscapes the basis for the almost static film. Nielsen was influenced by the early Romantic painting of Caspar David Friedrich

(1774–1840), a contemporary of Schubert and of von Schwind. The Germanic influence is thus filtered through the eyes of a Dane. Friedrich's landscapes are religious, mystical and austere in feeling. The same props and signs appear in Nielsen's inspirational paintings, and in the film itself. Friedrich is precise, however, where Nielsen/Disney is vague. His trees, for instance, play an important role in his paintings, symbolising the cross, rebirth and resurrection. Trees are important to Nielsen but as a pattern. Nielsen lacks the intensity of the devout Friedrich or the liberal Schubert.

Nielsen paints mist as a decorative device in a number of his inspirational paintings at the beginning of the sequence. Friedrich also uses mist but as more than decoration. It is symbolic of the obscurity of life and the constant danger of death. Friedrich's landscape *The Cross on the Mountains* (1808) (see Colour Plate 58) has similarities with the final shot of the *Ave Maria*. Although the film lacks the image of the cross, both depict romantic skies suffused with light. Both present hills, trees and a sunburst.

The intensity with which Friedrich painted trees can also be seen in his *Memorial Picture to Johann Emanuel Bremer* (c. 1818). Gothic churches and ruins appear in Friedrich's work and though no church as such appears in the *Ave Maria*, a Gothic ruin is seen as the pilgrims make their processional way. The most striking pictures in connection with Nielsen and Disney are Friedrich's *Abbey Among Oak Trees* (1809) and *Ruined Monastery in the Snow* (1817–1819). Both pictures have trees pointing into the sky. They are leafless whereas Nielsen's trees have the early foliage of spring. The Disney film echoes the processions of monks in both, dwarfed by the trees and ruins in the landscape around them (see Colour Plates 60 and 61). German Romanticism has an intensity which comes through in the cooler more mannered work of Nielsen, but the vision is distorted by Disney in his search for an emotional response which he feels is due to a religious climax. Disney commissioned the writer and novelist Rachel Field (1894–1942) to write new lyrics. These were sung by chorus and the soprano Julietta Novis. The Rachel Field lyrics used in the film are:

Ave Maria, Heaven's bride
The bells ring out in solemn praise
For you the anguish and the pride,
The living glory of our nights and days.
The Prince of Peace your arms embrace
While hosts of darkness fade and cower –
Oh, save us, Mother full of grace,
In life, and in our dying hour.
                Ave Maria!

In this connection it is worth noting that Disney and his colleagues 'went and looked at the Paramount version of "Ave Maria"' (story conference, 5 June 1939). I have not been able to identify this film, but it is possible that the Universal film *It's a Date* (1939) was the one seen by Disney. It starred Deanna Durbin, and closed on a rendering of the *Ave Maria* on stage, with a full choir of nuns in an ecclesiastical setting – a sort of open air cloister – and Deanna Durbin in close up wearing nun's habit. The popularity of *Ave Maria* is seen in two further examples: in a radio tribute Perry Como the popular singer claimed that his version of *Ave Maria*, sung in Yiddish, sold more records than anything else he sang throughout his career.[42] Tony Broughton, fourth generation of an acting family remembers his early days as a child actor in northern England variety concert circuits. The *Ave Maria* or 'Singing Nun Spot' was a regular, and immensely popular, feature.[43]

Disney intended the work to transcend all that had preceded it. 'The beauty,' he said at a meeting on 8 December 1938, 'we can get from controlled colour and the music everything we use here will be worth it. This stuff means more, it's richer, it's like a painting.' He was looking for ways of achieving on film the *impression* created by art and religion and continued:

> People go all over Europe to look at cathedrals, and when you go in they don't look like this – you don't see the beauty there. You have to get back and squint your eyes, or you have to see it at a certain hour or a certain minute of the day.

The 'you don't see the beauty there' is the speech of a man who has found the architectural heritage of Europe unimpressive except as a passing image or icon. Here, Disney and his colleagues were not driven by the religious belief which generated the music, painting and architecture that were their constant references. They brought instead the technological achievements of the New World; dissolves and pans which stretched the technicolor and camera resources, heavy use of the multiplane camera to achieve a three dimensional effect, with multi-directional sound. Using his nine speaker Fantasound system Disney wanted the music to move from left to right with the pilgrims and then appear to come up the main auditorium aisle as the camera enters the great forest of cathedral-like trees. He was also looking at ways of using scents and the smell of flowers and incense in addition to all the other technical gadgetry for which *Fantasia* is famous. 'I'm serious about this perfume thing,' he said on another occasion (story conference, 14 September 1938). Stokowski was also enthusiastic.[44]

When he was asked if the item was sectarian, Disney replied, 'The piece is non-sectarian. There's still a lot of Christians in the world, in spite of Russia and some of the others, and it would be a hell of an appealing thing from that angle. And if we go to a non-Christian country it's only four minutes long and can be snipped out and you wouldn't miss it' (story conference, 8 December 1938). Yet he called these four minutes 'precious' at the same meeting, and was to tinker with it almost up till the film's première. He said 'I'm looking at this and *Clair de Lune* (completed but dropped from the final version of the film) as a chance to – as a contrast to what we have before'.

The initial outline of 29 September 1938 clarified the religious aspect: 'We go inside the church for beautiful shots of light streaming through stained glass windows, illuminated paintings of several famous Madonnas' (see Colour Plate 59). Joe Grant commented on 8 December: 'Use the Botticelli Madonnas, they have more sex appeal'. The problem of the Madonna was to exercise Disney and his colleagues for months, though the locale of a real cathedral was quickly exchanged for trees in the open air. Disney attempted to create a magical illusion by use of special effects, and tried to clarify his views again and again:

> [The Madonna] is never really there – it is just a thought you are worshipping ... going right up into the sky and the sunburst thing [23 January 1940]. It should be more indefinite [7 February 1940]. The Madonna is just an illusion – we want to work it so it is just suggested [8 February 1940].

Two endings, one with and one without a Madonna, were worked out and a decision not taken until late July 1940.[45] There is an attempt here to balance the male dominance in the Moussorgsky piece with a female presence. Some idea of the abandoned Madonna image and church interior can be gauged from the illustrations by the Disney artists in Rachel Field's book of lyrics, where the pilgrims enter a real cathedral in drawings reminiscent of the work of Rockwell Kent. The illustrations end with a large rose window depicting Raphael's *Madonna and Child* in stained glass. The film version omits Madonna and church. Disney was expressing his doubts as early as the meeting on 8 December 1938, from which much of the information on the *Ave Maria* has been taken. 'I think we should find one [a Madonna] that is not attached to any definite religion', he said. His concern for the mass audience was always uppermost in his mind.

The programme synopsis of 1940 describes the *Ave Maria* as 'a universal symbol of Hope and Good ... In the dim light of first dawn ... the forest seems to have become the interior of a cathedral, immense, stately and beautiful beyond the dreams of human architects'. Screen cathedrals become products more desirable than real cathedrals. The film ends on a slow tracking shot through the forest which seems like the interior of a cathedral. We come through the trees, ending on a sunburst illuminating a hillside. At first sight this looks like a standard

Hollywood cliché, but we have seen that the imagery is much more complex in its associations, and it was technically difficult to film. It had to be shot three times; a wrong lens was used, then an earthquake shook the horizontal multiplane set-up and the whole thing had to be done again. Great care was taken with each of the four long shots that make up the five minutes of running time on the screen. The backgrounds were painted on glass three or four feet wide and then shot with the multiplane camera. Kay Nielsen's two-dimensional inspirational paintings were transformed into large glass paintings to create the effect of three dimensions. The result resembles a gigantic peep show of extraordinary intensity. At a screening of the film in 1996 the virtuosity and technical accomplishment had about them the aura of awe and wonder, despite the wobbly pilgrims. Disney noted the latter:

> *Walt* (looking at test film): Where do we get all that jitter in there?
>
> *Gail* (Papineau [Special Camera Effects]): It looks like it is from inking and painting.
>
> *Walt*: It's a lousy job. We can't use it. Both the lights and the figures jitter (story conference 2 August 1940).

So the scene was redone at great cost, but the sense of pageantry, religion and ritual which Disney wanted was dissipated in technical concerns. We are reminded of the loss to the Bach section of three dimensional viewing. And what would we make of the item if it possessed the multi-directional sound that Disney envisaged? Here is the showman at work, the magician who believes he can create magical worlds and hold an audience in thrall. Again he emphasised the processional: 'It must be like a spectacle on the stage. It can't be too literal in its interpretation ... It should be a big, organised thing – use a lot of showmanship. I would like to combine in this some of the abstract things we were trying to do in *Toccata and Fugue*. It must glorify the sacred side' (story conference 12 January 1940). Another difficulty was the rush to complete the film in time for its première. Time was against the crew working on the *Ave Maria* and this may have affected its final form. It remains a tantalising and beautiful fragment of technical virtuosity.

Disney felt constrained by his own house style. His frustration is expressed in his comments to a colleague who asked him if they were taking full advantage 'of the cartoon medium with a picture like this'. 'Excuse me if I get a little riled up on this stuff', said Disney at that meeting on 8 December 1938, 'because it's a continual fight around this place to get away from slapping somebody on the fanny or have somebody swallow something. So whenever it comes up I'm a little bit – I'm ready ... It's an experimental thing and I'm willing to experiment ... We have worlds to conquer here'.

Notes

1. A shortened account of this section appears in *A Reader in Animation Studies* ed. Jayne Pilling (London: John Libbey, 1997), 250–260.

2. 'Fantasia Edition.' *Walt Disney Studio Bulletin*, Vol. 3, No. 5, 15 November 1940 contains detailed lists of all the staff who worked on each section of the film. Courtesy Joe Grant.

3. See note 8 below on research by Karl Cohen and David Williams.

4. Information on Pierné is taken from *The New Grove Dictionary of Music and Musicians*, ed. Stanley Sadie (London: Macmillan, 1980), 736 and from Cyril W. Beaumont, *Complete Book of Ballets* (New York: Grosset & Dunlap, 1938), 546–550.

5. The difficulty that the Disney company has experienced in presenting the film is examined by the author in 'The Real *Fantasia* at Length, at Last', *The Times Saturday Review*, 25 August 1990.

6. Robert Graves, *The Greek Myths* (Harmondsworth: Penguin, 1955), Vol. 1, 361.

7. Ward Kimball, Interview on Television, *Walt Disney* (London: Thames Television, 27 April 1977).

8. Karl Cohen, 'Racism and Resistance: Black Stereotypes in Animation', *Animation Journal*, Vol. 4, No. 2, Spring 1996, 61; David Williams, 'Whatever Happened to Sunflower', *Animator*, No 28, 1991, 13.

9. John Canemaker, *Winsor McCay: His Life and Art* (New York: Abbeville, 1987), 157, and Crafton, *Before Mickey*, 250.

10. Culhane, *Walt Disney's Fantasia*, 138 and Canemaker *Before the Animation Begins*, 65–73.

11. Huemer, 'With Disney on Olympus: an Interview with Dick Huemer', *Funnyworld*, Vol. 17, 40.

12. Rick Altman, *The American Film Musical* (Bloomington & Indianapolis: Indiana University Press, 1987), 105–106.

13. Charles Solomon, *Enchanted Drawings: The History of Animation* (New York: Alfred Knopf, 1989), 69.

14. Helmut Farber, '*Fantasia* – Neuester orbis pictus', trans. author, *Suddeutsche Zeitung*, 14 April 1971.

15. Good accounts of the popularising of art through the distribution of the art print are given in William Gaunt, *Victorian Olympus* (London: Jonathan Cape, 1952) and in Mary Clive, *The Day of Reckoning* (London: Macmillan,1964).

16. *Arnold Böcklin*. Catalogue (London: Arts Council/Pro Helvetia, 1971). For more information on Böcklin see Dorothea Christ and Christian Geelhar, *Arnold Böcklin: Die Gemalde im Kunstmuseum Basel* (Basle: Öffentliche Kunstsammlung Basel & Eidolon, 1990); *German Masters of the Nineteenth Century* (New York: Metropolitan Museum of Art, 1981); *'In uns selbst liegt Italien': Die Kunst der Deutsch-Romer*, ed. Christoph Heilmann (Munich: Hirmer, 1987); *The Romantic Spirit in German Art 1790–1990*, ed. Keith Hartley (London and Edinburgh: South Bank Centre & National Galleries of Scotland, 1994).

17. Rolf Andree, Introduction *Arnold Böcklin*, Catalogue, 1971, 8. See also Franz Zelger, *Arnold Böcklin: Die Toteninsel* (Frankfurt: Fischer, 1991).

18. Claude Phillips, *Magazine of Art* (London: Cassell, 1885), quoted in Bernice Phillpotts, *Mermaids* (New York: Ballantine, 1980), 72.

19. Grant Wood (1891–1942) American artist. One of his most famous pictures is *American Gothic* (1930) at the Chicago Art Institute, but it does not display his

characteristic art deco style. Rockwell Kent (1882–1971), American artist and illustrator.

20. Gordon Legg, interview with Milton Gray, South Pasadena, California, 13 March 1976, 1. Courtesy Gordon Legg, who is the son of an English Methodist Minister who settled in Worcester, Massachusetts, where the boy Legg grew up, going out to California to visit relatives. He attended Chouinard School of Art in Los Angeles, but had to drop out of his last year owing to lack of funds. After work as a commercial artist he joined the Disney Studio in 1936, creating the great book for *Snow White and the Seven Dwarfs* (see Chapter 3). He designed many of the titles for the shorts, working directly to Walt Disney, and became famous for his delicacy of rendering and for his airbrush technique. Anxious to get into the story department, he was assigned to Sylvia Holland and her team on *The Nutcracker Suite* for *Fantasia*. He found Holland stimulating company, 'a real dynamic promoter,' he recalled. He then worked under Otto Englander on the *Pastoral* sequence.

    After *Fantasia* Legg produced some enchanting paintings for *Alice in Wonderland* before leaving the studio in 1941. After work for the Douglas Aircraft Corporation during the Second World War he returned to Disney for a brief period in the 1950s when he worked under Ward Kimball on *Mars and Beyond* (1957), *Goliath II* (1960) and other subjects. These paintings are again of exceptional quality. Gordon Legg retired in 1983.

21. Robin Allan, *Picture Books and Disney Pictures* (Manchester: Portico Library, 1990).

22. Helmut Farber, '*Fantasia* – Neuester orbis pictus'.

23. Jack Caldwell to Dick Huemer, inter-office memorandum, 'Entrance of Night Hours Bars 170–200', 27 October 1938. Courtesy Joe Grant.

24. Bamber Gascoigne, *World Theatre* (London: Ebury Press, 1968), 263.

25. '*Fantasia* Edition', 9. Courtesy Joe Grant. The information in this paragraph comes from this source.

26. Rick Altman, *The American Film Musical*, 202 ff.

27. Alastair Macauley, 'Disney's Dances', *Dancing Times*, December 1989 Vol. LXXX, No. 951, 264.

28. Brian Sibley, *The Book of Guinness Advertising* (Enfield: Guinness, 1985), 46.

29. *Heinrich Kley*, Catalogue (Munich: Galerie Wolfgang Gurlitt, 1962). In his introduction to an American edition of Kley's drawings George Grosz notes the 'remarkable observation of movement' in Kley's work. 'His sure rapid line roped in the grotesque creatures – parodies of humanity in animal forms, and people generally clad only in Adam's costume and struggling to escape their fates – who are at one and the same time the inhabitants of the world of his imagination, and the prey of his whirling, flying line ... Like Walt Disney, he humanises his beasts'.

30. Kley's satirical and erotic work expressed itself, like that of Sullivant, in the first decade of the twentieth century. His was too insolent a voice for the darker regime that followed the Weimar Republic, though he continued to paint industrial scenes during the Second World War. So little was known of him in the United States that it was presumed in error that he had died insane. (In England it was generally thought that the popular comic artist Heath Robinson was mad). Kley moved to a village outside Munich during the heavy bombing at the end of the Second World War, and died in 1945. His widow preserved some of his work and Munich mounted retrospective exhibitions in 1962 and 1964. The Disney family also owns a large collection of Kley paintings and drawings.

31. Walt Disney, quoted by Walt Partymiller, from a Disney TV programme c. April 1964.

32. Paul Valery, *L'Ame et la Danse*, quoted by Macauley, 'Disney's Dances', 264.

33. Harold C. Schonberg, *The Lives of the Composers* (London: Davis-Poynter, 1971), 343.

34. Quoted in Culhane, 185.

35. Walt Disney, quoted in Robert D. Feild, *The Art of Walt Disney*, 124.

36. Lotte H. Eisner, *The Haunted Screen* (London: Secker & Warburg, 1973), 285.

37. See Canemaker, *Before the Animation Begins*, 74–83 for a full account of Nielsen's Disney career.

38. Nielsen's three great murals in the Los Angeles area are:

    (i) *The First Spring* (see Colour Plates 62 and 63). This is a version of Genesis 1:25, 'And God made the beast of the earth after his kind, and cattle after their kind, and every thing that creepeth on the earth after his kind: and God saw that it was good'. The mural was painted for the Central Junior High School of Los Angeles and begun in 1942. It took Nielsen three years to complete and a year later, in 1946, the school was closed and the mural stripped from the wall. It was badly damaged. Following a public scandal, a new home was found for it in the library of the Sutter Junior High School which was then being built in the San Fernando Valley. Nielsen was with difficulty persuaded to repair his own work, after an understandably distressed refusal.

    The mural is enormous, stretching the width of the library and reaching from the top of the book stacks to the ceiling. It is painted with exquisite precision. The large figure is of the angel Gabriel shepherding a flock of animals and birds across an idealised landscape. Animals and birds pour out of the sky in a cloudburst of light. The words of Genesis run along the base of the mural, and Nielsen painted in small animals and plants at the request of the children who saw him repairing the work *in situ*.

    (ii) *The Canticle of the Sun* (see Colour Plates 64 and 65) is another huge mural in the library of the Emerson Junior High School, Westwood, Los Angeles. An almost naked figure strides across a landscape of hills, houses and a lake, with ploughman and shepherd at work in the fields. The picture has a brilliance of colour and composition to match *The First Spring*. In her 'Elegy' in *The Unknown Paintings of Kay Nielsen* Hildegarde Flanner writes, 'Exquisitness, grandeur and tenderness inevitably come to mind as one looks at this painting. It takes courage in our times to be so angelic'.

    (iii) *Altarpiece*. This is in the Wong Chapel of the First Congregational Church of Los Angeles. Based on the Twenty Third Psalm it depicts the shepherd climbing a rocky cliff with a lamb in his arms, and other sheep pasturing precariously below. It lacks the scale of the larger murals but has the same beatific calm.

    There is a fourth mural which I have not seen at Whitman College, Walla Walla, Washington, completed in 1953. It was Nielsen's last work and shows the death of early pioneers, with an idealised presentation of the future.

39. Susan E. Meyer, *A Treasury of the Great Children's Book Illustrators* (New York: Abrams, 1983), 209.

40. Robert Russett and Cecile Starr, *Experimental Animation* (New York: Da Capo, 1976), 74 and 92.

41. 'Even in its clearest portion a diffusion is used which makes it impossible for us to determine whether the pilgrims are men or women'; Wilfred Jackson, sequence director. Continuity outline, 'Ave Maria', 27 March 1940.

42. Perry Como, *Eightieth Birthday Interview* (London: Radio 2, 18 May 1992).

43. Tony Broughton, interview with author, Strines, Cheshire, 6 April 1992).

44. Reference may here be made to Aldous Huxley, *Brave New World* (Harmondsworth: Penguin,[1932] 1964), 133–136): 'A series of daring modulations through the spice keys into ambergris'.

45. Notes dictated by Jaxon (Wilfred Jackson) on changes suggested by Walt. 25 June 1940.

CHAPTER 8

The Experimental Forties

By the end of 1940 Disney had to make money quickly; the profits from *Snow White and the Seven Dwarfs* had been used up on *Pinocchio* and *Fantasia* as well as on the new studio at Burbank, and the war in Europe was closing overseas markets. Disney completed a live-action film with cartoon episodes called *The Reluctant Dragon* (1941), with one cartoon episode based on Kenneth Grahame's story from *Dream Days* (1898). The film is largely a live action documentary made in response to public demand for information about the workings of his studio. It was a stop-gap piece, acting as a framework for three different shorts in various stages of completion. Showing some of Disney's key artists at work, it also employed professional actors playing Disney personnel – one of them is Alan Ladd – combining fact and fiction within its live action framework.

The cartoon sections include a *Goofy* cartoon, 'How to Ride a Horse', and the story of an infant prodigy, 'Baby Weems'. This is told through story sketches and limited animation, a style that other cartoon studios would increasingly use in the late nineteen forties and fifties, turning away from naturalism and the illusion of reality, towards looser graphic expression.

The short cartoon version of *The Reluctant Dragon* ends the film. Like the best of the *Silly Symphonies* it has bold colours and sharply defined characters. The gentle mockery of Grahame's story is nicely captured and the irony of the text is given a visual complement through the animation and backgrounds; an edition of *The Reluctant Dragon* (1930) taken from Grahame's longer work, and illustrated by E.H. Shepard, was in the Walt Disney Studio Library.[1] The library card shows that the artists who worked on the film borrowed the book, and there is some reference to Shepard's pictures in the characterisation of the dragon, down to the feathery tuft on the ears. Albert Hurter provided a number of sketches of a dragon, knights in armour, villagers in medieval settings and comic incidents. The backgrounds are spare, and, like those for the *Pastoral Symphony*, inspired by Grant Wood's art deco Regionalist landscapes. Ken Anderson was the art director. There are caricatures of English 'types'; the blustering colonel figure, sporting a monocle, and an effete dragon who prefers tea and poetry to battle. The dragon resembles Oscar Wilde in shape if not in wit. Apart from the Grahame story the European influences on the rest of the film are minimal.

Animator's drawing of the Dragon, showing the debt to Shepard and to Hurter (smile and body language). © Walt Disney Enterprises, Inc.

Ernest Shepard: 'Not a word of truth in it'; illustration for The Reluctant Dragon. *The Disney Studio Library's copy of the 1930 edition borrowed by Walt Disney on 25 November 1938 and marked with his characteristic blue pencil. Illustration by E.H. Shepard copyright under the Berne Convention. Reproduced by permission of Curtis Brown, London.*

RELUCTANT

gin with. And if I *do* read other fellows my poetry, I'm always ready to listen to theirs!"

"Oh, dear!" cried the Boy, "I wish you'd try and grasp the situation properly. When the other people find you out, they'll come after you with spears and swords and all sorts of things. You'll have to be exterminated, according to their way of looking at it! You're a scourge, and a pest, and a baneful monster!"

Not a word of truth in it

Although the live-action footage shows a smiling work force, the reality was different. Industrial unrest led to the strike that began a month after the film's release.

At the same time Disney started *Dumbo* (1941), an outstanding film that owes little to Europe. It reflects Disney's love of trains and circuses and the anthropomorphised animals remind us especially of Kley. The Ringmaster has a German accent and comes out of nineteenth century melodrama. Adapted by Joe Grant and Dick Huemer from an American short story by Helen Aberson and Harold Pearl, *Dumbo* unfolds in

Heinrich Kley: Illustration 'Holiday Season' for Simpliccissimus. *In* Dumbo *the elephants are similarly crammed into the train.*

broadly homiletic terms, matching the bold animation and colour. The relationship between Dumbo and his mother emphasises the baby theme that has been noted, but the emotion is controlled and the animation by Bill Tytla and others deeply moving. This is relationship without the conscious charm of *Bambi*. The 'Pink Elephants' nightmare is anarchic, surrealistic and characteristic of Fleischer's New York animation rather than of Disney. Mark Langer has pointed out two distinctive styles in *Dumbo*, the West Coast style and the more 'cartoony' style emanating from New York.[2] Disney did not take a great deal of interest in the film, being occupied with *Bambi*, economic difficulties and the studio strike.

The strike began on 28 May 1941. It changed Disney the man and Disney the studio. At present we have little background to the strike itself except through the official histories,[3] but it is clear from the industrial unrest in Hollywood at the end of the nineteen thirties, that the Disney Studio would also be affected. The animators, like the clerical staff and make-up personnel, 'could not withstand the unionisation fever that has swept through Hollywood since April 1937'.[4] The success of *Snow White and the Seven Dwarfs* led to over-expansion without an adequate managerial structure. The move to the new Burbank studio involved petty bureaucracies and divisions, while salary anomalies and uncertainties led to jealousy. There was sexism with a fear of women taking power, and a feeling that the golden age promised by Walt Disney at the height of the creative euphoria generated by *Snow White and the Seven Dwarfs* was not forthcoming. The public response to *Pinocchio* and *Fantasia* had been disappointing and overseas income had fallen away because of the war in Europe. Desire for power was being sought democratically through the unions and politically through power seeking elements from outside the studios, such as gangland and the Mafia.[5] There had been a crippling strike at the rival Fleischer Studios in 1937, which had embittered Fleischer and his work force and caused him to move his studio from unionised New York to Florida.[6]

Another reason for unrest among the Disney animators and artists hinted at in the official biography by Thomas and made more explicit by Langer was the tension between the artists who had come from the East Coast and those Californians who had been with Disney since the early days. The two factions stayed apart and the studio was not the happy family which the publicity machine implied. *Snow White and the Seven Dwarfs* and its success, expansion and development with *Pinocchio* and *Fantasia* led to exhaustion. Disney was primarily concerned with product even though he designed his new premises with great care for the comfort and well-being of his employees. Driving himself, he expected his staff to be similarly driven and was surprised that the new premises did not generate the loyalty he had come to expect. All three feature films had been initiated in the old ramshackle Hyperion days – now, in spite of new and more congenial quarters, his staff was discontented. Wages were low, union activity expansive, bureaucracy heavy handed. It is clear from Disney's reaction that he had become divorced from the feeling on the shop floor. Still believing in his own benevolent paternalism, he was shocked and upset by the attitude of his employees, and in particular by that of a senior animator Art Babbitt who was one of the leaders of the strike. Disney had to reinstate Babbitt after the strike but he never forgave him and never spoke to him again.[7]

Disney handled the situation poorly and made the mistake of relying on the advice of his lawyer Gunther Lessing, a man disliked throughout the company. The strike dragged on through the summer of 1941; some of the best artists left, including Bill Tytla, and others were made redundant. Joe Grant was asked by the strikers if he would take Disney's place:

> It was a horrifying thought, and I said 'I don't want to hear that voiced again. It's absolutely ridiculous'. But the disillusioning job it did on Walt was devastating ... He couldn't conceive of himself being challenged in that way.

Contrary to the impression given by Richard Schickel that Disney kept his work and private life separate, his daughter Diane remembered the strike as a traumatic period. 'He talked endlessly about the strike,' she said. '... We lived through the strike.'

There is no doubt that this event, coming on top of the failure of his feature films to perform satisfactorily at the box office, changed Disney. The man became more withdrawn, less accessible, the studio more experimental, more eclectic in its search for material. By necessity it had to shelve the elaborate plans already in hand for further feature films, apart from *Bambi* which was in production but which was proving increasingly difficult to develop. The other projects were English classics and included Lewis Carroll's *Alice's Adventures in Wonderland*, J.M. Barrie's *Peter Pan*, and Kenneth Grahame's *The Wind in the Willows*, all in the early stages of production. They had been bought as properties in the late thirties along with many other European classics, and would surface again in one form or another after the war.

The reliance on Europe and its literary and artistic sources decreased. It was as if Disney kept them in a bank, hoping to make use of them when the situation became less volatile. The classical music items for the continuing *Fantasia* were shelved (see appendix A) and there were many other ideas which dated from the late nineteen thirties and early forties and which included European classics popular with both adults and children. Ninety seven out of a hundred and fifty titles in a Story Numbers list dated 12 October 1943 came from Europe. These included classics which were later filmed by Disney as either animated or live action films.[8] Some of the story sketches from this period suggest possibilities which animation has still not explored. Those for *Don Quixote*, to take one example, reached an advanced stage, and show a tantalising freedom of expression.[9] Bob Carr, one of the artists responsible, used the text of Cervantes' book as a training exercise for artists as early as 1940. His gouache sketches show an indebtedness to the European graphic line of Busch, Daumier and Randolph Caldecott (1846–1886). A scrapbook was also compiled of nineteenth century engravings and pictures including work by Doré (see appendix B).

The Walt Disney Company is still making capital out of the European or Middle Eastern sources that Walt Disney acquired in the late nineteen thirties. The debt to Kay Nielsen and *The Little Mermaid* (1989) has been noted; since then there have been *Beauty and the Beast* (1991), *Aladdin* (1992) which had become popular as a tale in Europe at the same time as the collected fairy tales of Perrault and Grimm, *The Hunchback of Notre Dame* (1996) and *Hercules* (1997). Other European and Asian stories continue to be developed.

However, in the strike-bound summer of 1941 Disney was invited by the US government to lead a delegation of artists on a goodwill tour of South America to counteract suspected Nazism there. It was an excuse to get away from troubles at home, and the visit was a success; Disney and his colleagues were relaxed and amiable ambassadors of goodwill, running animation workshops and inviting Latin American artists to cooperate on a number of projects. Some short subjects as well as two feature films, *Saludos Amigos* (1943) and *The Three Caballeros* (1945), were the result. The visit turned Disney's attention away from Europe as well as from the strike. When he returned in the autumn of 1941 the strike had been settled and he was able to continue his struggle with the intractible *Bambi* (1942).

This was based on Felix Salten's popular story which had been translated from the German in 1928. The producer/director Sidney Franklin bought the rights in 1933. Franklin had produced or directed a number of prestigious films including *The Barretts of Wimpole Street* (1933) and *The Good Earth* (1937). Later he was to make a live action story about a deer and a boy that would, like *Bambi*, have a traumatic effect upon the young of the next generation. This was *The Yearling* (1946). Franklin realised that the lyricism of Salten's book could not be captured by live action. In a letter of 20 April 1935, he wrote to Disney offering cooperation. 'It is something very close to me,' he said, 'as you already know, and, like yourself, I would want it to be one of the greatest things ever attempted and done'.[10] By the spring of 1937 Franklin had turned the rights over to Disney, continuing to act as a collaborator over the next four years. The film was in production for six years altogether and its opening credits contain this dedication: 'To Sidney A. Franklin our appreciation for his inspiring collaboration'.

Bambi was not the success that Disney had hoped for when it was first released, but it has gained in popularity, loved by children despite the horror of the death of Bambi's mother. It is also loved by adults and parents, and is the Disney film that many people remember. It has a clear story with dramatic episodes and bright, simple characters. The naturalistic animals are drawn with painstaking attention to detail; we forget this is an animated film, until episodes of broad caricature or comedy remind us that all is achieved by paint and brush. But a close examination reveals anomalies; perhaps the long gestation is responsible for the differences in rendering and in mood. Some sequences are elaborate, using layers of multiplane virtuosity (the opening scene in the forest at dawn is an example) while others are spare to the point of bleakness. Some animation is observed with attention to detail and care for the building of effect, for example, the 'Little April Shower' sequence, which owes much to the inspirational sketches of Sylvia Holland and is a masterpiece of observation and delicacy, combining the natural with the anthropomorphic (see Colour Plate 66). It has an understated quality which is reminiscent of the English watercolour school and the genius of Beatrix Potter. As well as the death of Bambi's mother, there are other powerful scenes, including the forest fire and the privations of winter. At times, however, the film is diffuse (the flight of the stags for instance); some scenes are comic (on ice) and some are stylised and expressionistic

Anonymous illustrations for the English edition of Bambi *(1928).*

(the stag fight). The many changes of policy between 1937 and 1941 are explained by Ollie Johnston and Frank Thomas in their book on the film;[11] an expansionist Disney began the work but had to cut back as economic difficulty arose, and at one point considered abandoning the project. The result is a film of extraordinary contrasts, combining self-consciousness with emotional strength.

The elemental scene of the death of Bambi's mother has had a powerful effect on cinemagoers, as powerful as the Queen-into-Witch scene in *Snow White and the Seven Dwarfs*. Disney tried to express visually the emotion of privation and death in Salten's book. That he struggled to express the scene is clear from the story meetings, where again and again he cut back from explicit violence on the screen until the scene has an austerity and visual understatement akin to Greek tragedy. Disney's intuitive response to trauma was expressed in the starkest terms, and the result is one of the most graphic and moving scenes in all his films (see Colour Plate 67).[12] Elsewhere the film varies in texture; this is not a real forest, but a painted tapestry of colours in which the chidren – Bambi and Thumper both have distinctive and American child voices – play. Their constant talk satisfies the child and adult as child in an identification process of and with childhood and memory. They convince as cuddly animals and children at the same time, and it is this conviction which renders the actuality of death all the more obtrusive and terrifying.

Jean de Brunhoff: Title page illustration for Babar's Travels *(1935). The eyes are dots but the animals no less sympathetic. As with animation, the artist's handling of the line is all important. Courtesy Hachette, Paris.*

Walt Disney and Europe

Salten's animals exist consistently in a world which is dangerous and violent; they have to learn to adapt to it and survive, or die, and their forest is an old one, the trees and roots and flowers wise in the ways of nature. It is a European forest. Disney's forest is American, and though it is based on photographs taken in Maine, it is a raw, Western forest with apparently only fir trees everywhere, except for the fall of leaf at autumn. Instead of the attention to natural detail that informed the *Nutcracker* suite, there is vagueness and generalisation. The flowers are Disney flowers hiding two blue eyes batting their lashes in a love duet. Where Disney has caricature and cartoon comedy, Salten has clarity and dignity: 'Out of the earth came whole troops of flowers like motley stars, so that the soil of the twilit forest floor shone with a silent, ardent colourful gladness. Everything smelled of fresh leaves, of blossoms, of moist clods and green wood'.[13] Salten has life and death balanced throughout the book; the great questions that children ask are not balked, nor are they manipulated. '... A fox tore to pieces the strong and handsome pheasant who had enjoyed such general respect and popularity. His death aroused the sympathies of a wide circle who tried to comfort his disconsolate widow'.[14] The ironic tone softens the harshness of the situation. Salten imbues the book with a detached observation. A visual equivalent for this in animation was feasible, but it would have demanded qualities for which Disney was only partially equipped, with a response to his source which he could not understand or absorb. He did not learn. Instead, his film shifts from bright cartoon style to naturalism and then back again in an attempt to match the ironies of the written word.

The forest scenes were largely designed by a Chinese artist, Tyrus Wong, who had emigrated to the United States at the age of nine, and his was a powerful influence, according to a senior animator, Marc Davis. Jim Algar commented on the 'moody oriental touch of never being tightly finished'. There is a sense of alienation experienced by the European viewer, which is explained by the strangeness of the environment portrayed by Wong.

Disney wanted comedy and he developed the characters; the child Peter Behn who took the voice of Thumper was such a personality in his own right that the role of Thumper was expanded, softened, rounded, the eyes enlarged, the snout reduced, the cheeks puffed out like a baby's. Jean de Brunhoff, another artist who deals with the anthropomorphising of animals in the *Babar* books, handles the appeal of his elephant heroes in a very different manner. He invites the reader to make the emotional adjustment as he or she gazes at the pictures of Babar and his family. The characters have small eyes and no expression – they are almost mask like – and we must, as when we see plays acted behind masks, make the imaginative leap ourselves into the emotion expressed. Disney forces the emotion by the appeal to the large close up of the baby-like animal,

Rico Lebrun: A page of his sketchbooks showing the articulation of animals. Courtesy David Lebrun.

and this applies in particular to the young Bambi and Thumper. The Pavlovian response to laughter and tears as shown on baby faces in close up is automatic; but Disney also wanted realism, and the two styles do not mix. The sexuality that is coyly presented in the 'Twitterpated' sequence is another example of the uneasy blend of cartoon and realism. That Disney worked painstakingly at perfecting realism, particularly in the rendering of the deer, is well documented. Lee Blair found the process tedious.

> I couldn't stand it. Perce Pearce (the associate producer) was enamoured of the New York stage, and he would say, 'Now when Bambi's mother comes out into the meadow and she senses danger, smells Man in the distance and looks around, imagine Katharine Cornell would be doing that.' And we couldn't figure out what the hell ... For Christ's sake, it's a deer you know ... It was too Godddamned close ... So I was going to quit ...

Disney turned to a European artist for help in achieving realism in drawing the animals, particularly deer. He asked the Italian Rico Lebrun (1900–1964) to give the artists special lessons in animal articulation and anatomy. Lebrun's sketchbooks for the use of the Disney artists reveal a graphic control and observation which the artists found inspiring; all those who remembered him spoke of his genius. The result of his teaching, as well as visits at Disney's request, to the local Griffith Park Zoo, was the search for the imitation of reality. The conclusion to this was Disney's capitulation to the live action camera in his documentary films, beginning with *Seal Island* in 1948.[15]

It is a relief to turn from the complexity of *Bambi* to the studio's work in wartime, when it was forced to employ many graphic devices scarcely used for its entertainment films. At first Disney hated the war as it would curtail his output, his control, and would lead to his being forced to make propaganda films for the government. 'The great panjandrum was as odd a fish as you ever heard of,' commented Joe Grant. 'Who else on the eve of war would have shouted, "War? That's a lot of hooey! There won't be a war"?' The war in fact saved Disney; it gave him breathing space and time to realign his product. Short schedules forced the studio into producing limited animation, offering stylised solutions to military problems in training films and educational programmes. It led to the experimental work of the forties which the studio would never repeat; the limited animation story 'Baby Weems' for *The Reluctant Dragon* was designed by two newspaper men Joe Grant and Dick Huemer and it is to the newspaper and the political cartoon in particular that the studio turned for inspiration in the films it produced for and about the war.

The studio was commandeered and Disney quickly adapted to making informational and propaganda films, first for the Canadian government and then for the various US war departments. It is part of this complex and multifaceted man that he could turn the studio almost overnight to the production of both short and long instructional films needed in a hurry. To speed the process up, limited animation was used, creating sharp, succinct cartoons that are no longer publicly shown. The influence of the political cartoon is clear, especially in allegory and satire, and used by Hogarth, Rowlandson and Gillray onwards. In *Education for Death* (1943) there is savage political satire. This film stresses the indoctrination of Nazi youth and shows Germania as an overweight Sleeping Beauty rescued by a knight in armour who turns out to be Hitler. He has great difficulty in carrying this lady off on his charger. The immediate connotation is Gillray and Rowlandson with their contemporary social commentaries in political cartoon (see Colour Plates 68 and 69); the Disney artists paid tribute also to political cartoonists of the day from both sides of the Atlantic, men like David Low, Louis Raemakers and George Grosz.

Metamorphosis is used to telling effect; a Bible is transformed into *Mein Kampf*, a crucifix into a Nazi sword. A marching soldier is blinkered, muzzled and chained before going to his death in war. The end of the film consists of a slow dissolve replacing the marching soldiers with crosses and helmets in a cemetery stretching across the screen. Colour and shadows add expressionistic force, and there is a reminder of the end of *All Quiet on the Western Front* (1930). Some of the most convincing animation of humans in any Disney film is evident here, especially that of the child Hans and his mother. The animator was Milt Kahl, a great admirer of the German artist Kathe Kollwitz (1867–1945), whose comments on political and social events led to her virtual incarceration under the third Reich. The conviction of Kahl's animation makes the debt to Kollwitz the more moving.

In *Der Führer's Face* (1943) surrealism is used as well as allegory. The landscape itself has become Nazified, so that trees, bushes and houses are shaped like Hitler or a swastika, in a nightmare dreamed by Donald Duck. Abstraction and expressionism combine in a form that is reminiscent of the anarchy of the 'Pink Elephants' scene in *Dumbo*. The studio had the technical skills necessary; a shorthand was found via the political cartoon to instruct, inform and influence.

These techniques were used in Disney's personal war film, *Victory Through Air Power*, (1943) based on the book by a distinguished Polish aviator Major de Seversky, advocating aerial strength. The ideological content makes for uncomfortable viewing since it insists on pervasive bombing, graphically animated, and ignores potential civilian casualties, but the animation is extraordinarily powerful, drawing upon a wide range of graphic styles from simple cartoon to visual metaphors of complex ingenuity. The world is represented as a clock, the years marked out in bold upright figures. As 1939 appears, the dove of peace flies off screen, and flames engulf the numbers. Maps and symbols are brightly coloured and mobile. Crete is seen as a map from the air when a mailed fist enters the screen and brands a giant swastika across the island. The axis power is a giant iron wheel attacked by allied hammers. The American eagle fights the Japanese octopus on a map of the Pacific, the octopus relinquishing its tentacles from one possession and then another. Jim Algar, who directed half the film, described it as a continuous running editorial cartoon.

Another war project based on a European source was Disney's plan to make a film of Roald Dahl's story *The Gremlins*. Dahl was then serving as a Flight Lieutenant with the RAF in Washington DC. He visited the studio in early 1942, but plans for the film developed slowly and the RAF had some authority in the contract which caused difficulty. Audience research showed lack of public interest in continuing war themes. By the end of the year Disney dropped the idea, though Dahl's book, with Disney illustrations, was published on both sides of the Atlantic.[16] Dahl later insisted that his own work was 'too English. He [Disney] was not into it. He was a hundred per cent American boy ... He had to go to Europe; he just wanted a good fairy tale'.

In his scholarly study of the studio at war, Richard Shale[17] also points out Disney's interest in educational and instructional films, though recognising that there would not be sufficient economic justification for a major investment. Latin America led Disney along another path, that of technological experiment. The Latin American features were cobbled together in a hurry, reflecting little of Europe's influence except indirectly through the Spanish and Portuguese colonial legacy. The Disney artist who responded warmly to Latin American culture was a woman, Mary Blair (1911–1978), who, as we shall see, influenced all the feature films from 1943 to 1953. These included *The Three Caballeros, Make Mine Music, Melody Time, The Adventures of Ichabod and Mr Toad, Cinderella, Alice in Wonderland* and *Peter Pan*. She also influenced the colour and design of other films as well as part of Disneyland.[18]

The Latin American films were received enthusiastically in South America, although some countries were angry that they had not been represented in the package. *The Three Caballeros* (1945) is particularly anarchic and extravagant, an extraordinary contrast to *Bambi*. It has a hectic surreal element running through it, with outbursts of frenzy and a relentless pace. There is a sexual obsession along with an anxiety to inform, a continuous orgasmic wish fulfilment expressed in Donald's relationships with live action women. This was a period when servicemen were separated from their womenfolk by the aftermath of war.

The studio publicity boasted that the film combined live action and animation for the first time, though this was of course not true. Disney had used it in a limited way for his *Alice* Comedies in 1923, and the device was as old as animation itself. Max Fleischer had used it successfully in his *Out of the Inkwell* series in the nineteen twenties. However, to combine live action and animation in colour was certainly new and Disney continued, with varying degrees of success, to marry the two forms until his death. It had to wait for new technology to be convincing; its aesthetic success is still debated in later Disney films, for example *Who Framed Roger Rabbit* (1988). It reveals Disney's passion for the technologically innovative rather than for artistic achievement. The artistry was by the way – sometimes it helped, sometimes it didn't.

Disney admired ostentation and egotistical flair in an artist. Hence his admiration for Stokowski, and his invitation to an artist who was one of the best self-publicists for his art of this century. Salvador Dalí (1904–1989) joined the Disney Studio after he had finished work on the dream sequence for Hitchcock's *Spellbound* (1945). Surrealism and psychoanalysis were fashionable in Hollywood at the time and both Disney and Dalí thought they would benefit from working together, but the partnership did not last long, though the two men got on well. Perhaps Dalí was too flamboyant – he would make a great entrance at the studio with his hat and cape, but there was room for only one genius at the Disney studio. Dalí began work on *Destino* in January 1946[19] but only a few seconds of the film were completed; the many paintings and story sketches suggest an interesting project and it would have been a suitable subject for the package films that were to follow. John Hench was assigned as Dalí's assistant, because, he recalled:

I was able to speak a little French, which was about as bad as his [Dalí's] French. We hit it off very well, and Walt liked him ... It was a diurnal dream story, dealing with time and the impossibility of dealing with destiny. There was a ballet, a girl changes forms ... but it withered.

The paintings and story sketches – it is difficult to tell Dalí apart from Hench – are elaborate and detailed, full of Dalíesque iconography; broken statuary, deserted landscapes, lonely figures dwarfed by incongruous forms. The sketches indicate loss, decay and abandonment, and while they led to nothing complete, they add to the picture of destabilisation at the studio, a mood reinforced by the first film that Disney released after the war, *Make Mine Music* (1946).

This film has never been revived, and apart from some sections being shown on TV, is forgotten or confused with another package film released by the studio two years later, *Melody Time* (1948). Indeed, some of its parts were united with *Melody Time* and released, only in the United States, as *Music Land* (1955). At a rare screening of the entire film at a retrospective *Tribute to Walt Disney* at the National Film Theatre in 1970, David Rider said, 'Of the ten sections, seven are perfectly satisfactory...and in some cases they are quite excellent'.[20]

In contrast to the anarchy of *The Three Caballeros* this film displays a melancholy and sense of loss new to Disney. Mary Blair and John Hench were the art directors, with Elmer Plummer (who had designed the inspirational paintings of the mushrooms for the *Nutcracker Suite*). Art deco and surrealism form part of the disparate short films that make up the package, but it lacks the cohesion of its predecessor *Fantasia*. Whether Dalí affected the work of the studio or not, surreal imagery prevails in three of the items, with European sources evident in at least half of the sections; but the melancholy is new. There is also wit and satire, a legacy from the war films, and evidence of the guiding hand of Joe Grant, the production supervisor, and the astringency of Jack Kinney who directed four of the pieces. The obsession, however, with loss of love and of the loved one occurs in eight out of the film's ten short pieces. Since the film is so little known, and since it is a fascinating collection of pieces with both New and Old World connotations, it is worth examining in detail.

The art deco titling invites the audience to share in a world of dreams, since the opening image is of a cinema lit from top to bottom announcing the opening credits, with the popular artists from radio and film, whose voices Disney uses to give the film added publicity. As we go inside, lobby cards in the foyer continue the credits until we find ourselves in the auditorium, looking at a programme announcing '*Make Mine Music*: A Musical Fantasy in Ten Parts', and then the individual titles for the

first item appear. We are already encountering a film within a film, distanced not only by the wealth of opening captions but also by the individual poster captions that introduce each section. There is a world of difference here between what became known as 'the poor man's *Fantasia*' and *Fantasia* itself. That film boldly opened with one credit card only; this one opens with many, leading us by literacy into a fantasy less audacious, more uncertain.

The first item 'The Martins and the Coys', illustrating a popular hill-billy legend in traditional though unremarkable form, recalls the *Silly Symphonies*. The second item is 'Clair de Lune', abandoned from *Fantasia* (see Appendix A); it has been taken off the shelf and diminished with new popular music and lyrics, 'Blue Bayou', still contemplative and sad in mood. The delicacy and grace of the animation, based on Sylvia Holland and Josh Meador's inspirational sketches, depicts herons in stillness and in flight. The subtitle 'A Tone Poem' is apt, for the piece contrasts dark and light with little or no story content. There are colour

Sylvia Holland: Inspirational chalk drawing on black paper for 'Clair de Lune', an item that was intended for Fantasia, *but later released with new music and included in the package film* Make Mine Music *(1946). Josh Meador also provided inspirational pastel sketches.*
© Disney Enterprises, Inc.

Josh Meador: Landscape drawing. Joshua Meador (1911–1965) was one of Disney's most loyal animators and special effects artists. Courtesy Elizabeth Meador.

gradations from deep black through a range of blues to silver and white, some almost abstract, with technical virtuosity in the use of the multiplane camera and slow dissolves. The item, designed specifically for Debussy, is a revelation when shown with its original music, orchestrated and conducted by Stokowski.

The third item is 'All the Cats Join In' played by Benny Goodman and his orchestra, using limited animation in art deco style and telling the story of a bobbysoxer and her friends enjoying themselves at the local soda fountain. Pace, colour and styling are as lively as the music, an all-American piece owing nothing to Europe. Another tone poem, 'Without You' employs abstract imagery and visual metaphors such as rain and colours dissolving on a window pane that blend into tears and stars, a mixture of imagery without narrative. There is an attempt here to avoid personality animation, comedy, or any of the effects which the studio had used successfully in the past. The search is away from formulae, however debatable the taste; abstract expressionism and surrealism are present, and once again there is a reminder of Fischinger combined with Dalí. The tone is melancholy, matching the sadness of the popular ballad expressing loss of the loved one. The music by the Latin American composer Osvaldo Farres suggests that this was an item intended for one of the Latin American films; it echoes in style and colour the 'Baia' number in *The Three Caballeros*. There is also an echo of the experiments

Story sketch for 'Without You', a brief semi-abstract item from Make Mine Music.
© *Disney Enterpises, Inc.*

by Fischinger and others with the colour organ. The studio publicity of
the day announced that:

> The rise and fall of the voice, and its characteristic colour are
> completely welded to the image of scenes in sunshine and rain that
> the audience sees...a way will be found to determine colour schemes
> for voices, and in time people will refer to 'mauve whispers, taupe
> groans, orange yells' ...

The next item, echoing Currier and Ives baseball prints, illustrates a
well known American ballad 'Casey at the Bat' and is incomprehensible
to Europeans with no knowledge of baseball; it has the look of a comic
strip and relies on the narration by a popular film comedian Jerry
Colonna. The next piece is 'Two Silhouettes' or 'A Ballade Ballet' and
combines live action in silhouette of two classical ballet dancers with
animation. The latter is mostly special effects, mist, stars, Disneydust
and so on and there are two cupids who emerge from and open the
heart-shaped doors at the start of the piece. The studio publicity
announced:

> 'Two Silhouettes' is a unique blending of the arts expressed in animated
> paintings and combining the persuasive power of song with the
> rhythmic grace of the ballet. Dinah Shore will sing the title ballad ...

Eric Gurney: Models of 'Peter and the Wolf' from Make Mine Music. *The final version of the hero is less Russian.*
© *Disney Enterprises, Inc.*

with the ballet designed and interpreted by David Lichine and Riabouchinska (of the Ballets Russes) ...

This is Europe filtered through the Midwest; satire, comedy, caricature, have been abandoned for the Hallmark greeting card. Sylvia Holland's influence can be traced from inspirational sketches made on her return to Disney in 1946. Joe Grant said they 'tried a lot of trick photography, riding a tightrope ... a little sugary'. The resulting kitsch lacks the robust vulgarity which Germany lent even, for example, to the Beethoven section of *Fantasia*. Dinah Shore's delicate singing is welcome.

It is claimed that *Peter and the Wolf* had been intended as one of the replacement items for the extended *Fantasia*, though this is not certain. Prokofiev dedicated the piece to Disney, saying, on a visit to the studio in 1938, 'I have composed this with the hope that I would get to see you and that you would make a cartoon with my music'.[21] Sylvia Holland advised the artists on the Russian backgrounds which have a naive simplicity that is not matched by the over-articulate commentary. There is some fine animation and the snow scenes are beautifully rendered.

'After You've Gone' interprets Benny Goodman's jazz quartet in a swirl of metamorphosed instruments which dance in surrealistic skies and plunge into stylised seas. It is a bravura piece of animation, matching image to sound with confidence and precision. It was much praised by critics when the film was first released.

'Johnny Fedora and Alice Blue Bonnet' tells the story of two hats in love against a violent urban background. The style is magazine art, with the eponymous hero encountering road works, a pack of city dogs, a drunken tramp who takes him to a variety hall of doubtful repute which is raided by the police after a brawl. Johnny is abandoned in the gutter to be blown through the streets and almost lost down a drain in company with broken bottles and cans. Of course the story, sung by the Andrews

Sisters, ends happily, but the overriding mood is one of frustration, loss, and despair. Expressionistic use of colour and background is matched by the limited animation which underlines the tense, restless isolation of the city.

When satire was used, as in *The Dance of the Hours*, there was genuine understanding of, and love for, the dance form that was parodied. When opera is the target of satire, as in 'The Whale Who Wanted to Sing at the Met' the results are equally successful. It is the last item of the film and the longest at fourteen and a half minutes. It is also the most tragic of all Disney's films. Willie, the Whale who can sing in tenor, baritone and bass, is harpooned at the end and although we see him with harp, wings and halo 'in whatever heaven is preserved for creatures of the deep still singing in a hundred voices, each more golden than before ...'

Still: Willie the Whale singing Pagliacci in his imagined debut at the Metropolitan Opera House, New York; from 'The Whale Who Wanted to Sing at the Met', the final item in Make Mine Music. © *Disney Enterprises Inc.*

the overwhelming emotion is one of grief that he and his voice is lost to us for ever on earth.[22] So powerfully animated is the character of Willie, so skilful is the reality of his personality, so convincing his imagined début at the Metropolitan Opera House and his success there, that it comes as a shock when we return to the real situation where 'the stubborn deluded' impresario harpoons Willie at sea, believing him to have swallowed three opera singers. Nelson Eddy narrates and sings this short tragedy with commendable reserve and tongue-in-cheek dignity.

Make Mine Music was not a great success although audience research (with adults) indicated that a similar compilation film would be popular. Compilation was not new to Disney; he had been using it since *Fantasia*, but it was an economic necessity now, until he had made up his mind about the future direction of the studio. Jack Kinney, who directed four of the ten items, remembered that some artists thought Disney had lost interest in animation which, on *Make Mine Music*, gave them more freedom. Disney said 'The cartoon film wasn't flexible enough. It forced me to make either a cartoon short seven or eight minutes long or a feature seventy or eighty minutes long. And I had a lot of ideas I thought would be good if I could fit them between those two extremes'.[23] The eclecticism, the experimental work, the nervous tension, the satire, limited animation, stylisation and abstraction, the sadness, melancholy and sense of loss are all here in *Make Mine Music*. They vanished as soon as Disney felt secure enough to return to the safety of the full length feature. His staff were glad to give up the compilation films; the public kept asking for a full story again from Disney. I recall the intense public excitement when the studio announced that it would make *Cinderella* (1950).

There were, however, still four more years of the forties, and Disney needed revenue. The eclecticism continued, and there is a continuing sense of uncertainty. Other studios were winning the Academy Awards now, and a sharper graphic design was being employed by Disney's rivals at MGM and at Warners. The best shorts of this period came from those studios, and from new talents such as Chuck Jones and Tex Avery. Live action was beginning to dominate the scene at the Disney Studio. *Song of the South* (1946) was largely live action with brief cartoon inserts of the Uncle Remus stories. The animation is charming with anthropomorphised animal characters that take us back both to Europe and Africa (see Colour Plate 70). The backgrounds remind us of the work of the American artist Thomas Hart Benton (1889–1975). Against the advice of two of his closest colleagues, Joe Grant and Dick Huemer, Disney made *Fun and Fancy Free* (1947). This is a flaccid tale about a circus bear called Bongo with much repetition from earlier work. The second half retells an earlier Mickey Mouse short and is a version of 'Jack and the Beanstalk', with Donald Duck and Goofy sharing Mickey's adventure.

This brief survey of the decade following the thirties shows the paucity of material emanating from Europe. The choice of European work had been made ten years before and the use of that material evaporated in the less optimistic forties. The studio's work became interesting in quite a different way, as it cobbled together stories out of unfinished fragments, shorts, and even story sketches. This can be seen in a brief examination of the next compilation feature.

This was *Melody Time* (1948), which is understandably confused with its predecessor *Make Mine Music*, since it is also made up of short pieces with no apparent connecting thread. It lacks the unifying art deco style of the earlier film and the themes of isolation and loss are less evident. Indigenous stories form a proportion of the whole and a folklore consultant is credited. The debt to Europe is indirect, through Romantic imagery. Unlike the credits for the earlier film, which presented a sequence of art deco tableaux within the framework of a cinema, those for *Melody Time* are taken from various sources, including an animated paintbrush, a device dating back to the earliest days of animation, which links it to the magic of the artist-cum-conjuror that is a characteristic of that period.[24] This variety of imagery at the opening reflects the confusion of the film itself.

The first item 'Once Upon a Wintertime' is indebted to the American Christmas card and has some characteristic Mary Blair backgrounds (see Colour Plate 71). The effects animation is expressionistic; the landscape turns blue reflecting the young hero's misery, and later the sky becomes black, with clouds pursuing the hero in his bid to rescue his girl trapped on the ice. There is a reminder of Paul Grimault's animated film *Le Petit Soldat* (1947), which had wide circulation, though there is no direct evidence that the Disney artists saw the film.

'Bumble Boogie' follows, a boogie-woogie treatment of Rimsky Korsakov's *Flight of the Bumble Bee* which had been intended for the extended *Fantasia*. It is very different in design and story from the original treatment, and owes more to the abstract patterns of musical shapes that characterised the Benny Goodman piece 'After You've Gone' in *Make Mine Music*. The piano features as an opponent to the diminutive bee who finds the world of flowers and leaves turning into an instrumental nightmare. The transmogrifying shapes – piano keys becoming in turn petals, a moving staircase, a caterpillar, a giant cobra – occur at lightning speed. Abstraction and colour are reminiscent not only of Fischinger's work, but also of the anarchic imagery of the Latin American period, and the experimentation following Dalí's visit in 1946. Dalí's dream landscapes are present throughout, and particularly at the end. The piece is brief, violent, febrile. Nothing like it would ever come out of Disney animation again. Nor was this experimental work popular with the senior men remaining at the Studio. Milt Kahl, who later animated Shere Khan in *The Jungle Book* (1967) recalled seeing the rushes for 'Bumble

Dick Kelsey: Story sketch for 'Trees'
from Melody Time.
© *Disney Enterprises, Inc.*

Boogie' and said, 'I thought it was terrible, just terrible and ... it just rankled me, and Walt says 'What's the matter with you?' And I said, 'How any man could put his money in a piece of shit like that, I just can't understand it".

Mary Blair's romantic landscapes dominate 'Johnny Appleseed', a story about the real life pioneer John Chapman, who planted apple trees across the states of Ohio and Indiana. Disney supported Mary's designs, though the animators found it difficult to match her style. There is an echo of Grandma Moses in the deliberate naivety of Blair's work, but it is also reminiscent of other artists; Le Douanier Rousseau and Gauguin come to mind. The boldness of her colour and design attracted Walt Disney. Marc Davis, who worked closely with her said:

> She could put things together that no other colourist including Matisse could equal. She had very poor eyesight. She had seven pairs of glasses and contact lenses. Her colour was inside her – it just came naturally ... Our people didn't know how to interpret her flat images ... Walt was embarrassed by his lack of education, but her work *read* to him.

There follows the story of a naughty baby tug in New York Harbour, 'Little Toot', who redeems himself by helping a ship in distress. It was based on a successful American children's story by Hardie Gramatky

E.H. Shepard: Illustration (1931) for Kenneth Grahame's The Wind in the Willows. *Toad is 'the rower – a short, stout figure – splashing badly and rolling a good deal, but working his hardest'. Illustration by E.H. Shepard copyright under the Berne Convention. Reproduced by permission of Curtis Brown, London.*

Disney's likeable Toad as mountaineer: This sketch is seen briefly in the film, but plays no part in the book. Toad, with the voice of Eric Blore, is one of the most delightful English characters of any Disney film.
© Disney Enterprises, Inc.

and like the indigenous 'Casey' ballad in *Make Mine Music*, shows Disney's increasing use of American subjects.

Next there is a short item illustrating Joyce Kilmer's poem 'Trees'. The song has become debased through its immense popularity, but Disney is nothing if not a popular entertainer, and his artists see only the truth and feeling expressed in Kilmer's poem and Oscar Rasbach's music; there are moments of lyrical intensity expressed graphically which demonstrate the Disney artists' absorption of the European Romantic convention through film. Apart from some simple animation of animals and birds the item is expressed directly through the story sketches of one artist, Dick Kelsey, with special effects in the hands of Ub Iwerks. A storm is visualised with great economy; a landscape is revealed to be only a reflection in a water drop on a bough; an autumnal sky is, by symbiosis, a leaf blown away from a giant close shot to a long shot of leaves against a wintry sky. Never, in the whole canon of Disney art, has there been such a concentrated piece of direct impressionism, coupled with a deeply felt Romanticism that takes us directly back to Friedrich. The touch is precise, the montage confident, only wavering at the portentous ending with its religious overtones.

The next item is 'Blame it on the Samba', a reminder of the Latin American films, with Donald Duck and his Brazilian friend the parrot José Carioca in a zany mixture of animation and live action. It has the febrile energy of its predecessors and owes nothing to Europe. The seventh and final piece in *Melody Time* is 'Pecos Bill', the story of a boy, raised, Mowgli-like by coyotes, to become a hero of the Wild West. There are some delightful moments, but it has all been done before in other Disney films and there is a dire live action framework to this story, featuring Roy Rogers and his horse Trigger, an attempt to create audience interest through the use of a star name. The film ends abruptly.

After *Melody Time* Disney abandoned experiment. By the end of the forties, when the financial position had improved, he concentrated on live action films and, in animation, returned to projects initiated before the war. The economic means and the drive required for an animated feature exhausted him. Some of his talented artists had left during the strike, and others were called up for active service. Finally he turned back to old projects that had been initiated in the expansive days of the late thirties. One of these was Kenneth Grahame's *The Wind in the Willows* and it was squashed into a half hour film, the other half consisting of Washington Irving's *The Legend of Sleepy Hollow*. The result, *The Adventures of Ichabod and Mr. Toad* (1949), the last film of the decade, is an uneasy partnership of two classics, one English and one American. Even given half an hour, Grahame's plot is not sufficient for the Disney story artists; hastily told elements outside Grahame are introduced including a new character called Winkey, the owner of a shady tavern.

There is little opportunity to study either Rat, Mole or Badger, though there are some reminders of Ernest Shepard's drawings, and Toad himself is delightful, with the voice of Eric Blore, complemented by a Lancastrian horse called Cyril who looks remarkably like George Formby. Toad's escape from the Tower of London is also influenced by Shepard but there is no time to convey either Grahame's story or his celebration of Edwardian tranquillity. Basil Rathbone is given little opportunity as narrator; the riverside is barely glimpsed and the Wild Wood is ignored. Disney was not capable of understanding the story's lyricism or tenderness and he ignored the terror, though we have seen — and shall see — that his artists were able to absorb the Englishness of other works they adapted. The book concludes: 'He was indeed an altered Toad! After this climax the four animals continued to lead their lives, so rudely broken in by civil war, in great joy and contentment ...'.[25] The film ends with Toad going off in an aeroplane on another new craze.

The Legend of Sleepy Hollow by Washington Irving forms the second half of the film, offering a contrast between the Old World and the New. Bing Crosby narrates and sings with assurance and there are charming New England landscapes inspired by Mary Blair and John Hench. Ichabod's ride through the forest and his encounter with the Headless Horseman is splendid *Grand Guignol*. There is still a struggle to delineate the human form in animation; in an anonymous note attached to some story sketches for the film is the comment (which has the ring of the outspoken Milt Kahl): 'Looks like the guys are afraid to animate him [Ichabod] — Jesus, he's a tall skinny guy ... If the guys can't make a personality like this come across we're limited to mice and bunnies!'.

This comment sums up the late forties, for it turned Disney's attention back to full length animated feature films, which contained the equivalent of mice and bunnies. The uncertainty that followed the strike and the loss of economic confidence led to a wide variety of work from the studio, a change in personnel, a search for short-term results with limited animation and experimental visual expression. Disney was no longer able to maintain total control of his empire, and much animation was done quickly and while he was either away, as with *Dumbo* or concentrating on live-action films.[26]

Mention should be made of a film also released in 1949. This was *So Dear to My Heart*, filmed largely in live action and on location. It is a modest, unself-conscious work whose freshness is augmented by stylised cartoon sections of great charm. It is the story of of a small boy and his pet lamb on a farm in the Midwest. When in difficulties the young hero consults his scrap book in the loft, and the homiletic pictures come to life (see Colour Plate 72). Columbus and Robert Bruce are invoked as heroic adenturers who conquer adversity because, in the words of the song, they 'Stick-to-it-ivity'. The animation is spare, succinct, evocative

Still: 'Stick-to-it-ivity', a short animated scene from So Dear To My Heart. *European cartography, Japanese engravings and American cartooning come together in a tale of the courage of Columbus and Robert the Bruce.*
© *Disney Enterprises, Inc.*

of period maps and engravings, and the film was described by C.A. Lejeune in her *Observer* review on 22 September 1949 as Disney's 'best film for years, a lovely film and a touching film.' Disney did not interfiere with the live action shooting, and the director Harold Schuster commented that 'Disney was a joy to have around'.[27]

The decade of the nineteen forties is one of great creative and artistic interest and is ignored by the standard reference books, and by The Walt Disney Company. It is not 'Disney' enough, and is little drawn upon by the Disney merchandising for its own mythologising and iconography. There is also evidence that Disney was driven by public demand to a return to the European classics which had led to his greatest success at the end of the previous decade, and it is difficult to see how else to interpret the use of Grahame, Perrault, Carroll and Barrie. Work had been done on these stories as far back as 1938, so it is not surprising that Disney and his colleagues took up the European threads once more. Another aspect needs emphasising; his artists as well as the public demanded a return to the 'Disney' with which they were familiar. Journalism of the day bemoaned the lack of a traditional Disney film, and the adults who had seen *Snow White and the Seven Dwarfs* now had children of their own. The popular culture of which he was part was now dictating to Walt Disney its own demands. The audience addressed would also be recognised as increasingly divided into groups, juvenile, adolescent and adult. Teenagers had been discovered.

In the next decade Disney returned to the European fairy tale and to the European classic for his animation; he also created a three-dimensional fairy tale of his own which, though inspired by many European sources, was completely American – Disneyland.

Notes

1. This is based on the author's visits to the Walt Disney Studio Library during July 1985. The system of issuing books using a card with the borrowers' names on it was useful for research, since it enabled identification of individual readers for each book. The system was continued until the library was disbanded in 1986, though some of the collection is still held in the WDI Information Research Center.

2. Mark Langer, 'Regionalism in Disney Animation: Pink Elephants and Dumbo', *Film History*, Vol. 4, 1990, 305–321. See also Karen Merritt, 'Narrative and Dumbo', unpublished paper, 1st annual conference, Society for Animation Studies, University of California at Los Angeles, 28 October 1989.

3. Good accounts are in Thomas, *The Walt Disney Biography*, 129–133 and in Holliss and Sibley, *The Disney Studio Story*, 42–45. See also Harvey Deneroff, 'The Disney Strike', unpublished paper, 3rd annual conference, Society for Animation Studies, Rochester, New York, 5 October 1991.

4. Murray Ross, *Stars and Strikes: Unionisation of Hollywood* (New York: Columbia University Press, 1941), 193 and 211.

5. Otto Friedrich, *City of Nets* (New York: Harper, 1987) 61–68.

6. Leslie Cabarga, *The Fleischer Story* (1976. Rpt., New York: Da Capo, 1988) 150, and Harvey Deneroff, '"We Can't Get Much Spinach": The Organisation and Implementation of the Fleischer Animation Strike', *Film History* Vol. 1, No. 1, 1987, 1–14.

7. *The American Animated Cartoon*, ed. Gerald and Danny Peary (New York: Dutton, 1980) 92.

8. Under the general title *Story Numbers* dated 12 October 1943, a typescript of twelve pages and headed 'Joe & Dick' in ms, contains five hundred and fifty three story titles; these include features, several hundred shorts and a number of military training films. Ninety seven can be identified by title as emanating from Europe and include many classics such as *Treasure Island* (made into a live-action feature in England in 1950), *Hansel and Gretel, Ivanhoe, The Three Musketeers, Robinson Crusoe, Swiss Family Robinson* (live-action feature 1960), *Arabian Nights* (The Walt Disney Company released *Aladdin* in the USA for Christmas 1992), *Peter Pan* (animated feature 1953), *Alice in Wonderland* (animated feature 1951), *Chanticleer* (the characters adapted for The Walt Disney Company animated feature *Robin*

Hood 1973), *Cinderella* (animated feature 1950), *Don Quixote, Midsummer Night's Dream, Pinafore* [sic], *Rose and the Ring, The Sword in the Stone* (animated feature 1963), *The Odyssey (Adventures of Ulysses), Idylls of the King* and many others. Courtesy Joe Grant (see Appendix B).

9. See Charles Solomon, *The Disney That Never Was* (New York: Hyperion, 1995) 162–168 for some remarkable sketches of the *Don Quixote* project. Joe Grant hoped for renewed interest in the story in 1998 (phone conversation with Joe Grant 4 January 1998).

10. Sidney Franklin, letter to Walt Disney, 20 April 1935. Walt Disney correspondence.

11. Ollie Johnston and Frank Thomas, *Walt Disney's Bambi* (New York: Stewart, Tabori and Chang, 1990).

12. On each ocasion of the six times the film has been seen in the cinema by the author, a child has had to be removed or comforted. At a lecture given by the author (Heritage Club, Buxton, 21 March 1991) two middle aged guests recalled the shock that the scene had caused them as children and the memory that had haunted them all their lives. The death is also remembered as taking place on screen, when in fact we only hear the shot that kills Bambi's mother.

13. Felix Salten, *Bambi*, trans. Whittaker Chambers (1928. Rpt., London: Jonathan Cape, 1961), 13.

14. Ibid., 101.

15. Ken Anderson maintained that Disney was a live-action film producer *manqué*. Interview with author, La Canada, California, 10 May 1985. When he had shown *To Kill a Mockingbird* (1962) to his family at home, Disney said, 'Why can't I make films like that?' Diane Disney Miller, Interview with author, Encino, California, 3 August 1986.

16. Roald Dahl, *The Gremlins*, illus. Walt Disney Studios (New York: Random House, 1943), (London: Collins, 1943).

17. Richard Shale, *Donald Duck Joins Up* (Ann Arbor, Michigan: UMI Press).

18. See Canemaker, *Before the Animation Begins*, 115–142 for a detailed biography of Mary Blair (1911–1978). See also the author's 'Mary Blair: An Indelible Imprint', *Animation Magazine* Vol. 8, No. 5, July 1995, 58–61.

19. David Smith, Walt Disney Archivist, letter to author, 28 August 1991.

20. David Rider, *Tribute to Walt Disney* (London: National Film Theatre, 1970).

21. Prokofiev, quoted in Thomas, *The Walt Disney Biography*, 158. Prokofiev visited Disney at the Studio on 28 February 1938. Letter to author from David Smith, 28 August 1991. The date of Prokofiev's visit suggests that the piece would have been chosen as part of the extended *Fantasia* repertoire.

22. The death of Willie caused distress for young members of the audience at its screening for a Disney retrospective *Disney Magic* (Los Angeles County Museum) 1 August 1986.

23. Walt Disney, quoted by Diane Disney Miller, *Walt Disney* (London: Odhams, 1958), 184.

24. Crafton, *Before Mickey*, 86.

25. Grahame's book was first published in 1908. This quotation comes from the 1963 Methuen reprint, 283, with E. H. Shepard's illustrations, which had first appeared in 1931. There was a copy with his pictures in the Walt Disney Studio Library.

26. Disney's increased commitment to live action films, many based on European sources, is beyond the scope of this study. He had achieved his first success with live action and animation in his *Alice* Comedies from 1923, and was fully aware of

the use of live action for special effects and rotoscope work. There was live action footage of the orchestra in *Fantasia* and live action and animation in *The Reluctant Dragon* (1941) and in the Latin American films.

Walt Disney produced many live action films either in England or Europe, or based on English and European sources. They include: *Treasure Island* (1950), *The Story of Robin Hood* (1952), *The Sword and the Rose* (1953), *Rob Roy, The Highland Rogue* (1954), *20,000 Leagues Under the Sea* (1954), *Darby O'Gill and the Little People* (1959), *Third Man on the Mountain* (1959), *Kidnapped* (1960), *Swiss Family Robinson* (1960), *Greyfriars Bobby* (1961), *In Search of the Castaways* (1962), *Miracle of the White Stallions* (1963), *The Moon-Spinners* (1964), *The Three Lives of Thomasina* (1964), *Emil and the Detectives* (1964), *Mary Poppins* (1964) – which contained some animation – and *The Fighting Prince of Donegal* (1966).

27. Harold Schuster, quoted in Maltin, *The Disney Films*, 190.

CHAPTER 9

From *Cinderella* to Disneyland

C inderella (1950) was the first animated feature film with a continuous narrative since *Bambi* eight years earlier, and it led to an economic success greatly exceeding that of *Snow White and the Seven Dwarfs*. Journalism of the period indicates relief that The Walt Disney Studio was returning to what popular cultural expectations demanded. 'A film even more enchanting than *Snow White and the Seven Dwarfs*' and 'presented in the manner that those who loved *Snow White and the Seven Dwarfs* will appreciate' are typical press comments not from the studio itself but from contemporary independent reports.[1]

The artists working for Disney all agreed that there was general satisfaction with the return to a single story feature; the public was tired of the package films, the compilations and the mixtures of live-action and animation, the experimental work of the middle forties, which had not done well at the box office. A generation was growing up that remembered the older Disney films, and the reissue of *Snow White and the Seven Dwarfs* reminded the public of its own and Disney's past.

Cinderella's success gave Disney increased confidence and led to his creation of Disneyland and to his manipulation of television as a means of purveying his product. In 1955 Disneyland opened. It was an immediate success. Disney exploited television, using it to promote his cinema releases; this brilliant move showed his ability to utilise new technologies while his fellow producers in Hollywood were still afraid of the new medium.

Every film of the nineteen fifties, every venture, made money apart from *Alice in Wonderland* (1951) and *Sleeping Beauty* (1959). This was the decade in which Disney returned to the classics and to Europe and European markets. He visited Europe in 1946, in 1949 and again in 1951. He was searching for universal themes once more, although there was doubt about which subject should be chosen first. Both *Peter Pan* and *Alice in Wonderland* had been in various stages of production since the first flush of success after *Snow White and the Seven Dwarfs*, but they had been shelved during the forties. Disney's choice of *Cinderella* was an arbitrary one. Jack Kinney, who had spent months working up a story board presentation of *Peter Pan* was disappointed when Disney chose *Cinderella* instead:

> Each board [for *Peter Pan*] carried more than one hundred sketches, close to 40,000 sketches representing a tremendous number of man

Hermann Vogel: 'King Rother puts the shoes on the princess's feet'; illustration from Epics and Romances of the Middle Ages *(1882). One of many variations on the Cinderella story.*

Ludwig Richter: Illustration for 'Cinderella' in Grimms' Fairy Tales. *'You tame pigeons, you turtle doves, and all you birds in the sky, come and help me...' Disney's heroine is also helped by the birds – and some valiant mice.*

hours ... It was a two-and-a-half-hour performance with no interruptions from the assembled group. At the end, I leaned on the last storyboard, completely pooped ... There was a long pause. The only sound was that of Walt's tapping fingers ... Finally his mind was made up. With a final accent on the arm of his chair, he announced, 'Y'know, I've been thinking of *Cinderella*.[2]

Cinderella (1950)

The decision to make this the first full length single story feature since *Bambi* is not surprising, in view of the story's popularity. In England, it is the most popular pantomime of all, and theatre managements can guarantee at least a ten per cent increase in receipts over any other show, because of the title alone. The universality of the tale has been noted, and there are many variations.[3] The Disney story men used Perrault's French version. Grimm has no fairy godmother, no pumpkin coach and gold rather than glass slippers. It contains cruel images which have neither been absorbed into the English pantomime tradition nor into the retelling of the story in book form. These images of punishment include the step-sisters cutting off toe and heel – at the stepmother's insistence – to accommodate the gold slipper. In Grimm the birds at Cinderella's wedding peck out the eyes of the ugly sisters, even though, as Ruth Bottigheimer points out, 'the girls' mutilation of their own toes and heels ... would seem punishment enough'.[4] Disney turned to the gentler tale of Perrault, which had been first published in 1697, though he borrowed the idea of Cinderella's animal helpers from Grimm, and invested the stepmother with the sadism that the German brothers make an explicit part of their tale.

The story reflected Disney's own career in its rags to riches theme, though his personality bore little resemblance to the passive heroine. Rather, it reflected a wish fulfilment on his part about the public role that he was to play. His public persona was designed to offer a masculine equivalent to the personality created in Cinderella, sweetness and kindness – in particular towards animals – being predominant. From this period it becomes more difficult to obtain primary source material about Disney; for example, the story conference discussion notes become less frequent. As he led the studio and the company to greater economic success, so he became more remote, relying on publicity to promote the avuncular image that was being promulgated through his new television shows. He made an admirable TV host and anchor man, settling comfortably into the role of public storyteller, and adapting to the new medium with characteristic aplomb. However, as 'Uncle Walt' came to be recognised by the American public, so the actual Walt Disney disappeared from public view.

Cinderella also contains the survival theme which is an element of all the features. John Hench, who was responsible with Mary Blair for the film's colour and styling, commented that 'artists can set our universe for us and all things revolve around survival, being kicked out of paradise and getting back in'. The film also represents Disney's own power of survival. The European influences though, unlike those in *Snow White and the Seven Dwarfs*, are interpreted entirely by American artists. The powerful creative Europeans had died or had left the studio, and the film is influenced by the style of cinema from the previous decade. Much depended on the new feature and it was largely shot in live action first, to avoid the expense of lengthy and costly animation. 'Only the animals were left as drawings, and story reels were made of those sketches to find the balance with the rest of the picture', as Frank Thomas and Ollie Johnston recalled.[5] Because of this there is visual uniformity throughout; the film does not contain dichotomies of style such as those noted in *Dumbo* or *Bambi* and although there is some French influence, the atmosphere is expressionistic and Germanic, filtered through Hollywood's own genre of *film noir* (see Colour Plate 74).

In spite of its colour, the feeling is dark, from the opening shot onwards. This is a close up of the inevitable Disney tome, heavily decorated. A theatrical light floods across it as the leaves open by magic. Here is an encapsulation of the Disney *œuvre*; the showman, entertainer, magician working the lights and creating magical effects and at the same time revealing the mystery of fantasy through the locked world of literature. The book as such is dark, shut up, bound by its own convention. In itself it is of no interest. Bejewelled and embossed it takes on meaning as an object from which essence can be extracted, like a magic lamp or box of delights. The dark colours prevail, blue, a deep red and purple in particular predominating; the evil stepmother is first seen from below outside a window, her head in shadow, her eyes smouldering in a similar manner to those of the cat Lucifer who is her feline companion. The suggestion that cat and mistress are familiar and witch is not made explicit nor does the stepmother have any special powers, but the comparison is nevertheless present, lending an undercurrent of fear to the stepmother's scenes. What she may do is always more alarming than what she appears to do. Expressionism enters at many levels – when the stepmother first guesses that Cinderella is the mysterious girl at the ball, her hatred spreads outwards till the whole room, the world she inhabits, becomes dark. She is powerfully animated and a successor, though less terrifying, to the Queen in *Snow White and the Seven Dwarfs*. She is also a forerunner of Maleficent in *Sleeping Beauty*, and is voiced by the same actress Eleanor Audley. In another example of expressionism, the shadows of a window spread across Cinderella's body like the bars of a prison, as she is forced reluctantly to approach the darkness of the bed in which the stepmother lies.

Other reminders of the German cinema are the angled shots of stairs and landings seen from a mouse's point of view as Cinderella's friends attempt to carry a heavy key up to her attic – the stepmother has locked her in, to prevent her from trying on the glass slipper. In a scene which presents all three participants in dramatic action, there is a shot of the stepmother climbing the stairs as we would see her from above were we Cinderella. She is in darkness, her face in shadow, only her eyes alight, the forehead black and masklike. We cut to a medium close shot of the mice looking down at us and at her, and then move into the attic room where Cinderella is brushing her hair; the angles and viewpoints change swiftly from subjective to objective and the audience observes the action through both means. There is a fluidity here which depends on the use of live action techniques and which is responsible for the richness of the visual narrative. It has a filmic thrust that keeps story and the subjective-objective relationshipo between viewer and film constantly engaged.

German influences include the castle, its columns, staircases, curtains and above all its rows and rows of guards dwarfing the isolated figure of Cinderella, likened to the military rally in Leni Riefenstahl's *Triumph of the Will* (1936). Jonathan Rosenbaum has traced Riefenstahl's influence elsewhere in Disney[6] though the artists themselves saw only the need, as Claude Coats remembered it, to 'emphasise the story'. John Hench pointed out the importance of underlining Cinderella's isolation and loneliness at the palace, 'to theatricalise, to show the baroque, the size and the exaggeration'. In this scene Hollywood cinema is also recalled in the huge staged musical numbers of Busby Berkeley.

Whether for economic or stylistic reasons, the screen is dependent on the characters in action, with much use of the close up or two shot. The *mise-en-scène* is spare apart from an elaborate set piece with a great deal of activity, when the mice and birds make Cinderella's ball gown, a reminder of the house cleaning sequence in *Snow White and the Seven Dwarfs*. On the whole the backgrounds are sketched in, using Mary Blair's inspirational paintings for colour and design. Claude Coats mentioned the research undertaken by his colleagues John Hench and Mary Blair who travelled to France to obtain firsthand impressions of country houses, farms and general atmosphere. There are reminders of Fragonard's insubstantial gardens and romanticised vistas in the opening shots with dripping foliage, and later in the garden where Cinderella meets her Fairy Godmother.[7]

The mice scenes are reminiscent of Beatrix Potter, whose work was widely admired in the United States.[8] In *The Tale of Samuel Whiskers* we follow the misfortunes of Tom Kitten behind the walls, when he falls into the clutches of rats, and in *Cinderella* we go behind walls and down mouse holes as we follow the adventures of the mouse heroes Gus and Jaq. In *The Tailor of Gloucester* mice are kept under tea cups by the cat Simpkin and in *Cinderella* Lucifer the cat does the same thing with Gus, the newcomer mouse. There is a mouse Cinderella in Potter's *A Cinderella Fantasy* which was an early idea for an illustrated book. We are reminded too of Aesop and his fable of the Town Mouse and the Country Mouse, which Disney had animated in 1936 as *The Country Cousin* in the *Silly Symphony* series.

The model for Cinderella herself is, of course, Snow White. The weakness in the animation of the human figure is more noticeable in the new film, in spite of increased sophistication with the use of rotoscope. Cinderella, though more convincing as a moving figure than Snow White, less gauche, less crudely drawn, is just as two dimensional. Contemporary reviewers commented that she was 'as nice a girl as you could meet anywhere in an advertisement for wheat flakes' (*New Statesman*) or 'dismally stiff' (*Observer*). Disney was still seeking the feminine ideal, imitating the real through rotoscope, instead of finding the truthful through the freedom of animation. The ideology of the late forties and early fifties is expressed in the Disney artists' attempt to create an idealised figure. She is the dutiful heroine who must stay at home and do all the housework; an example of Hollywood's reflection of post-war society's wish that American women would return to their pre-war domestic subserviance. She must also be seen to be an idealised figure who, though a skivvy, has to remain glamorous. Thus Disney imitates commercial Hollywood's aim to recreate life in its own image.

As popular artist Disney picked up on artistic styles of an earlier period. We have seen, for example, how the illustrated picture-book style of the early twentieth century influenced Disney's work of the nineteen thirties. Art deco, too, of the twenties and thirties was used by the Disney artists in the forties. In the new decade, Disney picked up on Hollywood *film noir* and what lies beneath the sub-text of *Cinderella* is its parallels with *film noir*; its darkened mirror reflection of reality, with heroines locked into a nightmare role of passivity. Although the two films are ten years apart, there are similarities between Hitchcock's *Rebecca* (1940) and *Cinderella* in the portrayal of Cinderella/Stepmother and the second Mrs De Winter/Mrs Danvers. The cartoon heroine (with the voice of Ilene Woods) looks and sounds like Joan Fontaine who plays the second Mrs De Winter. The voice of the stepmother (Eleanor Audley) sounds like Judith Anderson, who played the housekeeper Mrs Danvers in Hitchcock's film. The costume, stance and movement of both women are strikingly similar (see Colour Plate 73). The use of stairs and shadows remind us of the trapped heroine in *The Spiral Staircase* (1945). The nightmare of Cinderella's subservient position is also expressed dramatically through medium close shots when the ugly sisters attack her and destroy the dress that the mice have made for her. This is followed by an equally startling use of light and dark as the heroine runs sobbing away into the darkness and out into the garden. Her isolation is expressed in design. The Fairy Godmother is as convincing in movement and delineation as Cinderella herself is not – here is an ideal figure, but there is no struggle to idealise. Expressionism again is noted in the flight from the castle after midnight, with black and red riders chasing Cinderella's coach till it collapses and turns back into a pumpkin (see Colour Plate 75); as the romance leaves our heroine, so colour is drained out of the image to a monochrome grey.

Reviewing a revival of the film in 1991, Anthony Lane of *The Independent* wrote:

It somehow escapes the confines of the Disney tradition. There are moments which inhale the atmosphere of real films, or at least that particular brand of reality practised by American cinema of the period. ...Disney is still unsurpassed as an introduction to cinema; great simplicity is wedded to the first, gobsmacking realisation of what it is to have your feelings stretched and pummelled, and none of it against your will.[9]

Alice in Wonderland (1951)

'They talked me into making it' Disney told his colleague Jack Cutting, and Marc Davis said 'It's hard to make that transference to the screen ... all these visiting ladies would say, "Oh, Mr Disney, when will you do *Alice*?".' Disney felt bound to make the film although he did not feel comfortable with transferring the text to the screen. He thought the film was a failure and blamed Carroll; many of the artists concerned shared Disney's view.

> He had a date with destiny ... yet I don't think Walt ever found a way to get a handle on it (Jim Algar). None of us understood it (Ken Anderson). An awfully weak story, the picture doesn't have any substance (Milt Kahl). It didn't seem to flow (Bill Cottrell).

Even the most sensitive and articulate of Disney's associates, men like Marc Davis and Joe Grant, found it difficult. Marc Davis felt that the original was not well served, and Joe Grant pointed out that 'Walt couldn't understand the nonsense idea and ... the idea of peace was missing in Alice ... It was a bad time; Walt sort of lost interest and it became esoteric and out of his ken'.

The film had a long history. Disney had used a live child surrounded by cartoon characters in his first series the *Alice* Comedies (1923–1927), though these had no connection with Carroll's work. He then agreed to make an animated feature with Mary Pickford as a live Alice in the mid 1930s, but was uncertain about the scheme and then was unable to obtain the rights, since another film version was being made by Paramount (1933).[10] The United States was still in the throes of the 'Alice' fever occasioned by the arrival in New York of the eighty year old Alice Liddell for the celebrations in 1932 of the centenary of Carroll's birth. Disney produced a Mickey Mouse short called *Thru the Mirror* in 1936, in which Mickey dreams of climbing through the looking glass like Alice and having strange adventures with, among other things, a pack of cards.

It was not until after the success of *Snow White and the Seven Dwarfs* that Disney began serious work on his version in 1938. A long analysis of the book was made by a story artist Al Perkins, who concluded that

'To make a successful picture, we must get the spirit of the book onto the screen...rather than merely reproducing the appearance of the characters (as Paramount did)'. The project received much attention and an English artist David Hall (1905–1964) made over 400 extraordinary paintings and sketches for it which were never used.[11]

Little is known of David Hall beyond the fact that he was born in Ireland and emigrated to America. After leaving Disney in 1940 he worked as art director for MGM and 20th Century Fox, producing set designs for costume epics such as *Quo Vadis* (1951) and *The Greatest Story Ever Told*, on which he was working when he died of a heart attack at the age of 58 in 1964. Hall's pictures are highly idiosyncratic, packed with energy and imagination. They exhibit an understanding both of the dreamlike oddity of Alice's adventures, and of their possible realisation in animated form. He also presents aspects of the nightmare that hovers behind Carroll. His pictures show Alice as a child moving in both space and time – she appears four times in different sizes as she falls down a rabbit hole of roots, waterfalls and underground stars and sun. We see her growing larger and smaller in a series of sketches that indicate brilliantly how the animation of the figure would appear.

Little of Hall's work remains in the final version, although his talking 'Drink Me' bottle is transferred into the Talking Doorknob, which allowed an opportunity for puns – 'You did give me quite a turn' it says to Alice. Dinah, Alice's cat, is also in Hall's pictures, and she appears at the beginning of the Disney film. Hall's White Rabbit, too, has spectacles while Tenniel's does not, and these are retained in the final version. Hall's surrealism permeates the drawings, with hoses and shears trimming the Queen's garden unaided, counterpanes with eyes appearing to underline the dreamlike quality of the Mad Hatter's Tea Party. Hall's pictures are a delight and their quality may be seen in the Methuen edition of 1986.[12] Gordon Legg also provided inspirational paintings for the film. He painted a series of water-colour and gouache pictures of Alice, the Mock Turtle and Gryphon (see Colour Plate 76), and the garden of the Queen of Hearts. These capture in a precise way the dreamy lunacy of Carroll.

The artists kept trying to add gags of their own to Carroll and Disney asked them to return to the text. From the story meetings of 1938 and 1939 we can observe the way Disney used his sources and manipulated them for the mass audience which he interpreted as similar to himself. The confidence and optimism of the Disney of the thirties changed to a less assertive perception, with the result that the film becomes a curious mixture of reverence for its original and diverse transatlantic interpretations of it. The assumptions that Disney made and his utilisation of Carroll must be seen in their context, the hectic gestation period not only of *Pinocchio* and *Fantasia* but also of *Bambi*.

At a story conference as early as 10 December 1938 Disney commented: 'When you get down to it and analyse it, it was just a book to the people of that period. It was just a screwball book. Today it is kind of old and punny [sic]'. At the same meeting fear was expressed that 'the authorities on *Alice*' might object to the Disney version:

Joe: If there is a Carroll society, we'd better bring them in.

Walt: To hell with them. Ignore them. They are liable to bother you. We can get the spirit of the book.

The following month on 14 January 1939 he said:

It must be funny, I mean funny to an American audience. To hell with the English audiences or the people who love Carroll ... I want to put my money into something that will go into Podunk, Iowa, and they will go in and laugh at it ...

Here lies the complexity of the Disney adaptation of European sources; we have the arrogance of the American populariser with the optimism of the New World – before the war and its economic hardship brought a reconsideration of alternative ways of using animation – when *Snow White and the Seven Dwarfs* was breaking box office records all over the world. In the same year, while discussing a short Donald Duck subject, involving spoofs of old masters, he said:

You could make reproductions [of the spoof old masters with Donald Duck]. I'd like to have a set myself for a den or something. A lot of people would be crazy to get them. The ones that holler bloody murder, we don't give a damn about them. The controversy is swell publicity. The public at large is going to get a big kick out of it.[13]

With the *Alice* project he was contending with 'culture' of which he was afraid and for which he had such contempt as a populariser, and at the same time adding the brusque confidence of the New World and his own technological sophistication. He kept referring to the 'spirit' of Carroll but wanted to 'throw out the English expressions that are too English'. However, at the meeting on 14 January 1939, when a colleague Dorothy Blank suggested that Alice might be a modern American child Disney was quick to reply, 'She'll be English. We won't let the English think she isn't', and then he went on to criticise the story men and women about their lack of humour:

You haven't improved on the book; I would rather do it the way it is in the book ... When you get through with the damn thing it's going to be *Alice in Wonderland* and an *Alice in Wonderland* that everyone can like and enjoy ... and I know for one thing as a kid, I got a big

John Tenniel (above): Illustration for Through the Looking Glass and What Alice Found There *(1872). 'Now let's consider who it was that dreamed it all.' By arrangement with Macmillan Children's Books, London.*

John Tenniel (below): Illustration for Alice's Adventures in Wonderland *(1865). '"There's plenty of room!" said Alice indignantly, and she sat down in a large arm-chair.' By arrangement with Macmillan Children's Books, London.*

kick out of the characters ... Gees, I think you've got to get closer to the book.

When examining Tenniel, Disney said they would 'have to sort of adapt Tenniel's drawings to our own style. I think cute little colouring would add fascination to it' (22 March 1939). Discussion centred upon Alice herself, and the kind of 'good English' that Disney wanted her to speak. Bill Martin commented on the difficulty of adhering to Tenniel. 'The minute we depart,' he said, 'from that doleful sort of worn out look that the character has in the Tenniel illustrations, you have lost the Tenniel character' (6 May 1939). By November Disney was losing interest. 'I don't think there would be any harm in letting this thing sit for a while. Everyone is stale now ... I still feel that we can stick close to *Alice in Wonderland* and make it look like it and feel like it.'

By 1941 Disney considered using a live action girl, because of the difficulties of animation and because she was so central to the story, but dropped the idea later. This is all symptomatic of his uncertainty during the forties and it led him to invite the psychoanalyst Joseph Wood Krutch to offer some comments on the work. In 1945 Aldous Huxley came to work at the studio. His screenplay treatment for the film, lodged at the Walt Disney Archives, is a long and complex story involving a cruel governess, Dodgson himself being teased by undergraduates on account

Walt Disney and Europe

of his stutter, and Alice confessing to Ellen Terry how she coped with her fear by pretending to be in Wonderland. Queen Victoria also comes into the plot. Huxley attended the story meetings, making suggestions to Disney and his colleagues, but nothing came of this treatment; the idea of Huxley, Disney and Carroll combining through the medium of animation is a fascinating one but Huxley's ideas were very different from Disney's, and 'His vision was so bad that I don't know if he could see a cartoon on the screen' was Bill Cottrell's memory of him, and Joe Grant recalled that 'He was almost blind. I had to lead him to the car. He had no business to be brought in. Walt thought it was a good idea – to get a 'name' – silly'.

Various further treatments exist in the Walt Disney Archives, including variations on Huxley's framework, but by 1949 a story outline of sixteen scenes was written that is very like the final film. A scene with the Mock Turtle and Gryphon, however, was deleted. Discussion, analysis and illustration of the *Alice* theme continued from the late thirties until the film received its world première at the Leicester Square theatre, London, on 26 July 1951, which Disney and his child star, Kathryn Beaumont attended.[14] Disney was cautious even then; in a letter to his London representative Perce Pearce he said, 'I think it is about as good as can be done with it. I think it is going to be an exciting show. While it does have the tempo of a three-ring circus, it still has plenty of entertainment and it should satisfy everyone except a certain handful who can never be satisfied'.[15]

Disney tried to broaden the stories' appeal visually by slapstick and by a frenetic pace, not so much because he did not understand Carroll, but because he was afraid of Carroll, afraid of his quiet wit, his old-fashioned 'punny' humour, his gentle unfolding of events in a prose which matches the curious atmosphere of a dream bordering on the edge of nightmare. Disney was sympathetic to the dream state that the books invoke – both *Wonderland* and *Looking Glass* are drawn upon in the film – and spoke of this at an early conference: 'She thinks she dozes off, but woke up and saw this rabbit. That's the way a dream affects me. I dream that I am lying awake in bed and can't sleep ... Sometimes I keep dreaming all night. Gee! I'm sure sleeping.' (10 December 1938).

Disney's *Alice in Wonderland* is the last experimental work to be launched by the studio, and it is the late forties, the compilation films and the collections of stories flung together from Latin America which are the real bases for this curious film. For all its apparent homage to Carroll and to Tenniel it is really the most American of all the feature films for it finds an American equivalent to Carroll in its frantic dash from scene to scene. There is no Germanic influence. Certainly there is surrealism, dating back to *Dumbo* (1941) and to Dalí and the musical compilation films *Make Mine Music* (see Colour Plate 77) and *Melody*

Time. The surreal quality matches Carroll, particularly the conclusion which presents a kaleidoscopic jumble of images; the cards, led by the Queen of Hearts, chase Alice through a bleak Daliesque landscape reminiscent of that in the 'After You've Gone' section from *Make Mine Music*. There is also a reminder of the chaos at the end of *The Three Caballeros*, where the bombardment of sound and image exhausts, though Carroll holds Disney in check by a more balanced pace.

Disney is also echoing himself; the blooms in Disney's Garden of Wild Flowers sing and unite to cast Alice out of their Eden. This is a reminder of the musical flowers which terrify the protagonist in 'Bumble Boogie' from *Melody Time*. The trees through which Alice searches for the White Rabbit echo the stylised trees in 'Johnny Appleseed' and 'Trees' both also from *Melody Time*. The horror of nightmare is suggested when Alice finds herself moving in slow motion in her flight from her pursuers. Her adventure in the Tulgey Wood is her loneliest; lost, she is surrounded by creatures who remain alien but unlike the animals in Snow White's forest, they are unable to comfort her, dissolving like the tears they shed for her plight.

The 'three-ring circus' element is part of the film's strength; the anarchic, hectic pace, the vaudeville turns of the animals and characters, are mixed together with some attempt at English charm, or what is understood to be English charm and decorum. The characters speak in a variety of English and American accents.[16] The conflicting visual and verbal elements lend the film a dangerously poised elegance, with a threat of chaos lurking round the corner. Its episodic nature, criticised by both the Disney artists and the critics, comes from Carroll, but the density of background designs helps to produce a unity and depth. Once again it is to Mary Blair that we turn, seeing, from an examination of her original sketches, how closely her colour and design is maintained in the final film version (see Colour Plate 78). She was, with Claude Coats and John Hench, responsible for the colour and styling. Ken Anderson and Don Da Gradi, another unsung Disney artist, were also in the same unit.

The Alice that Disney finally decided to use was a cartoon figure, based on close observation, through rotoscoping, of a young English actress called Kathryn Beaumont, who first began working on the role when she was ten. She had read the book and recalled that her child interpretation of the character was her own. She had no voice coaching. She was filmed in live action and friends who saw the film recognised her characteristics.

The English countryside at the opening and closing of the film was carefully styled; there are no topographical mistakes like the American fencing in *Toad*. The animation is also richer than in *Cinderella*, less coarse, the *mise-en-scène* less concerned with the close up and dramatic interaction of characters. Before she goes down the rabbit hole Alice sings the song 'A World of my Own'; groups of flowers sway in the wind in long shot and when Alice lies down they bend and sway over her on a cut to a medium close shot at ground level so that we sense, with the child, the feeling of being close to the earth and seeing the natural world from the child's point of view. This scene, animated by Eric Larson, has a grace in its movement and pace which is lacking elsewhere, but Alice herself is one of the few Disney heroines to succeed as a cartoon character. Her adventures, the changes of size and the opportunities of displaying technical virtuosity add to the interest, but it is ultimately the acerbity of vaudeville, the piling up of assorted acts presented with a visual variety drawn from the experimental years, that give the film its density.

The struggle to reinterpret the original is not completely realised. Disney who had earlier wanted the White Knight to appear periodically as 'a sympathetic character', complained that it lacked 'heart'.[17] Seen today, the film grows in stature, refreshingly free from the cloying sentimentality that mars the Disney *œuvre*. It was not a success when first released, and was greeted with some hostility by the British press. William Whitebait of the *New Statesman* (4 August 1951), never willing to praise Disney, said 'This Disney film – almost his worst, by the way, on any grounds – has reduced adventure to a feeble series of 'turns' and repeated every cliché in the Disney repertoire.' He concluded his long review with 'This million-pound ineptitude deserves nothing but boos, and I wish cinema audiences were in the habit of according them'. Whitebait was unable to see any of the American qualities brought to the film, though other critics were less hostile, finding much to praise. Richard Mallett in *Punch* is worth quoting in some detail:

> I found much of it enjoyable and funny. It seems to me that the atmosphere of a dream, which is undeniably the atmosphere of the Alice stories, has been caught very often in the right way, even when the precise details of what is used to suggest it have been newly invented and were not thought of by either Carroll or Tenniel...I say it's brilliantly entertaining nonsense abounding in the right kind of comic ingenuity, and that a careful adherence to all the details of the original as written and drawn would have produced something that even devotees would have found less satisfactory.[18]

Peter Pan (1953)

Like *Cinderella*, *Peter Pan* relies on the interplay of character and dramatic tension to further the action, but moves away from the anthropomorphism of the earlier film. The characters are almost all 'straight' human beings; there were only four in *Snow White and the Seven Dwarfs*, six in *Cinderella* and thirteen in *Peter Pan* if the mermaids

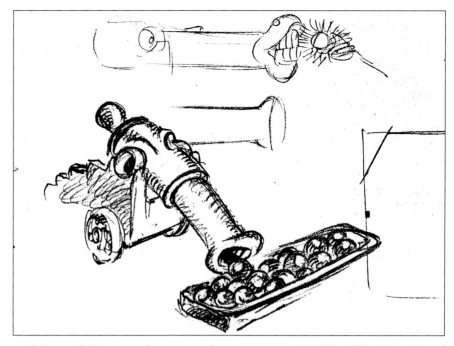

and the redskins may be counted as one example. The film, in spite of spectacular special effects and moments of visual beauty, has the feel of a stage play rather than a film. It lacks the cinematic muscularity of *Cinderella* or *Alice* and the characters come from melodrama; there is even a drowning sequence, with one of the heroines rescued in the nick of time. Hook comes out of the stage versions of Barrie, who started *Peter Pan* as a play before turning it into a novel. Hook is a traditional stage villain in action, facial expression and gesture, with long moustaches and period costume.

The desire to recreate ordinary human beings in cartoon form shows Disney's extended interest in animating not only the world of imagination through caricature and through exaggeration or distortion, but in imposing control on the real world. This would lead to the effigies of the Audio-Animatronics figures of Disneyland and the other parks. 'The Pirates of the Caribbean' attraction is an example of this and stems from *Peter Pan*.

There are no story conference notes available for *Peter Pan*, but we know that Disney bought the rights in 1939, and once again Albert Hurter provided doodles and sketches to suggest ways of approaching the story visually, and especially comically. There is evidence too that Disney knew the story well, as the library copy that he took out was marked with the blue pencil that he characteristically used.[19] This was illustrated by F.D. Bedford (1864–1954), whose delicate pictures match Barrie's imaginative vision.

PETER FLEW IN

THE BIRDS WERE FLOWN

Work continued in the late thirties; there are photographs of the artists in their offices with characters for the film pinned up on their boards and the early treatments were being produced under Joe Grant's and then Jack Kinney's auspices. An internal memorandum from Disney of December 1938 states that 'Joe Grant and Dorothy Blank are now the headquarters of *Peter Pan*' and a 'final' treatment by Kinney and his colleagues is dated 26 March 1946. Sufficient work had been done to present an early sequence for audience research purposes, on 9 December 1948. Another internal memorandum shows that the studio intended real children, including an adolescent Wendy 'being emotional about a Clark Gable type', to be part of a modern story and then being led into a cartoon fantasy based on Barrie. This shows the studio's uncertainty about audience level and appeal, and the problems posed by the story which Barrie himself revised many times in different forms. Barrie's original story quickly took on mythic proportions; the name Wendy for instance, was a Barrie invention and became popular almost immediately.

F.D. Bedford: 'Peter flew in'. Illustration for J.M. Barrie's Peter and Wendy *(1911) (left). The* Disney Studio Library *copy was borrowed and marked by Walt Disney with his blue pencil. The nursery of Disney's film and still more, the* Peter Pan *ride of Disneyland, recall Bedford's illustrations.*

F.D. Bedford: 'Mr and Mrs Darling and Nana rushed into the nursery too late. The birds were flown' (right). Illustration for Peter and Wendy. *Bedford's disturbing picture provides an adult dimension to the story. The Disney version, along with many others, simplifies and clarifies an uncomfortable original.*

The play itself was performed in London alone more than ten thousand times between its first performance in 1904 and Disney's film in 1953.[20]

The issues raised by the position of the child within fiction and the attitude of adults towards the child have been dealt with at length by Jacqueline Rose in her study of *Peter Pan*[21] and the parallels that are offered in the Disney film show an added concern about the Americanisation of the original.

The audience reaction to the Disney treatment of 9 December 1948[22] concentrates on viewers' concern for their memory of Barrie. Praise for the originality of the presentation is tempered by resentment at 'liberties taken with the original' and concern that 'the original story would be more appealing to the public' and 'is much better [than the Disney version] and should succeed with the audience because the story is well liked'. Praise that the 'sugary sweetness' and 'pansy' angle have been removed is qualified by 'past memories rebelling against this modern treatment'. Comment on the audience aimed at is also evident. The treatment is considered 'a cute story for kids', pleasing children 'but not adult audience', and the characterisation is enjoyed by some, hated by others. On being asked if they thought that *Peter Pan* 'could be made into a good Disney all-cartoon feature', thirty three of the audience replied 'yes' and one replied 'no'. No mention is made of the 1925 silent film made by Paramount nor does Disney himself refer to this version. The Jean Arthur/Boris Karloff stage revival of 1950 was a great success and Jack Kinney intended to use Jean Arthur as his voice for Peter. Wendy Toye, who choreographed this revival wrote: 'The New York production was done with great, great respect and love. We hardly altered a word of the script ... It introduced Barrie's "Peter" before Disney's arrived on the scene'.[23]

Disney's fully animated version extended the adolescent, sexually developing character of Peter, the first male Peter in the history of *Peter Pan*, using the maturing, broken voice of Bobby Driscoll. The style of dead-end performance from the animated Peter was no doubt to be as removed as possible from the 'pansy' Peter noted in the audience survey. This also explains the freedom from the sentimentality that marks Barrie.

Tinker Bell, a miniaturised adult fairy with sexual allure, is not a threat on account of her size. Donald Crafton[24] has shown the relation between the androgynous quality of the traditional stage Peter, played by a girl, and the problem of the dual audience of children and adults. From the audience research undertaken at this period, it is clear that Disney was thinking of both adults and children, since those who had been children when he first produced animated films were now the parents of children. There was a studio policy of re-issuing animated features about every seven years. With the advent of television, Disney astutely advertised his films for a market which anticipated a new Disney

'THIS MAN IS MINE'

film for children, or a revival which would add a patina to parents' nostalgic memories, sometimes traumatic, of their own first visit to a Disney film. This cycle of audience response is linked to the complex issues surrounding the marketing of the Disney product today.[25]

The film deals with the universal, not the particular. Escape, love and the denial of love, ageing and the acceptance of reality are all themes in Barrie and in Disney. Visually, the film echoes the universal. There are clear aerial views of London, but no sense of London surrounding the Darling household, nor of the Edwardian period in spite of the clothes and props; emphasis is on character, rather than on place.[26] The colour and styling is by Mary Blair (her last film) and her colleagues, and is similar to *Cinderella*. It remains an animated melodrama, escaping from stage confines in the flight over London to Never-Land, and in the return to London on Peter's flying ship. Human figures predominate; the only animals in the film are Nana and the Crocodile, though a seagull makes a brief appearance as a butt for an explicit 'fanny' joke.

'This man is mine': Illustration (left) for the story book version of Disney's Peter Pan.
© *Disney Enterprises, Inc.*

F.D. Bedford (above): 'This man is mine.' Illustration for Peter and Wendy.

Peter Pan was more successful than *Alice in Wonderland* and has proved popular in revival, forming the basis for at least two attractions at Disneyland.[27] It was well received by most British reviewers though C.A. Lejeune in the *Observer* summed up her caustic notice in the headline 'Pan-American'. The next feature film was also popular. This was *Lady and the Tramp* (1955), a nostalgic love story about dogs in a small town at the turn of the century, and set wholly in the United States. Its appeal to Edwardiana elicited a response from European as well as American audiences. It was Disney's first film in CinemaScope and contained some beautifully rendered backgrounds. However, the welcome acerbity of *Alice in Wonderland* and to some extent *Peter Pan* was replaced by a sentimentality bound up with Disney's naïvety unsympathetic to European taste. Like the other films of this period, the story had a long gestatory period.[28] For the first time the Walt Disney Studio made use of a multi-ethnic American society, with comments on Italian, German and Russian communities. Lady's capture and imprisonment in the dog pound, where she encounters a wide variety of types and classes of dog, are some of the most stimulating in the film. However, by this time Disney's interest lay in developing his first theme park, Disneyland, which he made into a three-dimensionalised cartoon; he turned his attention away from the animated films which had been his foundation and his source of power. The influences of Europe upon the workings of Disneyland will be examined in the next chapter.

Notes

1. Jonathan Routh, 'Cinderella', *Everybody's* July 1950, 18.

2. Jack Kinney, *Walt Disney and Other Assorted Characters* (New York: Harmony Books, 1988), 174. Jack Kinney also repeated the story to the author.

3. Information supplied by William Tyler, folklorist; and see Marian E. Roalke Cox, *Cinderella: Three Hundred and Forty Five Variants of Cinderella, Catskin and Cap O'Rushes* (London: Folklore Sciety, 1893). See also Susan Ohmer, '"That Rages to Riches Stuff": Disney's *Cinderella* and the Cultural Space of Animation', *Film History*, Vol 5, No. 2, June 1993, 231–249, for an astute analysis of *Cinderella*.

4. Ruth Bottigheimer, *Grimms' Bad Girls and Good Boys* (New Haven: Yale University Press, 1987), 36.

5. Thomas and Johnston, *Disney Animation: The Illusion of Life*, 330.

6. Jonathan Rosenbaum, 'Dream Masters 1: Walt Disney,' *Film Comment*, Jan/Feb 1975, 65.

7. John Canemaker has noted especially Fragonard's *Fête at Rambouillet*, Calouste Gulbenkian Museum, Lisbon. Interview with author, 9 August 1989.

8. Walt Disney had written to Beatrix Potter in 1936 asking for permission to make a film of *The Tale of Peter Rabbit*. Potter refused permission because, she said, 'my drawings are not good enough. To make Silly Symphonies they will have to enlarge them and that will show up all the imperfections.' Quoted in Judy Taylor, *Beatrix Potter: Artist, Storyteller and Countrywoman* (London: Warne, 1986), 184. English

companies have made both ballet and animated films using Potter's stories, and there is a mini-theme park in the Lake District.

9. Anthony Lane, 'A Brilliant and Wicked Way to Keep the Children in the Dark', *The Independent*, 10 August 1991.

10. J. B. Kaufman, 'Before Snow White', *Film History*, Vol 5, No. 2, June 1993, 160.

11. Lewis Carroll, *Alice's Adventures in Wonderland*, illus. David Hall (London: Methuen, 1986) and see also Canemaker, *Before the Animation Begins*, 153.

12. Thirty of Hall's illustrations for *Alice* first appeared in *Walt Disney's Surprise Package* (New York: Simon and Schuster, 1944), 43–61.

13. Solomon, *The Disney That Never Was*, 46.

14. Another version was made with American money in France, and premièred in Paris in 1949. Its English Alice, played by an adult actress Carole Marsh, inhabited a world of puppets created by Lou Bunin. The enterprising distributor of the film tried to release it in the United States at the same time as Disney's version. Disney claimed that this was a deliberate attempt to mislead the public into going to see the wrong film, pointing out that it had registered the title as long ago as 1938, and asked the courts for an injunction on Bunin's film for eighteen months. Disney lost the case. John Grant, *The Encyclopedia of Walt Disney's Animated Characters*, 219 and Howard Byrne, 'Only One Star is Human', *Illustrated* 29 May, 1948, 12. The Walt Disney Company however did prevent Bunin from access to Technicolor and the French/American version was forced to use the inferior Anscocolor process.

    Bunin's film is rarely screened. Giannalberto Bendazzi describes it as 'rhythmically weak, unimaginative and unoriginal', *Cartoons*, 140. On its first release, *Newsweek* praised the live actors who included Felix Aylmer as Dean Liddell and Pamela Brown as Queen Victoria, but complained that the film was a laboured and random approximation of Carroll. *Newsweek* 6 August 1951.

15. Walt Disney, quoted in Bob Thomas, *The Walt Disney Biography*, 174.

16. The mixture of voices comes from radio and vaudeville. Alice herself, played by Kathryn Beaumont is English, as is the Caterpillar of Richard Haydn, and Alice's sister is played by the English actress Heather Angel. Ed Wynn's Mad Hatter and Jerry Colonna's March Hare are American, and so is the Cheshire Cat of Sterling Holloway, while Tweedledum and Tweedledee, voiced by Pat O'Malley, have Lancashire accents. The Queen's gardeners have a mixture of cockney and north country accents.

17. Walt Disney, quoted in Diane Disney Miller, *Walt Disney*, 186.

18. Richard Mallet, *Punch*, 3 August 1951.

19. The Hurter sketches were discovered by the author at the Walt Disney Archives in an unopened bound book of story sketches of *Peter Pan*. They are not dated but follow a picture of pirates by D. McCarthy, dated 7 December 1939. There are a number of story treatments and suggestions, one of which refers to the children landing on the Empire State Building, which no doubt relates to the modern story which was at one time considered. Dorothy Blank comments in a note to Walt Disney of 1 November 1938 'It's a swell story but Mr Barrie has scattered it around and made it as confusing as possible'.

    The Walt Disney Studio Library's excellent arrangement of borrowers' names on the issue cards meant that, provided the cards still existed, those who had borrowed the book could be traced, and the date on which they borrowed the book verified. Disney borrowed *Peter Pan and Wendy*, illus. F.D. Bedford (Oxford: Oxford University Press, 1934). He borrowed it twice, on 1 December 1946 and on 1 October 1948. The text is marked with blue pencil.

20. R. L. Green, *Fifty Years of Peter Pan* (London: Peter Davies, 1954), vii.

21. Jacqueline Rose, *The Case of Peter Pan or the Impossibility of Children's Fiction* (London: Macmillan, 1984).

22. Card Walker to Walt Disney, internal memo., '*Peter Pan*: Non Critical Audience reaction,' 9 December 1948.

23. Wendy Toye, quoted in Green, 166.

24. Donald Crafton, 'Walt Disney's *Peter Pan*: Woman Trouble on the Island,', *Storytelling in Animation: The Art of the Animated Image* Vol. 2, ed. John Canemaker (Los Angeles: American Film Institute, 1988), 123–146.

25. Revival of the animated features is erratic, in the UK at least. *Snow White and the Seven Dwarfs* was revived in Britain in 1946, 1954, 1965, 1968, 1973, 1980, 1988 and 1992. There was probably also a revival between 1954 and 1965. The company now reissues the animated feature films on video.

    Work has begun on analysing the audience research undertaken by Gallup for Disney. See Susan Ohmer, '*Peter Pan* and ARI', unpublished paper for third annual conference, Society for Animation Studies, Rochester, New York, October 1991.

26. Disney returned to Edwardian London for *Mary Poppins* (1964) where the sense of place is more firmly extablished.

27 The Disney film was allowed to be the only version extant for ten years. This was by a 1939 agreement with the Great Ormond Street Hospital, by which Disney paid the hospital £5,000. [Law Report, 'Disney Productions fail in Appeal over *Peter Pan*,' *The Times*, 15 February 1967, 19.] After ten years other producers would be permitted to make a film, and since this study is of European influences upon Disney, it is worth noting that British justice prevailed in a case when the Disney corporation attempted to stop the making of such a film 'with a cynical disregard for their pledged word not to object' as Lord Justice Salmon put in his summing up at the Court of Appeal in 1967. In 1964 George Cukor and Mel Ferrer intended to make a film with Audrey Hepburn in the title role and agreed to pay the hospital £45,000. In breach of contract 'Disneys objected and so the hospital lost the prospect of a valuable contract'. The hospital sued Disney and the result was this appeal brought by the Disney corporation. 'Anyone might well be daunted by the prospect of litigation with such a large amd powerful corporation as Disneys' continued the Judge, 'who deliberately broke their word to secure a possible financial advantage to themselves ... and causing very serious financial loss to a hospital for sick children'. The Disney corporation lost the appeal.

28. Marty McNamara, 'Script Evolution and Story Adaptation: *Lady and the Tramp*', unpublished paper, fourth annual conference, Society for Animation Studies, California Institute of the Arts, Valencia, California, October 1992.

CHAPTER 10

From Magic Kingdom to Mowgli

Disneyland

Walt Disney spent his creative energy from the early 1950s onwards developing the idea of a theme park. Disneyland was an extension of the animated films, using the heritage of Europe and a nostalgia for an American past, wrapped up as a three-dimensional package as an experience to be enjoyed. Though Disney was never very interested in the merchandising spin-offs which his films and characters generated, he was conscious that they had given the company the economic freedom for him to pursue his ideas. A theme park however was not just a commercial plan of exploitation, though it was that too. It was a creative dream by the man who had seen the story of *Snow White and the Seven Dwarfs* grow in his mind until it could be realised dramatically through the animation skills of his staff.

There are many accounts of the park's inception, the difficulties Disney had in raising money, the rush to get the park opened on time and the overwhelming success of a second Disney 'Folly'.[1] The financial risk taken by Disney had its parallels nearly twenty years previously when he was pouring his energy and resources into the making of *Snow White and the Seven Dwarfs*. There is no record of any expression of doubt on his part during the making of the film; similarly, the public face that he presented during the making of his Magic Kingdom (under similar pressure and against concerted opposition) was always optimistic. His distress when his brother Roy opposed him, or his colleagues felt unable to support him, was described by Herbert Ryman (1910–1985). Ryman had worked for the studio in the late thirties and early forties before freelancing as designer and art director for other studios. He made the original aerial design for the park to Disney's suggestions and recalled:

> 1953 it was, 23 September. Phone rang. It was Dick Irvine at the studio saying Walt wanted to speak to me. Walt said, 'Come over'. 'But today's Saturday' I said. 'Sure,' he said, 'it's my studio. I can work on a Saturday.' 'But I'm not dressed,' I said. 'Come as you are. I'll be waiting outside for you.' So I went over to his office.
> Then he told me all about his plans and how he had to get designs up to New York immediately. I couldn't see how it could work, how I

could get it done in time. I said 'No.' He turned his back on me, turned his head and said, 'Will you do it if I stay?' I said 'Yes, if you stay Saturday and Sunday night.' He came over and said, 'What do you want to eat?' and we shook hands. I stayed with that project till after the Park opened.

Walt Disney, easily moved to tears, but rigidly controlled in his professional dealings, is here tellingly described exerting his power and charisma in the understated 'turned his head'. Harper Goff (1911–1997) was another colleague who first met Disney in London when both men were anxious to buy the same model engine in the Bassett–Lowke model railway shop. He designed the Nautilus submarine for Disney's live action film *Twenty Thousand Leagues Under the Sea* (1954). Goff worked with Disney on the early stages of Disneyland and remembered a moment when Disney broke down, almost alone and high up on the central scaffolding that was built in the middle of the park while it was under construction.

> It was nothing but a sea of drains and ditches and nothing above ground. 'I have half of the money spent,' he said, 'and nothing to show for it.' He said this with tears in his eyes. 'Nothing!' And he was not a fearful man.

Disneyland is like an animated cartoon with eleven out of its attractions in 1985 based on animated feature films. A number of others were based on or associated with live action films from the Disney Studio.[2] It is a controlled environment, with colour coded buildings, scaled down vistas and perspectives, so that the visitor, the 'guest', sees only what the designer has planned him or her to see. Thus, as John Hench said, 'We had total control, a visual literacy'. Hench was one of Disney's close collaborators on the development of Disneyland and he commented: 'Live action filming has to count on a lot of accidents, but in a cartoon we could gradually eliminate the things that contradicted what we were trying to say. With the background we had, this was a very easy thing to apply to the third dimension'.[3]

Disney began thinking about a park for employees and friends as early as 1948 and, in an internal memorandum, he outlined ideas for a 'Mickey Mouse Park' on vacant land near the studio:

> The Main Village, which includes the Railroad Station, is built around a village green or informal park. In the park will be benches, a bandstand, drinking fountain, trees and shrubs. It will be a place for people to sit and rest; mothers and grandmothers can watch over small children at play. I want it to be very relaxing, cool and inviting.[4]

It goes on to include a Western Village, shops, a Western museum, and some sort of fun fair; the European heritage which he added later is not mentioned at this stage, though it is present in the phrase 'village green'. The text is clearly Disney's own. The emphasis on comfort and safety, with concern for the users is part of the Disney ethos. His insistence on placing his audience in the forefront of all his discussions is characteristic; he wanted his audience, his 'American audience [from] Podunk Iowa' to enter into his dream. This plan was developed seven years later in 1955 when his speech writers wrapped up his ideas for public consumption in that formal Disneyesque style which is so different from the man himself: 'Disneyland is dedicated to the ideals, the dreams, and the hard facts that have created America ... with the hope that it will be a source of joy and inspiration to all the world'.[5] This is the formal Disney; the man is hidden behind the mask of the public persona which he cultivated, as his personal identity became more famous through television and through the increasing success of the Disney product. Nevertheless, the wishes expressed in that first memorandum, have been followed. It is still, today, a place of rest and recreation and, for the adult, nostalgia. The visitor is reminded of the past at every turn, from stepping out into Main Street to the end of the visit, where everyone has to leave by the same entrance/exit. Disney did not want the public to be disorientated by too many exits. Like a film inside a cinema, the park is hidden from view and only the vast car park, a horizontal equivalent to the expressionless face of the cinema, is a clue to the numbers of people that the park absorbs. Once through the tunnel that lies under the bank built to screen the Magic Kingdom from the outside world, one is inside a film, taking part in a western or adventure story, or experiencing the vicarious thrill of a night flight over Never-Land.[6]

Umberto Eco has drawn attention to the American passion for collection, the appetite for adding a detritus of the past, even vicariously through a variety of sources, in particular from Europe. His comments on the Hearst/Kane – San Simeon/Xanadu kaleidoscope can also be applied to Disneyland and its 'voracity of selection ... the fear of being caught up in this jungle of venerable beauties which unquestionably has its own wild flavour, its own pathetic sadness, barbarian grandeur and sensual perversity.' Eco continues by saying that 'the ideology of this America wants to establish reassurance through Imitation'.[7] Disney was obsessed with the enclosed, the miniature, the completeness and containable scale of Europe. When under stress in the nineteen forties he retreated to the small scale railway that he designed to go round his garden. He also made miniature stoves: 'Little tiny things he loved making ... He started making pot-bellied stoves on his little lathe,' recalled his friend the actor Richard Todd. 'They were all hand painted and they were like little Dresden pieces'. Another colleague Harry Tytle also

Grandville: Chapter heading for Gulliver's Travels (1840), Gulliver in Lilliput. Disney loved the miniature and planned a Lilliputland for which was not built, although Storybookland has a miniaturised landscape.

Madurodam, The Netherlands. This miniature town was visited by Walt Disney.

remembered how Disney enjoyed making miniature objects such as horse carriages and engines.

England especially is regarded by Americans as miniature and 'cute'. John Malcolm Brinnin, the American poet and biographer of Dylan Thomas wrote:

> Our history is brief, and our national character, compounded of so many heterogenous influences, still does not allow of definition ... Americans long for that which other peoples take quite for granted – the simple signs of speech, of place, of character and tradition that might tell them who they are.[8]

This is what Disney saw and remembered and what he sought in the creation of a world that would recreate that completeness, that sense of identity, but he went further, with the satisfaction of control over an environment which could not be defiled by life, that was perfect, brighter, cleaner, prettier, its dolls and puppets able to perform always at command; making art more perfect than life. The 'lifelong rage to order, control and keep clean any environment he inhabited' that Richard Schickel notes led also to the creation of the figures which populated his dream world.[9] As circus ring master his animals and clowns and performers had to obey his commands. He had visited the miniature village Madurodam in Holland with his colleague Bill Cottrell who recalled that 'The buildings were one inch or one and a half inches to the foot and you could walk through the streets ...'. The importance of Disney's visit to Europe in 1935 has been pointed out (see Chapter 2), and post-war visits led to increasing Anglo- and Europhilia. Here lay the seeds not only for the scale of Disneyland, but also for the Audio-Animatronics figures with which he would populate the individual attractions. The little articulated model man which he brought back from an early visit was the inspiration for one of the first of the theme lands that he planned for his Disneyland ideas, a Lilliputian Land. This never fully materialised, although there was a miniature landscape with village, castle and real plants of a miniature size in the Storybook Land attraction at Disneyland. However, based on the mechanical bird that he also brought back from Europe, the first Audio-Animatronics figures were birds for the Enchanted Tiki Room, a Polynesian show at Disneyland which was an immediate and long-lasting success; it was a particular favourite of Disney's.[10]

Another link with the animated film on which the Magic Kingdom is so carefully based is the appearance of living performers as cartoon characters. These are members of the Disney 'cast' wearing three-dimensional plastic heads. They emerge from secret entrances from time to time as if by magic, their heads frozen, inanimate grotesques of their cartoon originals which could be squashed or stretched into any conceivable shape or expression. These caricatured animals and comic figures with their giant masks, though fearful to the adult, attract children, who cluster round the performers-as-Disney characters. The power of the mask as icon is seen as protective, assuring. On the other hand, the nearly human all-electronic figure of Abraham Lincoln is the more alarming or threatening because of its similarity to and yet difference from its model, the real. Artifice here becomes morbid and points to the nightmare of a future where films like *Westworld* (1973) and *Blade Runner* (1982) may become reality. Disney as puppet master had no vision beyond the recreation of reality through his figures, and could not see how easily his benignity could become malignity. The Walt Disney Story, featuring 'Great Moments with Mr. Lincoln' attraction is bound up with the American ideal, with the desire to start afresh, to recreate, to encompass, to package, to package humanity. The puppets that were created for Disneyland resembled the cartoon characters – the more caricatured the more successful, the more real the more grotesque. Caricature, inherited from Europe and understood, absorbed through many forms including the theatre and illustration, is successfully presented in the context of the giant stage show or film experience that Disneyland actually demonstrates. Other more subtle ingredients such as idealism and the concept of beauty are more uneasily presented; Disneyland contains the same ingredients as the animated features; a complex awareness of a European heritage, a deliberate use of that heritage and a past with real cultural links with the present (see Colour Plates 79 and 80).

At first Disney searched unsuccessfully for a park that possessed the ingredients that he was looking for; the American parks depressed him with their squalor, their lack of organisation, haphazard and tiring acres of concrete, their surly personnel. In Denmark, he was impressed by the Tivoli Gardens. 'It was spotless and brightly coloured and priced within the reach of everyone,' he said. 'The gaiety of the music, the excellence of the food and drink, the warm courtesy of the employees – everything combined for a pleasurable experience'.[11]

His new imaginary world was made real by the same artists who had created his cartoon films. So there was a continuity in collective thinking and in practical ability. By utilising their skills, Disney combined a nostalgia for the past of America, (a past coloured itself by its own popularising through the cinema) and the fantasy of Europe, symbolised by the sight of Sleeping Beauty Castle pointing its pinnacles into the Californian sky beyond the confines of Main Street. This was a dreamscape made manifest. As in a dream the visitor glided as if by magic on a boat or train or cable car or monorail or 'people mover'; as in a dream, there was a smooth transference from one world to another; there was no need to walk, and the exhaustion caused by other parks and museums, a reminder of reality and of bodily limitations all too linked to the actual world, was at once removed.

Water featured as an element in many of the animated films; so with Disneyland. Water flowed everywhere, as a companion to the pedestrian or as a means of conveyance on a number of attractions, or as an adventurous accompaniment; on one ride the visitor goes in a boat on the Jungle Cruise behind a waterfall; the wish-fulfilment in this one small example can be be found in literature from *Lorna Doone* to *The Lord of the Rings*. It can also be seen in art, in the idealised landscapes of Claude, Poussin, Watteau, Fragonard. In the cinema an example comes to mind from DeMille's *Unconquered* (1947) where Gary Cooper rescues Paulette Goddard from a mighty waterfall and conveys her behind the fall to safety. In landscape gardening there is the example of the Villa D'Este,[12] the rococo water garden built on a mountainside near Rome. Cascades and fountains enchant the visitor on a series of stepped terraces (see Colour Plate 83). There is a walk through a grotto behind a waterfall. Water was one of the main ingredients used by The Grand Sophy, Shah Abbas the Great of Persia, when he redesigned Isfahan, turning it into a garden city of waterways and treelined walks; that city was also in a desert land.[13] Water was the accompaniment to many scenic parks, especially in France and Italy; there are reminders of the fountains of Rome and the waterfalls and fantastic water effects not only at the Villa D'Este but also at follies and cascades in English parklands, of which Chatsworth in Derbyshire is perhaps the most spectacular (see Colour Plate 84).[14]

It is difficult to remember that all the water in the Disney park is artificial in direction and flow, artificial in place. It has been diverted, pumped and projected over artificial rocks and into artificial lagoons and lakes and rivers. One of the artists who worked on Disneyland recalled the difficulty in creating the effect of a rainbow of coloured water as it fell over a waterfall, a reminder of the Beethoven section of *Fantasia* where cupids and fauns slide down a liquid rainbow. Disney wanted the water to fall with the distinct colours of the rainbow, but the engineer in charge said that it could not be done, was not physically possible and that the colours would blend and become muddy. Disney, for whom the word 'can't' was anathema, sacked the man on the spot and got one of his own artist designers working on the project; somehow, the effect that he wanted was achieved.

Christopher Finch has likened Disneyland to the great private parks of Europe, the enclosures for an élite like the court of Louis XIV at Versailles.[15] The icons are different, the privileged few have become the ordinary many who can afford the entrance fee, the public with whom Disney instinctively identified. Finch goes on to say that although separated culturally, 'Each in its own way celebrates similar pleasures

Walt Disney and Europe

and pieties. Each reflects the culture that produced it, removed from the everyday realities of life'.

Many people over the years have written about their reactions to Disneyland. Some have entered its gates prepared to loathe, but, overwhelmed by its charms have left with very different feelings. Others have refused to be seduced. I was not looking forward to my first visit, preferring my Disney on film and not in a three dimensional park. My diary for 18 May 1985 reads:

> The secret of the place, which no film or slide or photograph or even 3D picture can give, is the total three dimensional element of the fantasy.

> You become part of and enter into Walt's dream. The tat and kitschy quality which comes across in flat pictures dissolves when you go through those turnstiles. The lath and plaster is solid, the cardboard is so tough you never see it wobble. The paint is fresh, the flags flutter, the bands play, the people laugh and cry out for more, more security, more nostalgia, more happiness, more memories of a world better than our own. This is the technicolor experience wrapped round us so that, as in the days when we went to the movies we forgot our world of troubles for an hour or two, so here for a day the same emotional euphoria is generated. Is this bad? Is this, as critics say, like a drug, an escapist immature fantasy generated by an immature showman for cash? Or is it a work of art, as *The Wizard of Oz* or *Snow White and the Seven Dwarfs* or *Singin' in the Rain* are works of art, commercially manufactured products that transcend their age and have a meaning all to themselves as all great works of art should have?

Disney was continually changing Disneyland, tinkering, improving, altering. For him it was never static or complete and there are many stories about his passion for his park. He would stay overnight – he had a flat over the fire station on Main Street USA – and wander around the park looking for ways to improve or enhance his dreamscape. So he had wandered around the studio at night or at the week-end looking at his artists' work, surveying their scribbles and even the discarded material in their waste paper baskets. He would talk to people in the park, ask questions, invite comments. It was his new toy. Ray Bradbury, himself a teller of tales and a friend of Disney, recalled the European origins of the mythological centre of Disneyland. Bradbury is also an American from the Midwest living on the West Coast. He recalled that:

> Disney was only out to do one thing, to please himself. He saw a hunger, a need in himself and the world ... What happened with Walt is the same thing that happened to a lot of us later in our lives, that he went to Europe and he looked around the castles and the chateaux

and the parks, the architecture, the artistic influences and he came home and he said, 'Dammit! I'm gonna give this as a gift to my people'.

Jim Algar remembered an anecdote about Disney that took place soon after the park had been opened:

> The head gardener came to Walt and said: 'Look Walt, I've got a little problem I want to show you,' and he took him over to [a spot facing] the castle, and said, 'Look, I've got to have a sign here which says 'Keep off the grass', because look at the way everyone's trampling down these pansies trying to get a shot of the castle with their cameras. So can I have a little barrier here, a little fence?'
>
> Walt says, 'No. Wait a minute. Tell you what we'll do. We'll put a little rock walk right through there and we'll put up a sign that says "Best vantage point for filming the castle".'

Sleeping Beauty (1959)

By this time Disney was more interested in animation as support for his Magic Kingdom than in the creative process itself. Audiences were changing and the younger generation was seen as a specific target for film products; Disney's *Sleeping Beauty* (1959) was in production for at least six years, and there is a plot outline dating as far back as 15 May 1951. It was very expensive to make, was filmed in 70 millimetre and cost six million dollars, but it is innovative only in its technical presentation and design; its creative strengths derive from earlier work, in particular from *Snow White and the Seven Dwarfs*. The artists attempted to adapt to the new animation style of the fifties, learning from Disney's rivals at Warner Brothers and at UPA. There were no longer the talents at the studio, however, to make a transition, so while there is surface change, there is organic stalemate. Mary Blair had left and her absence was much felt; death or departure had removed the indigenous European talents who had enriched the work of the thirties and forties. Many had new careers as book illustrators; senior creative talents like Dick Huemer and Joe Grant who had survived the war and the strike had also gone – and Disney himself was absorbed with his new toy, Disneyland, taking some of his best artists over to work on the Magic Kingdom.

Ken Anderson and Don Da Gradi were nominally in charge of the production design for *Sleeping Beauty*, but the real artistic director was a young man whom Disney admired called Eyvind Earle (b. 1916), who was credited with 'colour styling' and his stamp is on every shot.[16] Earle was an artistic *enfant terrible* who had been working at the studio off and on as a freelance artist since 1951 and had painted backgrounds for *Peter Pan* and *Lady and the Tramp* as well as for a number of short subjects. His individual style is not obvious in these features, but there is a marked change of background style, entirely due to his talent, evident in some of the shorts of the period. Disney was searching for the look of what he called 'a continuing illustration'. While Earle's authority was questioned by some of the older artists, Disney was adamant in wishing to see Earle's style retained throughout. 'I wanted,' said Earle, 'stylised, simplified Gothic, a medieval tapestry out of the surface wherever possible ... Everything from the foreground to the far distance is in focus. That gives you more depth' (see Colour Plate 81). It also gives the viewer an unfocused visual viewpoint, so that the eye is free to wander over the huge Technirama surface, all of which is filled with crisp detail, whatever action is taking place. Earle's inexperience about the need to focus attention in background, through the use of light and design, is evident. Some of the backgrounds are in themselves very beautiful, the forest scenes in particular, although the castle backgrounds are less successful.[17] Gordon Legg remembers how the original Earle sketches were worked over:

> I saw these lovely Earle sketches, just gorgeous. I'd known his work. 'It's about time,' I said, 'that they had this man, stylistic, posterised' ... Then I saw some of the finished artwork. Lost all the great simplicity of design. He'd added pockmarks and knot holes and ruined it. 'What a shame,' I said, 'that they've Disneyfied your sketches.' 'What do you mean, 'they'?' he said. 'Those are all mine.'

Earle used a number of European references; Van Eyck, the Italian Primitives and their landscapes, Durer and Persian miniatures. He paid particular attention to the Duc de Berry's *Très Riches Heures* (see Colour Plate 82) and Olivier's *Henry V* (1944) which is not surprising since it is itself a designer's homage to the French paintings. Paul Sheriff and Olivier present integrated grace, Earle and Disney offer intermittent gracefulness. Frank Thomas also remembered that the artists were inspired by the style and colour of the English/Italian film *Romeo and Juliet* (1954). Directed by Renato Castellani this was shot on location in Italy and contains exquisite photography by Robert Krasker. The close shots of Aurora asleep look similar to those of Susan Shentall, the unknown girl chosen to play Juliet, lying in the crypt.[18]

The animated characters read uncomfortably against the elaborate backgrounds, and this Earle later accepted, admitting his inexperience. With the exception of *Dumbo*, a Disney feature was produced for the first time almost without Disney. In addition to this, there were changes of personnel during production with a consequent lack of coordinated effort.

To match Earle's angular and stylised forms, the animators sharpened the contours of their characters, which gives them a spiky contemporary look. There are few small creatures with which a young – or old –

member of the audience can identify. The human figures are stereotypically cardboard and there is little room for caricature or anthropomorphism. The references to *Snow White and the Seven Dwarfs* extend to the dialogue:

Aurora: He's tall and handsome and so romantic.

Dwarfs to Snow White: Was he strong and handsome? Was he big and tall?
Snow White: He was so romantic ...
Prince Phillip to Aurora: I'm awfully sorry – I didn't mean to frighten you.
Snow White to the animals: I'm awfully sorry – I didn't mean to frighten you.

The physical actions of Aurora on meeting the prince mirror precisely those of Snow White – she retreats shyly, hand up to her face, disappears behind a tree (Snow White behind a curtain) and then re-emerges to accept the young man's courtship. There are also direct plot elements taken from the earlier film but dropped from *Snow White and the Seven Dwarfs*, including the capture of the prince and his incarceration. Disney was concerned about the parallels with *Snow White and the Seven Dwarfs*. At a story meeting of 11 February 1953 he said, 'I worry about the Heigh-Ho-Derry-Do (song) now. If we could work on it, and keep it from being too much like *Snow White and the Seven Dwarfs* – even the girl's voice sounds like it'. Elaborate story ideas from the earlier film were utilised for the later, but the utilisation is mechanical, not organic, though there is some highly skilful animation, particularly of the three good fairies.

The film really comes alive with the arrival of the bad fairy Maleficent, following on from the Queen in *Snow White and the Seven Dwarfs* and the Stepmother in *Cinderella*. The gentlest of animators Marc Davis developed her role for animation, and when it was possible to get the busy Disney to attend meetings, he gave her some of his histrionic attention.[19] The last part of the film when she chases the prince and turns into a dragon is a *tour-de-force* of malignant terror. Maleficent is a stepmother figure like the Queen, but in some ways more disturbing for there is a real mother in this story, so helpless that she might as well, for a child watching the film, not exist. We can see how the new evil character has grown out of the original Queen; the cowl has been increased, with hornlike peaks, the collar stretched, the cloak extended to form gothic batlike folds. The black angularity and extensions have arachnid connotations. The face is long, mirroring the sharp angles of the clothing, the eyes large, pupils small, eyebrows arched and plucked; the *femme fatale* image is presented, with the accoutrements of power in the shape of a wand. The youthful appearance of the Queen with 'plenty of curves' as Disney demanded, has gone, replaced by exaggerations of all the signs that marked her – clothing, make up, facial characteristics. The element of caricature, however, adds to, rather than detracts from the conviction with which she is invested, leaving a void on the screen when she is not present. Children identify with the

Story sketch: Maleficent and her raven for Sleeping Beauty. *An early concept design, with the artist's note 'Bat wing effect from cloak'.* © *Disney Enterprises, Inc.*

sympathetic characters and no doubt this makes the film the more disturbing for them[20] but for adults the good fairies (three clones and direct descendents of the Fairy Godmother in *Cinderella*) are no substitute for seven individual dwarfs. The film was not successful perhaps because it did not appeal sufficiently to both adult and child and lacked the tight narrative of earlier Disney.

Disney recognised the failure. 'I sorta got trapped,' he said. 'I had passed the point of no return and I had to go forward with it'.[21] His obsession with the *femme fatale* continued into the sixties, with a comical emphasis added to the character. It is part of the European heritage which is completely absorbed into the new culture through animation. The picture book quality of the early features was developed through the work of living European artists; but the complexity of the earlier features, and in particular *Snow White and the Seven Dwarfs*, *Pinocchio* and *Fantasia*, had gone. The European references were now tacked on as decorative devices; the desire to create a new style, admirable in itself, failed through a misunderstanding of the capabilities of the medium, an attempt to reclothe an old shape. Eyvind Earle left the studio.[22]

The film was a critical and box-office failure, though it has since recovered its cost through re-releases and two video issues. Time has been kind to *Sleeping Beauty*; its superb technical presentation and growing period charm was noted on its 1996 cinema release.

One Hundred and One Dalmatians (1961)

Disney was prepared to economise on the next project, though he was not enthusiastic about an invention of his old colleague Ub Iwerks, a Xerox device for transferring the animator's drawings directly onto cel and avoiding the expensive tracing and inking process. This produced a rougher more obviously graphic effect than the hand-inked cel, which was traditionally done by highly skilled women tracers and painters. In the short cartoons the outlines were done in black, but on the features the animated figures would often be outlined using a variety of inks or paint to match the flesh tones, hair, or costume accordingly (see Colour Plate 73).[23] With the new Xerox process even the pencilling lines could be reproduced. It was a technique well suited to the first contemporary story – again European – that was the studio's next project.

The revolutionary graphic look gave the film a freedom of design, with its sketchy outlines emphasising their own essence as drawings. The Xerox effect was applied to the backgrounds too, so that for the first time character and background appeared to form part of one design, 'a true marriage between character and background', as Ward Kimball put it. It did not imitate reality – it looked what it was.

Dodie Smith's novel was published in 1956 to immediate success and, although the complex plot was changed and simplified, the spirit of the book was maintained, the film following its outline and above all its mood. An American friend of the author's had introduced the novel to Disney, himself a dog lover.[24] Disney was especially attracted to the episode where the puppies attempt to disguise themselves by rolling in soot. In 1959 he visited Dodie Smith at her home in Essex. 'Wow!' he exclaimed when he first saw her thatched cottage on a sunny July day. English author and American producer got on extremely well, and later Dodie Smith commented on Disney's gentle courteousness. She was delighted with the film.

Its look is quite different from any earlier feature, not only in style but also in the ability to rise to Dodie Smith's amiable fantasy, and to match her wit both visually and on the sound track. The impression is that a new set of artists has been at work, but the changes in personnel were minimal, with the exception of the departure of Eyvind Earle. Forty out of fifty-eight of the team that worked on the earlier film went on with *One Hundred and One Dalmatians*. This shows how quickly the studio could change visual direction given a crisis. Radical changes were made after the failure of *Fantasia*; after *Sleeping Beauty* there is a different, but equally noticeable change. There is a sense of freedom and of the stretching of artistic muscles in handling the contemporary work and process. Disney was again largely absent. Ken Anderson recalled: 'I did a lot of it while Walt was away'. This visual freedom is expressed everywhere, from the opening titles onwards, and was enjoyed by the production staff. Marc Davis, who animated Cruella De Vil, and Ray Aragon (b. 1926),[25] a layout artist, remembered it vividly and affectionately.

If Eyvind Earle put his stamp upon the earlier film then the responsibility for the new look is that of Bill Peet (b. 1914) and Ken Anderson (1909–1993).[26] Peet wrote the screenplay and designed the original storyboards while Anderson was both art director and production designer. Anderson's 'drawings gave a flavour to all the picture' said Ray Aragon and his feel for the book is explained by his generous acknowledgement to Ronald Searle (b. 1920). Searle and his wife Kaye Webb (editor of *Lilliput* and the founder editor of the children's Puffin Book series) visited the studio on 16 July 1957 and became friendly with Ken Anderson and other Disney artists including Marc Davis and Ward Kimball. Ronald Searle was well known in the United States, as was his contemporary British cartoonist colleague, Rowland Emmett, who also visited Walt Disney in the 1950s.[27] Life, *The New Yorker* and other magazines commissioned Ronald Searle's work. He was especially helpful to Anderson over topography, not only in London settings but also in country scenes in the English winter. Once the Searle connection is made, the witty use of line to express humour and character, can be noted in many of the film's scenes, not least in the opening credits.

Ronald Searle (left): Illustration for
The Rake's Porgress *(1955).*
© *Ronald Searle.*

Still (right): Roger and Pongo in
101 Dalmatians *(1961).*
© *Disney Enterprises, Inc.*

The film did not rely on songs or slices of vaudeville turns; the story was developed consistently with stylised characterisation; rotoscoping of the humans was abandoned, although there was close observation of live action footage. The people are caricatured, the young man Roger in particular bearing a physical resemblance to his dog Pongo, and his wife Anita looks like a real woman, *because* she is so obviously drawn. Cruella De Vil is another Disney villainess but there is comedy as well as evil in her portrayal. Contemporary satire of television lends the film, as well as the book, a social reference which is new to a Disney film; it is, however, the sense of place, the affection for and belief in a real Regent's Park in a real London, a real England in which the dramatic events occur which give the film the same kind of strengths which engage the reader of the book. London is 'there' in the film as it is on the page – the street lamps, railings, benches are right. Dodie Smith praised the depiction of the Suffolk countryside in snow, and there is a soft colour that catches the English light in a manner similar to the English water-colour school. The attention to correct detail is continued in the choice of voices, all clearly English (except some of the puppies) to match the various English 'types' ironically portrayed by Smith. The film finds a visual equivalent for her irony. The book, for example, opens with the narrative voice of the author, who immediately places the centre of her narrative firmly in the hands – or paws – of the hero and heroine, who are dogs: 'Not long ago, there lived in London a young married couple of Dalmatian dogs named Pongo and Missis Pongo'.[28]

The film places the narrative in the first person, but it takes a little while for the audience to realise, as we come in from establishing shots of London to Roger's flat, that it is Pongo who is talking. Dodie Smith's ironic prose is given emphasis by the irony implicit in the voice-over for the film.

The sketchy graphic outlines provide a freshness and suggest an alternative solution to a graphic problem for the first time in a Disney film. There is a hesitancy to the line, a grasping at alternative ways of expressing linear mobility or an awareness that there may not be a solution at all to the question of what is real, that what is being shown on film is only one way an artist has of expression; there may be others. Thus Daumier expresses the tragedy of the human condition through the anxiety of his febrile line; fear, exploitation, drunkenness, stupidity and avarice are made plain through linear alternatives. The link between Daumier and Searle in this context can be observed. Daumier, admired by the Disney artists, is an unconscious influence, just as he was for the dark areas that gave *Pinocchio* its deeper significance.

One Hundred and One Dalmatians received better notices than any Disney film since *Pinocchio* and was an immediate success with the public. 'The film turns out to be his best for a long time' said C. A. Lejeune in *The Observer* (31 March 1961) and added, 'The tone is firm, witty and engaging ... The new sureness of feeling is reflected in the draughtsmanship.' Dilys Powell in *The Sunday Times* on the same day was equally enthusiastic: 'It is a kind of rebirth of Disney, inventive all over again ... The movement within the frame remains elaborate, decorative and exciting'. Richard Mallett in *Punch* on 3 April pointed out its lack of sentimentality. '... No sign at all of the old Disney inclination towards chocolate-box charm ... Nearly every moment is cunningly contrived to please both the child and the adult ... All told, this is a winner'. Brenda Davies in the *Monthly Film Bulletin* echoed Mallett in her praise: 'The Disney cartoon team's danger has always lain in lapses of taste, so that it is especially pleasant to find a theme of infinite sentimental possibilities treated here with so much discretion.'

Disney, however, did not like the film. He was jealous that so much had been achieved without his control and told Ken Anderson 'No more of that *Hundred and One Dalmatians* stuff'. Ken Anderson later recalled that Disney 'didn't want lines. He was offended because [the film] was so stylised. He was a frustrated actor. Every line was a soft line and he was doing his level best to make it like live action'.

The Sword in the Stone (1963)

Disney had bought the rights for T.H. White's book in 1939, soon after its publication. It tells the story of King Arthur's boyhood as the lad

Wart, and his upbringing by the magician Merlin. The success of the musical *Camelot* in 1959 revived Disney's interest in a project which he felt earlier was too English, too localised as a property for a cartoon film.[29] Disney's instinct about the subject was right, for the film disappoints, in spite of the new linear and graphic freedom which is carried over from *One Hundred and One Dalmatians*. Disney's dislike for the previous film thwarted confidence and there was a large reduction in staff. Twenty-eight artists are credited compared with the fifty who had worked on *One Hundred and One Dalmatians*; Disney demoted Ken Anderson and forced him to disband his department.

Once again, Disney had little to do with the film, for the first time allowing a single director, Woolie Reitherman, to be in charge. Reitherman was an experienced animator who had been with the studio since the mid thirties; his animation of specatacular scenes made him famous throughout the studio and in the animation world generally. He had been responsible for animating Monstro the whale in *Pinocchio*, for the dinosaur battle in *Fantasia* and for Maleficent as the dragon in *Sleeping Beauty*, but lacked the finesse necessary for presenting the niceties of T.H. White's book. Bill Peet was again responsible for the story, and he decided to omit the book's English eccentricity; in any case the curious facetiousness of White's text, which dates it, could not have a visual equivalent in Disney animation.

Unlike *The Reluctant Dragon* more than twenty years earlier, there is no cheerful American reworking of an Old World story, but there is much dialogue rather flatly delivered. The beautifully stylised backgrounds (Ken Anderson was the art director) and the dark forests particularly are rendered with great delicacy. Some comic episodes are inventive, such as Wart's capture by Madame Mim, and her battle with Merlin. The colour and graphic style are fresh and lively, though less obviously linear than in *One Hundred and One Dalmatians*. Reviewers greeted the film warmly. Dilys Powell in *The Sunday Times* said, 'The great inventor and his collaborators – and too many people forget what an inventor Disney has been – still have jokes up their sleeves. The ones in *The Sword in the Stone* are agreeably free of Disney's occasional savagery' (15 December 1963). Richard Mallett in *Punch* on 25 December called it 'a good average Christmas Disney' though the *Monthly Film Bulletin* said 'Everything is empty vastnesses. Disney's world exists in a vacuum and is so remote it that it no longer holds its own truths'. The careful use of English voices is betrayed by young Wart's part being played by an American, or Americans, as the role was undertaken by a number of boys. The quaintness of a medieval England seen from across the Atlantic is not exploited and any sense of mystery or magic attaching to the legend of King Arthur, suggested in White's tale with some delicacy, is ignored. Dodie Smith had offered the simplest of ironies and of character types and this accorded well with the studio's own limitations. Ken Anderson and his colleagues grabbed their opportunity but they were not able to respond to or to reinvent the world created by T. H. White. The artists had difficulty in recalling *The Sword in the Stone* and made few comments in interview.

Mary Poppins (1964)

This is almost entirely a live action film, but if Walt Disney took little interest in either *One Hundred and One Dalmatians* or *The Sword in the Stone* he was fully engaged in the production of this film. There are some brief animated sequences which combine with the live action and the film's fantasy links it to its animated forerunners. Disney's daughter Diane had recommended the P.L. Travers books to her father in the 1940s but he could not obtain the rights because the author was unwilling to see a cartoon version. Four *Mary Poppins* books were published between 1934 and 1952 and when Disney suggested a live action version, Pamela Travers showed more interest. Disney called on her personally and she was attracted to his charismatic personality.[30] She agreed to a film version only after Disney accepted her terms that she should be consultant on the project. This was an unprecedented arrangement. She visited the studio in 1961 and expressed her reservations forcefully about the script changes from her books. Disney 'was unprepared for dealing with an author who not only held strong convictions about how her books should be dramatised but who expressed them so unequivocally'.[31] The film enlarged and simplified the books, and their creator objected to the 'prettying up' of her heroine, who was, she said:

> ... already beloved for what she was – plain, vain and incorruptible – (and now) transmogrified into a soubrette ... And how was it that Mary Poppins herself, the image of propriety, came to dance a can-can on the roof-top displaying all her underwear? A child wrote, after seeing the film, 'I think Mary Poppins behaved in a very indecorous manner'.

Indecorous indeed!

The acerbity of P.L. Travers' heroine has been softened, and although Mrs Travers criticised the role, she praised the professionalism of Julie Andrews and her performance, adding in spite of herself that 'there were moments in the film that showed me that she understood, even though not allowed to express, the essential quality of the original'.

The London of the Edwardian era is presented both in sets and in matte background paintings by the English artist, Peter Ellenshaw. He understood what Disney was looking for in terms of design and had painted special effects glass shots and projections for other live action

Disney films, going back to *20,000 Leagues Under the Sea* (1954). He provides a London of memory blended with fantasy; Main Street, Marceline is round the corner; America and Europe come together in nostalgic evocation, and Poppins is Disney idealised, himself the magician benign, firm, humorous, dispensing magic from on high. He was relaxed on the set and said later 'I never saw a sad face around the entire studio'.[32] The animated sections convey a rural charm that also links back to the Marceline of Disney's childhood, with farmyard scenes and a fairground carousel. The score by the Sherman brothers has a warmth that is matched by the sensitivity of Julie Andrews' singing and there are moments of extraordinary delicacy in the blending of live action with animation. In 'Feed the Birds' for example, the camera lingers on the real – the bird woman on the steps of St Pauls, and then soars up with animated birds to the dome and towers of the cathedral, which is suggested through painted backgrounds, taking it beyond the real to the fantastic. *Mary Poppins* combines Europe and America and presents a reworking of both cultures, balanced and assured. The actors are all English, with the exception of Dick Van Dyke who contorts his body as well as his cockney vowels, but brings great vitality to his role. The film was a huge critical and popular success. It was Walt Disney's personal epitaph to the cinema, the last feature film with any animation to be released while he was alive. He died on 15 December 1966.

The Jungle Book (1967)

Released ten months after Disney's death, *The Jungle Book* is an animated strip cartoon, with strongly anthropomorphised animal characters,

relying on well known star names to add individuality. Its energy owes little to Kipling's original and Disney told his artists to forget the book and get on with their own version. The result is a film of exuberance and comic energy with some richly observed character studies and visual humour. There is little of Kipling except the bare bones of plot and P.L. Travers' comments on film makers in general are appropriate here: 'It

Gustave Doré: Illustration for Chateaubriand's Atala *(1863).*

is as though they took a sausage, threw away the contents but kept the skin, and filled that skin with their own ideas very far away from the original substance'. Here, there is no attempt to anglicise the characters, as was the case with the films made from the Dodie Smith and T.H. White books. *The Jungle Book* offers a cheerful mixture of conglomerate accents, from the pukka English of George Sanders as Shere Khan, to the broad Liverpudlian vultures, who remind us of the Beatles, to the American accents of Phil Harris as Baloo and Louis Prima as the monkey King of the Jungle. An internationalism takes over, but the film is firmly set in the exotic east. Like the England of *101 Dalmatians* the jungle here is a real one in which we believe the characters live and move. The backgrounds are delicately painted settings with a reminder of Le Douanier Rousseau, the colour generous but restrained (see Colour Plate 85). The great size of the jungle and the bush country on its edges are suggested in all sorts of graphic ways, a convincing framework for the characters to act out their story. The characters, firmly established and animated with great skill, develop and react with one another both dramatically and comically. The film is a reminder not only of the studio's own past, but also of the anthropomorphic qualities of artists like Kley, Daumier and Busch. The energy of the story sketches by Ken Anderson, who had been with Disney for many years is carried through to the finished film, in animation by veterans like Frank Thomas, Ollie Johnston and Milt Kahl. It is a family film in more senses than one.

The Walt Disney Studio had come full circle, from short cartoons based on a series of gags that built up or succeeded each other in a linear form, to full character animation, part of a complex story with convincing backgrounds, based on the mythic fabric of fairy tales or classics. The first Disney animated feature films had strong European connections. In the uncertain forties Disney and his colleagues used animation in different and experimental ways; after the war, audiences were seen to be less homogenous and with the cloak of avuncular respectability, the Disney films became simpler in association, whatever their technical complexity. With *The Jungle Book* there was a return to grass roots.

In the last years of his life Walt Disney was reaching out to the future as well as returning to his roots. He was planning a second, much larger theme park in Florida and his Experimental Prototype Community of Tomorrow (now Epcot), an idea that was still in the embryonic stage when he died, and not properly realised when completed some years later. 'It will be a controlled community,' he said, 'a showcase for American industry and research, schools, cultural and educational opportunities...'.[33]

He also looked back to his own past. His love for the little town of Marceline in Missouri, which meant so much to him as a child and throughout his adult life, generated an idea for a theme park, with the tentative title of The Walt Disney Boyhood Farm.[34] The original Disney farmhouse was to be moved away from the road to allow for access by car. The idea was to have a living and organic farm that would, like Disneyland, be changing and developing from season to season and from year to year, based on the first decade of the twentieth century. There would be real animals and a swimming pool designed like a swimming hole with a wooden diving board as a reminder of the swimming holes of Disney's and countless other children's childhood. Steven Watts in his admirable account of Disney and the American way of life has pointed out the importance of nostalgia to Middle America and he asks, 'Why did American audiences respond so enthusiastically, even rapturously, to [Disney's] personal vision? ... The stable years he spent in Marceline were a brief respite from the geographic mobility and emotional turmoil that characterised the great bulk of his childhood ... His popular audience, many of its members also suffering from the dislocations of historical change, likewise yearned for the stability and comfort of a way of life that was vanishing'.[35]

Walt Disney became too ill to develop his idea and had to cancel visits to Marceline in the last year of his life. When his friend Rush Johnson, formerly Mayor of Marceline suggested that there should be a Walt Disney museum and library in Middle America, Disney's reply was characteristic: 'Rush, museums and libraries are for the dead'.

Notes

1. Good accounts of the inception and development of Disneyland are in Holliss and Sibley, *The Disney Studio Story* (1988), Bob Thomas, *The Walt Disney Biography* (1977) and Finch, *Walt Disney's America* (1975).

2. Disneyland now contains attractions associated with films other than those from the Disney Studio, for example the 'Indiana Jones™ and Temple of Doom' attraction.

3. John Hench, quoted in Finch, *The Art of Walt Disney*, 411.

4. Walt Disney, internal memorandum, quoted in Bob Thomas, *The Walt Disney Bigraphy*, 172.

5. Walt Disney, Dedication speech, quoted in *Walt Disney's Disneyland* (Los Angeles: Walt Disney Productions, 1971).

6. The three dimensionalising of experience was continued after Disney's death. A scheme in the early eighties for creating a new kind of attraction, involving the visitor in entering the vision of individual famous artists was discussed, and sketches and models made. The idea was to create the colours, shapes and style of an artist, Seurat for example (to give a comparatively simple case) and build up a 'ride' of his signifiers, creating a 3D *mise-en-scène* through which the visitor would travel in a car, as on a conventional 'ride'. The artist would thus be entered and visited in a way inconceivable except to Walt Disney 'Imagineers'. The visitor would be entirely in the hands of the creators of the 'ride' and would encounter the artist's vision and creativity via the mechanical control of the attraction's constructors.

   Another plan, also conceived with the art of Europe in mind, was to create a Temple of Art, a shrine containing the world's hundred most famous paintings. These were to be hung in a special gallery or galleries, called 'The Movement of Art' at Epcot in Florida. There are echoes here of the Victorian ethos of totality and inclusion represented by tomes like 'The Hundred Best Paintings' or 'The Hundred Best Poems'. When problems of security and conservation were analysed, The Walt Disney Company abandoned the plan. One of the instigators of these projects was Vince Jefferds who had been in charge of Disney's marketing department, and who purported to be himself an artist.

   This information is based on interviews with Michael Darby, Deputy Director of the Victoria and Albert Museum, who was the English specialist consultant on the project, London, 25 February 1985, and with Vince Jefferds, at Burbank, California, 21 May 1985.

7. Umberto Eco, *Travels in Hyperreality*, trans. William Feaver (1986. London, Picador, 1987), 23.

8. John Malcolm Brinnin, *Dylan Thomas in America* (1955. London: Arlington, 1988), 117.

9. Schickel, *Walt Disney*, 24.

10. 'At one point a cage of red and white lady parrots descended from the ceiling *à la Folies Bergères*, unconnected with the sound track which was what the birds were supposed to be singing ... The girl parrots had false eyelashes, mascara, lipstick and rouge ... But when the plastic flowers descend and begin crooning ...' Author's diary, 24 May 1985.

11. Walt Disney, quoted in Bob Thomas, *The Walt Disney Biography*, 193.

12. The Villa D'Este was built in the early seventeenth century by Cardinal Hippolytus Este, and was expanded throughout the next two centuries. The gardens lie on a steep slope and the fountains are operated by a diversion from the natural fall of the river. Each level opens up new vistas for the visitor, including a miniature Roman

area, and there is one grotto-like fountain which has a waterfall, behind which the visitor can walk.

13. Rose Macaulay writes in *Pleasure of Ruins* (London: Weidenfeld and Nicolson, 1953), 150:

'Isfahan ancient in history but made glorious by its Shahs, embellished with hundreds of palaces and gardens and mosques by the great Shah Abbas in the sixteenth century, who filled it with art, luxury and admiring foreigners and laid out the tremendous avenue of approach bordered with gardens, terraces, palaces, pavilions and running, cascading water ...

All over Persia the mud cities moulder, the Shahs' brilliant palaces crumble to earth ... But the gardens blossom, the fountains play; the fairy-tale cities live on in the mind like the chiming of bells.'

14. The grandest cascades and water effects in England are at Chatsworth House, Derbyshire, with its fountain, cascade and waterfall folly, where water falls from an apparently natural outcrop of rock, and an artificial weeping willow sprays water on unsuspecting visitors who step too close:

'Here art seems to have been most successful. In every direction masses of grey rock are strewn about in the most picturesque and unstudied disorder ... In some places we notice high piles of gritstone rising to a great elevation, their precipitous fronts clothed with mosses and creeping plants, and over which the water has been made to descend in beautiful cascades.' [James Croston, *On Foot Through the Peak*, (1876); Manchester: E.J. Morten, 1973: 140.]

15. Finch, *Walt Disney's America*, 46.

16. Catalogue, *Fine Art and Related Items* (Burbank: Howard Lowery, 25 August 1991), 56 and Canemaker, *Before the Animation Begins*, 163.

17. While visiting the Walt Disney Studio on 19 July 1989 the author met some of the senior animators who were about to leave for France to examine the châteaux of the Loire Valley. This was research for the animated feature *Beauty and the Beast* (1991) and the artists' comment was, 'We don't want to get the castles wrong again like we did in *Sleeping Beauty*'.

18. Reference to these two Shakespeare films was made in passing to the author by Frank Thomas.

19. Bob Thomas, *The Art of Animation* (1958), 109.

20. Nicholas Tucker, 'Arts in Society: Who's Afraid of Walt Disney', *New Society*, 4 April 1968, 502.

21. Bob Thomas, *The Walt Disney Biography*, 244.

22. Eyvind Earle has continued to paint in the same style and is now considered one of the most successful painters on the West Coast. His pictures of the Californian landscape and Pacific ocean combine power and an idiosyncratic personal vision.

23. For example, a cel of the wicked stepmother in *Cinderella* contains five different coloured inks for the outline; black for the eyebrows, light grey and dark grey for the hair and ruffs, flesh colour for the face and hands, and maroon for the dress. This form of inking and painting was extremely labour intensive but Disney liked his animation traditional and enjoyed the smooth polished look of the inked cel. There is a sensuous pleasure in the rounded forms and clean plastic outlines of the cel-painted character, as well as in the technical perfection of the hand inking and painting. This partly explains the very high prices for cels at art auctions. (See also *Producing an animated feature film* at the beginning of Chapter 3.) John Hench commented on the control that hand inking gave the artists: 'Through the line of beauty we had total control, total literacy'.

24. Valerie Grove, *Dear Dodie: The Life of Dodie Smith* (London: Chatto and Windus, 1996), 241.

25. Ray Aragon was born in 1926. The son of a Mexican father, he was born and brought up in Los Angeles in a working class atmosphere, 'with no books, no art, no nothing' as he put it, but he was a compulsive drawer. After serving with the army, he drifted into advertising. In order to study art at Chouinard and keep his family – he married in 1950 – he drove a truck from 4 pm till midnight, and then started at the college full-time from 9 am. In advertising he was earning between 60 and 80 dollars a week; at Disney he earned 85 dollars weekly. He was encouraged by Marc Davis who was teaching at Chouinard, to join the Walt Disney Studio, where he worked in the layout department under Don Griffith and Don Da Gradi. He expressed great respect for the latter's work and did layout drawings for *Sleeping Beauty* (1959), *101 Dalmatians* (1961) and *Mary Poppins* (1964) among others. His dancing graphic line and grasp of mass and detail recalls Daumier.

   Ray Aragon spoke of the support given by the Walt Disney Studio Library. 'Barbara Blake was a great library researcher,' he said. ' "Give me three hours" she'd say, if we had a problem. If they couldn't get it they sent a messenger to Fox or MGM and that afternoon a traffic messenger would come in with fifteen books and photographs, clippings. For example, a London kitchen that I needed...' Ray Aragon is still active in commercial art and animation.

26. Bill Peet's illustrated life story is in his *Autobiography* (1989).

   It is to be hoped that Ken Anderson's life story, and particularly his long and devoted service with Walt Disney will one day be chronicled. He was born in Seattle in 1909, the son of a travelling hardwood timber merchant. As a boy he was fostered out to a dictatorial aunt on a farm where he was badly treated. He ran away and lived wild in the woods for a month till found and brought back to his foster parents. Sleeping as a student above a library, he devoured books and finished his friends' assignments for a fee. A sympathetic academic, Professor Lionel Pries, introduced him to the world of music and the concert hall, and he was awarded an architectural scholarship to Europe. 'No one had won this scholarship west of the Mississippi' Anderson proudly recalled.

   He studied in Europe for two years, at L'École des Beaux Arts, Fontainebleau and at the American Academy in Rome. Art deco and art nouveau impressed him and he particularly enjoyed the warm colours of southern Europe, being drawn to Spain. He had a photographic memory and total recall. Joining the studio in 1934, he impressed Disney with his grasp of perspective; the latter liked Anderson's bright warm colour for *Ferdinand the Bull* (1938), based on his memories of Spain. He moved from animation to the story department, becoming story artist, colour stylist, art director and production designer for many of the feature films. Immensely gifted, he was deeply hurt by Disney's criticism of *One Hundred and One Dalmatians*. In 1962 he suffered two strokes but recovered and returned to work on *The Jungle Book* (1967), *The Aristocats* (1970) and other films until his retirement in 1978. He died peacefully in 1993 (see Colour Plate 86). See Canemaker, *Before the Animation Begins*, 168–182 and *Persistence of Vision*, ed. Paul Anderson.

27. Rowland Emmett was at least as well known as Searle in the late forties and early fifties. He and his wife Mary also visited the Walt Disney Studio and spent Christmas Day 1953 with Walt Disney who was working on *20,000 Leaguers under the Sea* at the time. Disney showed the couple round the studio and took them to his home. He was interested in filming *Anthony and Antimacassar*, a children's story written by Mary and illustrated by Rowland. It is a fantasy about a small china pig and a typically antiquated Emmett railway engine, who take to the rails together and encounter, among other things, a gang of pirates. Emmett recalled: 'The form (the film) should take could not be decided. It really boils down to this: all his characters

have three fingers only and I couldn't reconcile myself to that'. Quoted in Jacqui Grossart, *Rowland Emmett: From 'Punch' to 'Chitty-Chitty-Bang-Bang' and Beyond*, (London: Chris Beetles, 1988), 12–13.

28. Dodie Smith, *The Hundred and One Dalmatians* (1965; London, Piccolo, 1981), 9.

29. Holliss and Sibley, *The Disney Studio Story*, 76.

30. I am indebted to Brian Sibley for allowing me access to his private correspondence with the late P.L. Travers (1899–1996), and for granting me interviews about her work. Information comes from this source unless otherwise cited.

31. Holliss and Sibley, *The Disney Studio Story*, 82.

32. Ibid., 83 and 87.

33. Ibid., 83 and 87.

34. Information here is based on interviews with Rush Johnson and with his daughter Kaye Malins on 26 and 27 August 1994, Marceline, Missouri.

35. Watts, *The Magic Kingdom*, 6.

CHAPTER 11

Conclusion: 'Best Vantage Point for Viewing the Castle'

Animated feature films after Walt Disney

With the death of Walt Disney, my survey of the relationship between the man, the studio and Europe comes properly to an end, but the studio was so much part of the man that in order to complete the story, a brief outline is given here of the animated feature films that have been released since 1966. The European connection continued, leading to the revival of the company's film fortunes with a European fairy tale, *The Little Mermaid* in 1989. Several books have been written about the changes to the company in the last thirty years of the twentieth century[1] and Europe still continues to play a part in a global search for filmic or thematic material. Indeed there is more than ever a need for worldwide success, should a film fail to recoup its costs inside the United States alone. Disney learnt the lesson of losing his European and world markets back in 1940 during the Second World War, and the search continues for universal story material, much of which emanates from Europe.

Towards the end of his life Walt Disney was not always a creative presence in the animation department but the studio was producing a number of films based on European sources around the time of his death. Mention should be made of the *Winnie the Pooh* books by A. A. Milne (1882–1956), illustrated by E.H. Shepard (1879–1976), which Disney intended to use as material for a feature film. Because the studio felt the story was too juvenile to sustain interest for the length of a whole feature, it was released in 1966 as a 'featurette' of twenty minutes. Afraid of alienating American audiences, the studio introduced an American gopher, a burrowing rodent unknown to English audiences and gave Christopher Robin an American accent; the outrage in Britain caused the voice to be redubbed and the film was a popular, if not critical success. Mrs Milne was pleased with the result, though Shepard called it 'a complete travesty'.[2] The characterisation in the early films is charming, with sketchy backgrounds that approximate sympathetically to Shepard. The first film's success led to sequels and a compilation feature film in 1977. The characters continue their popularity both as Disney revisions of Milne and Shepard and in their original form.

Storyboard: The Aristocats *(1970).*
© Disney Enterprises, Inc.

The Aristocats (1970) and *Robin Hood* (1973) reflect the torpidity of The Walt Disney Company after the death of its founder. The former was begun before Disney died, but owing to the uncertainty prevailing at the studio after his death, it took another four years to be completed, and lacks spontaneity. Set in France it has some pleasant Parisian backgrounds (Ken Anderson was once again art director) and the film remains popular with the French. Although some of the finest talents still working at the studio were employed on both *The Aristocats* and *Robin Hood*, neither makes imaginative use of the animation medium and both rely on reworking earlier material. So long dependent on Disney himself, the artists relied on their memory of what he liked, rather than on their own judgement. Ken Anderson wept when he saw how his character concepts had been processed into stereotypes for the animation on *Robin Hood*.[3]

Ken Anderson: Story sketch of Friar Tuck for Robin Hood.
© *Disney Enterprises, Inc.*

The Rescuers (1977) is based on two stories by the English writer Margery Sharp, *The Rescuers* (1959) and *Miss Bianca* (1962). Beginning in New York and ending in the bayou swamps of Florida, it concerns the adventures of two mice who are members of the Rescue Aid Society, a United Nations of mice which has its headqarters beneath the mother building in New York. The hero and heroine set out to help a little orphan girl in the clutches of a classic Disney villainess Madame Medusa. Eleven years after his death, the shade of Disney was less restricting, and this modest film combines excellence of plot and characterisation with a freshness that avoids sentimentality. It was followed by *The Fox and the Hound* (1981) an entirely American project which was largely produced by a new group of artists and directors at the studio.

The Black Cauldron (1985) was released just after the advent of a new management team under the triumvirate control of Michael Eisner, Frank Wells and Jeffrey Katzenberg. This marked an end to the interregnum years after Walt Disney's death and confidence was regained, but not until after this expensive film had failed at the box office.

Based on Lloyd Alexander's five *Chronicles of Prydain* books (1964–1968), it concerns the struggle between good and evil in ancient Wales. Its long gestation from 1981 to 1985 and the many changes of plot and personnel during its production may partly explain the film's uneven quality. Characterisation is uncertain and the plot lacks cohesion, though there is much to admire technically and aesthetically. It explores the dark world of fantasy that J. R. R. Tolkien had initiated in his seminal epic *The Lord of the Rings* (1954–1955), and the plot structure is reminiscent of Tolkien, like so much fantasy written at that time. Other influences come from Hollywood and especially from the science fantasy *Star Wars* trilogy.

The next animated feature *The Great Mouse Detective* (1986) was more modest in scope and in budget. It is based on the Eve Titus story of 1974 *Basil of Baker Street* about a mouse Sherlock Holmes going to the aid of a little girl mouse in London, whose father is in the hands of an evil rat. It has interesting characters, and is refreshingly taut after the rambling *The Black Cauldron*, but it lacks conviction of place or atmosphere. London, so strongly defined in graphic terms in *101 Dalmatians*, is less firmly grasped. *Oliver & Co* (1988) updates Dickens' *Oliver Twist* to New York with dogs and cats as the main characters.[4] Once again Europe was the source for the new film and, despite crudely realised animation, it was suffcently successful at the box office to encourage the new regime of Eisner, Wells and Katzenberg to continue with animation. *Who Framed Roger Rabbit* (1988) followed, with its skilful blending of live action and animation. This story of Hollywood between the wars and the relationship between a real detective and cartoon rabbit was an enormous success; resources were made available at the studio to expand the animation unit and to increase output.

The Little Mermaid (1989) is based on Hans Christian Andersen's fairy tale and was considered as a possibility for animation as long ago as the late 1930s. The Danish artist Kay Nielsen (see Chapter 7) had worked on the project in 1939 when he was art director at the story department during the making of *Fantasia*. His concept paintings for *The Little Mermaid* of 1939 were originally intended for use in a film about Andersen and his work (see appendix B). His delicate pastel sketches were used as a basis for some of the story for the much later film, and Nielsen is given posthumous screen credit as a 'visual developer'.[5] The influence of the theatre on Disney animation now becomes noticeable; the show-stopping number forms part of this and subsequent films, and many of the senior creative and managerial posts at the studio were now held by men and women with stage experience, in musical theatre especially, on both sides of the Atlantic. This theatricality is noticeable in *Beauty and the Beast* (1991) and German expressionism through Hollywood is again an influence, as has been noticed with earlier Disney work. There are reminders of *Frankenstein* (1931) especially (see Colour Plate 87).

Merchandising, with the profits to be made by marketing of spin-off materials linked to the films is now a major factor in the success of film projects, and pre-publicity accounts for a large proportion of the budget. These films also, based on European fairy tales, have an epic dimension that gives them, for the first time since the death of Walt Disney, a classic status that refers us back to the earlier days of *Snow White and the Seven Dwarfs* and *Cinderella*.

A sequel to *The Rescuers*, *The Rescuers Down Under* was released in 1990. This time the intrepid mice Bianca and Bernard fly to the Australian outback to rescue a small boy and his animal friends from an evil trapper. There is a delightful absorption of the Australian landscape in the backgrounds to this enchanting film, with its unity of plot, characterisation and atmosphere. The proscenium arch as an extra dimension does not intrude and there are no songs. The film was modestly promoted and overshadowed by the success of *The Little Mermaid*. By complete contrast, *Aladdin* (1992) is the most American of all the Disney features,[6] and continues the new tradition with theatrically presented mammoth musical numbers. Its debt to Europe lies in its homage to the genius of the Hungarian Korda brother film makers and especially to Vincent Korda the designer of *The Thief of Baghdad* (1940)[7] and to the Richard Williams film *The Cobbler and the Thief*, begun many years ago but completed by other hands and released in 1996. The Disney *Aladdin* was enormously popular but its success was overtaken by that of the next animated feature *The Lion King* (1994).

The Lion King has been, at the time of writing (1998) the most successful animated feature ever produced. It is a skilful retelling of the Hamlet story with Biblical overtones, and the anthropomorphism makes it an ideal vehicle for animation. It is the story of a lion cub who matures and learns to control his fear enough to face the evil uncle who has usurped his rightful throne. There is a real feeling for the open landscape and skies of Africa as well as for the menace that lurks in its undergrowth. *Pocahontas* (1995) is an earnest attempt to treat an adult historical subject with tact and seriousness. It deals with, and alters, the real story of an Indian princess who fell in love with an English pioneer in the seventeenth century. Once again the proscenium arch is an unseen presence for some expansive and irrelevent theatrical numbers.

Music, an important element in any Disney film, becomes operatic in its intensity in *The Hunchback of Notre Dame* (1996). The film is a bizarre homage to the 1939 Hollywood version directed by William Dieterle and starring Charles Laughton. There are constant reminders of the earlier film, though Disney alters the tone and makes the tragedy end happily. The artists visited Paris to study the background as well as the work of Hugo himself and that of illustrators such as Gustave Doré – whom we have already seen as an inspiration to the men and women who worked for Disney himself.[8] Once again there are elaborate musical numbers. Disney has again come full circle, from the pioneering twenties when Walt Disney based his work on the inspiration of the silent cinema and live theatrical vaudeville, to the sophisticated nineties with a return

Marek Buchwald: Conceptual sketch of Notre Dame for the Disney film The Hunchback of Notre Dame *(1996).*
© *Disney Enterprises, Inc.*

to musical theatre. Disney in fact has taken the place of the great musicals that came out of America and were themselves based on the European tradition of musical comedy and operetta. Promoting its own stage versions of current animated films, the company has launched *Beauty and the Beast* and *The Lion King* in the theatre. Thus a film can have extended life through the theatre, and these stage versions have been produced not only on Broadway but also in London and in other major cities throughout the world.

Europe and classical myth inspired the next animated feature film *Hercules* (1997). This is a comic strip version and cheerfully inaccurate, influenced by the British cartoonist Gerald Scarfe (b. 1936) who was initially employed as inspirational artist, but who became production designer. His angular line and sharp visual commentary on human nature is captured admirably through animation; this is one of the least pretentious and most enjoyable of recent Disney features. European sources will, no doubt, continue to be utilised by the company in its global search for animation material.

Gustave Doré: 'Gargantua resting on the towers of Notre Dame'. Doré's illustrations continue to inspire the Disney artists. This scene from Rabelais' Gargantua and Pantagruel (1873) shows Doré's command of scale and dramatic sense. The Disney film of Hugo's novel also invites admiration of scale and contrasts between the individual and the crowd, between the city and the cathedral, between landscape and sky.

From Epcot to Disneyland Paris

During his last years Walt Disney turned his attention from animation to plans for a second theme park in Florida, which opened as Walt Disney World Resort in 1971 nearly five years after his death. He was interested in solving in the problems of urban pollution and community planning which he outlined as an Experimental Prototype Community

Illustration (1891) of gargoyles on Notre Dame. The grotesque fancy of the carving is taken up by the Disney artists in the animated gargoyle characters in The Hunchback of Notre Dame.

of Tomorrow (Epcot). Development for this did not begin until 1975 and Epcot eventually opened in 1982 in a very different form from that conceived by Disney. A third theme park, Tokyo Disneyland, opened in 1983 and attendance records for all the three parks were broken there on one day alone.[9] A fourth theme park, Euro Disneyland (EuroDisney for short), was opened in Paris in 1992. After an uncertain start, this park, renamed Disneyland Paris, is also a success. There are plans at the time of writing for more parks in Florida and in California. The income generated from the parks and from the attendant merchandising is enormous, but film is still the basis upon which the empire is built.

Euro Disneyland opened in April 1992 to a barrage of criticism from the French and British press.[10] Heavy losses in the first two years led to rumours that it would close, but a new name Disneyland Paris and new management from 1994 have led to increasing success. The park is under an hour's train ride from Paris, and there is a short walk from the specially built station through charming gardens and fountains to the gates of the park. The Disneyland Hotel which straddles the gates contains reminders of Disney films and characters, and is a combination of the discreet and the lavish. The appeal of this park is its overall design, a real sense of the *fin-de-siècle* art nouveau period which is most noticeable in Discoveryland and in the arcades of Main Street. Reminders of the Paris metro signs, Toulouse Lautrec posters and other turn of the century design motifs are rendered lovingly in pastiche. There is an exuberant blend of Europe and America in these areas, and the close attention to detail in the minutiae of rooftops, gilding, signs, tiles and so on reminds us of the finest of Disney's own animated films. This finesse is perhaps even more carefully attended to than in California, and displays an innate good taste lacking in some current feature animation.

The park is carefully modelled on Disney's own personally supervised first Magic Kingdom in California, though there are some new attractions, and, like all the other parks, it is constantly updated and altered. *Alice's Curious Labyrinth* is an active rather than passive adventure with the real problem of getting around a complicated maze on foot, which should surely delight a child. Lewis Carroll would have been the first to approve of the surprise appearance of his books' characters and the water squirts, which are fountains of little jets that seem to fly from one hidden spout to another. The comic Alice castle from which we can survey the rest of the park would have delighted Carroll.

The *Sleeping Beauty* castle is also imaginatively designed; there are treelike fronds to decorate the pillars, a series of stained glass windows and tapestries that tell the story, and in the dungeon a magnificent dragon that moves and spits fiery steam from its nostrils. Angular trees and rocks echo the precision of Eyvind Earle's paintings for the 1959 film of *Sleeping Beauty*, and there is also a reminder of the formal gardens of

France and her châteaux (see Colour Plates 88 and 89). Elsewhere the art nouveau decor acts as a cohesive design for all the park, including the Jules Verne moon rocket and airship. Disneyland Paris returns to Europe the sources that it has used and Americanised; the Magic Kingdom has come full circle just as modern Disney animated film returns to the stage from which it came (see Colour Plate 90).

Walt Disney and Europe

The power of a company to package dreams and to capitalise upon a people's expectations of happiness is as dynamic as ever. Ten days before the opening of EuroDisney in 1992 I watched a huddle of cold parents and querulous children line up in the large square dominated by Manchester's Gothic town hall. The towers and spires of Victorian Gothic however were being upstaged by a new castle which had grown overnight, by magic, its gold and green turrets of plastic vying with the sturdier stone embattlements of Alfred Waterhouse's 1868 building (see Colour Plate 91). This was the castle of *La Belle au Bois Dormant*, a miniature château promoting EuroDisney; and a moment later Mickey and Minnie came out among us like royalty to embrace the children and to receive homage. A child whose age could not at most have been more than three beamed at the giant grotesques. The little face lit up, shining with a delight which was transparent, naked and unashamed. The product reached out and touched.

How this has been achieved over a period of the last seventy years is a complicated and profound historiographical phenomenon. Its power is disturbing. It embraces psychology and religion, conscious and sub-conscious desires and fears, ideologies and marketing and determining standards in a mass communication environment. The abuse heaped upon the new theme park by the European press is an instance of the uneasy relationship between the American and the European. The press paid little attention to the popular rides and attractions of the park, which are the reasons for its existence, but concentrated on the cultural issues of imperialism and economics. It was felt that Europe has her own heritage and does not need a 'Magic Kingdom'; but this real European heritage gave Walt Disney the ideas for his first animated features which he in turn developed in his theme parks. The Walt Disney Company is returning to Europe the European stories and folktales and classics which it has kept alive – debased no doubt – through the films and latterly through the parks. The complexity of this dialogue between Walt Disney and his European sources, and especially with regard to the audiences that he conceived as both adults and children has been outlined above. Emphasis has been placed on the difficulty of identifying Disney the man, and Disney the studio before it developed into the enormous company that has expanded throughout the last two decades of the twentieth century. There are many other books to be written, not least one on the way the company is now itself exploiting the work of its founder.

Disney made use of graphic European traditions, in particular from Germany, for his animated feature films. The mass audience, comprising both adult and child, which was always at the forefront of his conscious thinking was appealed to by turns and by turns invited to extend its vision, via his technology of animation, to enjoy art and music and literature from the older cultures which in their turn were uneasily reinterpreted. Disney used the individual talents of artists who were either European themselves or influenced by the great illustrative tradition of Europe which culminated in the golden age of book illustration in the first decades of this century. I have drawn attention to some of the individual artists who worked under the name 'Disney', and the work of some exceptional talents has been emphasised. Disney drove himself and his staff to an over expansion which led to near collapse at the end of 1940; this caused him to look away from Europe for ideas, in a desperate bid to keep afloat with heavy debts and low box office returns. The cohesive vision collapsed into a series of experimental works, of package formation, of varying styles.

Disney's use of the European story after the war was a return to pre-war projects. The post-war feature films were less elaborate and more reliant on formulae that had proved successful or imitative of earlier filmic styles. Their success led to renewed confidence, taking Walt Disney away from animation to explore live action and the idea of the Magic Kingdom. Europe again, with a popular blend of the past and present, formed one of the bases of Disneyland.

After seeing the films for the last sixty years, and after studying the man and the work closely for the last fifteen years, I am still no nearer understanding the man. He is an alien to me, born of a harsh New World which is desperate to re-root itself through its European past. A gentle and much loved man by family and friends, his fierce independence and wounded vulnerability led to a ruthlessness which made him some bitter enemies. Many of his staff, however, served him loyally and with devotion through every vicissitude. He remains what perhaps he always was, an enigma. I do, however, now comprehend something of the mixture of past and present that he absorbed and recreated. Out of literature, art and music he and his colleagues produced a series of films which stand as works of art in their own right, transcending the ephemeral and continuing to evoke wonder and delight as the years go by. At their best, the Disney animated feature films universalise human experience; they are both vulgar in the old-fashioned sense 'of the people' and profound. I have tried in this book to throw some light on the European influences that contribute to this new American art form of the twentieth century.

Walt Disney's optimism was entirely transatlantic; his resources a mixture of the old world and the new. When he stopped the gardener from putting up a little fence to prevent us walking on the grass he said:

No. Wait a minute. Tell you what we'll do. We'll put up a little rock walk right through there and we'll put up a sign that says 'Best vantage point for filming the castle'.

Notes

1. See Bryman, *Disney and his Worlds*, 34–60, who points out that Eisner and his team capitalised on experimental work that had already been started by the outgoing chief executive, Ron Miller and his colleagues. See also John Taylor, *Storming the Magic Kingdom: Wall Street, the Raiders and the Battle for Disney* (London: Viking, 1988) and Ron Grover, *The Disney Touch: How a Daring Management Team Revived an Entertainment Empire* (Homewood, Ill.: Business One Irwin, 1991).

2. Holliss and Sibley, *The Disney Studio Story*, 85.

3. Ken Anderson quoted by Richard Dixon; interview with author, Southampton, 2 August 1971.

4. The short Disney cartoon *Mickey's Christmas Carol* (1983) is a reminder of how much Dickens and Disney have in common as popular artists. Both were workaholics producing work which varies enormously in style, content and quality, sensational melodrama and crude sentimentality jostling with deeply felt, moving expressiveness. Both utilised new technologies, recognising the value of marketing, and both used the media (theatre or TV) in order to promote their image. Both created a gallery of immortal characters.

5. Canemaker, *Before the Animation Begins*, 81.

6. Leslie Felperin has pointed out the self-referential element in *Aladdin* and its reliance on Western attitudes to the Middle East in her 'The Thief of Buena Vista: Disney's *Aladdin* and Orientalism' *A Reader in Animation Studies*, ed. Jayne Pilling (London: John Libbey), 1997.

7. J. B. Kaufman, 'Douglas Fairbanks, William Cameron Menzies, Alexander Korda – and *Aladdin*', published in Italian as 'Di nuovo *Aladdin*', *Cinemzero*, February 1994 (Supplemento No. 1a Cinemazero/Notizie Anno XIII°–N.2), 10–14.

8. Stephen Rebello, *The Art of the Hunchback of Notre Dame* (New York: Hyperion, 1996), 118.

9. Holliss and Sibley, *The Disney Studio Story*, 103.

10. Typical press comments may be gauged by these headlines: Peter Hillman, 'From Guest to Grumpy Overnight', *Observer*, 19 April 1992; Nick Gilbert, 'No Fun for Europe in divided Disney world', *Independent on Sunday*, 23 August 1992; '£23m loss reported by EuroDisney', *Independent*, 21 November 1992.

APPENDIX A

Continuing *Fantasia*

It was Walt Disney's hope to extend *Fantasia* by adding to or replacing some of its items for special release distribution. To gain a sense of the Disney Studio's concept of an ongoing concert feature, this appendix outlines some of the proposed items. See also the end of Chapter 5 Introduction to *Fantasia* for Disney's ideas about an ongoing concert feature film. See also Canemaker, 'The *Fantasia* That Never Was', 81 and Solomon, *The Disney That Never Was*, 120–151. There are many story sketches and inspirational drawings and paintings for these items in the Walt Disney Archives and elsewhere, and one of them, *Clair de Lune*, was completed.

Clair de Lune by Debussy

This is an impressionistic piece like the *Ave Maria* but without the latter's religious overtones. 'It has the restful effect that we need,' said Disney. 'You don't want too much effort in this – if you have too much going on, then you don't hear it'. And again, 'A much more effective picture than if you start putting in detail (on) the birds ... Hold it down to a simple type of animation' (story conference 8 December 1938).

Clair de Lune was shelved, and resurfaced in the package film *Make Mine Music* (1946) with a different sound track, using a specially written popular ballad called *Blue Bayou*. The visual presentation, however, was created for Debussy's music and which, like *Ave Maria* has little story, but much technical sophistication.

The piece observes two herons wading through bayou swampland; they fly off into the moonlight. This is all that occurs, although the *mise-en-scène* is complex and considerably more movement takes place within the frame, and with simulated camera movement than in the *Ave Maria*. At three and three-quarter minutes it is almost exactly a minute shorter, with eight shots as opposed to five, although the colour range of blue, black and silver is more muted than in the Schubert item. The frame is filled with detail of trees, swamp, water and reflections, as well as with the movement of the birds either wading, flying or quite still.

Sylvia Holland prepared a series of delicate pastels on black paper which bear a close resemblance to the final film in mood at least. Josh Meador also provided detailed inspirational chalk studies on black paper. The style of the film is impressionistic. There is a slow dissolve at the end of the opening shot of the full moon surrounded by clouds and stars. In a very slow mix, the picture becomes purely abstract before the image is redefined as a mangrove swamp. The heron sets up ripples which are handled unrealistically, a foretaste of the limited animation techniques that the studio would adopt later in the forties. As the heron flies up through the bayou trees the camera tracks with it and swings up and back, simulating the lazy flight of the bird. The spareness of Japanese painting is also suggested, though the inspirational work was by an Englishwoman. It is essentially cinematic, a camera's eye at work, as opposed to the theatricality of the *Ave Maria*. There is an overwhelming sense of melancholy evoked by the colour, the setting, the music. *Clair de Lune* has never been theatrically released with its original score. It was given a special screening at the Los Angeles County Museum in July 1986. This was part of a retrospective of Disney animated feature films, *Disney Magic*, curated by Charles Solomon. A specially restored print was shown by Scott MacQueen, the Walt Disney Studio Film Archivist, at the London Film Festival, 1998.

The Ride of the Valkyries by Wagner

Kay Nielsen and his assistant Bill Wallett prepared some beautiful pastels displaying a vigour absent from Nielsen's book illustrations and from the paintings for the *Ave Maria*. Perhaps it was Wallett who brought a virility that Nielsen lacked; it is difficult to tell which artist painted which pictures. There are at least a hundred and fifteen sketches in coloured crayon or gouache on black paper, showing the descent of the Valkyries from the clouds and their conducting of slain warriors to Valhalla. Disney was impressed by the storyboards presented by Nielsen and Wallett:

> I sure like this set-up, especially the colouring; the greys and blacks ... This would be a great subject. It would be controversial ... We haven't butchered it up or done anything where anybody could squalk ...(story conference 27 January 1941).

He commented on the need to differentiate the item from *Ave Maria*, and said that it would probably be a replacement. He was also becoming much more conscious of cost, a subject rarely mentioned in previous meetings. Here, however, it was referred to constantly, and it would do so throughout the remaining years spent on animation. 'If we can't do it for a set figure,' Disney said at the same meeting, 'then we better forget it.' And he was also aware of the difficulty of animating human beings realistically: 'You'll get embarrassing animation if you get Brunnhilde up there mugging, or one of those things'.

Sam Armstrong the director, with Nielsen and Wallett, presented these continuity notes: 'We deliberately worked away from the Germanic-Operatic type of staging and towards the older Norse legends and ancient traditions.' However, doubt was expressed about the suitability of producing the item in wartime. Two years later, after the extensions to *Fantasia* had been abandoned, the item was raised in an internal memorandum at Sylvia Holland's request. 'I wonder if its theme of a hero's death on the battlefield, and ascension into Valhalla in the arms of an armoured blonde, would win public acceptance at this time'. (Inter-office communication from Bob Carr to Ralph Parker, 9 July 1943. Courtesy Theo Halladay.)

The Swan of Tuonela by Sibelius

Most of the inspirational sketches for this item were by Sylvia Holland, and her colleagues Sam Armstrong and Joe Stahley, once again using coloured chalk and crayon on black paper. They have a still, unearthly quality not unlike Nielsen's – he was admired by Sylvia Holland. Nielsen was present at the story conferences early in 1941 when both the Sibelius and Wagner pieces were discussed. Over eighty enchanting pastels, most of them by Holland (see Colour Plate 92), were shown on a Leica reel to an enthusiastic Disney, but he was again concerned about cost. 'I think this can be done for less,' he said as soon as his attention turned from *The Ride of The Valkyries* to *The Swan of Tuonela*. He was also anxious to keep the Swan at a distance. 'Always keep her mysterious ... I like the interpretation here but I would like to see that Swan just a character that floats around and doesn't do any acting or emoting ... I'm crazy about them both. I'd like to see us do them' (story conference 27 January 1941).

Disney was again conscious of similarities between this item and the *Ave Maria*, but as John Canemaker points out in 'The *Fantasia* That Never Was', '*The Swan of Tuonela* achieves a similar feeling of spirituality and transcendence without resorting to non-secular and obvious religious symbolism'.

The illustrations show a funeral barge being launched and making its way through fantastic caverns on the river of death to the land beyond, where it is met by other spirits. Bob Carr who did research for it wrote, 'The Swan, from the start, has had all supporters, no critics. Stokowski was enthusiastic. It has survived every revision of every *Fantasia*-sequel programme' (inter-office communication, 9 July 1943). A year later, in a report on musical subjects in progress (7 April 1944, courtesy Joe Grant) Violet Tharpe noted that the music had been recorded by Stokowski and studio musicians. There was a layout running reel made up of partly rough layouts and story sketches.

The Insect Suite – various composers

This was to include *The Flight of the Bumble Bee* with the technically innovative idea of the bee chasing a floating blossom outside the parameter of the screen and invading the auditorium. The story sketches were by Curt Perkins or possibly Elmer Plummer and the music was recorded by Stokowski and studio musicians. With directional sound, this would have been a startling number. Quite a different boogie-woogie treatment of the music was given for a version called *Bumble Boogie* and shown in the package film *Melody Time* (1948).

Chopin's 'Minute' Waltz was conceived as a dragonfly ballet, the delicate drawings again probably by Sylvia Holland. 'The Mosquito Dance', from the story sketches by another English artist Johnny Walbridge, appears to be reminiscent of Winsor McCay's *How a Mosquito Operates* (1912). John Canemaker cites the 'exquisite black and white pastels probably by Elmer Plummer' for Grieg's 'Butterflies' as the most beautiful of all the inspirational drawings. 'If the subsequent film had adhered to the quiet beauty and texture of the original storyboard, 'Butterflies' might have become a new breakthrough in animation technique and direction' (John Canemaker, 'The *Fantasia* That Never Was', 139).

The Baby Ballet – various composers

Suggested by Joe Grant and with preliminary sketches by Mary Blair, this was about babies fleeing from anthropomorphised nappies and safety pins and being rescued by storks. Lee Blair worked out story board continuity and it was developed by Sylvia Holland, Ethel Kulsar and Curt Perkins. Tchaikovsky's 'Humoresque', one of a number of classical pieces suggested, was recorded by Stokowski and studio musicians.

Adventures of a Perambulator by John Alden Carpenter

Coloured ink and gouache sketches by Sylvia Holland show life from an infant's point of view. Bold and energetic, the pictures demonstrate Sylvia Holland's range and versatility.

Invitation to the Dance by Weber

This was to make use of two of the popular characters from *Fantasia* – the baby Pegasus from the *Pastoral* Symphony and Hop Low the mushroom from the *Nutcracker* Suite. The film was started but by July 1941 it had been taken out of production.

Other projects

Prokofiev's *Peter and the Wolf* formed part of the compilation film *Make Mine Music* (1946). It may have been conceived as part of the continuing *Fantasia* group; Sylvia Holland was clearly involved because she is mentioned in an internal memorandum by Bob Carr dated 9 July 1943. Prokofiev had visited Disney in 1938 and work was being done on story sketches in the early forties. Other classical music items under consideration included Ravel's *Bolero*, Saint-Saens' *Carnival of the Animals* and Debussy's *Sea Cycle*. In various inter-office memoranda, a large number of well known and less well known European classical pieces were considered and their availability and suitability for animation discussed (see Colour Plate 93).

Work is in progress on *Fantasia 2000*, which will combine some of the items from *Fantasia* with new classically inspired pieces. These include Respighi's *The Pines of Rome*, Elgar's *Pomp and Circumstance*, and Saint-Saens' *Carnival of Animals*.

Conclusion

By the summer of 1941 the studio was strikebound and the war only a few months away; the first animation projects to suffer were the *Fantasia* replacements. Many of the key personnel left or were laid off or called up and Disney had to turn to immediate short-term projects to keep the company going. John Canemaker and Charles Solomon reproduce a large number of illustrations in their accounts of this fascinating proposed extension of *Fantasia* which, however, was never seriously considered again in Walt Disney's lifetime.

Other unfinished European projects

A studio as imaginatively fertile as Walt Disney's would always have a large number of film projects in various stages of development. I am indebted to Joe Grant for allowing me to see an internal studio memorandum of 12 October 1943, entitled *Story Numbers*, which consists of twelve pages listing five hundred and fifty three titles with allocated numbers. Below is an extract from that list, containing stories from European sources, with their numbers, and in the order in which they appear. See also Chapter 8 *The Nineteen Forties*, note 8.

1004 *Treasure Island*
1005 *Hansel and Gretel*
1006 *Wind in the Willows*
1007 *The Bluebird*
1009 *Reynard the Fox*
1010 *Ivanhoe*
1011 *King Arthur Stories*
1012 *The Three Musketeers*
1013 *Robinson Crusoe*
1014 *Swiss Family Robinson*
1016 *Peter Pan and Peter Pan in Kensington Gardens*
1017 *Alice in Wonderland*
1018 *Chanticleer*
1020 *Cinderella*
1022 *Pied Piper of Hamlin or (Legend of Hamlin Town)*
1023 *Don Quixote*
1025 *Midsummer Night's Dream*
1026 *Pinafore*
1027 *Cabbages and Kings*
1028 *Robin Hood*
1046 *Rose and the Ring*
1104 *Perri*
1105 *The Sword in the Stone*
1108 *Black Beauty*
1110 *Crock of Gold*
1112 *Story of the Bible*

1113 *Harlequin*
1115 *Idylls of the King*
1116 *The Odyssey (Adventure of Ulysses)*
1117 *Punchinello*
1118 *The Tinder Box*
1119 *Thimbelina [sic]*
1120 *Water Babies*
1121 *Enchanted Island*
1122 *Little Claus and Big Claus*
1123 *Dante's Divine Comedy*
1125 *Mythological Research (Stories of Mythology)*
1127 *The Mysterious Island*
1128 *Bambi's Children*
1130 *Jack and the Beanstalk*
1158 *Penelope*
1160 *Andersen – Live Action Section*
1167 *Babes in the Wood*
1219 *The Emperor's New Clothes*
1223 *Boy Hero of Holland (Holland Mickey) (Leak in the Dike)*
1224 *King of the Golden River*
1228 *The Lion and the Mouse*
1229 *Boy Blue*
1231 *Three Little Bears (Goldilocks)*
1233 *Country Cousin Sequel*
1237 *The Nativity*
1259 *Wee Gillis*
1264 *The Magic Flute*
1265 *The Nightingale*
1267 *Pandora's Box*
1268 *The Sugar Plum Tree*
1270 *The Chocolate Soldier*
1272 *Cupid and Psyche*
1273 *Dog in a Manger*
1274 *Echo and Narcissus*
1276 *The Little Fir Tree*
1278 *The Golden Egg*
1279 *The House that Jack Built*
1280 *Little Bo Peep*
1281 *Little Goose Girl*
1282 *The Magic Horse*
1283 *Punch and Judy*
1284 *The Red Shoes*
1287 *House Boat on the Styx*
1295 *Barber of Seville*

1297 *Androcles and the Lion*
1298 *Dwarf Long Nose*
1318 *Donald Munchausen*
1322 *Mickey's Lilliputians*
1326 *Princess Who Couldn't Laugh*
1388 *Children of Tyrol (Tyrolean Children)*
1448 *The Spider and the Fly*
1472 *Faust*
1539–1543 *Training and propaganda films on Europe*
1551 *Gremlin Story Research*

Some of these stories were intended to be packaged together into a feature about the life of Hans Christian Andersen, to be made in conjunction with Samuel Goldwyn. Nothing came of this project and Goldwyn made his own film *Hans Christian Andersen* in 1952. Other stories could form part of a film on Greek mythology (Sylvia Holland produced inspirational drawings and paintings for this) (see Colour Plate 93). Some story numbers, based on Asian legends that have filtered into Europe are also in the list:

1015 *Arabian Nights*
1107 *Chinese Fairy Tales*
1266 *Omar Khayyam*
1277 *The Fisherman and the Genii*

Some of these projects, like *Aladdin* (1992), may yet reach the big screen, though they are unlikely to be realised in forms relating to the initial artwork.

Select Bibliography

Adams, Henry. *Thomas Hart Benton: An American Original*. New York: Alfred A. Knopf, 1989.

Adams, T. R. *Tom and Jerry: Fifty Years of Cat and Mouse*. London: Pyramid Books, 1991.

Adamson, Joe. *Bugs Bunny: Fifty Years and Only One Grey Hare*. London: Pyramid Books, 1990.

——. *Tex Avery King of Cartoons*. New York: Da Capo, 1975.

——. *The Walter Lantz Story: With Woody Woodpecker and Friends*. New York: Putnam's, 1985.

The Adventures of Mickey Mouse. Illus. Staff of The Walt Disney Studio. London: Harrap, 1931.

Aesop's Fables. Illus. Ernest Griset. New York: McLoughlin, n.d., c. 1880.

——. *Aesop's Fables*. Illus. Arthur Rackham. 1912; London: Heinemann, 1919.

Allan, Robin. 'Alice in Disneyland.' *Sight and Sound*, 54 (1985), 136–138.

——. 'The Artists of Disney.' *Manchester Memoirs*. Manchester: The Manchester Literary and Philosophical Society, 128 (1990), 91–106.

——. 'Fifty Years of "Snow White"' *Journal of Popular Film and Television*, 15 (1988), 156–163.

——. 'Make Mine Disney.' *Animator*, 19, April/June 1987, 28–31.

——. *Picture Books and Disney Pictures*. Programme. Manchester: The Portico Library, 1990.

——. 'The Real *Fantasia*, At Length At Last.' *The Times Saturday Review*, 25 August 1990.

——. 'Still Is the Story Told.' *Storytelling in Animation: The Art of the Animated Image*. Vol. 2. Ed. John Canemaker. Los Angeles: The American Film Institute, 2 (1988), 83–92.

——. 'Sylvia Holland: Disney Artist'. *Animation Journal* Vol 2, No. 2, Spring 1994, 32–41.

——. 'Time for Melody.' *Animator*, 27 August 1990, 9–12.

Allen, Tom. 'Animation After Disney.' *Village Voice*, 26 September 1977.

Altman, Rick. *The American Film Musical*. Bloomington and Indianapolis: Indiana University Press, 1987.

The American Animated Cartoon. Gerald Peary and Danny Peary (eds). New York: Dutton, 1980.

The American People: In Their Stories, Tall Tales, Traditions, Ballads and Songs. B.A. Botkin (ed). London: Pilot Press, 1946.

Anderson, Susan M., and Robert Henning Jnr., et al., comps. *Regionalism: The California View. Watercolours 1929–1945*. Santa Barbara: Santa Barbara Museum of Art, 1988.

Animation Journal. Ed. Maureen Furniss. Vols 1–6 (1992–1997).

Arabian Nights. Illus. Edmund Dulac. 1907; New York: Weathervane Books, 1985.

Arndt, Walter. *The Genius of Wilhelm Busch*. Berkeley: University of California Press, 1982.

Arnold Böcklin. London: Arts Council/Pro Helvetia, 1971.

The Art of the Animated Image: An Anthology. Charles Solomon (ed). Los Angeles: The American Film Institute: 1987.

The Art of Disneyland 1953–1986. Burbank: Disney Gallery, 1988.

The Art of Grim Natwick, Catalogue, Burbank: Howard Lowery, 1991.

The Art of Marc Davis. Catalogue, Burbank: Howard Lowery, 1993.

Arthur Rackham. David Larkin (ed). New York: Peacock Press/Bantam Books, 1975.

Les artistes de Disney. Catalogue. Paris: Librarie Seguier, 1987.

The Artists of Disney. Intr. John Russell Taylor. Catalogue. London: Victoria and Albert Museum, 1976.

Atkinson, Alex, and Ronald Searle. *The Big City or The New Mayhew*. London: Perpetua Books, 1958.

Ave Maria. Illus. The Walt Disney Studio. New York: Random House, 1940.

Ayer, Jean. *Donald Duck and His Friends*. Illus. The Walt Disney Studio. Boston: D. C. Heath, 1939.

Babbitt, Art, and Richard Williams. 'Goofy and Babbitt.' *Sight and Sound*. Spring 1974, 94–95.

Baigell, Matthew. *Thomas Hart Benton*. New York: Harry N. Abrams, n.d., 1975.

Bailey, Adrian. *Walt Disney's World of Fantasy*. Limpsfield, Surrey: Dragon's World, 1982.

Bailey, Colin. *Caspar David Friedrich*. London: National Gallery, 1991.

Balbach, Manfred. *Rothenburg ob der Tauber*. Starnberg: Joseph Keller, 1989.

Barrie, J. M. *Peter Pan and Wendy*. Illus. F. D. Bedford; London: Hodder and Stoughton, 1911.

——. *J. M. Barrie's Peter Pan and Wendy*. Retold by May Byron. Illus. Mabel Lucie Attwell. London: Hodder and Stoughton, n.d.

——. *The Walt Disney Illustrated Peter Pan and Wendy*. Retold by May Byron. 1953; Leicester: Brockhampton Press, 1956.

——. *Peter Pan in Kensington Gardens*. Illus. Arthur Rackham. London: Hodder and Stoughton, 1906.

Barrier, Mike. 'Building a Better Mouse.' *Funnyworld*, 20 (1979), 6–22.

——. *Fifty Years of Animation: Building a Better Mouse*. Catalogue. Washington: Library of Congress, 1978.

——. 'The Moving Drawing Speaks.' *Funnyworld*, 18 (1977), 17–37.

——, and Milt Gray. 'Bob Clampett: An Interview with a Master Cartoon Maker and Puppeteer.' *Funnyworld*, 12 (1970), 13–37.

—— *et al*. 'An Interview with Carl Stalling.' *Funnyworld*, 13 (1971), 21–27.

Barsacq, Leon. *Caligari's Cabinet and Other Grand Illusions*. Boston/New York: New York Graphic Society, 1976.

Baruch, Dorothy Walter. *Walt Disney's Pinocchio*. Boston: D. C. Heath, 1940.

Baur-Heinhold, Margarete. *Baroque Theatre*. Trans. Mary Whittall. London: Thames and Hudson, 1967.

Beaumont, Cyril W. *Complete Book of Ballets*. New York: Grosset and Dunlap, 1938.

Beck, Jerry, and Will Friedwald. *Looney Tunes and Merry Melodies: A Complete Illustrated Guide to the Warner Bros. Cartoons*. New York: Henry Holt, 1989.

Behlmer, Rudy. *America's Favourite Movies: Behind the Scenes*. New York: Frederick Ungar, 1982.

Benayoun Robert. *Le dessin animé après Walt Disney*. Ed. Jean-Jacques Pauvert, Paris: Société Française des Presses Suisses, 1961.

Bendazzi, Giannalberto. *Cartoons, Le cinema d'animation, 1892–1992*. Paris: Liana Levi, 1991.

Bendazzi, Giannalberto. *CartoonCento anni di cinema d'animazione*. Venice: Marsolio, 1988.

——. *Cartoons: One Hundred Years of Cinema Animation*. London: John Libbey, 1994.

Bierbaum, Otto Julius. *Franz Stuck*. Bielefeld and Leipzig: Delinagen and Klafing, 1899.

Bjurström, Per, et al., comps. *Bauer*. Catalogue. Stockholm: Nationalmuseum, 1981.

Blair, Preston. 'The Animation of *Fantasia*.' *Cartoonist Profiles*, 49 (1981), 16–25.

Blamires, David. 'The Early Reception of the Grimms' Kinder und Hausmärchen in England.' *Bulletin*. Manchester: The John Rylands Library, Autumn 1989.

——. *Happily Ever After: Fairytale Books Through the Ages*. Catalogue. Manchester: John Rylands University Library, 1992.

Blanc-Gatti, Charles. *Des sons et des couleurs*. Paris: Editions d'Art Chromophonique, n.d., c. 1935.

Blitz, Marcia. *Donald Duck*. New York: Harmony Books, 1979.

Blum, Daniel. *A Pictorial History of the American Theatre*. Philadelphia: Chilton, 1960.

——. *A Pictorial History of the Silent Screen*. London: Spring Books, 1953.

Bódy, Verushka, and Peter Weibel. *Clip, Klapp, Bum: Von der visuellen Musik zum Musikvideo*. Cologne: Dumont, 1987.

Bottigheimer, Ruth B. *Grimms' Bad Girls and Bold Boys: The Moral and Social Vision of the Tales*. New Haven: Yale University Press, 1987.

Bradbury, Ray. 'Walt Disney, His Beauties and Beasts.' *Los Angeles Times*, 21 October 1973.

Brinnin, John Malcolm. *Dylan Thomas in America*. 1955; London, Arlington Books, 1988.

Bristol, George T. ' "Snow White": Inanimate Characters become a Force in Merchandising.' *Dun's Review*, April 1938, 13–17.

Brown, Margaret Wise. *Little Pig's Picnic and Other Stories*. Illus. The Walt Disney Studio. Boston: D. C. Heath, 1939.

Browne, Georgiana. *Water Babies' Circus and Other Stories*. Illus. The Walt Disney Studio. Boston: D. C. Heath, 1939.

Brumbraugh, Florence. *Donald Duck and His Nephews*. Illus. The Walt Disney Studio. Boston: D. C. Heath, 1940.

Bryman, Alan. *Disney and His Worlds*. London: Routledge, 1995.

Buberl, Brigitte. *Erlkönig und Alpenbraut: Dichtung, Märchen und Sage in Bildern der Schack-Galerie*. Munich: Lipp, 1989.

Busch, Wilhelm. *Neues Wilhelm Busch Album*. Berlin: Germann Klemm. n.d. c. 1930.

Byrne, Howard. 'Only One Star is Human.' *Illustrated*, 29 May 1948, 12–15.

Cabarga, Leslie. *The Fleischer Story*. 1976; New York: Da Capo, 1988.

Canady, John. 'The Art, So to Speak, of Walt Disney.' *New York Times*, 28 October 1973.

Canemaker, John. 'The Abstract Films of Oskar Fischinger.' *Print*, 37 (Mar/Apr 1983), 66–72.

——. *Before the Animation Begins: The Art and Lives of Disney Inspirational Sketch Artists*. New York: Hyperion, 1996.

——. *Dreams in Motion: The Art of Winsor McCay*. Catalogue. Katonah, New York: Katonah Gallery, 1988.

——. 'Elfriede! On the Road with Mrs Oskar Fischinger.' *Funnyworld*, 18 (1977), 4–14.

——. 'The *Fantasia* That Never Was.' *Print*, 42 (1988), 76–87, 139–140.

——. *Felix: The Twisted Tale of the World's Most Famous Cat*. New York: Pantheon Books, 1991.

——. 'Grim Natwick.' *Film Comment*, Jan/Feb 1975, 58–61.

——. 'Profile of a Living Animation Legend: J. R. Bray.' *Filmmaker's Newsletter*, January 1975, 28–31.

——. 'Secrets of Disney's Visual Effects: The Schultheis Notebooks.' *Print*, Mar/Apr (1996), 66–73, 118.

——. 'Sylvia Moberly Holland.' Catalogue. *Animation Art*. Burbank: Howard Lowery, 5 August 1990, 49–50.

——. *Winsor McCay: His Life and Art*. New York: Abbeville, 1987.

—— and Marc Davis. 'Remembering Grim Natwick.' Catalogue. *The Art of Grim Natwick*. Burbank: Howard Lowery, 9 November 1991.

Capell, Richard. '*Fantasia* or the New Barbarism.' *Musical Opinion*, November 1943, 41.

Care, Ross. 'Symphonists for the Sillies: The Composers of the Disney Shorts.' *Funnyworld*, 18 (1977), 38–48.

Carey, Frances, and Antony Griffiths. *The Print in Germany: The Age of Expressionism*. London: British Museum Publications, 1984.

Carr, Dorothy. 'Alice in Movieland.' *The Amateur Theatre and Playwrights' Journal*, 1 (1934), 29–35.

Carroll, Lewis. *Alice's Adventures in Wonderland*. Illus. David Hall. Afterword, Brian Sibley. London: Methuen, 1986.

——. *The Annotated Alice: 'Alice's Adventures in Wonderland' and 'Through the Looking Glass.'* Ed. Martin Gardner. Harmondsworth: Penguin, 1965.

——. *Jabberwocky*. New York: Disney Press, 1992.

Castle, Charles. *Oliver Messel*. London: Thames and Hudson, 1986.

Cawley, John. 'Walt Disney "The Gremlins." An Unfinished Story.' *American Classic Screen*, 1980, 8–11.

Chasins, Abram. *Leopold Stokowski: A Profile*. New York: Hawthorn, 1979.

Chaucer, Geoffrey. *The Canterbury Tales*. Illus. Gustaf Tenggren. New York: Golden Press, 1961.

Christ, Dorothea and Christian Geehlar. *Arnold Böcklin: Die Gemälde in Kunstmuseum Basel*. Basle: Öffentlich Kunstmuseum Basel and Eidolon, 1990.

Christie's Animation Art. Catalogue. Los Angeles: Christie's, 7 June 1997.

Clive, Mary. *The Day of Reckoning*. London: Macmillan, 1964.

Cohen, Karl. *Forbidden Animation: Censored Cartoons and Blacklisted Animators in America*. Jefferson: McFarland, 1997.

——. 'Racism and Resistance: Black Stereotypes in America.' *Animation Journal* Vol 4, No. 2, Spring 1996.

Collodi, Carlo (Carlo Lorenzini). *The Story of a Puppet or The Adventures of Pinocchio*. Trans. M. A. Murray. Illus. C. Mazzantini. New York: Cassell, 1892.

——. *Pinocchio The Story of a Puppet*. Illus. Charles Folkard. London: Dent, 1911.

——. *Pinocchio*. Trans. Bianca Majolie. Unpublished: Walt Disney Productions, 22 November 1937.

Commire, Anne. *Something About the Author*. Detroit: Gale Research Book Tower, 1971–1983.

Cook, Olive. *Movement in Two Dimensions. A Study of the Animated and Projected Pictures which preceded the Invention of Cinematography*. London: Hutchinson, 1965.

Corn, Wanda M. *Grant Wood: The Regionalist Vision*. New Haven: Yale University Press, 1983.

Cornelissen, Julia, comp. *The Illustrators: The British Art of Illustration 1800–1991*. Catalogue. London: Chris Beetles, 1991.

Cosandey, Roland. *Langages et imaginaire dans le Cinéma Suisse d'animation*. Étagnières-Genève: Groupement Suisse du film d'animation, 1988.

Cox, Marian E. Roalke. *Cinderella: Three Hundred and Forty Five Variants of Cinderella, Catskin and Cap O'Rushes*. London: Folklore Society, 1893.

Crafton, Donald. *Before Mickey: The Animated Film 1898–1928*. Cambridge, Mass.: MIT Press, 1982.

——. Emile Cohl, *Caricature and Film*. Princeton: Princeton University Press, 1990.

——. 'Walt Disney's *Peter Pan*. Woman Trouble on the Island.' *Storytelling in Animation: The Art of the Animated Image*. Vol. 2. Ed. John Canemaker. Los Angeles: American Film Institute, 1988.

Crowther, Bosley. 'Yes, But is it Art?' *New York Times*, 17 November 1940.

Culbert, David. ' "A Quick, Delightful Gink". Eric Knight at the Walt Disney Studio.' *Funnyworld*, 19 (1978), 13–17.

Culhane, John. *Walt Disney's Fantasia*. New York: Harry N. Abrams, 1983.

Culhane, Shamus. *Talking Animals and Other People*. New York: St. Martins Press, 1986.

——. *Animation from Script to Screen*. London: Columbus Books, 1988.

Czeslochowski, Joseph S. *John Steuart Curry and Grant Wood*. Columbia: University of Missouri Press, 1981.

Dahl, Roald. *The Gremlins*. Illus. The Walt Disney Studio. New York: Random House, 1943. London: Collins, 1943.

Dalby, Richard. *The Golden Age of Children's Book Illustration*. London: Michael Omara Books, 1991.

Dante. *Inferno*. Illus. Gustave Doré. 1861; Paris: Hachette, 1865.

Dardis, Tom. *Some Time in the Sun*. 1976; New York: Limelight Editions, 1988.

Davies, Russell. 'Disney's World.' *The Listener*, 16 February 1984, 8.

Davis, Marc, and John Hench. 'Two Disney Artists.' *Crimmer's: The Harvard Journal of Pictorial Fiction*. Cambridge, Mass.: Harvard University Press, Winter, 1975, 35–44.

de Brunhoff, Jean. *Babar's Travels*. London: Methuen, 1935.

Delehanty, Thornton. 'A Curious Bystander at *Fantasia*.' *New York Herald Tribune*, 20 October 1940.

Deming, Barbara. 'The Artlessness of Walt Disney.' *Partisan Review*, Spring 1945, 226–231.

Deneroff, Harvey. ' "We Can't Get Much Spinach!" The Organisation and Implementation of the Fleischer Studio Strike.' *Film History*, 1 (1987), 1–14.

——. 'The Disney Strike.' Unpublished Paper, Proceedings of Third Annual Conference, Society for Animation Studies, Rochester, New York, October 1991.

Denton, Ralph. 'Review of *Fantasia*.' *Picturegoer*, 29 November 1941.

De Roos, Robert. 'The Magic Worlds of Walt Disney.' *National Geographic*, 124 (1963), 158–207.

De Seversky, Alexander D. *Victory Through Air Power*. New York: Simon and Schuster, 1942.

Dickens, Charles. *A Christmas Carol*. Illus. Arthur Rackham. 1915; London: Heinemann, 1952.

Dill, Janeann. 'Jules Engel: Film Artist A Painterly Aesthetic.' *Animation Journal*, Vol. 1, no. 2, Spring 1993, 51–73.

Disney Discourse: Producing the Magic Kingdom. Eric Smoodin (ed). London: Routledge, 1994.

'Disney Productions Fail in Appeal over *Peter Pan*.' *The Times*, 15 February 1967.

Disney, Roy. 'My Unforgettable Brother, Walt Disney.' *Readers Digest*, March 1969, 133–139.

'Disney's *Snow White and the Seven Dwarfs* is the Fourth.' *Pic*, 31 May 1938, 34–36.

Disney, Walt. 'The Art of Animation and the Wisdom of Walt Disney.' *Wisdom Magazine*, 22 (1959), 64–80.

——. 'Dedication Speech.' *Walt Disney's Disneyland*. Guide. Burbank: Walt Disney Productions, 1971.

——. 'Growing Pains.' *Journal for the Society of Motion Picture Engineers*. January 1941.

——. 'The Inside Story of the Filming of *Pinocchio*.' *News of the World*, 21 March 1940.

——. 'The Marceline I knew.' *The Marceline News*. 2 September 1938.

——. 'Why I Chose *Snow White and the Seven Dwarfs*.' *Photoplay Studies*. Vol. 3, pt. 10, n.d., 7–8.

Doré Gallery. London: Cassell, n.d. 1880.

Doré's Illustrations for Rabelais. New York: Dover, 1978.

Dorfman, Ariel, and Armand Mattelart. *How to Read Donald Duck: Imperialist Ideology in the Disney Comic*. Trans. David Kunzle. New York: International General, 1975.

Doyle, Richard. *In Fairyland: A Series of Pictures from the Elf-World*. 1870; London: Michael Joseph/Webb and Bower, 1979.

The Drawings of Heinrich Kley. Intr. George Grosz. Los Angeles: Borden Publishing Co., 1947.

Dreams for Sale: Popular Culture in the 20th Century. Richard Maltby (ed). London: Harrap, 1989.

Duca, Lo. *Le dessin animé*. Paris: Prisma, 1948.

Dunlop, Beth. *Building a Dream: The Art of Disney Architecture*. New York: Abrams, 1996.

Durham, Michael. 'The Marketing of Mickey Mouse.' *The Independent on Sunday*, 5 April 1992.

East of the Sun and West of the Moon: Old Tales from the North. Illus. Kay Nielsen. 1914; Ware: Omega, 1986.

Eco, Umberto. *Travels in Hyperreality*. Trans. William Weaver. London: Picador, 1986.

Edera, Bruno. *Full Length Animated Feature Films*. Ed. John Halas. London: Focal Press, 1977.

——. *Histoire du Cinéma Suisse d'animation*. Yverdon & Geneva: Cinematique Travelling, 1978.

Eine lustige Gesellschaft: 100 Münchener Bilderbogen in einem Band. Zurich: Olms, 1978.

Eisenstein at Ninety. Ed. Ian Christie. Catalogue. Oxford: Museum of Modern Art, 1988.

Eisenstein on Disney. Ed. Jay Leyda. London: Methuen, 1988.

Eisner, Lotte. *The Haunted Screen*. London: Secker and Warburg, 1973.

Emmett. *Saturday Slow*. London: Faber, 1948.

Engel, Jules. 'Teaching Animation.' *Millimetre*, 14 (February 1976), 30.

——. 'The United Productions of America: Reminiscing Thirty Years Later.' Ed. William Moritz. *ASIFA Newsletter*, 12 (December 1984), 14–17.

Engen, Rodney. *Richard Doyle*. Stroud: Catalpa Press, 1983.

——., *et al.*, comps. *Richard Doyle and his Family*. London: Victoria and Albert Museum, 1983.

'Fantasia.' *Hollywood Citizen News*, 20 January 1941.

'*Fantasia* Edition.' *Walt Disney Studio Bulletin*, 15 November 1940.

Farber, Helmut. '*Fantasia* – Neuester Orbis pictus.' Trans. Edith Wilson. *Suddeutsche Zeitung*, 14 April 1971.

'Father Goose.' *Time*, 27 December 1954, 30–34.

The Favourite Album of Fun and Fancy. Illus. Ernest Griset. London: Cassell, n.d., c. 1880.

Feild, Robert D. *The Art of Walt Disney*. London: Collins, 1944.

The Fifty Greatest Cartoons. Jerry Beck (ed). Atlanta: Turner, 1994.

Film Architecture: Set Designs from Metropolis *to* Blade Runner. Dietrich Neumann (ed). Munich/New York: Pastel, 1996.

Finch, Christopher. *The Art of the Lion King*. New York: Hyperion, 1994.

——. *The Art of Walt Disney*. New York: Abrams, 1973.

——. *Special Effects: Creating Movie Magic*. New York: Abbeville, 1984.

——. *Walt Disney's America*. New York: Abbeville, 1975.

Fine Animation Art & Related Items. Catalogues. Burbank: Howard Lowery, 3 December 1990, 7 April 1991, 25 August 1991, 5 April 1992.

Fischinger, Elfriede. 'Writing Light.' *Relay*, 2 (May 1984).

Flans, Robyn. 'Joe Grant: *Fantasia* Revisited.' *Disney News*, 25 (1990), 31.

Francisco de Goya: Prints in the Collection of Manchester City Art Galleries. Catalogue. Manchester: City Art Gallery, 1984.

French, Philip. 'Return of "Fantasia".' *The Observer*, 1 April 1979.

Friedrich, Otto. *City of Nets*. New York: Harper, 1987.

From Mouse to Mermaid: The Politics of Film, Gender and Culture. Elizabeth Bell *et al.* (eds). Bloomington and Indianapolis: Indiana University Press, 1995.

Gabler, Neal. *An Empire of their Own: How the Jews Invented Hollywood*. New York: Doubleday, 1988.

Gascoigne, Bamber. *World Theatre*. London: Ebury Press, 1968.

Gatzke, H. W. *Germany and the United States*. Cambridge, Mass.: Harvard University Press, 1980.

Gaunt, William. *Victorian Olympus*. London: Jonathan Cape, 1952.

German Books from the Romantic Period. Catalogue. Manchester: John Rylands University Library, 1988.

German Masters of the Nineteenth Century: Paintings and Drawings from the Federal Republic of Germany. Ed. John P. O'Neill. New York: Metropolitan Museum of Art, 1981.

Gifford, Denis. *The Great Cartoon Stars: A Who's Who*. London: Jupiter, 1979.

——. 'Stars in Line: From Comic Strips to Movie Stardom.' *Movie*. 15 (1980), 298.

Gilbert, Dorothy B. *The American Federation of Arts: Who's Who in American Art*. New York: R. R. Bowker, 1962.

Gilbert, Joan. 'Disney's Marceline Memories'. *Rural Missouri*, January 1990, 5.

'Girls at Work for Disney.' *Glamour Magazine*, April 1941, 50–51.

Grahame, Kenneth. *Dream Days*. Illus. Maxfield Parrish. 1898; Edinburgh: Paul Harris, 1983.

——. *The Golden Age*. Illus. Maxfield Parrish. London: John Lane, 1900.

——. *The Wind in the Willows*. Illus. Ernest Shepard. 1931; London: Methuen, 1963.

Grandville's Animals: The World's Vaudeville. Illus. Grandville. London: Thames and Hudson, 1981.

Grant, John. *The Encyclopedia of Walt Disney's Animated Characters*. London: Hamlyn, 1987.

Graves, Robert. *The Greek Myths*. Harmondsworth: Penguin, 1955.

Green, Richard L. *Fifty Years of* Peter Pan. London: Peter Davies, 1954.

Greene, Katherine and Richard. *The Man Behind the Magic: The Story of Walt Disney*. New York: Viking Penguin, 1991.

Grimm, Joseph, and William. *Fairy Tales*. Trans. Margaret Hunt. Illus. Hermann Vogel *et al*. 1944; Ware: Omega, n.d.

——. *Hansel and Gretel and Other Stories*. Illus. Kay Nielsen. 1925; Ware: Omega, 1985.

——. *Kinder und Hausmärchen*. Illus. Hermann Vogel. Munich: von Braun and Schneider, 1922.

Grimms Märchen. Illus. Ludwig Richter. Erlangen: Karl Muller, n.d.

Groll, Gunter. '*Fantasia* – die Grosse Farbenorgel.' Trans. Edith Wilson. *Suddeutsche Zeitung*, 14 April 1971.

Grossart, Jacqui. 'Rowland Emmett: from *Punch* to *Chitty-Chitty-Bang-Bang* and Beyond,' *Chris Beetles Catalogue*, London, 1988, 12–13.

Grove, Valerie. *Dear Dodie: The Life of Dodie Smith*. London: Pimlico, 1996.

Grover, Ron. *The Disney Touch: How a Daring Management Team Revived an Entertainment Empire*. Homewood, Ill.: Business One Irwin, 1991.

Haack, Friedrich. *Die Kunst des XIX Jahrhunderts*. Esslingen: Paul Neff, 1913.

Haggin, B. H. 'Music.' *The Nation*, 10 May 1941, 566.

Halas, John. *Design in Motion*. London: Studio, 1962.

Halas, John, and Roger Manvell. *Art in Movement: New Directions in Animation*. London: Studio Vista, 1970.

Hambley, John, and Patrick Downing. *Thames Television's The Art of Hollywood: Fifty Years of Art Direction*. London: Thames Television, 1979.

Hamilton, James. *Arthur Rackham: A Life with Illustration*. London: Pavilion, 1990.

Hand, David Dodd. *Memoirs*. Cambria, Ca.: Martha Hand, 1991.

Harris, Joel Chandler. *The Essential Uncle Remus*. Ed. George van Santvoord and Archibald C. Coolidge. Illus. A. B. Frost. 1949; London: Macmillan, 1967.

——. *Uncle Remus*. Illus. A. T. Elwes. London: Routledge, n.d.

Hawthorne, Nathaniel. *A Wonder Book and Tanglewood Tales*. Illus. Gustaf Tenggren. Boston: Houghton Mifflin, 1923.

Heller, Nancy, and Julia Williams. *The Regionalists*. New York: Watson-Guptill, 1976.

Henderson, Marina. *Gustave Doré: Selected Engravings*. London: Academy, 1975.

Hermann Vogel Album. Munich: Brown and Schneider. n.d. 1896.

Heuring, David, and George Turner. 'Disney's "Fantasia": Yesterday and Today.' *American Cinematographer*, 72 (1991), 54–65.

Hillmore, Peter. 'From Guest to Grumpy Overnight.' *Observer*, 19 April 1992.

Hoffmann, Detlef. 'Disneyworld: Vormarsch auf die Geschichte oder Rückzug in die Geschichte' Trans. Detlef Hoffmann. *Geschichts-didaktik*, 1 (1983), 31–41.

Holliss, Richard and Brian Sibley. *The Disney Studio Story*. London: Octopus, 1988.

——. *Walt Disney's Mickey Mouse: His Life and Times*. London: Fleetway, 1986.

——. *Walt Disney's* Snow White and the Seven Dwarfs *and the Making of the Classic Film*. New York: Simon and Schuster, 1987.

Hollister, Paul. 'Genius at Work: Walt Disney.' *Atlantic*, December 1940, 689–701.

Holme, Bryan. *Enchanted World: The Magic of Pictures*. London: Thames and Hudson, 1979.

Horvath, Ferdinand H. Catalogue. West Plains, Mo.: Russ Cochran, n.d., c. 1985.

The Hospital Centenary Gift Book. Ed. Robert Ollerenshaw. Illus. Walt Disney Studio. London: Harrap, 1935.

Howell, Betje. 'Herbert Ryman: Californian Painter.' *American Artist*, 1969.

Howell, Blair. 'Frank Thomas and Ollie Johnston: Too Creative to Retire.' *Storyboard*, 1 (1988), 14–27.

Hudson, Derek. *Arthur Rackham: His Life and Work*. London: Heinemann, 1960.

Huemer, Dick. 'Huemeresque.' *Funnyworld*, 18 (1977), 15.

——. 'Huemeresque: The Bilking of Bunny.' *Funnyworld*, 20 (1979), 23–26.

——. 'Huemeresque: Thumbnail Sketches.' *Funnyworld*, 21 (1979), 41.

——. 'With Disney on Olympus.' *Funnyworld*, 17 (1976), 37–45.

Hughes, Robert. 'Disney: Mousebrow to Highbrow.' *Time*, 15 October 1973, 54–57.

Hulett, Steve. 'The Making of *Snow White and the Seven Dwarfs*.' *Walt Disney's* Snow White and the Seven Dwarfs. New York: Viking Press, 1979.

Hurter, Albert. *He Drew as He Pleased*. Intr. Ted Sears. New York: Simon and Schuster, 1948.

Huxley, Aldous. *Brave New World*. 1932; Harmondsworth: Penguin, 1964.

——. *Letters of Aldous Huxley*. Ed. Grover Smith. New York: Harper and Row, 1969.

The Illusion of Life: Essays on Animation. Alan Cholodenko (ed). Sydney: Power, 1991.

The Imagineers. *Walt Disney Imagineering*. New York: Hyperion, 1996.

'In uns selbst liegt Italien': Die Kunst der Deutsch-Römer. Christoph Heilmann (ed). Munich: Hirmer, 1987.

Jackson, Kathryn, and Byron Jackson. *Tenggren's Cowboys and Indians*. Illus. Gustaf Tenggren. New York: Golden Press, 1968.

Jackson, Kathy Merlock. *Walt Disney: A Bio-Bibliography*. Westport: Greenwood Press, 1993.

Jacobs, Lewis. *The Rise of the American Film, A Critical History*. New York: Harcourt, Brace, 1939.

Jerrold, Blanchard and Gustave Doré. *The London of Doré*. 1872; Ware: Wordsworth, 1987.

Johnson, Diana L. *Fantastic Illustration and Design in Britain, 1850–1930*. Rhode Island: Museum of Art, Rhode Island School of Design, 1979.

Johnston, Ollie and Frank Thomas. *The Disney Villain*. New York: Hyperion, 1993.

——. *Walt Disney's* Bambi. New York: Stewart, Tabori and Chang, 1990.

Jones, Chuck. *Chuck Amuck*. New York: Farrar Straus Giroux, 1989.

Julliard, Jacques. 'Cette souris est-elle dangereuse?' *Le Nouvel Observateur*, 3–9 June 1986.

Jungersen, Frederik G. *Disney*. Copenhagen: Det Danske Filmuseum, 1968.

Justice, Bill. 'From "Snow White" to Disney World (and Almost Everything Inbetween.)' *Animato*. 20 (1990), 38–41.

Kalkschmidt, Eugen. *Ludwig Richter*. Bonn: Wahlband, 1940.

Kaufman, J. B. 'Before Snow White'. *Film History*, June 1993, 158–175.

——. 'Norm Ferguson and the Latin American Films of Walt Disney, in *A Reader in Animation Studies*. ed. Jayne Pilling. London: John Libbey, 1997.

——. 'Three Little Pigs – Big Little Picture.' *American Cinematographer*, 69 (1989) 38–44.

Kay Nielsen. Ed. David Larkin. Peacock Press/Bantam Books, 1975.

Keith Haring, Andy Warhol and Walt Disney. Bruce D. Kurtz (ed). Munich: Prestel, 1992.

Kempe, Lothar. *Ludwig Richter*. Dresden: Sachsen, 1954.

Kent, Rockwell. *It's Me O Lord*. New York: Dodd, Mead, 1955.

Kimball, Ward. 'Disney Animator.' *The Illustrator*, Winter 1977, 4–8, 28–30.

——. 'Disney's World of Motion.' *The Horseless Carriage Gazette*, Sept/Oct 1982, 34–39.

Kinney, Jack. *Walt Disney and Assorted Other Characters*. New York: Harmony Books, 1988.

Kipling, Rudyard. *The Jungle Book*. 1894; London: Macmillan, 1972.

——. *The Second Jungle Book*. 1895; London, Macmillan, 1913.

Klein, I. 'At the Walt Disney Studios.' *Cartoonist Profiles*, 23 (1974), 14–18.

——. 'When Walt Disney Took Another Step.' *Cartoonist Profiles*. 33 (1977), 72–75.

Kley, Heinrich. *The Drawings of Heinrich Kley*. New York: Dover Press, 1961.

——. *Heinrich Kley*. Catalogue. Munich: Galerie Wolfgang Gurlitt, 1962.

——. *More Drawings by Heinrich Kley*. New York: Dover Press, 1962.

Knight, Charles Robert. *Life Through the Ages*. New York: Knopf, 1946. Orlando, Fl.: National History Prints, 1991.

Krause, Martin and Linda Witkowski. *Walt Disney's* Snow White and the Seven Dwarfs: *An Art in its Making*. New York: Hyperion, 1994

La Fontaine, Jean de. *Fables*. Illus. Doré. London: Cassell, n.d. 1867.

Lambert, Pierre. *Pinocchio*. Rozay-en-Brie: Démons et Merveilles, 1995.

Lambourne, Lionel. *Ernest Griset*. London: Thames and Hudson, 1979.

——. *An Introduction to Caricature*. London: Her Majesty's Stationery Office, 1983.

Lane, Anthony. 'A Brilliant and Wicked Way to Keep the Children in the Dark.' *Independent*, 10 August 1991.

Langer, Mark. 'Regionalism in Disney Animation: Pink Elephants and *Dumbo*.' *Film History*, 4 (1990), 305–321.

Langewiesche, Karl Robert. *Ludwig Richter, der Feierabend*. Leipzig: Blaüen Bücher, 1941.

Laqua, Carsten. *Wie Micky unter die Nazi fiel: Walt Disney und Deutschland*. Hamburg: Rowohlt, 1992.

Larson, Judy L. *American Illustration 1890–1925: Romance, Adventure and Suspense*. Catalogue. Calgary: Glenbow Museum, 1986.

Leaf, Munro. *The Story of Ferdinand*. Illus. Robert Lawson. New York: Viking, 1936.

Lebrun, Rico. *Drawings*. Intr. James Thrau Soby. Berkeley: University of California Press, 1961.

——. *Paintings and Drawings: 1946–1961*. Intr. Peter Selz. Los Angeles: University of Southern California, 1961.

Leeper, Janet. *Edward Gordon Craig: Designs for the Theatre*. Harmondsworth: Penguin, 1948.

Lehmann-Haupt, Christopher. 'Hating to Love Walt Disney.' *New York Times*, 29 October 1973.

Lejeune, C. A. *Chestnuts in Her Lap*. London: Phoenix House, 1948.

Lenburg, Jeff. *The Encyclopedia of Animated Cartoons*. New York: Facts on File, 1991.

Levin, Bernard. 'A Wondrous Journey.' *The Times*, 16 February 1991.

Los Angeles: 1900–1961. Los Angeles: History Department of Los Angeles County Museum, 1961.

Lotman, Jeff. *Animation Art: The Early Years, 1911–1953*. Atglen, Penn.: Schiffer, 1995.

——. *A Salute to Walt Disney Animation Art: The Early Years 1928–1942*. Catalogue. Philadelphia: Philadelphia Art Alliance, 1990.

Lotze, Dieter P. *Wilhelm Busch: Leben und Werk*. Stuttgart: Belser, 1982.

Low, David. 'Leonardo da Disney.' *New Republic*. 5 January 1942.

Lowery, Howard, and Paula Sigman Lowery. 'Walt Disney Studio Character Model Statues'. *Fine Animation Art*. Burbank: Howard Lowery. 3 December 1990, 17, 59.

Ludwig Richter Buch für Kinde und Kinderfreunde. Leipzig and Berlin: A. Anton, n.d.

Maas, Jeremy. *Victorian Painters*. London: Barrie and Jenkins, 1984.

Macauley, Alastair. 'Disney's Dances.' *Dancing Times*, 70 (1989), 261–264.

Macauley, Rose. *Pleasure of Ruins*. London: Weidenfeld and Nicolson, 1953.

Madurodam. Official Guide. The Hague: Madurodam, n.d. 1992.

Mallett, Richard. '*Fantasia* Review'. *Punch*, 16 August 1941.

Mallory, Michael. 'Disney's Secret Films.' *Disney News*, 26 (1991), 25–27.

Maltin, Leonard. *The Disney Films*. 1973; New York: Crown, 1984.

——. *Of Mice and Magic*. New York: Plume, 1983.

Manvell, Roger., Brian Sibley *et al.* 'Animated Cinema.' *The Movie* 33(1980), 641–659.

Martin, André. 'Pourquoi il faut voir, revoir et revoir encore les films de Oskar Fischinger.' Programme. Ottawa: International Animated Film Festival, 1976.

Martindale, Andrew. *Gothic Art*. London: Thames and Hudson, 1967; 1993.

Mayer, J. P. *British Cinemas and their Audiences*. London: Dennis Dobson, 1948.

Mayersberg, Paul. 'Arts in Society: The American Nightmare.' *New Society*, 11 April 1968, 537.

Mayerson, Mark. 'Right and Wrong.' Unpublished Paper, Proceedings of First Annual Conference, Society for Animation Studies, University of California at Los Angeles, October 1989.

Mendgen, Eva. *Franz von Stuck*. Cologne: Benedict Taschen, 1994.

McNamara, Marty. 'Script Evolution and Story Adaptation: *Lady and the Tramp*.' Unpublished Paper, Proceedings of Fourth Annual Conference, Society for Animation Studies, California Institute of the Arts, Valencia, California, October 1992.

Merritt, Karen. 'The Little Girl/Little Mother Transformation: The American Evolution of Snow White.' *Storytelling in Animation: the Art of the Animated Image*. Vol. 2. Ed. John Canemaker. Los Angeles: The American Film Institute, 1988.

——. 'Narrative and *Dumbo*.' Unpublished Paper, Proceedings of First Annual Conference, Society for Animation Studies, University of California at Los Angeles, October 1989.

Merritt, Russell. 'Disney War Cartoons.' *Animation Magazine*. 2(1989). 33.

——. 'Analysis of *Pinocchio*.' Unpublished Paper, Proceedings of First Annual Conference, Society for Animation Studies, University of California at Los Angeles, October 1989.

——and J. B. Kaufman. *Nel Paese delle Meraviglie: Walt Disney in Wonderland*. Pordenone: Edizione Biblioteca dell'Immagine, 1992.

Meyer, Susan E. *A Treasury of the Great Children's Book Illustrators.* New York: Abrams, 1983.

Mickey fait du camping. Illus. Walt Disney Studio. Paris: Hachette, 1933.

Mickey Mouse: Fifty Happy Years. David Bain and Bruce Harris (eds). London: New English Library, 1977.

Miller, Diane Disney and Pete Martin. *Walt Disney.* London: Odhams, 1958.

——. *Mein Vater Walt Disney.* Trans. Irene Esser. (Germany): C. Bertelsmann, n.d.

Moffatt, Derry. *Dumbo: Based on Walt Disney Productions' Full-Length Cartoon Feature Film.* London: New English Library, 1975.

Mohn, V. Paul. *Ludwig Richter.* Bielefeld and Leipzig: Velhagen and Klafing, 1896.

Moritz, William. 'Abstract Film and Colour Music.' *The Spiritual In Art: Abstract Painting.* Ed. Edward Weisberger. New York: Abbeville, 1986, 296–310.

——. 'The Films of Oskar Fischinger.' *Film Culture,* no. 58–59–60 (1974), 37–188.

——. 'Fischinger at Disney, or Oskar in the Mousetrap.' *Millimetre,* 5 (February 1977), 25–28, 65–67.

——. 'The Importance of Being Fischinger.' Programme. Ottawa: International Animated Film Festival, 1976.

——. *The Private World of Oskar Fischinger.* Los Angeles: Laser Disc Visual Path Finders, 1989.

——. 'Towards a Visual Music.' *Cantrill's Film Notes.* Melbourne: University of Melbourne, August 1985, 35–42.

Morley, Sheridan. *Tales From the Hollywood Raj: The British Film Colony On Screen and Off.* London: Weidenfeld and Nicolson, 1983.

Moure, Nancy Dustin Wall. *Drawings and Illustrations by Southern Californian Artists Before 1950.* Laguna Beach: Laguna Beach Museum of Art, 1982.

'Mouse and Man.' *Time.* 27 December 1937, 19–21.

Muir, Percy. *English Children's Books.* London: Batsford, 1954.

Murphy, Robert. 'Grim Natwick.' *Animator,* 27 (August 1990), 20–22.

Muybridge, Eadweard. *The Human Figure in Motion.* 1887; New York: Dover, 1955.

Nash, George. *Edward Gordon Craig.* London: Her Majesty's Stationery Office, 1967.

The New Grove Dictionary of American Music. H. Wiley (ed) Hitchcock and Stanley Sadie. London: Macmillan, 1986.

The New Grove Dictionary of Music and Musicians. Stanley Sadie (ed). London: Macmillan, 1980.

Noake, Roger. *Animation: A Guide to Animated Film Techniques.* London: MacDonald Orbis, 1988.

Norman, Geraldine. *Biedermeier Painting.* London: Thames and Hudson, 1987.

'The Nutcracker Suite from Walt Disney's* Fantasia.' London: Collins, n.d. 1940.

O'Brien, Flora. *Walt Disney's Goofy.* London: Ebury Press, 1985.

Oestrich, Friedrich. *Arnold Böcklin.* Cologne: Bastei, 1968.

Ohmer, Susan. '*Peter Pan* and ARI.' Unpublished Paper for Third Annual Conference, Society for Animation Studies, Rochester, New York, October 1991.

——. ' "That Rags to Riches Stuff": Disney's *Cinderella* and the Cultural Space of Animation.' *Film History*, Vol. 5, No. 2, June 1993, 231–249.

Olenius, Elsa, comp. *Great Swedish Fairy Tales*. Trans. Holger Lundbergh. Illus. John Bauer. New York: Delacorte Press, 1973.

Opie, Iona and Peter. *The Classic Fairy Tales*. London: Book Club Associates, 1974.

Opperby, Preben. *Leopold Stokowski*. Speldhurst: Midas, 1982.

Optische Poesie: Oskar Fischinger Leben und Werk. Catalogue. Frankfurt: Deutsches Filmmuseum, 1993.

Otto Hunte: Architekt für den Film. Alfons Arns and Hans-Pieter Reichmann (eds). Frankfurt: Deutsches Filmmuseum, 1996.

Passeron, Roger. *Daumier*. Trans. Helga Harrison. New Jersey: Poplar Books, 1981.

Paul, William. 'Pantheon Pantheist.' *Village Voice*, 2 August 1973.

——. 'Art, Music and Walt Disney.' *Movie*, 24 (1977), 44–52.

Peet, Bill. *Autobiography*. Boston: Houghton Miflin, 1989.

Perrault, Charles. *Fairy Tales*. Trans. S. R. Littlewood. Illus. Honor C. Appleton. London: Herbert and Daniel, 1911.

Persistence of Vision. Paul Anderson (ed), 5 (1993), 60.

Phillips, Claude. *Magazine of Art*. London: Cassell, 1885.

Picturing Childhood: Illustrated Children's Books from University of California Collections 1550–1990. Ed. Karen Jacobson. Catalogue. Los Angeles: UCLA, 1997.

Pitz, Henry C. *Illustrating Children's Books: History – Technique – Production*. New York: Watson-Guptill, 1963.

——. *200 Years of American Illustration*. New York: Random House, 1977.

Poltarnees, Welleran. *Kay Nielsen: An Appreciation*. La Jolla: Green Tiger Press, 1976.

Porcher, Jean. *Les Très Riches Heures du Duc de Berry*. Paris: Nomis, n.d.

Public and Private Life of Animals. Pierre Jules Hetzel (ed). Illus. Grandville. 1877; London: Paddington, 1977.

Rawls, Walton. *Disney Dons Dogtags: The Best of Disney Military Insignia from World War II*. New York: Abbeville, 1992

A Reader in Animation Studies. Jayne Pilling (ed). London: John Libbey, 1997.

Realms of the Mind: British Fantasy Art and Illustration. Catalogue. London: Sotheby's 30 October 1997.

Rebello, Stephen. *The Art of the* Hunchback of Notre Dame. New York: Hyperion, 1996.

——. *The Art of* Pocahontas. New York: Hyperion, 1995.

—— and Jane Healey. *The Art of* Hercules: *The Chaos of Creation*. New York: Hyperion, 1997.

'Rediscover Starevitch.' *International Animation Film Centre Newsletter*. Annecy: Annecy Festival, March 1991.

Reilly, Frank. 'The Walt Disney Comic Strips.' *Cartoonist Profiles*, Winter 1969, 14–18.

Reisner, Mark. *Cadillac Desert: The American West and its Disappearing Water*. New York: Viking, 1986.

Renault, Christian. *Disney de Blanche Neige à Hercule: 28 long métrages d'animation des Studios Disney*. Paris: Dreamland, 1997.

Retrospective Exhibition of the Walt Disney Medium. Catalogue. Los Angeles: Los Angeles County Museum, 1940.

Richter, Ludwig. *Für's Haus*. Leipzig: Alphons Durr. n.d.

Rider, David, and Ken Wlaschin. 'Tribute to Walt Disney.' Retrospective Programme. London: National Film Theatre, 1970.

Roberts, Fulton. *Chanticleer and the Fox*. Illus. Marc Davis. New York: Disney Press, 1991.

Robinson, David. 'The Art of Animation.' *Movie*, 15 (1980), 292–296.

Robinson, Jerry. *The Comics: An Illustrated History of Comic Strip Art*. New York: Berkley, 1974.

The Romantic Spirit in German Art 1790–1990. Ed. Keith Hartley et. al. Catalogue. London and Edinburgh: South Bank Centre and National Gallery of Scotland, 1994.

Rose, Jacqueline. *The Case of Peter Pan or the Impossibility of Children's Fiction*. London: Macmillan, 1984.

Rosenbaum, Jonathan. 'Dreammasters 1: Walt Disney.' *Film Comment*, 11 (Jan/Feb 1975), 64–69.

Ross, Murray. *Stars and Strikes: Unionisation of Hollywood*. New York: Columbia University Press, 1941.

Rothenburg ob der Tauber: Worth Seeing, Worth Knowing. Rothenburg: Tourist Information Office, 1990.

Routh, Jonathan. 'Cinderella.' *Everybody's*, July 1950.

Rudström, Lennart. *In the Troll Wood*. Trans. Olive Jones. Illus. John Bauer. London: Methuen, 1978.

Russell, Herbert. 'L'Affaire Mickey Mouse.' *New York Times Magazine*, 26 December 1937.

Russett, Robert, and Cecile Starr. *Experimental Animation*. New York: Da Capo, 1976.

Ryman, Herbert. *Paintings and Drawings*. Catalogue. Los Angeles: Fotoset, n.d.

Sala, Charles. *Caspar David Friedrich: The Spirit of Romantic Painting*. Paris: Terrail, 1994.

Salten, Felix. *Bambi*. Trans. Whittaker Chambers. 1928; London: Jonathan Cape, 1961.

Savory, Jerold J. *Thomas Rowlandson's Doctor Syntax Drawings*. London: Cygnus Arts, 1997.

Sayers, Frances Clarke. 'Walt Disney Accused.' *Hornbook Magazine*, 40 (December 1965), 602–611.

Schickel, Richard. *Walt Disney*. London: Weidenfeld and Nicolson, 1968.

Schidlower, Daniel, *et al. Qu'est ce que le musicalisme?* Paris: Galerie Drouart, 1990.

Schneider, Steven. 'The Animated Alternative.' *Art in America*, 69 (December 1981), 121–127.

——. That's All Folks! *The Art of Warner Bros. Animation*. New York: Henry Holt, 1988.

Schonberg, Harold C. *The Lives of the Composers*. London: Davis-Poynter, 1971.

Searle, Ronald. *The Rake's Progress*. London: Perpetua, 1955.

Sehlinger, Bob. *The Unofficial Guide to Disneyland*. New York: Menasha Ridge Press, 1985.

Seldis, Henry J. *Rico Lebrun*. Los Angeles: Los Angeles County Museum of Art, 1967.

Sendak, Maurice. '*Pinocchio*: At 38 He's Still a Hero.' *Los Angeles Times*, 17 December 1978.

Shale, Richard. *Donald Duck Joins Up: The Walt Disney Studio During World War II*. Ann Arbor, Michigan: UMI Research Press, 1982.

Shannon, Leonard. 'When Disney Met Dalí.' *Modern Maturity*. Dec. 1978 – January 1979, 50–52.

Shepard, Ernest H. *The Pooh Sketch Book*. Ed. Brian Sibley. London: Methuen, 1982.

Sibley, Brian. *The Book of Guinness Advertising*. Enfield: Guinness, 1985.

——. *Books to Begin With: An Exhibition of Children's Books*. Lamberhurst: Scotney Castle, 1981.

——. 'The Enchanted Realms of Walt Disney.' *Movies of the Forties*. Ed. Ann Lloyd and David Robinson. London: Orbis, 1982.

——. Letter to the Editor. *The Listener*. 25 February 1984, 18.

——., and Richard Holliss. *Disney Retrospective*. Programme. London: National Film Theatre, 1989.

Sklar, Robert. *Movie-Made America: A Social History of American Movies*. New York: Random House, 1975.

Smith, Dave (David R.). *Disney A to Z*. New York: Hyperion, 1996.

Smith, David R. 'Ben Sharpsteen: 33 Years with Disney.' *Millimetre*, 3 (1975), 38–45.

——. 'Disney before Burbank.' *Funnyworld*, 20 (1979), 32–38.

——. 'The Sorcerer's Apprentice: Birthplace of *Fantasia*.' *Millimetre*, 4, February 1976, 18–24, 64–67.

——. 'Ub Iwerks, 1901–1971.' *Funnyworld*, 14 (1972), 33–47.

——. 'Up to Date in Kansas City But Walt Disney Had Not Yet Gone as Far as he Could Go.' *Funnyworld*, 19 (1978), 22–34.

Smith, Dodie. *The Hundred and One Dalmatians*. 1965; London: Piccolo, 1981

Smoodin, Eric. *Animating Culture: Hollywood Cartoons from the Sound Era*. Oxford: Roundhouse, 1993.

Snow White and the Seven Dwarfs. Modena: Figurini Panini, 1980.

Snow White and the Seven Dwarfs: The Original Disney Story. London: Editions Magazines, 1987.

Solomon, Charles. 'Disney Magic: The Animated Features.' *Members' Calendar*, Los Angeles County Museum of Art, July/Aug 1986.

——. *The Disney That Never Was*. New York: Hyperion, 1995.

——. 'Disney Villainesses: Images of the Evil and the Ecstasy.' *Los Angeles Times*, 9 September 1980.

——. *Enchanted Drawings: The History of Animation*. New York: Alfred Knopf, 1989.

——. 'Was She a Snow Job?' *Los Angeles Times*. 16 July 1983.

Stadler, Edmund. *Adolph Appia*. London: The Victoria and Albert Museum, 1970.

Stahl, P. J. *Poor Minette*. Trans. Julian Jacobs. Illus. Grandville. London: Rodale Press, 1954.

Starewicz 1882–1965. Jayne Pilling (ed). Edinburgh: Filmhouse, 1983.

Stevenson, Robert Louis. *Treasure Island*. Illus. N.C. Wyeth. 1911; London: Gollancz, 1990.

Stokowski, Leopold. '*Fantasia* Impromptu: Interview with the Editor.' *Royal College of Music Magazine*, 67 (Easter 1971).

Stone, Dominic R. *The Art of Biedermeier*. Secaucus, New Jersey: Chartwell Books, 1990.

The Story of Walt Disney World: Commemorative Edition. Burbank: Walt Disney Productions, 1976.

Storytelling in Animation: The Art of the Animated Image. Vol. 2. John Canemaker (ed). Los Angeles: American Film Institute, 1988.

Strauss, Theodor. 'Stokowski Has His Say.' *New York Times*, 5 January 1941.

Strzyz, Klaus and Andreas C. Knigge. *Disney von Innen*. Frankfurt: Ullstein, 1988.

Swanson, Mary. *From Swedish Fairy Tales to American Fantasy: Gustaf Tenggren's Illustrations 1920–1970*. Minneapolis: University of Minnesota Art Museum, 1987.

——. *Gustaf Tenggrens Illustrationer 1920–1970*. Stockholm: Nationalmuseum, 1990.

Swift, Jonathan. *Gulliver's Travels*. Illus. Grandville. n.d.

Swingewood, Alan. *The Myth of Mass Culture*. London: Macmillan, 1977.

Taylor, Deems. *Fantasia*. New York: Simon and Schuster, 1940.

Taylor, John. *Storming the Magic Kingdom: Wall Street, the Raiders and the Battle for Disney*. London: Viking, 1988.

Taylor, John Russell. *Strangers in Paradise: The Hollywood Emigrés, 1933–1950*. New York: Holt, Rinehart and Winston, 1983.

Taylor, Judy. *Beatrix Potter: Artist, Storyteller and Countrywoman*. London: Warne, 1986.

Thomas, Bob. *Disney's Art of Animation: From Mickey Mouse to Beauty and the Beast*. New York: Hyperion, 1991.

——. *Walt Disney: An American Original*. New York: Hyperion, 1994.

——. *The Walt Disney Biography*. London: New English Library, 1977.

——. *Walt Disney: The Art of Animation*. New York: Golden Press, 1958.

Thomas, Frank and Ollie Johnston. *Disney Animation: The Illusion of Life*. New York: Abbeville, 1981.

——. *Too Funny for Words*. New York: Abbeville, 1987.

Thorp, Margaret Farrand. *America at the Movies*. London: Faber, 1946.

Treasures of Disney Animation Art. Intr. John Canemaker. New York: Abbeville, 1982.

Tucker, Nicholas. 'Arts in Society: Who's Afraid of Walt Disney?' *New Society*, 4 April 1968, 502–503.

The Unknown Paintings of Kay Nielsen. David Larkin (ed). New York: Peacock Books/Bantam Press, 1977.

'"The Valuator" Interviews Walt Disney.' *The Valuator*. Summer 1966, 11–13.

Vampira (Maila Nurmi). 'The One – The Only Vampira.' *Fangoria*. 30 (1983), 26–29.

Van der Post, Laurens. *Venture to the Interior*. London: Hogarth Press, 1952.

Vaughan, William. *German Romantic Painting*. New Haven: Yale University Press, 1980.

Verne, Jules. *Twenty Thousand Leagues Under the Sea*. Illus. William McLaren. London: Dent, 1966.

Von Hoffmansthall, Hugo. *Everyman*. Programme. Los Angeles: Hollywood Bowl, 1936.

Wagner, W. *Epics and Romances of the Middle Ages*. Ed. W. S. W. Anson. Illus. Hermann Vogel. 1882; London: Routledge, 1917.

'Walt Disney: Great Teacher.' *Fortune*, August 1942, 90–95, 153–156.

Walt Disney Magic Moments. Milan: Arnoldo Mondadori, 1973.

Walt Disney Productions The Jungle Book. Modena: Figurine Panini, 1983.

'Walt Disney – Teacher of Tomorrow.' *Look*. 8 (1948), 23–27.

Walt Disney's Alice in Wonderland. Burbank: Walt Disney Productions, 1951.

Walt Disney's Bambi. New York: Golden Press, 1949.

Walt Disney's Disneyland. Burbank: Walt Disney Productions, 1971.

Walt Disney's Fantasia. Programme. New York: Walt Disney Productions, n.d. 1940.

Walt Disney's Fantasia. 50th Anniversary Programme. [USA]: Walt Disney Company, n.d. 1990

Walt Disney's Mary Poppins. London: Sackville Smeets, n.d. 1965.

Walt Disney's Mickey's Christmas Carol. Paulton, Bristol: Purnell Books, 1984.

Walt Disney's Pinocchio: *Overall Continuity Outline*. London: Collins, 1939

Walt Disney's Snow White and the Seven Dwarfs. Illus. Gustaf Tenggren. New York: Grosset and Dunlap, 1938.

Walt Disney's Snow White and the Seven Dwarfs. Manchester: London Editions Magazines, 1987.

Walt Disney's Snow White and the Seven Dwarfs. 1937; New York: Harry N. Abrams, 1987.

Walt Disney's Snow White and the Seven Dwarfs. New York: Viking, 1979.

Walt Disney's Snow White and the Seven Dwarfs *Golden Anniversary*. 1987: Prescott, Az: Gladstone, 1987.

Walt Disney's Surprise Package. Adapt. H. Marion Palmer. New York: Simon and Schuster, 1944.

Walt Disney's The Sword in the Stone. London: Purnell, 1963.

Walt Disney Studios. *Die Kleine Schweine.* Berlin: Williams, 1934.

Walt Disney Studio Staff. *Mickey Mouse Movie Stories.* Illus. Walt Disney Studio Staff. London: Dean, n.d. 1932.

Walt Disney Studio Staff. *Mickey Mouse Movie Stories.* Intr. Maurice Sendak. Illus. Walt Disney Studio Staff. New York: Harry N. Abrams, 1988.

Warner, Marina. *The Inner Eye: Art Beyond the Visual.* London: South Bank Centre, 1996.

Warwick, Alan. 'Cinderella.' *Picturegoer.* 20 December 1950, 10–12.

Watts, Steven. *The Magic Kingdom: Walt Disney and the American Way of Life.* Boston/New York: Houghton Mifflin, 1997

Waugh, Evelyn. *The Loved One.* London: Chapman and Hall, 1948.

Weber, Eva. *Art Deco in North America.* London: Bison Books, 1985.

Werner, Jane. *Walt Disney's* Cinderella. Illus. adapt. Retta Scott Worcester. New York: Simon and Schuster, 1950.

Whicker, Alan. 'The House the Mouse Built.' *Punch.* 27 July 1971, 86–87.

White, Colin. *Edmund Dulac.* New York: Charles Scribner's Sons, 1976.

——. *The Enchanted World of Jessie M. King.* Edinburgh: Canongate, 1989.

——. *The World of the Nursery.* London: The Herbert Press, 1984.

White, T. H. *The Sword in the Stone.* London: Collins, 1939.

'The Wide World of Walt Disney.' *Newsweek,* 31 December 1962, 50–53.

Williams, David. 'Whatever Happened to Sunflower?' *Animator.* 28(1991), 13.

Willis, Susan. '*Fantasia*: Walt Disney's Los Angeles Suite.' Unpublished Paper, University of California at Santa Cruz, n.d. c. 1985.

Women and Animation. Jayne Pilling (ed). London: British Film Institute, 1992.

The Wonderful World of Walt Disney: Gala Collection. Angus Allan (ed). London: F. K. S., 1973.

'A Wonderful World: Growing Impact of the Disney Art.' *Newsweek,* 18 April 1955, 26–30.

The Wonderful Worlds of Walt Disney: America. London: Grolier, 1965.

'The World According to Disney'. Susan Willis (ed). *South Atlantic Quarterly.* Vol. 92, No. 1 (Winter 1993).

The World Encyclopedia of Cartoons. Maurice Horn (ed). New York: Chelsea House, 1980.

Wunderlich, R., and P. Morrissey. *The Desecration of* Pinocchio *in the United States.* Unpublished Paper. Minneapolis: The Children's Literature Association, 1981.

Zelger, Franz. *Arnold Böcklin: die Toteninsel.* Frankfurt: Fischer, 1991.

Unpublished Sources

Interviews with the author

Jim Algar, Carmel by the Sea, California, 8 June 1985.

Ken Anderson, La Canada, California, 10 May 1985, 17 July 1989.

Ray Aragon, Woodland Hills, California, 6 November 1989.

Art Babbitt, Los Angeles, 3 June 1985.

Kathryn Beaumont, Burbank, California, 11 July 1985.

Lee Blair, Soquel, California, 8 June 1985.

Sue Bottigheimer, Stony Brook, New York, 6 May 1985.

Ray Bradbury, Los Angeles, 6 June 1985.

John Canemaker, New York, 7 May 1985, 22 July 1985, 9 August 1989.

Adriana Caselotti, Los Angeles, 7 July 1985, 1 August 1986, 11 June 1989.

Tony Cierichietti, Los Angeles, 12 June 1985.

Claude Coats, Burbank, California, 2 May and 31 May 1985.

Jack and Camille Cutting, Studio City, California, 26 June and 2 July 1985.

Roald Dahl, Telephone interview, London, 11 December 1984.

Marc and Alice Davis, Los Angeles, 11 and 18 June 1985, 12 August 1986.

'Disney Magic', Los Angeles County Museum transcripts, California, 13 July 1986.

Richard Dixon, Southampton, 7 August 1971.

Eyvind Earle, Telephone interview, California, 15 July 1989.

Jules Engel, Los Angeles, 14 May 1985.

Elfriede Fischinger, Los Angeles, 20 and 23 May 1985, 31 July 1986.

Harper Goff, Studio City, California, 7 July 1985.

Joe and Jennie Grant, Glendale, California, 30 May, 11 and 25 June 1985, 14 August 1986.

Theo Halladay, Tarzana, California, 26 June and 10 July 1989.

John Hench, Glendale, California, 22 May 1985, 29 June 1989.

Don Iwerks, Burbank, California, 20 June 1985.

Vince Jefferds, Burbank, California, 21 May 1985.

Rush Johnson, Marceline, Mo., 26 August 1994.

Ollie Johnston and Frank Thomas, Burbank, California, 4 June 1985.

Bob Jones, Fullerton, California, I and 4 November 1989.

Milt Kahl, Marin County, California, 9 June 1985.

Ward Kimball, San Gabriel, California, 16 May 1985.

Jack and Jane Kinney, Sunland, California, 10 June and 1 July 1985,
2 July 1989.

Eric Larson, Glendale, California, 19 June and 10 July 1985.

David Lebrun, Venice, California, 2 June 1985.

Gordon Legg, Pasadena, California, 21 June 1989
and interview with Milton Gray, 31 March 1976.

Helen and Robert Mackintosh, Los Angeles, 31 July 1986.

Kaye Malins, Marceline, Mo., 26 August 1994.

Jim Mason, Burbank, California, 5 June 1985.

Elizabeth Meador, Glendale, California, 28 October 1992.

Bill Melendez, Los Angeles, 22 October 1992.

Diane Disney Miller and Ron Miller, Encino, California, 5 August 1986 and
Interview with Richard Holliss and Brian Sibley, Encino, September 1986.

William Moritz, Studio City, 22 May 1985.

Grim Natwick, Telephone interview, California, 2 July 1985.

Herb Ryman, Van Nuys, California, 7 and 13 July 1985, 13 August 1986.

Retta Scott (Worcester), Telephone Interview, California, 1 November 1989.

Mel Shaw, Los Angeles, 6 July 1985.

Brian Sibley, London, 26 September 1984 and 5 June 1987.

Richard Todd, London, 7 December 1984.

Adrienne Tytla, East Lyme, Conn., 8 August 1989.

Harry Tytle, Glendale, California, 12 July 1985.

Select Filmography

Animated feature films

The short animated films are listed in Maltin *Of Mice and Magic*, 343–354. The first complete filmography of all the silent shorts has been issued by Russell Merritt and J.B. Kaufman in their *Nel Paese delle Meraviglie: Walt in Wonderland*, 174–226. Brief descriptions of the sound shorts are given in Holliss and Sibley, *The Disney Studio Story*. The animated features have full credits in Maltin *The Disney Films* and in John Grant, *Encyclopedia of Walt Disney's Animated Characters*. The following is a list of the animated feature films produced under the personal supervision of Walt Disney, with a list of those produced by the studio after his death.

1937 *Snow White and the Seven Dwarfs*
1940 *Pinocchio*
1940 *Fantasia*
1941 *The Reluctant Dragon* (live action with three complete animated sections and other animated scenes)
1941 *Dumbo*
1942 *Bambi*
1943 *Victory Through Air Power* (animation with live action commentary)
1943 *Saludos Amigos* (animation with live action links)
1945 *The Three Caballeros* (combination of live action and animation)
1946 *Make Mine Music* (live action silhouettes in one section)
1946 *Song of the South* (live action with brief animated sections)
1947 *Fun and Fancy Free* (animation with live action link)
1948 *Melody Time* (animation with some live action combined)
1949 *So Dear To My Heart* (live action with brief animated sections)
1949 *The Adventures of Ichabod and Mr Toad*
1950 *Cinderella*
1951 *Alice in Wonderland*
1953 *Peter Pan*
1955 *Lady and the Tramp*
1959 *Sleeping Beauty*
1961 *101 Dalmatians*
1963 *The Sword in the Stone*

1964 *Mary Poppins* (live action with brief combination of live action and animation)

1966 Death of Walt Disney on 15 December

1967 *The Jungle Book*

1970 *The Aristocats*

1971 *Bedknobs and Broomsticks* (live action with brief animation combined)

1973 *Robin Hood*

1977 *The Rescuers*

1977 *Pete's Dragon* (live action with brief animation combined)

1977 *The Many Adventures of Winnie the Pooh* (made up of three featurettes)

1981 *The Fox and the Hound*

1985 *The Black Cauldron*

1986 *The Great Mouse Detective* (UK title: *Basil – The Great Mouse Detective*). This was the last animated film to be supervised by any of Disney's own contemporaries.

1988 *Oliver & Company*

1988 *Who Framed Roger Rabbit* (live action with animation combined)

1989 *The Little Mermaid*

1990 *The Rescuers Down Under*

1991 *Beauty and the Beast*

1992 *Aladdin*

1994 *The Lion King*

1995 *Pocahontas*

1996 *The Hunchback of Notre Dame*

1997 *Hercules*

1998 *Mulan*

Index

Note: Colour plates are referred to, for example, as **CP1**; black and white illustrations in the text are given a page reference in **bold figures;** n refers to an endnote.